GANGSTERS
AND
GUNMEN

GANGSTERS
AND
GUNMEN

A Time Warner Paperback

This first edition published in 2004

ISBN 0-7515-3588-5

Produced by Omnipress, Eastbourne

Printed in Great Britain

Time Warner Books
Brettenham House
Lancaster Place
London WC2E 7EN

Photo credits: Popperfoto

CONTENTS

PART ONE
AMERICA

A Short History

Throughout history crime has existed in one form or another. Crime is not only committed by individuals but by groups as well. Crime knows no boundaries, has existed since the beginning of time, and is a lifestyle for many people.

Since the beginning of the early 1900s, organized crime has existed in the United States. This brief history will show when, where and why the Mafia came to the United States, who organized it, and how it differed from its origins in the European Mafia.

As early as the ninth century, Sicily was occupied by Arab forces. The natives of the country were persecuted and took refuge in the surrounding hills. The Sicilians formed a secret society to unite the natives against the invading Arabs and Normans. This secret society was called 'Mafia' after the Arabic word meaning refuge. The intention of this society was to form a sense of family based on their ancestry and Sicilian heritage. In the 1700s the wealthy were given pictures of a black hand, which was a silent request for money in return for protection. If the recipients didn't pay the money, they could expect violence such as bombings, kidnappings and even murder.

In 1876, Mafia Don Rafael Palizzolo, ran for

political office in Sicily. Using a gun for persuasion he forced people to vote for him. After being elected, he promoted Mafia Don Crispi as Prime Minister and together they put Sicily under government control. They also redirected government funds to the society known as the Mafia.

The largest Mafia site in the United States in the 1800s was New Orleans. David Hennessey, who was Police Chief at the time, discovered the existence of this secret society whilst investigating the murder of an Italian immigrant. Hennessey was, however, assassinated before this murder case could go to trial. Twelve men were charged with his assassination but were lynched by a newly formed vigilante group. Although the Italian Ambassador demanded that the vigilantes be tried, President Harrison overrode the decision and gave a large sum of cash to the families of the lynched men as a form of settlement. This case was widely publicized because of its foreign implications and the involvement of the President of the United States.

Vito Cascio Ferro, who is believed to be the one man primarily responsible for establishing the communication between the Sicilian and American Mafia, fled to the United States in 1901 to escape arrest. He formed a group called the 'Black Hand' whose members consisted of hardened criminals and fugitives from Sicily. He was known as the Father of the American Mafia.

In 1924, Mussolini was determined to rid Italy of the Mafia, so many of its members fled to the United States. All the time the number of members in the organization was increasing. These fleeing Italians were well aware there was money to be made in the United States through extortion, prostitution, gambling and bootlegging, and it wasn't long before every large city had its own Mafia section. When Prohibition was introduced, which was a legal ban on the manufacture and sale of alcohol, it generated a wave of illegal activity due to the fact there was big money to be made. Gangsters would openly flaunt their wealth and power and many young men became leaders in the New Age American Mafia.

Charles 'Lucky' Luciano

One of the most powerful mafia bosses of the 20th century, Luciano teamed with Meyer Lansky and Bugsy Siegel to form a national crime syndicate and became known as the 'Boss of Bosses'.

Charles Luciano was born in 1897 in Lercardia Friddi, in Sicily. His parents worked hard to provide for the family, but somehow they knew there must be a better way of life. They had heard about the promised land of America from their friends. But the stories about plentiful work and good schools soon proved to be just that – fabricated stories.

The Lucianos set sail for America in 1906 and arrived at New York harbour in November. In his youth, Luciano was permanently in trouble with the police. His first arrest was in 1907 for shoplifting, and during that year he started his first racket business. For just a penny or two a day, Luciano offered younger and smaller Jewish children his personal protection against beatings on the way to school. It was easy money – if they didn't pay, he simply beat them up.

One Polish kid, Meyer Lansky, who appeared to be a weakling, refused to pay Luciano. Luciano fought him one day and was surprised at how hard Lansky fought back. After that they became close friends, a friendship that lasted even after Luciano was deported to Italy some years later.

As a teenager, Luciano became an expert at various vices – particularly narcotics. When he was only eighteen he was convicted of peddling heroin and morphine and was put in a reformatory for six months. However, this did not curtail his activities and on his release he resumed his narcotics dealing. By 1916, Luciano was a leading member of the notorious Five Points Gang and named by police as the prime suspect in a number of murders. His notoriety grew as did his circle of underworld friends.

By 1920, Luciano had become a big name in bootlegging rackets with the help of Lansky and his previous partner Benjamin 'Bugsy' Siegel. They had also become familiar with Joe Adonis, Vito Genovese and most important among Italian gangsters, Frank Costello. In fact it was Costello who introduced him to other gangsters like Big Bill Dwyer and Jews like Arnold Rothstein, Dutch Schultz and Dandy Phil Kastel. Luciano was impressed by the way Costello bought protection from city officials and the police – an important ingredient in any big-time criminal setup.

A BRUSH WITH MASSERIA

Luciano later joined forces with Joe 'the Boss' Masseria, but soon realized that Masseria did not see the future in the same way that he did.

Luciano was becoming very impatient with the way Masseria was handling business, letting many opportunities go by that could have made them a lot of money. Masseria, however, would not do business with any non-Italians and, being aware of Luciano's ambitions, felt that he was a threat to him. It was at this time that he committed an act that would prove fatal to him, but launched Luciano into gangland stardom.

Whilst Luciano was standing on Sixth Avenue in New York, a limousine drew up beside him. Three armed men leaped from the vehicle and forced him into the back of the limousine. This proved to be a very long ride. They applied sticking tape to his mouth and then came the kicks, punches and knife wounds. Luciano, certain that he was about to die, became weaker and weaker with each attack until he eventually passed out. Hours later, however, he regained consciousness only to discover that he was on the beach. Tearing off the tape he managed to stagger almost a mile before reaching a police booth at the Tottenville Precinct. Ignoring his bribes and pleas for a taxi, the police took him to hospital, where they began to ask a series of questions. Luciano would say nothing, and denied that he had recognized the men who had taken him for the ride. Fed up with the incessant questions he eventually blurted out in anger, 'Don't you cops lose any sleep over it, I'll attend to this thing myself.'

At first Luciano had no idea who would want him dead, so he turned to his friend Meyer Lansky for an answer. It didn't take Meyer very long to come up with not only the answer, but also a solution. Meyer explained that it was Masseria who had arranged the beatings and that it would be a good idea to join forces with Masseria's arch-enemy, Salvatore Maranzano.

Several months later, after recovering from the beatings, Luciano did just that. He had a secret meeting with Maranzano and together they put into action one of gangland's biggest purges. It became known as The Castellammarese War.

THE WAR

The Castellammarese War broke out between the numerous forces of Joe the Boss and those of a fast-rising New York *mafioso*, Salvatore Maranzano. Dozens of gangsters were killed over the next two years. Luciano avoided the conflict as much as he could, and made the most of the time by cementing relationships with the younger members of the Maranzano outfit. Luciano soon emerged as the leader of this new-found clique.

The war continued into 1931 with Maranzano winning, but with Masseria still very powerful. This was when an impatient Luciano made his move. Three of his men and Bugsy Siegel shot Joe the Boss to death in a Coney Island restaurant. The assassination made Maranzano the victor in the War and, in way of thanks to Luciano, made him the Number Two man in his new Mafia empire. Maranzano proclaimed himself the 'Boss of Bosses' in New York and set up five crime families under him – Gambino, Genovese,

Bonanno, Colombo and the Lucchese family. But that was only the start of Maranzano's plans; he was determined to become the supreme boss of the entire Mafia in the United States.

To achieve his goal he compiled a list of two gangsters who had to be eliminated: in Chicago, Al Capone, and in New York, Charles Luciano. Luciano, however, learned of Maranzano's plans in advance. Maranzano had planned to summon Luciano and Vito Genovese to his office for a conference. He had lined up a murderous Irish gunman, Mad Dog Coll, to assassinate the pair. Instead, moments before Coll arrived, four of Lansky's gunmen, pretending to be government agents, entered Maranzano's office, and shot and stabbed him to death.

'LUCKY' LUCIANO

Luciano was now at the top. He appeared menacing, thanks to a scar he received in 1929 when knife-wielding kidnappers severed the muscles in his right cheek. This left him with an evil droop to his right eye. He inherited the name 'Lucky' for being a whiz at selecting winning horses at various race courses.

Life was tough in the 1930s for the average American. Following the Depression numerous people were left homeless and without jobs. This was not the case, however, for Lucky Luciano and his band. Luciano reaped enormous profits from gambling, drinking and prostitution. Prostitution was indeed Luciano's forte, and he soon mastered

15

the art of pimping. One weakness he had, however, was the fact that he liked to sample the goods himself, which caused him to contract gonorrhoea seven times and syphilis once. Luciano was beginning to express doubts about the viability of his prostitution business and felt that more money could be extracted if he were to syndicate every whorehouse in New York and put all the madams on a salary. The madams who did not fall into line ended up in hospital, and the rest were worked like dogs.

When Special Prosecutor Thomas Dewey and his team of twenty racket busters went after a conspiracy in the prostitution business, they secretly set up a massive raid on approximately eighty brothels. Forty of these raids were successful and almost one hundred madams and girls were brought in.

It was then that Luciano got caught. Lucky had worried about his prostitution business for good reason. Following the raid, the prostitutes were talking, the madams were talking, and soon the clients of the women were talking. As the weeks went by, Dewey realized that he had an unassailable case against Luciano in just this one field.

A warrant was issued and Luciano was eventually arrested in Hot Springs, Arkansas. Soon Lucky's greatest fear came about – he was put on trial. All of Dewey's witnesses were convincing, and they corroborated with ease the fact that Luciano had been running an illegal vice business. He denied all the charges, but the jury was convinced by the evidence and found him guilty of all

16

charges. Much to his surprise, he was handed a sentence of thirty to fifty years' imprisonment.

NOT SO LUCKY

So Luciano's luck had at last run out. He was shipped out of Sing Sing to the Clinton State Prison at Dannemora, near the village of Malone in upstate New York.

Dannemora, the third-oldest maximum-security institution in the state, was a cold, neglected, inhuman place where men like Luciano were supposed to repent their sins. He was confined in his cell for fourteen to sixteen hours a day from July 1936 until the spring of 1942. Out of sight, out of mind – or so the authorities assumed.

Luciano and his Syndicate friends back in New York city were influential enough to ask the warden for one important favour. To allow Lucky to have unrecorded visits from friends and family – the requests were granted. This was their big mistake as it meant that Luciano was able to run his empire from within the walls of Dannemora.

Although Luciano was not even eligible to apply for parole until April 24, 1956, his trusted friend Meyer Lansky put out feelers in 1942 that suggested Lucky could help the United States war effort in Sicily and at home. Naval Intelligence got wind of the idea and eagerly decided to approach Luciano with their proposal. All they had to do now was to get him out of Dannemora and send him to a more secure location. The place they had in mind was Great Meadow Prison in Comstock,

New York. Luciano was delighted and jumped at the opportunity to leave Dannemora. On May 12, 1942, he headed for Great Meadow Prison.

THE DEAL

Luciano was a model prisoner during his time spent at Great Meadow. He had frequent visits by his friends, especially Meyer Lansky. The Allies in war-torn Europe were about to launch an invasion of Sicily. The United States could use some help in acquiring intelligence on German troop movements and other vital military information. The US had reason to believe the Mafia wanted the armed forces off the island, so that they could return to peaceful times. Naval Intelligence made numerous unrecorded visits to Great Meadow to enlist the help of Lucky. Lucky assured them that he could get word to the Mafia leaders on the island of Sicily asking for their help. Luciano did indeed contact his Mafia associates and the deal was made.

In January 1946 Thomas Dewey granted commutation of sentence with the condition that Luciano be deported to Italy. On Sunday, February 10, 1946, Luciano set sail away from America aboard the SS *Laura Keene*.

The Italian government set strict rules in that Luciano could venture no more than a few miles from Naples and had to tell them about any visitors from outside Italy. This was a rule he broke frequently, and he still managed to conduct business back in the United States through runners and via the telephone.

Luciano died of a heart attack on January 26, 1962, when he was scheduled to meet a scriptwriter who was to do a story about his life. It was only after his death that Luciano was allowed to come back to the United States. He is buried at St. John's Cemetery in New York City.

'Lucky' Luciano's life has been romantically portrayed in films such as *Lucky Luciano* (1974), *Gangster Wars* (1981), *Mobsters* (1991), *Billy Bathgate* (1991) and *Hoodlum* (1997).

Meyer Lansky

In the rise and fall of underworld fortunes,
Meyer Lansky was immune to replacement
because he was too valuable an asset.
Despite this fact, he was never an initiated member
of the Mafia because Lansky was not an Italian.

Under the rule of the Czars, Jews in Poland suffered greatly. There were restrictions on their business practices and by the end of the 19th century many Jews felt the pressure to emigrate. Among those who emigrated was Max Suchowljansky who, in 1909, left his wife and three children behind in Grodno to start a new life in America. Two years later, ten-year-old Meyer and his mother, brother and sister followed their father to New York City. Meyer thought New York was both an exotic and exciting place to live.

Shortly after moving to the United States Max had Americanized their surname by shortening it to Lansky. Meyer's mother Yetta was the dominant influence in his young life, as his father was never able to overcome his depression due to living in abject poverty.

Meyer was determined to help his family and took to gambling on the streets of the Lower East Side of New York. Hidden in a hole in his mattress was an ever-increasing bankroll which Meyer won by playing these street corner gambling games.

Meyer soon noticed that the Jews of the Lower

East Side were frequent targets of the organized
Irish and Italian gangs. One day, while walking
home from school, Meyer himself was set upon by
a group of Sicilians, boys much older than himself,
who demanded money from him. The leader of
this group was Salvatore Lucania, who would
become better known to the world as Charles
'Lucky' Luciano. Luciano liked picking on
solitary Jews because they rarely fought back, but
this time was different – he had cornered a small,
but dangerous opponent. 'We both had an instant
understanding,' Luciano remembered later. 'It was
something that never left us.' Luciano and the
Sicilians let Meyer pass without paying. From this
encounter Luciano and Meyer formed a lifelong
friendship.

Just before his fifteenth birthday, Meyer left
school. Determined that his eldest son would do
better than himself, Max got his son a job as an
apprentice in a tool-and-die operation, in the hope
that one day Meyer would be a mechanical
engineer. Meyer earned 10 cents an hour for a 52-
hour working week, and when he was given a raise
to a dollar an hour, he felt this was a joke as he
could make that amount in just a few rolls of the
dice. He continued to work at the tool-and-die
shop, but he knew he would never be a professional
worker. The most important education he was
getting came after he clocked off from work and he
and an Irish friend worked as strong-arm men in a
craps game run by Yudie and Willie Albert.

Within a few years, Meyer was known to the
union as a *shtarke* – a strong-arm man who would

21

do violence for a price. It was as a *shtarke* that Meyer's name first appeared on police records. In 1918, when Meyer was only sixteen, he was arrested and charged with felonious assault, only to have the charges dismissed. A little later he was arrested again, this time for disorderly conduct. It is alleged that Meyer was leaning on some of the local prostitutes on Madison Street in an effort to become a pimp. He pleaded guilty and received a $2 fine.

In 1921 Meyer quit his job at the tool-and-die shop and would never work for anyone again.

THE INFLUENCE OF BUGSY

As youngsters Meyer and his friends were beaten up daily by the Irish boys. Standing up to the Irish and Italian gangs meant that Meyer and his friends needed to organize their own protection society. Between 1914 and 1920, Meyer and his younger brother Jake, were joined by Meyer 'Mike' Wassell, Red Levine, Tabbo Sandler and Doc Stacher, who would remain a lifelong friend of Meyer's. Around this time, Meyer Lansky also met and became close friends with another man who would accompany him on his rise to the top of the Syndicate – 'Bugsy' Siegel.

Meyer met Benny Siegel on a street corner in the poverty-stricken Lower East Side of Manhattan when they were both still in their teens. The two were involved in a fight that arose from a street corner craps game. Meyer saw Benny reach for a gun and point it at one of the combatants. Just as

22

the sound of police whistles could be heard, Meyer hit Siegel's arm and forced him to drop the gun. The two youngsters ran away although Benny could barely contain his rage at the older boy.

Despite the somewhat rocky beginning, Meyer and Siegel became fast friends and were soon to be the terrors of their neighbourhood. Meyer was without a doubt the brains of the outfit while Benny, better known as 'Bugsy', was the brawn.

Lansky and Siegel were complete opposites. Benny was a flashy dresser who was always quick to fight, while Meyer was the thinker, the one who never let his emotions overrule his head. Despite these differences, the two boys were closer than brothers.

The Bugs and Meyer mobsters were equal opportunity thugs. They liked to shakedown Jewish moneylenders and storekeepers as well as Irish and Italian shop owners and gamblers. No one was safe from the gang.

Thanks to Meyer's experience with cars and mechanics, the Bugs and Meyer Mob became active in car theft and hijacking. The gang quickly became known as experts in 'transportation' with no job too big or too dangerous. To cover their illegal activities they used a car and truck rental garage that served as a warehouse for their illicit gains.

THE BRAIN

Arnold Rothstein was known to the underworld as A.R. or the 'Brain'. In the years before Prohibition, he was arguably the most important and powerful gangster in the United States.

Rothstein was a gambler and definitely the man to go to in New York City if you wanted to make a deal. He associated with killers and politicians alike and there was probably nothing he couldn't fix. Rothstein made his fortune by making deals and finding opportunities and, like a modern venture capitalist, he financially supported others who came to him with risky propositions. He also had the gift of being able to detect a good bet, either at the gaming table or on the street, and had an eye for young hoods with potential.

Rothstein was inspirational to many people, not just young gangsters like Lansky, but he also provided the basis for the character of Meyer Wolfsheim in F. Scott Fitzgerald's masterpiece *The Great Gatsby*.

By the early 1920s, Rothstein knew there was an easy way to make a lot of money due to the social experiment known as Prohibition. He knew that a constitutional amendment wouldn't stop people from drinking, it would only serve to drive the drinking underground. The law of supply and demand, therefore, dictated that the price of alcohol was going to go through the roof and Rothstein was determined to be in charge of this supply.

However, Rothstein was not the type of man who got his hands dirty, he needed partners. He was looking for men who were smart enough to realize that there was still a market for high class, expensive liquor and who were tough enough to survive in the world of bootlegging. Rothstein knew where to find just such men – he turned to a pair of up-and-coming gangsters from Manhattan – Meyer Lansky and Charles Luciano.

Meyer met Rothstein at the Bar Mitzvah of the son of a mutual friend, and he told Meyer he was impressed with the young man. He invited Meyer to his exclusive apartment at the Park Central Hotel. It was here that they had a six-hour conversation about the future. Rothstein wanted Meyer to go into business with him running booze.

A similar meeting was held with Charles Luciano, and seemingly had a profound influence on the Sicilian. Luciano wrote in his autobiography: 'He taught me how to dress, how not to wear loud things but to have good taste. He was the best etiquette teacher a guy could ever have – real smooth.'

Unlike other bootleggers who only wanted to make a quick buck on cheap booze, Rothstein was intent on building a network of bootleggers who would only sell the best alcohol money could buy. He knew that if he could get a reputation for selling quality, people would be prepared to pay for it. Rothstein developed contacts with distilleries in Scotland who would sell him grade A whisky which he then transferred to Irving 'Waxey' Gordon in Philadelphia.

Rothstein refused to allow his minions to cut the whisky with cheaper alcohol and prohibited them from ripping each other off. To defy 'The Brain' was to dice with death, and between them Rothstein, Lansky, Luciano and Gordon developed a distribution system that made them all very wealthy men.

The economics of bootlegging were actually a little more complex than Luciano remembered. The supply of the illegal whisky had to be regular, so Customs and Federal Agents had to be controlled, and that cost money. There also had to be plants to cut the whisky in, so Lansky and Luciano went into the real estate business. They needed bottles that looked like the originals, so they bought a bottling company. They needed labels that looked exactly like the Johnny Walker, Haig & Haig and Dewers labels, so Lansky bought a printing operation complete with colour presses. And lastly, lots and lots of trucks to deliver the illicit booze.

ETHNIC DIFFERENCES

By the start of Prohibition, Luciano, along with the Bugs and Meyer mob were widely known in the underworld. At this time, Guiseppe, Masseria and Sal Maranzano were not-so-gently pushing for Luciano to join their gangs. Luciano, however, was holding out because of his close friendship with Meyer. He was able to see past Lansky's Jewish heritage, something neither Masseria or Maranzano could do. They wanted Luciano to dump Lansky and take over the territory the Bugs and Meyer gang had established.

The relationship between Luciano and Lansky was quite complex and very unusual for its time. Masseria and Maranzano, who headed the two most influential Italian gangs on the East Coast refused to associate with anyone who wasn't a Sicilian. They were firm believers in the old way of doing things.

Luciano and Lansky, however, didn't let their different ethnic backgrounds stand in the way of friendship, partnership and profit. These differences were often the source of jokes between the men, but still their wave of crime grew and prospered. They bought boats for picking up loads of bootleg scotch and trucks to transport it. Lansky and Siegel ran profitable gambling houses and Luciano became an important bordello owner. The gang hit the pawnbrokers and moneylenders in the ghettos, and the insurance salesmen who collected nickel and dime premiums, who proved to be easy targets. In fact they had so much money coming in it was hard to keep track of it.

The group soon looked for other ways to put their money to work for them. They bought into established bookmaking operations, the first step in what would become a nationwide gambling syndicate.

By this time the Italians and Jews of the Luciano and Bugs and Meyer mobs had attracted the attention of not only Rothstein, but of Maranzano and Masseria. As a powerful Italian, Luciano was drawn into the battle between the two old-timers despite his reservations. As a Jew, Lansky could only sit back and watch the battle and try to help his Sicilian friend. Maranzano having come out the eventual winner in his battle with Masseria, adopted the title of *capo di tutti capo* (boss of bosses), and this is where Lansky and Siegel would step in, working closely with Charles Luciano, to bring true 'organization' to organized crime.

Lansky and Luciano summoned all the major underworld leaders to New York. Their proposition was to have a loose-knit Syndicate of gangs, stressing that there would be no one boss to whom they would have to answer. The Syndicate, Lansky and Luciano said, would serve as a co-operative venture to halt the tit-for-tat bloodshed that had claimed so many lives in the past few years. The Syndicate would simply be a crime cartel.

With Maranzano out of the way, Luciano and Meyer took their show on the road and went from city to city selling the idea of the Syndicate. It was clear that this was a new day for the underworld. Luciano, who because of his extroverted personality took most of the spotlight, refused to accept the sealed envelopes filled with money that was the Mafia tradition. He pointed out that the old Mafia traditions were fine for Sicily, but in America they would all work for each other, whilst still running their own outfits.

BACK TO GAMBLING

When Prohibition ended, Meyer returned to his first love, gambling. In 1933, every state, with the exception of Nevada, made gambling illegal. In New York, there was a huge underground gambling network. The games were held on street corners, in back rooms and often in suites of hotels. These were only temporary set-ups and in many cases, the games were rigged. Their operators didn't worry about their reputations for fairness because they would be running the game from a different site by the next day.

During the August racing season in upstate Saratoga Springs, New York turned a blind eye to illicit gaming. Saratoga was a spa community known for its sulphur springs as well as its race track and casino. It also acted as a summer camp for people roasting in the city 190 miles south. The racetrack opened during the Civil War and after the war Southern horse owners migrated north during the steamy summer months and brought with them the gambling games from the Mississippi riverboats. By the 1890s, the casinos of Saratoga rivalled those of Europe's most glamorous spas. In fact Saratoga's two principal hotels on the main street, the Grand Union and the United States, were the two largest hotels in the world. The city, however, was permeated with the Mob influence.

By the time Meyer Lansky and Lucky Luciano were in a position to have an effect on the market in Saratoga, Rothstein was already in charge of the spa town. He paid off the local officials and imported his dealers from New York, still making sure that others did the real dirty work. Lansky and Luciano were brought in to fix things with the local police as well as to run the dining room and entertainment. It was with Rothstein's help that Meyer, Siegel, Luciano and Costello perfected the business of casino and hotel operation.

Lansky and his chums approached the casino

operation with the same scruples as they had in bootlegging. They knew the percentages were in their favour and that the short-term gains from running a crooked game could never match the almost unimaginable profits from a fair casino.

'Everyone who came into my casino knew that if he lost his money it wouldn't be because he was cheated,' Meyer said proudly.

Meyer recruited the best dealers and croupiers he could find and paid them a salary plus a commission. This instilled loyalty and made the dealers pay closer attention to the games and to each other.

In the years leading up to World War II, Lansky had slowly but surely developed a reputation that attracted the highest rollers and most influential gamblers. Having learned the tricks of the trade at the Saratoga Springs casinos, Lansky began to branch out. In New Orleans, for the 1932 Democratic National Convention, Meyer and his friend Doc Stacher met with Louisiana Governor Huey 'Kingfish' Long. They arranged for the governor to open a Swiss bank account so that he could accept the $3 to $4 million in cash annually that the mobsters were prepared to pay for the privilege of running casinos in the Big Easy.

The Governor, who was impressed by the sophisticated way they handled themselves, gave his visitors from New York carte blanche. The opening of the famous Blue Room at the Roosevelt Hotel and of the Beverly Country Club, also in New Orleans, was the beginning of the nationwide development of casinos.

Following his success in New Orleans, Lansky moved further north to Hot Springs, Arkansas. Here he worked a similar deal and put Owney 'Killer' Madden, a former operator of The Cotton Club in Harlem, in charge. The Hot Springs set up was so luxurious and safe that it became a haven for gangsters who were on the run. During the 1950s Hot Springs was unlike any other town in the South, and it ended up having the largest illegal gambling operation in the United States. There was a race track, there was a system of bribery, there were pay-offs, but most of all there were people there who were above the law.

Exercising considerable political muscle, Lansky proceeded to expand his gaming empire into Kentucky and eventually Florida.

The illegal casinos became known as 'carpet joints', and breathed life into the depressed South Beach communities of Hollywood, Hallendale and Opalocka. Just across the county line from Miami, some small-time casinos and bingo houses provided Lansky with the perfect set up for a south Florida empire.

However, not everyone was so ambivalent towards the carpet joints that were going up on the outskirts of Broward County. More than once, some high-minded citizens would approach a judge for an injunction, preventing the gamblers from operating on a particular site. It meant the carpet joint owners had to find another place to operate from, which created significant problems for Lansky. So Meyer sent his brother Jake down to Broward County with a sackful of cash.

More than two dozen local organizations began receiving generous and helpful donations from the new owners of the bingo parlour. This ploy worked and there were no more complaints from citizens.

AND NOW TO CUBA

With carpet joints running from Saratoga to Key West, Lansky attracted the attention of many different government officials. Some were on his payroll, while others were his sworn enemies. However, the most powerful government official to be drawn to Lansky wasn't even American. He was Cuban dictator Fulgencio Batista.

In 1952, when Batista seized power, Cuba was known as the Paris of the New World. Europeans and Americans alike flocked to the sunny beaches, dancing, drinking and smoking cigars. Although gambling was big in Cuba, Batista had a problem. The games, it seemed, were seen as crooked and no one was playing. Tourism started to falter as gamblers bypassed the Cuban casinos in favour of the more honest Puerto Rican joints – things started to look bad for the dictator.

Batista somehow needed to inject some honesty into his games, and so he turned to Meyer Lansky. Lansky was appointed Batista's advisor on gambling reform and was given the authority to clean up the crooked gaming houses.

Lansky went to Havana and immediately began to clean up the crooked casino bosses. He ordered operators to start running a clean game, and dealers and croupiers, who were crooked, to be deported. He started the practice of dealing Blackjack from a six-deck shoe, which not only helped the house in terms of percentage, but minimized cheating by the dealer and player.

While his reformed Montmartre Club was the in-place in Havana, Meyer had long expressed an interest in putting a casino in the elegant Hotel Nacional, which overlooked El Morro, the ancient fortress guarding Havana harbour. Meyer planned to take a wing of the 10-storey hotel and create luxury suites for high stakes players. Batista endorsed Lansky's idea over the objections of American expatriots like Ernest Hemingway and the elegant hotel opened for business in 1955 with a show by Eartha Kitt. The casino was an immediate success.

That spring, Lansky began working on his own casino, a 21-storey, 440-foot skyscraper called the Riviera. When it opened it would be the largest casino-hotel in the world outside Las Vegas.

LAS VEGAS

In the mid-40s, things were pretty hot for Benny Siegel in New York. He was the key suspect in a murder and Meyer Lansky was having a hard time keeping him under control. The two were still as close as ever, but Benny was not happy under Meyer's leadership. Meyer decided that Bugsy needed to go out on his own and so he headed for Los Angeles to bring the operations in California under the Syndicate's control.

Bugsy was a big success out west and began to

expand the Syndicate inland. He looked east to Nevada, and saw a small town at the southern tip called Las Vegas. Although Siegel wasn't the first man to build a casino in Las Vegas, he was the first mobster with Syndicate connections to realize that putting a casino in Las Vegas could mean a licence to print money for the mob.

In 1943 Siegel tried to buy his way into a partnership with the owners of the Last Frontier in Vegas, using mob money. The owners went public with Siegel's action and rejected him. So Siegel and Lansky acquired El Cortez, a downtown hotel and casino, instead. Meyer did not share Siegel's enthusiasm for Las Vegas, but did put a $60,000 investment in El Cortez and became a silent partner. Soon after the men bought the casino, Siegel sold the operation and netted a $166,000 profit – a 27 percent return on their investment in just six months.

By now the Las Vegas real estate market was booming and Lansky allowed Siegel to reinvest the money from the sale of El Cortez into a bigger casino that he was about to build – the Flamingo – and he bought a 66 percent stake in the casino. However, Siegel totally lacked his friend Meyer's sense of control and the project got out of hand. There were incredible cost overruns and delays caused in part by Siegel's ignorance of how to build a hotel of the magnitude of the Flamingo and partly because of the booming post-war construction industry.

Back in Havana, the Syndicate had a meeting in secret, and Lansky was forced to tell the bosses that the cost of the casino would far exceed the $1 million that had been quoted. In fact, Meyer admitted, the Flamingo was likely to cost the Syndicate about $6 million before it would be completed. Immediately, there were calls for Siegel's head, but Lansky was able to pacify them with promises of huge inflows of cash once the building was completed.

Meyer talked the men into giving Bugsy until the spring to turn a profit, and then went to Las Vegas to try and talk some sense into his old friend. Benny had turned decorating control over to his girlfriend Virginia Hill, who was in many ways responsible for the overruns. When Meyer returned from Las Vegas, he was quite dejected. He told his associates that Siegel was 'so much in that woman's power that he cannot see reason'. Luciano told Lansky that Bugsy would have to get things under control or he would order that their old friend be killed.

Siegel managed to get the casino completed by his self-imposed December 1946 deadline, but not the hotel portion. On December 26, the casino opened, but nothing went right for the mobsters. In short, the guests at the Flamingo cleaned the casino out of $75,000 in the opening evening.

Siegel managed to struggle on for two weeks before realizing that the casino would have to close. Back in Cuba, Lansky once again saved Benny's life by coming up with a plan to put the Flamingo in receivership and setting up a new syndicate to buy out the old corporation. Luciano backed Lansky's plan, despite reservations by a number of other bosses.

In March, the Flamingo reopened and by April it was starting to get out of the red. In May the casino turned a profit, but for some reason it was too late to save Benny. In mid June, 1947, sitting in his apartment in Beverly Hills, Benny Siegel was gunned down by an unknown killer.

Shortly after Siegel died in California, two men working for Meyer Lansky walked into the Flamingo and announced that they were taking over. Maurice Rosen and Gus Greenbaum had worked for Lansky in Miami, Havana and New York, which gave a great deal of strength to the theory that in the end, Lansky had ordered his best friend killed. Lansky, however, denied having anything to do with Benny's killing.

JEWISH HERITAGE

Meyer Lansky's religious upbringing and cultural background as a Jew played conflicting roles during his lifetime. As time went by and Lansky grew older, his Jewish heritage came to mean more and more for him. He visited Israel for the first time when he was almost sixty years old, and the visit to the Holy Land re-ignited a passion for his culture.

By 1970, hounded by the police, the FBI and under surveillance at every turn, Meyer Lansky decided to join his friend Doc Stacher in Israel. After living in Israel for several months, Lansky decided to take advantage of the country's unique immigration law, the Law of Return, which states that every Jew in the world is eligible to become an

Israeli citizen – save for those with 'a criminal past'.

Lansky engaged several attorneys in order to secure his rightful place as an Israeli citizen. It was looking favourable for Lansky and his second wife, Teddy, until the Israeli press caught wind that Meyer Lansky, the chairman of the mob board of directors was in Tel Aviv. Photographers stalked the Lanskys and newspapers speculated that he was planning on continuing his racketeering in Israel. Although it would have been an easy thing to do, Lansky by this time was close to retiring.

When Israel's Prime Minister Golda Meir found out Lansky was connected to 'the Mafia' she intervened and Lansky was turned out of the country.

Lansky then travelled to Zurich and quickly left Switzerland for South America. He was trying to stay one step ahead of the FBI who wanted to arrest him on racketeering charges. But Paraguay would not accept him either and he was placed on an aeroplane whose final destination was Panama City, Florida. There would be no escape for Lansky this time.

As soon as Meyer's plane touched down in Florida, FBI agents arrested him and he was held until he posted a $250,000 bail. From jail, Lansky checked into the Mount Sinai Hospital for observation – the stress of the 13,000 mile journey from Tel Aviv to South America through Latin America to Florida had taken its toll on the heart of the seventy-year-old Lansky.

In the Federal court in Miami, Meyer Lansky was convicted of contempt of court for failing to return from Israel two years earlier to answer a grand jury's questions. He was sentenced to a year-and-a-day in jail.

Lansky was next tried for tax evasion, despite his ill health and need for oxygen and almost constant medical attention. The jury in this case took little time in finding against the government and for Lansky. Meanwhile, the Fifth Circuit court overturned his contempt conviction. Finally, the third case which had precipitated Lansky's deportation from Israel, was dropped by the government after an unfavourable ruling by the judge.

Lansky survived another six years after his final court battles. In that time he never gave up hope of returning to Israel either as a tourist or as a citizen. But his health became poor and on January 15, 1983, Meyer Lansky, the mastermind of the mob, died at his home.

It was through Meyer Lansky's guidance that the Syndicate was able to prosper in the United States. He might not have been the one to suggest the idea that the mob get involved in narcotics, but his system of co-operation between various gangsters regardless of race or ethnic background paved the way for today's organized gangs. Even though he saw himself as an honest citizen whose vision had been perverted by others with fewer scruples, there is no doubt that Meyer Lansky was a criminal through and through.

Benjamin 'Bugsy' Siegel

*As Benjamin 'Bugsy' Siegel stood just a fraction
under six-feet tall, with a thick head of black hair
and piercing blue eyes, he appeared to be a gangster
sent from central casting in Hollywood. He was
charming with the ladies and a sharp dresser,
athletically inclined and fearless.*

This is the story of 'Bugsy' Siegel – a man who
rose from the depths of poverty to the pinnacle
of mob life, but whose arrogant pride would be his
downfall. 'Bugsy' Siegel was one of the most
ruthless killers in the Mafia. He began his rise in
New York's Hell's Kitchen and ended up by
building up the gambling industry in Las Vegas.

Benjamin Siegelbaum was born in 1902 in the
Williamsburg section of Brooklyn. It was here that
thousands of Irish, Italian and Jewish immigrants
had settled, all struggling to make a life for
themselves in the New World. The streets of Hell's
Kitchen were a perfect breeding ground for crime.

Benjamin's parents raised five children, including Ben, on the meagre wages of a day labourer.
Ben saw how hard his Russian-born father worked
for pennies and vowed that he would rise above
this life. He knew he was destined for bigger things.

39

Ben's best childhood friend was Moey Sedway, who was willing to go along with whatever plan Ben was hatching. Their favourite pastime was a small extortion racket launched against the street vendors. Ben would go up and ask the vendor for a dollar and when he turned away from his kart, Ben would have Moey splash the wares with petrol and set light to it. The next time the boys came around, the vendor was usually willing to pay up. Ben and Moey then moved on to a protection scam, taking money from the vendors on Lafayette Street in return for making sure no one else pulled the same rip-off.

It was while Ben was running this protection racket that he met another immigrant teenage outlaw with big plans, Meyer Lansky. Together, these two youngsters would build up a gang of killers that became first the underworld's murder-for-hire squad and later an integral part of the national crime Syndicate.

Lansky, who had already had a run-in with a young Salvatore Lucania, later known as Lucky Luciano, saw that the Jewish boys of his Brooklyn neighbourhood needed to group together in the same manner as the Italians and Irish. The first person he recruited for his gang was Ben Siegel.

Siegel's gang mates included Abner 'Longie' Zwillman, who later ran the rackets in New Jersey; Lepke Buchalter, the head of Murder Inc. and the only top mobster to get the chair; Lansky's brother, Jake; and a young boy named Arthur Flegenheimer, who would go on to make a name for himself as Dutch Schultz. Benny and Meyer

Lansky were so close that the gang became known as the 'Bugs and Meyer Mob'.

MURDER INC.

It wasn't long before the Bugs and Meyer mob was running street corner gambling games, protection rackets and a stolen car ring. But murder wasn't something that they had tackled – until now.

Charlie Luciano went to prison on a narcotics charge in 1915, and served six months of a one-year prison sentence. Both Bugsy and Lansky remained close to the Sicilian. On his release, Luciano was hot for revenge. He knew who had set him up for the drug charge – the son of an Irish cop. Luciano wanted the kid dead and was prepared to take quick action.

Lansky and Siegel waited a full year to exact revenge. Then, Lansky told Luciano to take a holiday out of town and to make sure he had a solid alibi. While Luciano established the precise and verifiable details of his alibi, Siegel and Lansky went to work. Soon afterwards, there was a massive manhunt for a missing 19-year-old Irishman, the son of a Brooklyn cop. Charlie was hauled in for questioning, but his alibi held. The boy's body was never found.

The killing would have repercussions for Siegel nearly a decade later. In the fallout of the killing, a local woman started to lean on the trio, saying unless they paid up, she would go to the police with information about the boy's disappearance. Lansky, Luciano and Bugsy paid a visit to the

41

woman's apartment and savagely beat her as a warning to keep her mouth shut. They were caught in the act by police, who hauled them down to their headquarters. The woman, who had apparently got the message they were trying to impart, failed to show up for the court date.

Eight years later, Siegel ran into the woman in a bar. She started mocking Ben and told him he had been wet behind the ears and 'wouldn't have known what to do with me anyway'. Ben did not take this chastising lightly and decided to show her that he had grown up and learned what to do with women. He followed her home, and as she approached an alley, Siegel pulled her into the dark and raped her. He was arrested, but Lansky had a few 'persuasive' words with the woman and the charges were dropped.

After the Irish boy's disappearance, Siegel, Lansky and Luciano kept low profiles, working mostly on floating craps games, small-time union head-busting and robbery. The Bugs and Meyer mob was known as a stick-up and burglary operation, running gambling ventures in Brooklyn but roaming far from home – Harlem and other Manhattan areas – to commit their robberies. The gang was already known for its viciousness; they weren't afraid to use knives or fists to beat up whoever got in their way.

THE MOB IN FULL SWING

By the end of World War I, the Bugs and Meyer mob was in full swing, operating closely with

Lucky Luciano and his right-hand man, Frank Costello. Although the Sicilians and the Jews were separate gangs, there was more than a loose connection between the two groups.

While the rest of the world was occupied with the fighting over in Europe, the Bugs and Meyer mob were busy terrorizing the people of New York. Their targets were mainly pawnbrokers, money-lenders and immigrant businessmen. While Bugs remained a hothead who liked to fight first and ask questions later, Lansky and Luciano were making plans to break into the big time.

Unlike other gangs who spent their illicit earnings as soon as they acquired it, Meyer and Charlie put their money aside in a special fund. As the war came to a close, neither man had any idea as to what the bankroll would be used for, but they both knew that to hit the big time they had to have capital behind them.

Meyer, always the businessman, read up on management practices and investment policies. He told Benny to case out a local bank to see if it was worth putting the funds in. But Benny returned from the visit unimpressed, saying that it was not safe to deposit their savings there as anyone could break in and steal all the money.

Two weeks later, the Bugs and Meyer mob returned to the bank – not to make a deposit, but to hold the place up. They overpowered the aged, half-blind security guard and escaped with $8,000.

Robbery, street corner craps and protection rackets were providing the gang with a quick infusion of funds, but Lansky, Siegel and Luciano were smart. They knew that it wouldn't be long before their luck ran out. They started to look for different ways to break into the huge illegal gambling market in New York. They decided to use the money they had put away to buy into an established bookmaking operation, and to buy the protection of the police and politicians who ran the Lower East Side.

This was when the Bugs and Meyer mob came to the attention of the real powers in New York City, Joe 'The Boss' Masseria and the Big Man himself, Arnold Rothstein.

In early 1919, a craps game that was operating under the protection of Meyer was raided by a group of men who proceeded to beat up the game's organizers, bodyguards and customers. The hoods told Lansky that this was a warning – unless tribute was paid, killings would follow.

Meyer and Bugs, however, remained determined. They hunted down the Italian who led the raid and were prepared to exact revenge when the man told them that Joe the Boss would make them pay with their lives. They backed off and regrouped. Masseria had decided to bring the Lower East Side under his control and the Bugs and Meyer mob was standing in his way. Masseria was an old-time gangster who was not interested in co-operating with non-Sicilians and he was set on obtaining the mob's money for his own purposes.

Bugs, in his usual style, was ready to go in shooting. It didn't seem to matter to him that Masseria had a 200-man army and that the Bugs

and Meyer mob was at best two dozen strong.
Siegel's honour was at stake and he wouldn't go
down without a fight. This time, Lansky agreed
with his boyhood friend. He knew that every other
mobster in the city was gunning for Joe the Boss
and that now was the time to go on the offensive.

Siegel and several other toughs from his gang
returned to Masseria's East Side lieutenant and
this time they didn't back down. A huge fight
broke out and the Masseria boys were driven off.
By the time the battle was over, the cops had
arrived and Lansky, Siegel and some other Bugs
and Meyer hoods were arrested. The charge was
disorderly conduct and carried a $2 fine. The fight
sent a clear message to Masseria – the Lower East
Side belonged to the Bugs and Meyer mob.

PROHIBITION

The Volstead Act of 1919 made the manufacture
and sale of alcohol illegal in the United States, and
for gangsters like Bugsy Siegel, this was a licence
to steal.

Across the country this law was flouted –
speakeasies and gin joints sprang up with amazing
frequency. Bootleggers smuggled booze across
every border, in trucks, boats and through pipelines. Judges were reluctant to enforce the
penalties of the Volstead Act and police would turn
a blind eye for a price. Prohibition did little to
curb the consumption of alcohol and only served
to provide the underworld with access to easy
money.

In New York, Arnold Rothstein knew a good thing when he saw it. Rothstein wanted to make money during Prohibition, but he wanted to do it high class. To do this, however, he needed partners. This was when he turned to Charlie Luciano and the Bugs and Meyer mob. He summoned them to his Central Park residence, where Meyer Lansky and Charlie Luciano were offered their chance at the big time.

The meeting lasted for more than six hours. Rothstein proposed that under the direction of the Bugs and Meyer mob – specifically Lansky (he had no patience for a man of Bugs's temperament) – Dutch Schultz would take over the New York bootlegging operation and Longy Zwillman, Lansky's close friend and kindred intellectual spirit, would run North Jersey.

As a cover-up for their rum-running operation, Siegel and Lansky operated a car and truck rental operation through a garage on Cannon Street in Brooklyn. Ironically, Lansky's skill as a businessman made the rental business almost as much of a success as the bootlegging.

While Lansky watched over the gang's ever-increasing businesses, Bugsy was the one who craved the excitement of taking a shipment of illegal booze or hijacking another gang's property. One such hijacking took place after Bugsy found out that a shipment coming in on the South Jersey Shore belonged to Joe Masseria.

Lansky and Siegel, still anxious for revenge for Masseria's attempted power grab in Brooklyn, travelled down to Atlantic City and set up an ambush. They felled a tree and then hid in the nearby woods, waiting for the truck convoy to approach. Thanks to a $2,000 bribe, Siegel knew exactly when and where the shipment would be coming.

The shipment of top-grade scotch whisky was on its way from Masseria's boats to another Rothstein partner, Irving Wexler, better known as Waxey Gordon. Waxey planned to mix the scotch with some of his homemade Philadelphia rotgut and sell it at a quick profit. The raid was dangerous for several reasons. First, Masseria was still a force to be reckoned with on the East Coast. He still controlled his 200-man force and had many ways of reaching the boys if it all went wrong and they were forced into hiding. Second, Waxey Gordon was the boss of Philadelphia and would be out for blood when his investment failed to arrive. And finally, the Bugs and Meyer gang was going against Arnold Rothstein, who was Gordon's Philadelphia partner. Rothstein had forbidden his minions from stealing from one another and the penalty for such insolence would most likely be death.

Exactly as planned, the trucks arrived on the deserted road. On seeing the tree lying across the road, the driver of the first truck stopped the convoy and jumped out to move it. As soon as the group approached the tree, a shower of bullets rained down on them and sent them scrambling for cover. A furious gun battle ensued, and three of Masseria's men were shot. As the battle turned in favour of Siegel and his men, they emerged from the woods and began clubbing and beating the remaining Italians who had surrendered.

In the course of this savagery, one of Masseria's men recognized Meyer Lansky. Through Masseria, Waxey Gordon learned that the Bugs and Meyer mob was responsible for his loss, but because he didn't want Rothstein to know he was working with the Brain's despised Sicilian adversary, he kept his mouth shut. Gordon, however, did not forget, and he vowed to get revenge.

BUGSY AND SCARFACE

About the time Lansky was meeting with Rothstein to set up the bootlegging operation, Bugsy was helping out an old friend in a jam, Alphonse Capone, who was a boyhood friend of Bugsy's from his days in the Williamsburg section of Brooklyn. Capone wasn't a member of the Bugs and Meyer mob, he worked for and idolized Johnny Torrio, the bantamweight killer who would one day help Luciano and Lepke Buchalter found the Syndicate.

Capone, like Siegel, wasn't afraid to kill. Following his suspected involvement in a murder, Capone was forced to move west to avoid the law. Before leaving town, Capone went to his friend Ben Siegel and asked for help. Ben arranged for Capone to hide out with one of Siegel's aunts until things cooled down. It was clear, however, that even with friends like Bugsy, Al would have to leave New York.

Capone went west to join his mentor Torrio, but still remained close to Siegel and Luciano. Ben's success as a bootlegger would spur on the young

Scarface, who was now part of the Big Jim Colosimo gang in Chicago.

Big Jim was even more shortsighted than Masseria, and felt that the old rackets of prostitution and gambling were the way to go and forbade his gang from getting involved in rum-running. The leaders of the Bugs and Meyer mob were afraid that because of Big Jim's reluctance to get into bootlegging some other gangs would get into Chicago and lock them out. They hired Frankie Yale to go west and take care of Big Jim.

After Colosimo's death, Johnny Torrio took over with Capone as his lieutenant. They had no reluctance to get into the alcohol business and invited Siegel and Luciano into the city. Siegel, Lansky and Luciano made sure that they treated their friends in Chicago well. They split the profits equally between the two cities and built up a loyalty that would serve them well into the future.

THE END OF JOE THE BOSS

One of the most memorable moments in the history of organized crime must be the slaying of Joe 'the Boss' Masseria. His death, which ended the Castellamarese war between Masseria and his rival, Sal Maranzano, helped shape the face of organized crime as it exists today. Gangsters who moved up in ranks thanks to Masseria's death continued until the last decade to run the national crime syndicate, and the system that was put in place after Masseria's death still thrives in the United States.

By the end of the 1920s, Masseria had convinced Charlie Luciano to join his team. Charlie continued to interact with Siegel and Lansky, but he was occupied with the war between the Masseria and Maranzano gangs. Both Masseria and Maranzano wanted to be *capo di tutti capo*. Maranzano had a plan to unite all of the Italians in New York under an umbrella group that would put an end to the hijacking, kidnapping and murder that had gnawed away at the gangs during Prohibition. To do this, however, he would have to go through Joe the Boss. On the other hand, Masseria's philosophy was one of confrontation, not co-operation.

For nearly two years, the gangs waged war on each other. The friction was eating up both sides, but it soon became clear to Siegel and Lansky that Maranzano was winning. Sal had also been lobbying for Luciano's loyalties and even though Lucky was working for Masseria, Maranzano still wanted his help. The men of the Bugs and Meyer mob met with Luciano and hatched a plan.

Accompanied by Ben Siegel, Luciano met with Maranzano on the neutral ground of the Bronx Zoo. It was there that Luciano agreed to join Maranzano's gang. Although he would be Maranzano's lieutenant, he would still maintain his own operations with the Jewish gangsters as well as share in the Sicilian's spoils. His initiation fee was to be Joe Masseria's life.

Luciano invited his boss to Scarpato's restaurant in Coney Island on April 15, 1931. During the meal, which allegedly lasted for more than three hours,

Luciano excused himself to use the bathroom. As Masseria sat at the table where he and his loyal lieutenant had been planning the eradication once and for all of the Maranzano gang, a crew of gunmen rushed in and shot him to death.

Leading this charge was Benny Siegel, guns blazing. Six bullets found Joe the Boss who was desperately trying to find a place to hide. With Joe either dead or dying, the four gunmen, Siegel, Vito Genovese, Albert Anastasia and Joe Adonis, rushed from Scarpato's into the waiting car. The driver, Ciro Terranova, was so nervous that he stalled the car twice trying to get away. Siegel, awash in an adrenaline rush, slugged Ciro and pushed him out of the way. The four gunmen escaped before the police arrived and found the boss of bosses dead.

IN NEED OF REST

After the deaths of Joe Masseria and the mysterious killing of Arnold Rothstein, Waxey Gordon decided the time had come to even the score with Siegel and Lansky. From inside jail (where he had been sent by the IRS thanks to information leaked from the Bugs and Meyer mob), Waxey hired the Fabrazzo brothers to take out the Brooklyn boys once and for all. The Fabrazzos and Waxey's lieutenant, Charlie Sherman, broke into the Grand Street hideout of the Bugs and Meyer mob and managed to plant a bomb in a fireplace.

Bugs and Meyer were in the building at the time

51

when Siegel spotted the bomb, and they managed to throw it out of a window before it exploded. The blast hurt Siegel, but Meyer was unharmed. Ben, despite his injuries, hunted down the Fabrazzo brothers and made sure that they never took on another contract. Andy Fabrazzo was found stuffed in a sack in North Jersey and Louis was gunned down on a Manhattan street.

Tony Fabrazzo was as crooked as his brothers, but he wasn't involved in the attempt on Bugsy and Lansky. The deaths of his brothers made him realize how dangerous Siegel was, and he decided to protect himself. He let it be known that he was 'writing his memoirs' and was planning to give them to an attorney who would make sure the authorities got them if something happened to his client. One of the longest chapters of the book would be the section on the nationwide kill-for-hire squad led by Benjamin Siegel. Unfortunately for Tony, the mob got wind of his plans before he had a chance to put pen to paper. Siegel decided to take care of Tony himself and he set about creating an airtight alibi.

Bugsy told his friends that he was not well and needed to rest up after the bombing. He checked himself into a local Catholic hospital, and for two days he rested just like anyone else who had been through such a traumatic experience. Then, one night, he told the nurse that he was very tired and was going to bed early. He asked her to close the door and make sure that he was not disturbed.

As soon as the nurse left, Ben jumped out of bed, dressed and placed pillows under the sheets to make it look like a body was in the bed in case someone checked on him. He then climbed down the fire escape and met up with a couple of his gang members at the corner.

They drove down through Brooklyn to Tony Fabrazzo's house. Siegel knocked on the door and Fabrazzo's elderly father answered. 'We're detectives,' he told the old man. 'Where's Tony?'

Tony was in the kitchen when his father hurried in to deliver the message. Tony strutted to the front door with his family behind him. Tony should have recognized the trio, but when he saw them he didn't react like a man who was about to be killed. Fabrazzo presented an easy target to the killers and they took full advantage. Three shots rang out and Tony, in full view of his mother and father, fell dead to the floor of his boyhood home.

Bugsy returned to the hospital and was back in bed before anyone noticed he was missing. He remained in his bed for two more days until he was visited by a couple of his gang members. Then, he quickly packed his things and checked himself out. Later, it was learned that his mob had been watching the hospital and had noticed a couple of Fabrazzo's friends circling the block looking for a place to park. The Bugs and Meyer mobsters figured they were out for revenge and that the healthiest place for Bugsy was as far away from the hospital as possible.

THE WEST COAST ASSIGNMENT

The murder of Fabrazzo was not one of Ben's

smartest moves. His victim knew him and Tony's friends knew that Bugsy had been a key part of Fabrazzo's tell-all book. Over time Ben's alibi, so carefully constructed, began to crumble and he was forced to go underground.

Other problems were also becoming apparent. Ben and Meyer were as close as brothers, but Bugsy wasn't happy standing in Meyer's shadow. In normal gangster behaviour, when number two gets tired of being an underling, he conspires to bump off the boss. But even in Bugsy's twisted mind, killing Lansky wasn't something he cared to contemplate. As Bugsy became more and more unsettled, Meyer decided to set up the West Coast assignment specifically for Bugsy.

Although it took about four years, eventually New York became too hot for Siegel following the death of Fabrazzo. It was time for him to leave. The Syndicate board of directors met and conferred about Bugsy's fate, and it is a testament to the loyalty between Lansky and Siegel that the Syndicate allowed Bugsy to live. Normally gangsters who have become liabilities to the mob are taken out in classic mob style. Regardless of his skill and value to the mob, if Siegel hadn't been a blood brother to Lansky, he probably would have ended up on the bottom of the East River – instead he would go to the West coast.

At this time the western United States was almost untapped in terms of organized crime. There were gangs here and there, but the national Syndicate had only got as far as Hot Springs, Arkansas.

The strongest gang in California was headed by Jack I. Dragna, president of the Italian Protective League (or IPL). The IPL was a benevolent society for Italian immigrants who had come to the Gold Coast, but in reality, the League was little more than a Mafia muscle outfit preying on the same immigrants it claimed to protect. Dragna and his number two, Joe Ardizzone, had their fingers in gambling, bootlegging, extortion and smuggling.

Dragna's real name was Anthony Rizzoti, and like so many others in organized crime, he held Charlie Luciano in the highest regard. Luciano, who was at the time imprisoned in Dannemora State Penitentiary, sent word to Dragna that the Syndicate was moving in and he could either take part or be taken apart.

Dragna wisely decided to co-operate. He did, however, resent the intrusion of the Jewish gangster from New York and bided his time looking for a chance to get rid of Bugsy.

Bugsy, his wife and their two daughters showed up in California and immediately rented a 35-room mansion owned by singer Lawrence Tibbet. The white brick palace in the upscale Hollywood suburb of Holmby Hills was complete with swimming pool and a private marble bath for Bugsy.

When he got to Hollywood, Siegel looked up an old friend from Williamsburg who had made it big in the movies – George Raft. He and Bugsy had kept in contact with one another over the years and formed a mutual admiration society. Together, Raft and Siegel became regulars at Santa Anita Racetrack, betting huge sums of money on the horses. It was Raft who opened the door to Siegel's first West Coast racket.

Following Lansky's example, Siegel let Dragna handle the gambling operations while he went after the unions. His first target was the relatively easy-to-tackle extras union. Quickly, Bugsy and his old pal Moey Sedway, who had followed his boss west, infiltrated the union and began extorting money from movie moguls who needed the extras to make their films.

Raft also introduced Ben into the high glamour world of the film stars. Starlets were taken with Ben's suave appearance and good looks, and the men were in awe of his masculinity. He soon became the talk of the town and no party was complete unless Bugsy Siegel was there. Siegel had a torrid romance with a wild French actress named Ketti Gallian. But Bugs was fickle and soon he was moving from starlet to starlet, including Jean Harlow.

Once Siegel and Sedway had control of the extras union, they began to move in on the stars. At one of those Hollywood parties, Ben would point out that the star would be unable to work on his next picture if the producer couldn't hire any extras. In his first year in Hollywood, Bugsy received more than $400,000 in one-way 'loans' from movie stars, the same people who were so desperate to have him at their parties.

TRANSAMERICA WIRE

It certainly seemed that if Bugsy was in town, murder couldn't be far behind. Siegel, arguably the gambling grandfather of organized crime was also the head of Transamerica. This was a wire service which was set up to compete with the Continental Wire Service as part of the organized crime extortion scheme.

Wire services were operating from a nationwide network and would report anything that might affect betting or the outcome of a race. It was vital that bookmakers had a quick, discreet and reliable method of reporting the results of races. The Wire services provided this service and the information supplied included the condition of a certain track, any change in jockey, up-to-the-minute betting odds and, of course, results. It also informed the bookies if there was unusually heavy betting on any one particular horse.

However, race results via the legal Western Union wire were restricted by law. They were only allowed to give the outcome of the race after it had been officially declared. This could result in a delay of several minutes, maybe due to a photo-finish, or an objection by a jockey. This delay, however, left it open for 'past posting'. This involved corrupt punters placing a winning bet after a decision has been reached. So this meant that no serious bookmaker would attempt to operate their business without the back-up of an illegal wire.

At the beginning of the 1940s, two major wire services were in operation – Continental Wire Service, operated by a Chicago gangster named James Ragan and Transamerica Wire, which operated with the full backing of the Syndicate.

One of Siegel's major priorities in the pre-war 1940s was to endeavour to get California bookmakers to subscribe to the Transamerica wire to try and oust the opposition. It took Siegel almost six years to build up his wire network, but he was finally able to eliminate Continental (including James Ragan), through the usual mob strong-arm tactics. Ragan was gunned down in the streets of Chicago, which caused Continental to fall apart rapidly, giving Transamerica the chance to completely take over.

However, following his success, the Syndicate informed Bugsy that they would now be handling the wire business. Bugsy was far from happy because he was earning a good living from Transamerica. Siegel told the Syndicate, quite adamantly, that he would continue to run the wire services his own way and they were not going to take the profits of his hard work. Siegel must have realized at that time that he was writing his own death sentence.

BENNY IN LAS VEGAS

Siegel could see that there were opportunities to be made out west and so he decided to make his move. In fact, Bugsy Siegel is mainly remembered for his success in building up gambling houses in Las Vegas. In truth, Bugsy's work in Las Vegas came at the very end of his career and probably contributed to him being killed in the prime of his life.

Bugsy was convinced that Las Vegas had something else going for it that no other place in the

United States had at the time, the reason – it was legal to gamble in Nevada. In the 1940s, Nevada's gaming laws were expanded to allow off-track betting on horse races, and it was this that first attracted Siegel, thanks in part to his involvement in Transamerica Wire.

Lansky and his buddies on the East Coast ran a number of carpet joints in Florida that operated on the fringe of the law and Jack Dragna and Bugsy managed a couple of floating casinos that operated outside the 3-mile US territorial limit. But setting a permanent, lavish casino in Las Vegas would give the mob an entry into a legitimate business that was almost a licence to print money.

After couple of unsuccessful attempts to buy already established gambling joints in the city, Bugsy met Billy Wilkerson. Billy was getting ready to build the most luxurious hotel Vegas had ever seen, complete with individual air conditioners, tiled bathrooms and two swimming pools. Bugsy had just managed to buy a controlling interest in the project when Wilkerson's cashflow dried up. Siegel wanted to create an oasis in the desert where travellers from both coasts could come for sun, fun, gambling and entertainment. Ben called his dream 'The Flamingo'.

However, things were not easy and there were difficulties right from the start. Construction materials were hard to come by, were very expensive, and transportation to and from Vegas was difficult. Bugsy was a gangster, not an architect, and some of the builders working on the project were taking him for a ride, and robbing him of what they could get their hands on.

Ben had already convinced his fellow racketeers to invest money into his Flamingo venture, luring them with stories of immense wealth and quick profits. But the building costs soon spiralled out of control, and the original $1.2 million costing quickly escalated to $6 million. Lansky, Luciano and the other investors started to become increasingly concerned about Ben's dream in the Las Vegas desert.

By December 1946 the casino had not produced any revenue and was bleeding the mob treasury dry. At a conference in Havana, Cuba, attended by Meyer Lansky, Frank Costello, Luciano, Vito Genovese and Joey Adonis, Lansky revealed even more disturbing news. Ben Siegel had apparently been creaming money from the mob and stashing it away in Swiss bank accounts. The solution for anyone who steals from the Syndicate is death.

Luckily for Bugsy, Meyer wasn't ready to give up on him yet. He stood up to the Syndicate and recommended a stay of execution until after the opening of the Flamingo casino. If it turned out to be a success, then there would be plenty of ways to make Benny pay back the money. If it didn't make money, then Fischetti could carry out the contract.

Just after Christmas the Flamingo's casino was ready to take its first customers. He pulled out all the stops, hiring famous names to do the entertainment, but it was a disaster.

With the hotel rooms unfinished and the inclement weather conditions, Siegel's guests gambled at his casino and took their winnings back home with them or spent it in other downtown hotels. Lansky reluctantly reported to the Syndicate that the Flamingo's opening had been a flop. The gangsters were enraged and assembled in Havana, demanding that Fischetti fulfil the contract at once. Again, Meyer tried everything he could to save his friend, saying that he was sure Las Vegas could be a very profitable venture. The Syndicate agreed to a short delay and asked their lawyers if it was possible for the original Flamingo corporation to be put into receivership to stop any more losses. The mob could then move in and buy out the legitimate partners. The plan was reluctantly agreed and Bugsy was given yet another reprieve.

THE DEATH OF BUGSY SIEGEL

Bugsy gave up on the Flamingo in the early part of January. He ordered that the resort be closed until the hotel itself could be finished. Fortunately for Ben, his staunchest allies remained Meyer Lansky and Charles Luciano, who continued to believe that money could and would be made in Las Vegas.

Bugsy devoted every waking hour to making sure the Flamingo was ready for its grand reopening in March. Having been given this second chance, Ben made sure that he didn't waste any time. The casino reopened in March and by May, it appeared that Bugsy's dream would finally come true. The resort reported a profit of over $250,000 for the first half of 1947, including the disastrous month of January.

With the Flamingo now running at a profit Ben felt he could now relax. Siegel had named the Flamingo after his pet name for his mistress Virginia Hill. Virginia was a notorious blackmailer and she thrived in Hollywood, where she made plenty of money out of closet homosexuals who did not want their secret life revealed to the public. Although Siegel was married with two daughters, he still had an insatiable sexual appetite and pursued many girls, but he always came back to Hill. Possibly because she was just as ruthless as he was and he loved her for it. What he didn't know, however, was that she was spying on him for the Chicago branch of the Syndicate.

On June 8, 1947, the Chicago mob called Virginia Hill and instructed her to go to Paris. She was a money courier for the Mafia and it was not unusual for her to fly to various destinations to deposit dirty money in Syndicate accounts. Bugsy asked if she would join him but she told him she had to fly to Paris to get some wine for the Flamingo. Involved in his business activities Bugsy hardly paid any attention.

On the evening of June 20, 1947, Siegel was at home in the bungalow he and Virginia shared in Hollywood. Finally Ben felt things were going his way and he was looking forward to his daughters coming out from the East Coast to spend the summer with him.

At about 10:30 p.m. a fusillade of bullets crashed through the living room window. The first shot hit Bugsy in the head, blowing his eye fifteen feet from his body. Four more bullets hit his body, breaking his ribs and ripping through his lungs. Bugsy Siegel, at only 42 years old, was dead.

Only five people, all relatives, attended Ben's funeral. Exactly who killed Bugsy Siegel has never really been answered, but there are no shortage of theories. Before Siegel's body was even cold, two of Meyer Lansky's top operatives, Maurice Rosen and Gus Greenbaum, walked into the Flamingo and announced that the Syndicate was taking over.

Virginia Hill's body was found in Austria in 1966, dead from Mercury poisoning.

Alphonse 'Scarface' Capone

Al Capone is probably America's best known gangster and the single greatest symbol of the collapse of law and order in the United States during the 1920s Prohibition era. Capone had a leading role in the illegal activities that lent Chicago its reputation as a lawless city.

Along with thousands of other Italians, the Capone family moved to Brooklyn near the Brooklyn Navy Yard. It was a harsh start in the New World. Number 95, Navy Street was a cold-water tenement flat that had no indoor toilet or furniture.

Capone was born on January 17, 1899, in Brooklyn, New York. His parents Gabriele and Teresina had him baptized 'Alphonsus Capone' and he grew up in a very rough neighbourhood. Shortly after Al was born, Gabriele moved the family to better lodgings in an apartment over his barber shop at 69, Park Avenue in Brooklyn. This move introduced Al to cultural influences well beyond those of the Italian immigrant community. Most of the people living around Park Avenue were Irish, although Germans, Swedes and

Chinese also lived in the neighbourhood. There is no doubt that this exposure would help him in his future role as the head of a criminal empire. It was here that he would meet his future wife Mae and the gangster Johnny Torrio.

A few blocks away from the Capone house on Garfield Place was a small unobtrusive building that was the headquarters of one of the most successful gangsters on the East Coast.

JOHNNY TORRIO

Johnny Torrio was a new breed of gangster, a pioneer in the development of a modern criminal operation. His administrative and organizational skills transformed crude racketeering into a kind of corporate structure, taking advantage of every opportunity as it emerged. It was from Torrio, that a young Capone learned invaluable lessons that were the foundation of the criminal empire he later built in Chicago.

Torrio was known as a gentleman gangster who had his finger in many pies, including being in charge of a number of whores and brothels. He was a role model for many boys in the community. Capone, like many other boys his age, earned pocket money by running errands for Johnny Torrio. As time went by Torrio learned to trust the young Capone and gave him more to do. This gave the young Al the opportunity to learn by watching Torrio and the people in his organization.

Kids growing up in immigrant Brooklyn went around in gangs – Italian gangs, Jewish gangs and

Irish gangs. They were not the vicious urban street gangs of today, but rather groups of territorial neighbourhood boys who hung out together. Capone was a tough, scrappy kid and belonged to two gangs, the Brooklyn Rippers and the Forty Thieves Juniors. Despite Al's relationship with the street gangs and Johnny Torrio, there was no indication that Al would choose someday to lead a life of crime.

Although Al was a bright child at school, at the age of fourteen he lost his temper with his teacher, she hit him and he hit her back. He was expelled and never went to school again. Al still lived at home and was a well-behaved and sociable boy.

For approximately six years, between various swindles he worked faithfully at exceptionally boring jobs – a clerk in a sweetshop, a pinboy in a bowling alley, and a cutter in a book bindery. One person that had a lasting influence on Al was Frankie Yale. Originally from Calabria, Francesco Ioele (called 'Yale'), was both feared and respected. Unlike the peace-loving and apparently respectable Johnny Torrio, Frankie Yale built his turf on muscle and aggression. Yale opened a bar on Coney Island called the *Harvard Inn* and hired, on the recommendation of Johnny Torrio, the eighteen-year-old Al Capone.

'SCARFACE'

Capone's job at the *Harvard Inn* was to be a bartender, bouncer and, when necessary, to wait on tables. In his first year, Capone became popular with both his boss and the customers. But one day while he waited on the table of a young couple his luck was to turn. The girl was beautiful and the young Capone was completely captivated. He leaned over her and said, 'Honey, you have a nice ass and I mean that as a compliment'.

The man who was accompanying her was her brother, Frank Gallucio. He immediately jumped to his feet and punched the man who insulted his sister. At this Capone flew into a rage and Gallucio pulled out a knife to defend himself. He slashed Capone's face three times before grabbing his sister and leaving the inn. Although the wounds healed well, the long ugly scars haunted him for the rest of his life.

Capone's incident with Gallucio caused a bit of an uproar. Gallucio had reported back to Lucky Luciano with his grievance and Luciano immediately went to Frankie Yale. When it came to Yale's attention, all four men came together and forced Capone to apologize to Gallucio. Capone learned from the experience, if nothing else, to restrain his temper when it was necessary.

Seeing another side to Capone, Yale took him under his wing. He impressed upon the young Capone how business can be built up through brutality. Yale was both a resourceful and violent man who had prospered by strong-arm tactics. Yale specialized in extortion, loansharking, taking money from pimps and bookmakers, and offering 'protection' to local businesses. Yale needed employees who could not only break arms and heads but would be prepared to kill.

Although Yale was a powerful influence on Capone's development, other influences had a very moderating effect on Al. At the age of nineteen, he met a pretty blonde Irish girl named Mae Coughlin, who was two years his senior. Her family was comfortable and solidly middle class. Mae's family were not supportive of her relationship with Capone and it was not until after their baby was born that they actually married.

Albert Francis Capone was born December 4, 1918, and Johnny Torrio was appointed his godfather. While Sonny, as he was known all his life, seemed okay at birth, he was in fact a victim of congenital syphilis. Years later, Al confessed to doctors that he had been infected before he was married, but he believed that the infection had gone away.

With a beautiful respectable wife and a baby to support, Al now focused on a legitimate career. He stopped working for Frankie Yale and moved to Baltimore where he worked as a bookkeeper for Peter Aiello's construction firm. Al did very well. He was smart, had a good head for figures and was very reliable.

However, Capone abandoned his acquired cloak of respectability when his father died on November 14, 1920, of heart disease at the age of fifty-five. He resumed his relationship with Johnny Torrio, who had during the intervening years greatly expanded his racketeering empire. Torrio had left Brooklyn some years ago and was now operating in Chicago. The opportunities there were enormous – gambling, brothels and illegal alcohol.

Torrio asked Capone to join him in Chicago and early in 1921 Al accepted. Armed with his knowledge of business and his experience with the brutal Frankie Yale, Capone had a good resume for a career in crime.

A CRIMINAL EMPIRE IN CHICAGO

Chicago was a perfect place to build a criminal empire. Political corruption was a tradition in the city, breeding an atmosphere in which crime flourished. The city became known for its wealth and sexual promiscuity and by the time Al Capone came to the city in 1920, the flesh trade was becoming the province of organized crime. The mastermind behind this business was 'Big Jim' Colosimo together with his wife and partner, Victoria Moresco, a highly successful madam. Together their brothels were earning an estimated $50,000 per month.

Big Jim owned one of the most popular nightclubs in the city – the Colosimo Cafe. Nobody gave a damn that he was a pimp, and indeed it never stopped him from hobnobbing with the rich and famous. Among his distinguished guests were Enrico Caruso and the famous lawyer Clarence Darrow. Big Jim was a true product of Chicago society – handsome, generous, gaudy and larger than life.

As his vice business grew, Big Jim brought in the discreet Johnny Torrio from Brooklyn to operate and help him expand his empire. It was the best decision he could have made because Torrio expanded their business without attracting attention. Torrio was a serious businessman, unlike Big Jim, who loved to drink, smoke, swear and womanize.

Big Jim's downfall was when he met Dale Winter, a pretty young singer who stole his heart. He foolishly divorced his loyal wife Victoria and immediately married the young singer. Word of Colosimo's foolishness got back to Frankie Yale, who immediately took the opportunity to muscle in on Colosimo's huge empire. On May 11, 1920, Yale assassinated Big Jim in his nightclub.

The police eventually figured out who the murderer was and they arrested him in New York. However, the only witness to the murder, a waiter, flatly refused to testify against Frankie Yale, which rendered the police powerless. Although Yale was able to avoid prosecution, his attempt to take over Colosimo's empire failed. Torrio was able to maintain his grip on the vast multimillion-dollar-a-year business he had built for Big Jim and with a big boost to business from Prohibition, Torrio now oversaw thousands of whorehouses, gambling joints and speakeasies.

It was into this vast criminal enterprise that Torrio brought 22-year-old Al Capone from his honest bookkeeping job in Baltimore. With his business acumen, Al soon became Torrio's partner rather than his employee. He took over as manager of the Four Deuces, which was a speakeasy, gambling joint and whorehouse all in one. Soon, Al's brother Ralph 'Bottles' Capone would come to join him in Torrio's business.

It was about this time that Al became associated with a man that would be his friend for life, Jack Guzik. Guzik came from a large Jewish Orthodox family who made their living through prostitution. Guzik was a devoted family man who acted like an older brother to Al, and took him under his wing. Once again, Capone showed his ability to step outside the Italian community as he had in marrying his Irish wife. Now his closest friend was Jewish. Capone's lack of prejudice and ability to create alliances outside of the Italian gangster community proved to be invaluable in shaping his future.

Al, now financially secure, was able to buy a house for his family in a respectable neighbour-hood. 7244 Prairie Avenue, was home not only to Mae and Sonny, but also his mother and other siblings. Al posed to his neighbours as a dealer in second-hand furniture and went out of his way to maintain a façade of respectability.

CAPONE TAKES CHARGE

For several years after Capone arrived in Chicago, things were comparatively quiet among the various gangs. But things were to change when William E. Dever succeeded the particularly corrupt Mayor 'Big Bill' Thompson. With the city now in the hands of an earnest reformer, the daily process of payoffs and corruption became more and more difficult. Torrio and Capone decided to move many of their operations out of the city into the suburb of Cicero, where they could buy off the

entire city government and police department.
Shortly after opening up a brothel in Cicero,
Torrio took his elderly mother back to live in Italy,
leaving Capone in charge of the business. Capone
made it clear that he wanted to be in total charge
of the town. He installed his older brother Frank
as the front man with the Cicero city government.
Meanwhile, Ralph was given the job of opening up
a working-class brothel called the Stockade, while
Al focused on gambling. He took an interest in a
new gambling joint called the Ship, and also took
control of the Hawthorne Race Track.

If it hadn't been for a young journalist named
Robert St. John who worked for the *Cicero
Tribune*, Capone's conquest of Cicero would have
remained unopposed. St. John exposed the rackets
that Capone was running in the city, and his
editorials proved effective enough to threaten
Capone-backed candidates in the 1924 primary
election.

Things became ugly on election day, as Capone's
forces kidnapped opponents' election workers and
threatened voters with violence. As reports of the
violence spread, the Chicago Chief of Police
rounded up 79 police armed with shotguns. The
police, dressed in plain clothes, arrived in Cicero
in unmarked cars under the pretence of protecting
workers at the Western Electric plant there.

Frank Capone, who had just finished nego-
tiating a lease, was walking down the street when
the convoy of Chicago policemen approached him.
Someone recognized him, the police all climbed
out of their cars, and in seconds Frank's body was

riddled with bullets. The police called it self defence, since Frank had drawn his own revolver on seeing the police approaching him. Al was enraged and made the situation worse by kidnapping officials and stealing ballot boxes. One official was murdered and when it was all over, Capone had won his victory for Cicero.

Capone threw a lavish funeral for his brother – the flowers alone, provided by racketeer florist Dion O'Banion – cost $20,000.

Capone kept his temper under control for several weeks until Joe Howard, a small-time thug, assaulted Capone's friend Jack Guzik. Apparently Guzik had turned him down for a loan. Capone tracked Howard down in a bar and shot him dead, after he foolishly called Capone a 'dago pimp'.

Capone got away with murder, mainly because eyewitnesses suddenly developed faulty memories. The publicity surrounding the case, however, gave him a notoriety that he never had before

After only four years in Chicago, and still only 25 years old, Capone was a force to be reckoned with. Wealthy, powerful, master of the city of Cicero, he became a target for lawmen and rival gangsters alike. He was keenly aware that his could be the next gangster funeral and the fragile peace that Torrio had constructed with other gangs was being blown apart by Prohibition. Gangland murders were now reaching epidemic proportions.

Attempts on Capone's life were never successful. He had an extensive spy network in Chicago, from newspaper boys to policemen, so that any plots were quickly discovered. Capone, on the other hand, was skillful at isolating and killing his enemies when they became too powerful. A typical Capone murder consisted of men renting an apartment across the street from the victim's residence and gunning him down when he stepped outside. The operations were quick and complete and Capone always had an alibi.

While Capone's name was often linked with these murders, the fact was that there were many other gangsters responsible that Capone and Torrio had tried to keep in line. One such gangster was Dion O'Banion. O'Banion was known for his bizarre behaviour which included shooting a man in front of a crowd of people for no apparent reason, and then killing a man after meeting him at Capone's Four Deuces, which dragged Capone into a murder investigation needlessly. There was a growing sense of realization that something had to be done.

On November 10, 1924, Dion was in his flower shop fixing flowers for a funeral when three gangsters came into the shop. Dion's employee left the men alone to their business. O'Banion, who thought they had come to pick up a wreath, greeted the men and prepared to shake hands. One of the men pulled O'Banion's arm and knocked him off balance. Dion's employee heard six gun shots and ran to help his boss who was lying on the floor in a pool of blood. The three men had vanished and none of Dion's likely murderers ever came to trial.

Dion's funeral was a celebration for Torrio and Capone because they took over Dion's excellent bootlegging territory and they had finally rid themselves of a dangerously unpredictable colleague. What they didn't appreciate at the time was exactly how Dion's death would affect them personally. From that moment on, Capone and Torrio looked over their shoulders constantly for 'Hymie' Weiss and another Dion associate, Bugs Moran.

'Hymie' Weiss's real name was Earl Wajcie-chowski, which he shortened to Weiss. The nickname 'Hymie' stuck somehow and everyone assumed he was a Jewish gangster, when he was in fact a very devout Catholic. George Moran was a violent and unstable man who got the nickname 'Bugs' because everyone thought he was nuts or 'buggy'.

Torrio was so concerned for his life that he decided to leave Chicago and headed for Hot Springs, Arkansas. Capone was just as worried but instead of running, took every possible security measure. Over the next two years, the former colleagues of Dion O'Banion would make a dozen attempts to assassinate Capone. Capone made sure that he was never alone. He only travelled by car, sandwiched between bodyguards, with a trusted, armed chauffeur named Sylvester Barton, making most of his journeys after dark.

In January of 1925, twelve days after the Weiss-Moran gang tried to assassinate Capone, Johnny Torrio came back to Chicago. He and his wife Ann had just returned from a shopping trip and got out of their car to walk to the door of their apartment building. Torrio walked behind her carrying packages. Weiss and Bugs Moran jumped out of a car and, thinking that Torrio was still in his automobile, fired wildly, wounding the chauffeur. When they finally saw Torrio, they shot him in the chest and neck, then his right arm and his groin. Moran held a gun to Torrio's temple and pulled the trigger, but the firing chamber was empty and poor Johnny Torrio, the peacemaker, heard only a faint click.

The hospital was a dangerous place for a gangster and as the security was inadequate, Capone arranged to protect Torrio himself following his brush with death. Al decided to sleep in Torrio's room, thereby making sure that his beloved mentor was safe.

Everyone was shocked when only four weeks after the shooting, Torrio appeared in court to face charges on a brewery raid. The frail, shaken man pleaded guilty and was given a sentence of nine months. Things were made easier for him because he became close friends with the sheriff, who made sure that there were no more assassination attempts while he was in jail, and he was treated like a privileged gentleman.

Torrio had had enough of his life of violence and wanted to retire and live quietly on his substantial earnings. He called Al to the jail in Waukegan in March of 1925 and told him that he was retiring from the Chicago rackets and going to live abroad. Torrio was turning over his vast assets to Al and the rest of the Capone brothers. It was an amazing legacy – nightclubs, whorehouses, gambling joints, breweries and speakeasies. Capone's power had suddenly increased immensely.

A MAJOR FORCE

After inheriting Johnny Torrio's empire, it was obvious that his new status had changed Al Capone. He came out of hiding and he became a major force in the Chicago underworld. He did all he could to make himself seem available, a man with nothing to fear. Always immaculately dressed, quiet, another political fixer going about his daily rounds. Capone's political flair, and his urge to be seen in public, was unique among racketeers, who as a rule hated any publicity.

Capone had built a fearsome reputation in the ruthless gang rivalries of the period, struggling to acquire and retain 'racketeering rights' to several areas of Chicago. That reputation grew as rival gangs were eliminated or nullified, and the suburb of Cicero became, in effect, a fiefdom of the Capone mob.

However his newfound freedom did not last long. His involvement with the accidental killing of prosecutor William McSwiggin in the spring of 1926, caused Al to go into hiding. During his time away from Chicago, he reconsidered his image and even thought about retirement.

By July of that year, Capone had returned to Chicago with a new philosophy. Capone was tired of the endless killing, and decided to organize a Peace Conference at which a reprieve was agreed – all parties agreed that there were to be no more killings, and no past murders were to be avenged.

For two months the gangs stood by the agreement, but in January 1927 one of Capone's friends was found murdered. In response, Capone invited over several news reporters in order to announce his retirement. But despite all his good intentions, it was clear to everyone who knew him that Capone may have had the desire to retire, but he didn't have the will.

THE SULLIVAN RULING

In May 1927, the Supreme Court Sullivan Ruling finally gave the Internal Revenue Service the ability to investigate Capone, but it was to take a very long time. Capone had always made sure that all business dealings were done through third parties, with any transactions made in cash – so this made his criminal activity difficult to trace.

Whilst the investigations were taking place, Capone escaped from the Chicago winter and left for Miami, where he had cleverly used a middleman to buy his Palm Island estate.

The following summer, he moved his official headquarters to the Lexington Hotel and began to diversify his business dealings. Yet again he ran into trouble with the North-Side gang, but this time he was not alone.

Capone's close friend and associate Jack McGurn had had two attempts made on his life by North-Side's new leader Bugs Moran, and now McGurn was ready to take revenge. Before he did anything, McGurn allegedly set up a meeting with Capone in the winter of 1928 to plan what would be one of the most notorious gangland killings of all time – the St. Valentine's Day Massacre.

ST VALENTINE'S DAY MASSACRE

The St. Valentine's Day Massacre took place on February 14, 1929. This was during the height of Prohibition and the never-ending competition between gangster rivals Al 'Scarface' Capone and George 'Bugs' Moran. Of course bloody warfare was nothing new to the authorities of Chicago.

Four of Capone's men entered a garage at 2122 N. Clark Street. The building was the main liquor headquarters of bootlegger George 'Bugs' Moran's North-Side gang. Two of Capone's men were dressed as police, and consequently the seven men in the garage thought it was a police raid. As a result, they dropped their guns and put their hands against the wall. Using two shotguns and two machine guns, the Capone men fired more than 150 bullets into their victims. Six of the seven killed were members of Moran's gang; the seventh was an unlucky friend. Moran, who was probably the real target, was across the street when Capone's men arrived and stayed away when he saw the police uniforms. As usual, Capone had an alibi – he was in Florida during the massacre.

Investigators on the scene found the St. Valentine's Day Massacre to be somewhat puzzling. The victims were mobsters, with an endless supply of weapons and well known for their brutality. Why would they turn their backs and face the wall for anyone without putting up a fight? That was one of many questions to be answered.

Another question came about after an eyewitness gave her account of what happened on that night in 1929. She lived directly across the street and had a perfect view of the garage. She claimed to have seen two uniformed policemen exit the garage while escorting two plain clothed men who held their hands up in the air, as if they were under arrest. Of course, this comforted the shaken woman, thinking that the loud gun fire that she had just heard had been resolved and the parties responsible were being taken into custody. However, the Chicago police had no record of any such activity at 2122 Clark Street until they arrived on the scene to find the horrifying blood bath.

When it comes to suspects, there was a whole range of possibilities. In the case of the St. Valentine's Day Massacre, the person with the greatest motive was not difficult to come by. Although he claimed to be in Florida at the time of the murders, Al Capone was, without hesitation, the one and only suspect in this infamous crime. It was well known that Capone was continuously expanding his territories by getting rid of rival gangs. Capone's fortune was estimated at $60,000,000 and that kind of money gave Al Capone one of the oldest and most common motives in murder mystery history. He had to take down 'Bugs' Moran at any cost. But as one of the leading gangsters in Chicago, Moran was not an easy person to get rid of. So in order to get rid of

Moran, Capone chose to start at the bottom and get rid of Moran's outfit, leaving him defenceless.

When the bodies were discovered splattered on the floor of the garage, it seemed at first glance, that not one single person could have survived the force of the attack. However, this proved to be untrue, when one investigator on the scene found Frank Gusenberg lying amongst the bloody corpses, breathing heavily and choking on his own blood. Immediately, the unconscious victim was taken to hospital where investigators waited with anticipation for their only possible lead to wake up and point a finger at the men who were responsible. Their greatest fear was that he would die before they had the opportunity to question him, but eventually he did wake. When he was asked for the identity of the killer, he simply stated 'I'm not gonna talk,' before he laid his head back and died. Without Frank Gusenberg's testimony and with only a few eye witnesses outside the garage, the investigators had to return to the scene of the crime and try to piece the murder together with what information they had.

After a re-enactment of the crime, authorities concluded that the two men dressed as policemen entered the garage and acted as if they were police on a routine investigation. The Moran outfit automatically assumed that they were policemen on a routine sting. It was obvious that they didn't suspect anything questionable with the two uniformed killers or they certainly would have never been killed without a fight. But as it was, the mobsters seemed to have co-operated with the

costumed officers and consequently let the fake
policemen disarm them and force them up against
the wall. As soon as their backs were turned, the
two men in plain clothes entered with guns and
shot them down.

The eye-witnesses were therefore accurate in
some respects when they claimed to have seen two
policemen arresting two men. What they had
actually seen was four brutal murderers making
their cleverly planned getaway. If a neighbour or
neighbours looked out after such rapid and
explosive gunfire, what better way to calm their
nerves, than by letting them think that everything
was under control. And indeed it was under control. The mysterious killers drove away into the
night, long before anyone thought to call the
police, because the neighbours presumed from
what they saw that the police were already there.

Al Capone was never arrested for the crimes,
and the mysterious gunmen were never identified.

PUBLIC ENEMY NUMBER ONE

Oblivious to the sensational publicity of the St
Valentine's Day Massacre, and its catalytic effect
on the government's desire to put him away, Capone
took no measures to tone down his violent criminal
activities.

Although he preferred to stay at a distance from
the murders he ordered, on occasion Capone
would deal with certain people personally. The
most infamous being the brutal murders of his hit
men Scalise, Anselmi, and Giunta.

Capone had been informed that Scalise and Anselmi had been disloyal to him, which according to Capone was unforgivable. Standing by the old Sicilian tradition 'hospitality before execution' he invited them to a veritable banquet. However, once the feast was over, the men were beaten to death with a baseball bat and then shot with a single bullet in the back of the head.

Meanwhile the government was launching its crusade against Capone aiming to get enough evidence to prove his income tax evasion and Prohibition violations. Soon after this upsurge in government interest, Capone was arrested in Philadelphia for carrying a concealed weapon. While he was in jail, Eliot Ness, a law-enforcement agent with the US Treasury Department's Prohibition Bureau, began his campaign to shut down Capone's breweries. By the time of his release in March 1930, Frank Loesch, the head of Chicago Crime Commission, had released his Public Enemies list and Al Capone was named as Public Enemy Number One.

ELIOT NESS AND HIS TEAM

In 1931, three legal indictments were brought against Al Capone. The first dealt with violations between the years 1925–1929, the second charged Capone with 22 accounts of tax evasion totalling over $200,000, and the third was brought according to the evidence provided by Eliot Ness and his team.

With evidence that could potentially imprison

Capone for 34 years, his lawyers approached the US Attorney and made a deal for a short sentence if he pleaded guilty. The trial began on June 16, 1931, but Capone's deal did not hold up. At his sentencing hearing on June 30, Judge Wilkerson made it clear that no bargaining was to be done with a Federal court. This obviously shocked Capone, and he withdrew his guilty plea. The trial was rescheduled to start on October 6, 1931.

The only chance of reducing his sentence now was if he could influence the jury, and during the summer before the trial, Capone's gang began the process of bribing and threatening all of the twelve jurors.

Realising what Capone would do, Judge Wilkerson made other plans. On the day of the trial he openly switched juries with another trial. The following day, after nine hours of deliberation, the new jury found Capone guilty of some, but not all, counts of tax evasion.

A week later, Al Capone was sentenced to eleven years' imprisonment, and a total of $80,000 in fines and court costs.

THE END OF AN ERA

Al Capone's sentence began at the US Penitentiary in Atlanta, but his crime Syndicate provided him with money and a privileged existence, so he was soon moved to Alcatraz.

Unable to contact the outside world or buy himself a better lifestyle than the other prisoners, Capone continued to serve his sentence, which due to good behaviour was eventually reduced to six years and five months. Having suffered from congenital syphilis all his life, Capone's condition deteriorated, and the last year of his term was spent in the hospital section. He was released in November 1939, and treated in a Baltimore hospital until spring 1940.

The rest of his life was spent peacefully living at his Palm Island estate. He died from a cardiac arrest, at the age of 48, on January 25, 1947.

Dion O'Banion

O'Banion was raised in the Little Hell district of Chicago's North Side. He was a choir boy at Holy Name Cathedral by day and a street punk by night in the concrete jungle of whorehouses and pubs. As he got older, he became a singing waiter in some of the dive bars on Eire and Clarke. As the customers listened to O'Banion's sentimental Irish ballads and the booze slowly got the better of them, Dion would pick their pockets. After the bars had shut, O'Banion prowled the streets looking for victims to mug.

Charles Dion O'Banion was born on July 8, 1892 to Irish immigrant parents in Aurora, Illinois, west of Chicago. As a child Charles, or Deanie, as he was better known, loved practical jokes, and he pulled them with regularity on his friends. Simply, he loved to have fun.

His mother died when he had just turned six. Over the next few years, life for Charles passed uneventfully. His father, however, seemed unable to continue living in a house with too many memories, and they relocated again in 1901 to Chicago. The move was to an Irish neighbourhood that was seeing a steady influx of Sicilians, an area that had one of the highest murder rates in the city.

The rents in the city were much higher than Mr. O'Banion expected and out of desperation chose a flat in an area affordable to a tradesman. Unknowingly, he naively moved his family into probably one of the worst spots in Chicago, Kilgubbin, an area nicknamed 'Little Hell'.

There were many temptations for a boy like Deanie who was looking for fun. Saloons, honky tonks, billiard parlours, gambling dens, pawn shops selling anything, garish vaudevilles and prostitutes. Deanie was, for a short time, an altar boy, and he also sang in the church choir at Holy Name. Although he possessed a lilting Irish tenor he had no interest in pursuing a vocal training.

He had started to grow restless, seeing his friends who bunked off school making money from the opportunities derived from street life. He listened intently to their adventures about picking pockets and chasing drunks. Only a few nickels, dimes and quarters perhaps, but they were having a lot more fun than Deanie it seemed. His father barely eked out a living and Deanie wanted more.

PART OF A GANG

With three of his best friends, Earl Wojciechowsky, Vinny Drucci and Georgie Moran, he joined the Market Street Gang whose existence relied on supplying local 'fences' with the merchandise they black marketed. They were a gang of teenage thugs who preyed on pedestrians and store owners alike, perpetrating shoplifting sprees, purse snatchings and occasionally robberies at gunpoint.

The gang was also called upon to act as 'sluggers' by major newspapers in town that had to compete against one another: the *Chicago Tribune*, the *Chicago Herald* and the *Examiner*. A 'slugger' literally beat newsstand owners who refused to sell the competitive paper.

Deanie launched his slugging career with the *Tribune*, but switched allegiance when mob boss Moses Annenberg offered him more money.

One afternoon, whilst Deanie was playing with some friends near the streetcar tracks, he ran in front of a Chicago Surface Lines trolley. He was thrown onto the cobblestones, and knocked unconscious. Passersby rushed him to a hospital where doctors at first thought he would die. He survived, but he had a splintered left leg which never quite healed correctly, leaving him with a rolling gait.

Once back on his feet Deanie went back to work for Annenberg. Annenberg was very impressed with O'Banion, as he seemed afraid of no one and somehow managed to actually earn respect from those he accosted. His Irish charm did him proud. Annenberg's praise for Deanie attracted the attention of other members of the underworld. One such person being Charles Reiser, a safe-breaker who was looking to recruit new blood. From Reiser, Deanie and his friends learned the tricks of the trade and tested their newly-acquired knowledge on the back room safes in local shops. Sometimes, the boys' keenness outdid their experience, like the time they blew out an entire wall of a factory leaving the safe firmly locked. Deanie picked himself up from the rubble, brushed the brick dust from his face, and thought it was the best laugh he had had in years.

During one of these safebreaking outings in early 1909, Deanie was arrested and served three months in the city's House of Correction. Two years later, he did another brief sentence for assault. Deanie, who liked the open streets, vowed he would never serve time again, and he never did.

With his newfound fame as a jailbird, threats were becoming common. Deanie felt it would be a good idea to carry a revolver as well as the brass knuckles he visibly wore. Practising his skill on the rooftops, Deanie and his friends took their aim on pigeons and rats. Deanie became an excellent marksman and carried his favourite gun, a .38, with him all the time and in all probability used it for more than just show. His bankroll increased with each job he performed for Reiser, Annenberg and others. Car jackings, warehouse robberies, and the occasional beating. He broke off his ties with the Market Street Gang as he was enjoying the life of a freelancer. His friends Weiss, Drucci and Moran started to emulate everything their friend did, including the way he walked and talked – he was their hero.

Earl Weiss, called 'Hymie' by the group, was born in Poland in 1898 and had emigrated to America a short time later. By his teens he had become Deanie's closest friend. Having been the first boy Deanie met on the pavements of Little Hell, Weiss provided a good balance in their relationship – he was as serious as the Irishman was flambuoyant.

Vinny Drucci, despite Deanie's adopted dislike

for most of the other Italian kids in Kilgubbin, proved himself to be an invaluable and loyal friend, and is said to have masterminded most of the heists they pulled.

George 'Bugs' Moran was born in Minnesota, in 1893, and relocated with his parents to Chicago's North Side where he immediately became a petty thief. More than the other gang members, Moran imitated Deanie almost to the point of idolatry, aping the way he wore his hat at a jaunty angle and the manner in which he tossed his head to one side when he laughed.

Annenberg introduced the boys to the political decision-makers who called upon the mobs to help 'steer' the outcomes of elections in the 42nd and 43rd wards. Deanie and his gang soon discovered that this 'job' was a good earner. Soon the lads of Kilgubbin were driving their own cars up and down the old neighbourhood and the people would wave and smile at the lovable 'ward boys'. Even the cops, either on horseback or in squad cars, would give them right-of-way. Deanie, especially, had by now become almost an icon. His father, Charles O'Banion, believed his son had found an honest City Hall job and boasted that his son never forgot his dad. He would flash the new wristwatch or the diamond ring his son had just bought him.

Though everything seemed to be going well for the gang somehow they yearned for something bigger.

THE ARRIVAL OF PROHIBITION

Prohibition started out as an experiment. The First

World War had ended in 1918 and Congress was made to believe that the nation had to release its dependency on liquor. By January 1919, the necessary number of states accepted the bill introduced by Senator Andrew J. Volstead of Minnesota and his law became constitutional.

Deanie saw Prohibition as an opportunity to make plenty of money. America was definitely not ready for an alcohol-free life and Deanie and his pals could just imagine the revenue that awaited them in the black-market distribution and sales of beer and whisky.

Even before the law came into effect, the mobs were making preparations, and Deanie was no exception. He decided to concentrate on the provision of beer. Months before Prohibition was effected, he made contacts with would-be underground beer suppliers in Canada and arranged for shipments to start immediately, concentrating on only the best quality beers.

Government enforcement of the new law proved futile, it seemed those who didn't drink before, drank now. Meeting this demand was the objective of the gangs in any way possible. Deanie performed the city's first liquor hijacking on December 19, 1921 when he spotted a truckload of Grommes & Ullrich whisky held at a stop sign in Chicago's downtown area. Pushing the startled driver out, he drove the truck to Maxwell Street, where he deposited the precious cargo with one Samuel J. Morton, whose garage served as a depot for stolen vehicles.

Owners of saloons would pay exorbitant prices

for alcohol rather than let their businesses suffer. Deanie was able to sell the entire hijacked load in 20 minutes over Morton's shop telephone.

Determined to be one step ahead, Deanie and his boys started to eliminate any looming competition. It was thanks to the O'Banion mob, that thousands of speakeasies on the North Side were able to survive, and indeed thrive, during the Prohibition.

His power became extensive, and with pay-offs the officials learned to look the other way. By 1922, his bootlegging business was well established and making around $2 million a year. The public had come to recognize that his was high-quality beer stock.

In the meantime Deanie's personal entourage had grown. He needed more men that he could trust in order to help him run his operations. One of these was an old friend Sam 'Nails' Morton, the fence in whose garage he had deposited his first load of hijacked whisky. Morton, it appeared, was not scared of anything. He was a war veteran who had won the Croix de Guerre for bravery, and who now made a living by disguising and selling stolen cars. It was to Morton that Deanie entrusted his whisky disbursement. Another new member to the O'Banion cause was a somewhat comical figure called Louis 'Two Gun' Alterie, who owned a vast ranch in Colorado. Louis was a former gunman for the South Side's Terry Druggan gang and a union muscleman who loved the Western cowboy motif. Along with the ever-faithful Weiss, Drucci and Moran, these made up Deanie's little gang.

Everything ran smoothly and it appeared that

Deanie suffered no real interference in the running of his enterprise. He became apprehensive though when he heard that two men named Johnny Torrio and Al Capone had encroached on his own profitable Gold Coast.

RIVALRY

From time to time, Deanie's gang would hijack a convoy of beer trucks belonging to the heavily Italian South Side mob organization under Johnny Torrio. In retaliation, Torrio's desperadoes would counteract by heisting O'Banion freight. Fearing open warfare, which would seriously inhibit the free flow of money under more peaceable conditions, Torrio called Deanie personally and asked if he was willing to compromise.

What Torrio suggested was that they share proceeds from various breweries on the North Side, including the prosperous Sieben Brewery on Larabee Street. In return, Deanie would have an equal share in a number of Capone-run distilleries and gambling establishments in the suburbs.

Deanie accepted the treaty reluctantly, with a resolve to watch the Italians constantly to make sure that they were not making any underhand deals. And so it was that Deanie became a member of the Chicago area combine that was divided into a number of territories: Torrio/Capone had the Loop and much of the vast South Side, along with a number of suburbs; Deanie retained the North Side; the Genna family and 'Diamond Joe' Esposito had Little Italy southwest of the Loop; Edward 'Spike' O'Donnell had the Kerry Patch district far south; William 'Klondike' O'Donnell had the Far West Side; Terry Druggan and Frankie Lake had the Near West; Joe Saltis and Frankie McErlane had the Stock Yards neighbourhood; and finally Roger Touhy had the far suburbs.

However, before the night was over, Deanie was back to his old tricks, hijacking Capone's as well as others' trucks. He seemed to be taunting the Italians into action.

When the Genna gang began to undercut O'Banion's prices for whisky, O'Banion demanded that Torrio and Capone did something about it. When this request fell on stony ground, O'Banion took stronger measures himself, hijacking a $30,000 shipment of Genna whisky. The Gennas decided to kill him then, but were talked out of it by Mike Merlo of the Unione Siciliane.

In May of 1924, O'Banion learned that a police raid would be taking place on Sieben's Brewery. He acted quickly and sold the brewery to Torrio and Capone – the raid took place on the day of the transfer. This insult was intolerable, and Torrio and Capone now took sides with the Gennas. O'Banion's words were, 'Tell them Sicilians to go to hell,' which only infuriated them further.

A PASSION FOR FLOWERS

Dion O'Banion, now twenty-nine, got married on February 5, 1921 in a spectacular ceremony at Holy Name Cathedral. His bride was an angel-faced eighteen-year-old called Viola Kaniff, a recent graduate of an Iowa boarding school. The marriage proved to be a happy one and his adoration of Viola helped to calm him down considerably. Because he now felt the need for some respectability, he bought half interest in a legitimate enterprise – William Schofield's Flower Shop, located at 738, North State. In total contrast to his gangster surface, he loved flowers. He had a passion for arranging them into lovely bouquets, centrepieces and wreaths for special occasions. He worked hard at his new venture, never missing a day in the shop, often working late into the evening and at weekends. His employees found him a joy to work with, and most evenings he proudly brought home one of his original designs to Viola.

But Deanie was still a gangster in the true sense of the word, and he had a special telephone in the back of the shop to take orders for beer.

Schofield's became the florist for mobdom. Whenever someone was shot, stabbed or taken for a ride, Schofield's was asked to make the floral arrangements for the funeral. In a token of good gesture, Capone and Torrio often placed large orders for someone they had killed, but whom they thought deserved a grand send-off just the same. Deanie, in return, would offer them a discount for their beneficence.

CICERO, ILLINOIS

Cicero, Illinois, was just one of the many sleepy towns growing slowly beyond Chicago, that was until the early 1920s when Torrio and his mob moved in. With an ever-growing reform movement taking place within Chicago, the mob laid low in Cicero, introducing it to all the latest vices. Capone changed his mob headquarters from his Loop address to the Hawthorne Hotel in Cicero, where the municipal government had already proved that it was open to bribes. Mayor Joseph Klenha, although not outwardly supportive of mobster takeover, lacked the gumption and, indeed the forces, to fight the gangsters.

Twenty-Second Street, a main thoroughfare that ran straight through to Chicago, became a place of fun, frolic and mostly sin, much to the annoyance of the docile residents. Cicero police drove meekly around the hustle and bustle and just kept on going. No cop would intervene; they had all heard about Capone's reputation.

Money poured into Cicero. But, as had happened in Chicago, reform was once again taking its effect. The suburban Democrats thought they could win the vote and throw out Republican Klenha and rid Cicero of all the vices that he allowed. But what they didn't know, was the power behind Capone. Nor did they know that Capone had got wind of their plot through Republican boss man Eddie Vogel.

On April 1, 1924, the day that Cicero's mayor would be elected, nearly 250 thugs, two dozen of whom were supplied by Deanie, rode into Cicero's town square. Their black limousines formed a solid line with several men crouched inside each car, and two more on the running boards carrying a Thompson gun. Everyone knew exactly what this meant – Capone was here to stay.

As soon as the polls opened, the gangsters were there to threaten and harass, forcing people to vote for Klenha. The few citizens who dared to decline were grabbed, dragged to the limousines and never seen again. Everything possible was done to ensure that Klenha retained the vote, even down to the thugs filling blank voting forms and signing them themselves.

William Dever, the Mayor of Chicago, did everything he could think of to appease the situation. He redirected seventy city detectives to Cicero, but by the time they arrived in the terrified town, the damage had been done. The only small satisfaction for the conservative faction at the end of the day was that Al Capone's younger brother, Frank, was shot by an unmarked police squad. The people of Cicero at least had the gratification that Al Capone would remember Cicero's election day fiasco as a very, very costly victory.

For Deanie's part he demanded a large financial payback. Reluctantly, Torrio allotted him a large section of Cicero's beer rights and a quarter percentage of Cicero's most popular gambling hall called The Ship.

This was to be the first of a series of incidences that would lead to the death of Dion O'Banion.

Without seeking approval from Torrio, Deanie convinced the owners of several saloons on the West Side of Chicago to move their speakeasies to his area within Cicero. Consequently, his area began earning $100,000 every month, five times the amount agreed with Torrio. and more than the Capone-run saloons earned throughout the rest of the village. To pacify the now irate Capone, Torrio tried to bargain with the Irish trickster. If Deanie would allow Capone to take back a piece of his built-up business, Papa Johnny would hand over to him a like amount of their brothel business in nearby Forest View.

Deanie was angry and told them where they could put their deal, pointing out that his religion was totally again prostitution. By this time Deanie's tricks and insults had started to annoy members of the Italian Outfit. Six of these were the Sicilian-born Genna brothers who controlled the district immediately west of the Loop called Little Italy. Killers without a conscience, they were not to be messed with.

While Deanie was busy tending to his Cicero concerns, the Gennas began marketing, quite successfully, their caramel-coloured manufacture in the North Side. When Deanie discovered a reduction in his whisky sales, and found out the reason, he in turn stormed to Torrio to complain. Probably because of the earlier rebuff from Deanie, Torrio told him there was nothing he could do as it was totally out of his control. Deanie knew exactly what that meant – the Mafia.

A NASTY TRICK

In early May 1924, Deanie informed Torrio that he was getting out of the rackets. He had had enough of the gang warfare and as he was still a young man, only 31, wanted to spend more time with his wife, perhaps retire on his investments to another

98

state. He asked Torrio if he would be interested in buying out his share in the Sieben Brewery for $500,000. Torrio was delighted. He thought this would finally pacify the Gennas and Capone, who both had a dislike for O'Banion. As a final request, Deanie asked Torrio to meet him at the brewery at sunrise of the following Monday to inspect the next big shipment.

On May 19, 1924, early in the morning, Torrio surveyed Sieben's with proud ownership. Deanie had shown him round and now stood next to him, the cheque for $500,000 made out to him in his vest pocket, watching the trucks being loaded with a never-ending supply of barrels.

No sooner had the last truck been loaded, than from all directions, blocking all exits, came a troop of blue uniforms led by Chief of Police Morgan Collins. Torrio panicked – he knew that under the law a second offence for bootlegging could mean jail time. At the Federal Building downtown, Deanie on the other hand seemed totally unperturbed. Torrio watched O'Banion pay his $7,500 bail and left the courtroom, whistling.

Within the week, Torrio learned from a police informant the real reason for Dion O'Banion's high spirits. The Irishman had known of the raid in advance, and had made sure that Torrio was on the spot in the hope of him receiving possible conviction.

Deanie, still smiling at his ruse, bolted with his wife and bodyguards to Louis Alterie's Colorado ranch for a holiday which was to last from July through to early October. Whilst in Colorado he bought a 2,700-acre estate for cash.

As the 1924 city elections drew nearer, the Democratic Party wanted to make sure of Deanie's patronage that year. So, on November 1, they threw him a testimonial dinner at the Webster Hotel on North Lincoln Park Avenue, where they presented him with a $1,500 platinum watch. However, three days later, still wearing the gift, he and his North Side lads caused havoc at the polls by 'persuading' the public to vote Republican. And of course the Republicans were victorious.

The tension had still not subsided between him and the Gennas. In fact, it reached a climax the night of November 3. Stopping by The Ship gambling hall in Cicero to collect his share of the October proceeds, he learned that one of the Genna brothers, Angelo, had lost $30,000 at the tables the previous evening. When Torrio recommended that the debt be written off as 'professional courtesy', O'Banion sneered. He immediately telephoned Angelo and told him to pay up within a week or he would have to face the consequences. His friend, Hymie Weiss, tried to warn Deanie not to be so impetuous and suggested he trod a little more lightly.

Torrio immediately summoned Capone and the Genna brothers to counsel. Dion O'Banion had insulted the brotherhood, betrayed their trust, and continued to make a farce out of the combination they had all worked so hard to preserve. They said he failed to understand Italian tradition and their decision was unanimous – thumbs down.

To make matters worse the Unione Siciliane

President Mike Merlo, who previously talked the Syndicate out of assassinating O'Banion, died on Saturday, November 8. Torrio ordered $10,000 from Schofield's Flower Shop, Capone $8,000, while Deanie told them he would prepare the wreaths himself as his own tribute.

Deanie was hard at work in Schofield's back room preparing wreaths and trying to clear a backlog of work. For some reason he seemed to be especially tired that morning, and it was around 11.30 when the bells over the street door rang. Deanie went out to greet his customers, still carrying a pair of clipping shears in his left hand. Three men entered, one of whom he instantly recognized as Frankie Yale. Asking if they were from Mike Merlo's, he held out his hand to greet Yale. Instinctively Deanie knew that something was wrong, and the two strangers fired – two bullets into his chest, two in his throat, and another blew his jaw away.

If Deanie had recognized the two men accompanying Yale, he would not have been caught unawares, for they were the most brutal assassins in the Syndicate, Juano Scalise and Alberto Anselmi.

Deanie's body lay in state for nearly a week at Sbabaro's Funeral Home, and on November 14, Dion O'Banion was buried at Mount Carmel Cemetery. Twenty thousand spectators crammed the grounds.

No one was ever prosecuted for the murder. Frankie Yale was detained at the LaSalle Street train station where he was boarding a train to New York, but had a perfect alibi.

Arnold Rothstein

*Rothstein received his nickname, 'The Big Bankroll',
because he always insisted on carrying a huge bankroll
of $100 bills. He wanted to be able to immediately
finance any deals he made. Rothstein once stated that he
was willing to bet on anything but the weather – the
weather was the only thing he could not fix.*

Arnold Rothstein was actually born in the
United States, unlike many of the underworld
figures. He was born in 1882 on East 47th Street
in Manhattan, the second of five children. He was
not a happy or outgoing child like his siblings, in
fact Arnold spent many hours alone in cellars and
closets choosing dark places in which to play. At
the age of three he took an intense dislike to his
older brother Harry. So much so that he was found
one night by his father, standing over Harry
holding a knife in his hand.

Arnold seemed to live in the shadow of his older
brother, lacking an identity of his own. He fell
behind at school and even dropped two classes to
end up with his younger brother Edgar. When
Harry Rothstein was thirteen he informed his
parents that he wanted to study to become a rabbi.
Abraham, his father, was delighted with this news

and chastised Arnold for not being proud of his religion. Arnold quit school for good in 1898 at the age of sixteen and found his vocation on the streets. He began shooting dice for nickels and dimes and kept a daily record of his winnings. He could be regularly found in pool halls, a place where betting was rife. As gamblers waited around for the results there was usually a billiards table to occupy their time. Rothstein earned a reputation at the billiards table and his pocket money began to grow.

Rothstein became a regular at Hammerstein's Victoria Theatre where there would be a craps game running every Monday. The popular game attracted people like Monk Eastman and Herman 'Beansie' Rosenthal. Rothstein's success and his increasing bankroll made him a popular figure at the game and at other gambling spots. He started lending money to several of the players, and made a dollar interest for every four he loaned. If Rothstein experienced any problems in retrieving the loan he would call in his new-found friend Monk Eastman. No one put up any resistance when they were threatened by the thug Eastman.

During his early gambling days, Rothstein, still only sixteen, befriended Timothy D. Sullivan, Tammany Hall's East Side political boss. Sullivan was known as 'Big Tim' and Rothstein spent a lot of time at his headquarters. He ran errands for Sullivan and served as a translator for his Jewish constituents. Sullivan soon realized that Rothstein was a young man with a future, while, Rothstein found in Sullivan the father figure he had been so desperately looking for.

At the age of seventeen, Rothstein took a job as a travelling headwear salesman. Never having been really happy at home he decided to move out. His job took him to New York, Pennsylvania and West Virginia, and after two years into the job he received a telegram informing him that his brother Harry had died of pneumonia.

ARNOLD AND THE ACTRESS

Following the death of his brother Harry, Arnold tried very hard to make it up with his father. He moved back home, worked at his father's factory, stayed away from the poolrooms and even attended the synagogue. But his efforts failed and after an argument he left home again feeling that he was unloved and unwanted.

Rothstein moved into the Broadway Central Hotel and started work as a cigar salesman, which kept him in close contact with gambling houses, hotels and saloons. He became a regular at a poolroom owned by John J. McGraw, the manager of the New York Giants baseball team. After much practice, Arnold gained the reputation of being one of the best pool players on Broadway.

It was at this stage of his life that Arnold started carrying a large sum of money around with him, and flashing it at every opportunity, believing that 'money talks'. He made a good living as a cigar salesman, and managed to accumulate $2,000. He decided that this was sufficient to gain entry into the gambling world. He quit his salesman's job and with 'Big Tim' Sullivan's backing, in 1902 Rothstein began working on his own. Rothstein prospered from his gambling endeavours and he was still lending money at exorbitant interest rates. He invested his income in legitimate businesses as a silent partner, and became part owner of a car dealership and several drug stores.

By 1906 his bankroll had grown from $2,000 to $12,000. He felt that if he flashed his 'roll' it would serve as a sign of his ability and success and earn him respect.

In 1907, Arnold met Carolyn Greene, a nineteen-year-old Catholic actress. Before proposing to her, Rothstein had Carolyn checked out thoroughly. He introduced her to his father, who told him quite bluntly that he would have nothing more to do with him if he married outside of the Jewish faith. Rothstein once again left his parents' house with a feeling of being unloved. However, his father's wishes had no effect on his plans to wed Carolyn. On August 12, 1909 Rothstein and Greene were married in Saratoga, New York right at the heart of horse racing season.

THE PROMISE

Arnold had promised Carolyn that he would retire from gambling once he had made a lot of money. At Saratoga he pawned all of the expensive jewellery he had given Carolyn in order to obtain cash, he felt this was better than borrowing the money at a higher interest rate. By the end of the honeymoon, Rothstein had won $12,000 and returned all the jewellery he had pawned to Carolyn.

When the couple returned to New York, Arnold decided to open his own gambling house. He rented two properties on West 46th Street, one of which they lived in, while the other was fitted out with roulette wheels and poker tables. Rothstein then went to his friend 'Big Tim' Sullivan to discuss protection. Sullivan was delighted that his protégé had got married and his wedding gift to the couple was 'protection' but with a price. Rothstein had to take on William Shea, a deposed building inspector, as his partner.

Shea, a self-proclaimed anti-Semite, distrusted Rothstein from the beginning of their relationship and felt that his partner was always cheating him.

One night at Jack's, a popular Manhattan hangout, Rothstein walked in and was invited to sit down with a group of men as they discussed baseball and prizefights. One of these men was Jack Conway, a Philadelphia sportsman and accomplished jockey, who happened to be an expert pool player. During this talk it came out that Conway was probably the best amateur pool player in the country. Rothstein, unaware that he was being set up, sensed a challenge and jumped at it.

The two men agreed to play to 100 points for $500, and it took place at John McGraw's Billiard Parlor. The game started on a Thursday night at 8.00 p.m. By the time it was over, at 4.00 a.m. Saturday morning, some thirty-two hours later, Rothstein was rumoured to have won over $10,000. The game received so much publicity that it was reported in two New York City newspapers.

To increase the winnings at his gambling house, Rothstein was in constant search for what the gamblers called 'marks'. A mark was a wealthy individual who enjoyed gambling and believed he could 'beat the house'. Rothstein realized that using attractive women could be a great help in bringing in the marks. One of the women Rothstein utilized was Peggy Hopkins, a beautiful ex-show girl. One night Hopkins brought in Stanley Joyce, a man she later married, and Percival H. Hill, of the American Tobacco Company. While Joyce lost $17,000, the unlucky Hill ended his night of gambling by signing over an IOU to Rothstein for $250,000. Rothstein wondered if he would have any trouble collecting the debt and his wife, Carolyn, urged that if he did collect, that he keep his promise to her and retire from gambling.

When morning arrived, Rothstein took a cab to the offices of the American Tobacco Company and collected a certified cheque for a quarter of a million dollars. He did not, however, keep his promise to his wife.

THE RAIDS

In 1912 'Big Tim' Sullivan's mental state started to deteriorate. Sullivan was institutionalized before being placed in a home in Williamsburg. Occasionally Sullivan would slip past his attendants and return to his old stomping grounds. In September 1913 Sullivan disappeared after an all night card game with his guards. A few days later his body was found on the railway tracks near the Westchester freight yards, and investigation showed that Sullivan was dead before the train ran over his body. 'Big Tim's' funeral was attended by more than 25,000 mourners.

With Sullivan in the grave, Rothstein's new protection came from an even higher source – Tammany Hall boss Charles F. Murphy and his closest advisor, Tom Foley. The year 1913 was a watershed year for Rothstein – the year he would move to the top due to his relationship with Murphy.

In 1910, as a favour to Foley, Rothstein bailed a confidence man out of jail. This made him realize just what high premiums could be charged for this service and he went into the bonding business for himself. Rothstein began to work with reputable bonding and surety companies, paying them a lower interest rate for the money he borrowed than he charged for his own services. Rothstein proved himself to be a highly successful businessman and Murphy, Foley and James J. 'Jimmy' Hines, all came to rely on Rothstein and his services. These services included anything from posting a bond to having a ballot box rigged in their favour. Rothstein became the pipeline between Tammany Hall and the underworld and he was getting richer because of it.

Rothstein received cash for everything he did. Carolyn and Arnold moved up in the world to an apartment at the corner of Broadway and 52nd Street. Their new home had eight rooms and two baths, as well as separate quarters for a butler and a maid.

THE HOLD-UP

In the early morning of May 16, 1917 Rothstein was rolling dice in a floating craps game at the Hotel St. Francis on West 47th Street. Around 3.00 a.m. five gunmen entered the hotel lobby. They gained access by bribing the elevator boy, who doubled as an errand runner for the gamblers. Rothstein knew most of the players in the room. As well as professional gamblers the group included stockbrokers, doctors, actors, attorneys and businessmen. One man, however, a two-bit gambler, had the distinction of being present at several games that had recently been held up. As the masked gunmen entered the room Rothstein's first reaction was to drop his bankroll, estimated to be $60,000, to the floor and kick it under the carpet. His next response was to keep his eyes on the inside accomplice throughout the whole ordeal as he had seen Rothstein drop the money. When he was searched they only found $2,600 in his watch pocket. When the gunmen left, he bent down and picked up the hidden wad of cash.

Rothstein went to the police station and identified two of the robbers from mug shots. On August 22, 1917 Rothstein appeared in court and testified against the two gunmen. The two men were convicted and sentenced to Sing Sing. One of the men, Albert Johnson, vowed to get even with Rothstein. Two months later Johnson escaped. The police notified Rothstein of the escape, and he was advised to leave town until Johnson was recaptured. Rothstein declined, saying that that it would tarnish his fearless reputation. Albert Johnson was killed a few weeks later by a security guard in Detroit while trying to rob a bank.

Two years later Rothstein was a participant in another floating craps game, this time on West 57th Street. The police received a tip-off and raided the game. One of the officers pounded on the door and demanded entry, but they were met by a volley of bullets that crashed through the door, luckily only causing three minor flesh wounds.

The officers cried out, 'This isn't a stickup, it's the police,' at which point the door was quickly unlocked. The police searched and arrested 20 men, but no gun was found. A patrol wagon was summoned and the men were escorted to it. As the police were leaving the building a bystander pointed out to one of the officers a figure hiding on the second floor fire escape. Two officers re-entered the building and climbed out on the fire escape where they discovered Rothstein hiding with a revolver. He was charged with assault and subsequently provided bail money for all the gamblers who had been arrested.

Dominic Henry, with the help of an assistant United States attorney, pushed for an indictment, saying that the police had not properly identified themselves. When the case was called, Rothstein's attorney requested a dismissal, which the judge readily agreed to. Later, one of the newspapers hinted that Rothstein had paid $32,000 to get the case quashed. An investigation followed and in a strange turn of events Inspector Henry found himself indicted for perjury. He was convicted and sentenced to five years in prison. This incident showed the power of Rothstein's influence.

THE 'BLACK SOX' SCANDAL

Arnold Rothstein was rumoured to be the mastermind of the 'Black Sox' scandal, which entailed the fixing of the 1919 World Series.

In 1919, baseball was truly America's favourite pastime. Considering themselves grossly underpaid, eight members of the Chicago White Sox, led by first baseman Chick Gandil, conspired to lose the World Series to the Cincinnati team. That was if they could find a gambler willing to pay them to lose. Gandil approached Abe Attell, a former featherweight boxing champion, and who, in retirement, served as Arnold Rothstein's bodyguard. Gandil told Attell that, for $100,000, he could guarantee that his teammates would lose to Cincinnati. It is reported that Rothstein rejected Attell's initiative, sensing that Attell wanted to build his own reputation as an important gambler. However, through another intermediary Rothstein arranged to pay the White Sox players $80,000 on the condition that they lost the game. They did, and Rothstein made a significant sum betting against Chicago.

The American League did not respond until over a year later after the completion of the 1920 season. At that time all eight players involved were banned from playing baseball for life. Ban Johnson, the president of the American League, was certain of Rothstein's participation in the fix and openly said so. To which Rothstein responded, 'My only connection was to refuse to do business with some men who said they could fix it ... I intend to sue Ban Johnson for libel...'

Rothstein travelled to Chicago to testify before a grand jury investigating the fixed games. An attorney representing Charles Comiskey, the owner of the White Sox, believed Rothstein, as did the members of the grand jury. Despite the fact that Rothstein was cleared and never charged his name will forever be linked to Major League Baseball's darkest hour.

ROTHSTEIN AND THE PROHIBITION

Prohibition was probably the greatest day for organized crime in America. Little did Rothstein realize with the arrival of the Volstead Act that he would be one of the founding fathers of organized crime in the United States. In fact, at the time, Rothstein actually believed the new law would be effective.

One of Rothstein's first ventures into rum running came after a meeting with Waxey Gordon and Detroit bootlegger Maxie Greenberg. Greenberg had started smuggling in whisky from Canada, and realizing at once how profitable this venture was, he wanted to expand but needed $175,000 to do so. He travelled to New York in the hope that he could obtain financing from

Rothstein, through Waxey Gordon. Gordon knew Rothstein having previously worked for him as a labour enforcer.

Rothstein met the two in Central Park. Sitting on a park bench, he listened intently to their plan to smuggle in Canadian whisky. The following day the three men met again, this time in Rothstein's office where he made a counterproposal. Rothstein would finance the venture, but the liquor would be purchased and brought in from Great Britain. Gordon, acting as middleman, asked to be included in the deal and was cut in for a small 'piece'. From this 'piece' Gordon was to launch a successful rum-running empire and become a very wealthy man. After Rothstein ended his partnership with the two in 1921, he continued to help finance them. Gordon took over two large warehouses when they split, one in the city and the other on Long Island. Rothstein would later use Gordon's speedboats to smuggle in diamonds and narcotics.

Rothstein got out of the rum-running business for one reason, because he couldn't control it. While he would continue to bankroll rum running operations throughout the 1920s, Rothstein would focus on letting other individuals take the risks while he collected the profits.

ROTHSTEIN AND NARCOTICS

Rothstein was not a pioneer in the field of dope peddling, but he was introduced to the potential of making big money by both Lucky Luciano and Waxey Gordon. By the mid-1920s many of

Rothstein's big money ventures had gone by the wayside. He decided that it was time for a change and decided to devote his efforts to organizing drug trafficking. His interest was in wholesaling, not the street pushing of narcotics. Coming in at this level, his only competition came from unscrupulous members of the medical profession. Rothstein's goal was far higher and he set out to regulate supply and demand and organize the drug trade on an international basis.

Rothstein employed several men to work for him. Among them were Harry Mather, 'Dapper Dan' Collins, Sid Stager, George Uffner, and Jacob 'Yasha' Katzenberg. Rothstein then purchased Vantines, a well-known importing house. Vantines had a legitimate reputation and shipments arriving from China and the Orient received only a fleeting inspection. In addition to Vantines, Rothstein bought several antique shops and art galleries to serve as legitimate fronts for his drug trafficking business.

As more and more drugs came into the city it created a new generation of drug pushers and addicts. Rothstein's bail bond business increased dramatically due to the increased amounts of arrests. Ironically, Rothstein never made any money from his ventures in narcotics, because every single dollar he received was put back into the business. He died unfortunately while his drugs consortium was still in full swing.

THE END OF A LEGEND

A man was reported to have been shot at 10.53

p.m. on Sunday, November 4, 1928, and by midnight it was confirmed that the man was forty-six-year-old Arnold Rothstein. He had been shot in the abdomen and found near the employee's entrance of the Park Central Hotel.

Earlier that evening, Rothstein had arrived at Lindy's restaurant on Seventh Avenue. Rothstein used Lindy's as his office and had regular meetings in a private booth he held there. One of the men waiting to see him that night was Jimmy Meehan, who ran the Park City Club.

At about 10.15, Rothstein received a telephone call. After a short conversation he hung up and asked Meehan if he would walk outside with him. He told Meehan that George McManus wanted to see him at the Park Central. He then pulled a gun out of his pocket and handed it to Meehan saying, 'Keep this for me, I will be right back'. Rothstein then left and walked up Seventh Avenue.

George McManus was a bookmaker and gambler, who was well connected in the city. He had one brother in the police force and another serving as a priest. Several weeks earlier, Rothstein had attended a high-stakes poker game run by McManus. The game started on September 8 and continued into the morning of September 10. By the end of this very lengthy card game, Rothstein owed a lot of money. When Rothstein walked out, without so much as signing an IOU, a couple of the players became irritated.

A week passed and Rothstein still held off paying his debts, possibly hoping to make the gamblers sweat and maybe take a lesser payoff.

The players however were beginning to pressure McManus since he was the host and had promised them that Rothstein would make good.

As the weeks passed, the pressure began to get to McManus who began drinking and threatened Rothstein. On Sunday night November 4, McManus called Rothstein from room 349 in the Park Central Hotel, where he had registered as George, requesting that Rothstein come over right away.

The conversation and events that took place after Rothstein arrived are still a mystery. But it is known that shortly after he entered room 349, Rothstein was shot once in the lower abdomen. The revolver was tossed out of a window where it bounced off the hood of a parked taxi and landed in the street. Rothstein was later found walking down the service stairs, clutching his stomach and asking for a cab to take him home.

A police officer arrived who immediately called an ambulance and Rothstein was taken to New York's Polyclinic Hospital where he underwent an operation to remove the bullet. It had entered just above the groin and travelled downwards severing an artery. Rothstein had sustained tremendous internal bleeding and left the operating room in a coma.

Rothstein's wife and two brothers, Jack and Edgar, were immediately summoned to the hospital. He regained consciousness on the Monday morning and told his wife he wanted to go home. Carolyn saw him again late on the Monday afternoon. Once again he asked to go home and stressed that he didn't want to be left alone. As he tried to get out of bed, he fell back and became unconscious once again. Rothstein never regained consciousness and died the following morning at about 10.20.

Rothstein was buried the following day in Union Field Cemetery in Queens. Inside the closed casket he was dressed in a white skullcap with a purple-striped prayer shawl over a muslin shroud.

After the shooting, McManus went into hiding. Three weeks later McManus arranged for his own arrest in a Broadway barbershop, but as no witness could place him in the room at the time of the shooting, he was acquitted. The gamblers who had taken part in the marathon poker game were also arrested, but they all had ironclad alibis for the night of November 4 and were soon released. Rothstein's murder remains officially unsolved.

The organizer of organized crime was gone. Despite his wealth, power and influence, Rothstein will be remembered most for the future underworld leaders he helped along their way. In addition to Waxey Gordon, who has already been mentioned, other major underworld personalities that came under Rothstein's wing were Jack 'Legs' Diamond, Charles 'Lucky' Luciano, Meyer Lansky, Frank Costello and Lepke Buchalter. In the end Lucky Luciano, Meyer Lansky, Frank Costello and Lepke Buchalter took over the Rothstein empire.

Jack 'Legs' Diamond

Legs Diamond wasn't well liked. In fact, he never had a friend he didn't betray, killing many of them. Legs was notorious for the double cross, an art admired by many fellow mobsters – except that he took it to the extreme. Unsurprisingly, Legs had to pay the ultimate price. But before he was hit by his enemies, Legs Diamond became a power in New York's underworld. He was known to be completely without remorse, or any other form of conscience.

New York was in the depth of the Depression in 1931. Although many people were out of work and poor during this time, speakeasies and nightclubs owned by the gangsters seemed to thrive. One mobster who was right at the forefront of the action was Jack 'Legs' Diamond. Diamond became known to the Underworld as 'the Clay Pigeon' purely because he had been shot at so many times, and yet he had survived.

HIS RISE TO FAME

Born in 1896, John T. Nolan, better remembered as Jack 'Legs' Diamond was given his nickname either because of his skill on the dance floor, or

118

because of his ability to outrun any pursuing police officer.

Diamond began his career as a petty thief on the streets of New York, gradually working his way up to become a bodyguard to Jacob Orgen. Orgen was a New York City labour racketeer known as 'Little Augie' Orgen, who had made his way up the ranks as a slugger for 'Dopey' Benny Fein. On October 15, 1927, Orgen was walking down the street with Diamond when an automobile containing Louis 'Lepke' Buchalter and Jake 'Gurrah' Shapiro pulled up alongside them. Buchalter and Shapiro opened fire killing Orgen and seriously wounding Diamond.

On his release from hospital, Diamond divided his employer's businesses with his killers, Lepke and Shapiro, keeping the bootleg liquor and narcotics trade for himself.

Diamond opened up the Hotsy Totsy Club on Broadway between 54th and 55th Street, using Hymie Cohen as his front man. It was from this club that a number of gangland killings were carried out. Eventually, on 13 June 1929, Diamond and his right-hand man, Charles Entratta, were forced to flee. They had killed a rival named William 'Red' Cassidy at the bar of the Hotsy Totsy when it was unusually full of both employees and customers. Cassidy was standing at the bar causing trouble. Things got totally out of hand when Cassidy insulted Diamond by calling him a pimp. He was shot along with an innocent bystander, Simon Walker. It was later thought that Walker was probably Cassidy's assistant, since he had arrived with him and was also wearing two guns.

119

Both Diamond and Entratta immediately went underground, and then organized a series of contracts to eliminate any witnesses. Four of these witnesses mysteriously disappeared – three of them being the cashier, a waiter and the hat-check girl – thus hampering the police investigation. Tired of hiding, Diamond and Entratta eventually gave themselves up. They were charged with the murder but subsequently released for lack of evidence. But Diamond was to pay in another way.

While Diamond had been underground he discovered that a large part of his bootlegging interests had been taken over. The main part had been seized by a man called Arthur Flegenheimer, better known as 'Dutch' Schultz. Diamond at once set out to regain his territory. It was during this dispute that Diamond got the backing from Arnold Rothstein. To endeavour to put an end to the feud Rothstein and Schultz reluctantly agreed to meet at the Harding Hotel. It came to light that both Schultz and Diamond had similar reservations and it was obvious that neither of them trusted the other. Schultz is reputed to have said 'I don't trust Legs. He's nuts. He gets excited and starts pulling a trigger like another guy wipes his nose.'

They subsequently worked out a deal which would result in Diamond receiving a substantial settlement in return for his mid-town rights. The outcome, however, was that Joey Noe, the man who had set up the meeting, was shot as soon as he left the building. Shultz believed it was the dirty work of Diamond out to get revenge. Diamond became elusive and so a vendetta was launched on his brother Eddie, who was suffering from consumption and had been sent from Denver for treatment. Eddie's car was showered with machine gun fire, but miraculously he survived the attack. Diamond immediately turned his forces on Shultz's men and of course Shultz retaliated.

IMPOSSIBLE TO KILL

Despite the many assassination attempts on Diamond he always seemed to survive, and gained the reputation of invulnerability. It was said in the twenties that 'the bullet hasn't been made yet that can kill Legs Diamond'.

He was shot in October 1924, but was still able to drive himself to Mount Sinai Hospital for treatment. The second attempt was when he survived the murder of Jacob Orgen. The third came in October 1930 when he was in his hotel suite at the Monticello with a chorus girl named Kiki Roberts. In a machine-gun attack ordered by Schultz he was the receiver of five bullets. Once again, against all medical expectations he survived.

Amazingly, following an attack in April 1931 he survived yet again. This time he was left with a bullet in the lung, one in the back, another in the liver and, rather less seriously, one in the arm.

Now Diamond, with the help of his new friend Garry Scaccio, turned his attention to Albany in upstate New York. He attempted to muscle in on some local bootleggers, Grover Parks and James Duncan. After being tortured and released, Parks and Duncan went to the police. Scaccio was convicted and sentenced to ten years' imprisonment. Diamond, however, was released and promised to look after his family. This was a promise he very quickly forgot.

THE END

By now Legs Diamond had fallen out with most of the leading figures in the Underworld, and in a typical gangland execution, he was finally shot dead on December 18, 1931. He was asleep in his room at 67 Dove Street, Albany, when three men entered his room. This time the killers took no chances and held his head while firing bullets through it. Three soft-nosed bullets ripped through Diamond's head, all entering on the left side. From the deep powder burns surrounding the wounds, detectives surmised the death weapons had been pressed directly against their target.

Despite it all, Diamond's wife, Alice, loved him to the end. The former Alice Schiffer washed the blood from the slain gangster's face with her handkerchief and kissed his cold cheeks wildly.

It has been suggested that perhaps Alice ordered the hit on her husband because she was jealous of his relationship with Kiki Roberts, but it seems unlikely. More probably his death was connected to his work. There were many possible reasons – the fact that he could no longer be trusted; his forgotten promise to Scaccio; the fact he wanted a larger share of Joey Fay's nightclub rackets; and of course the bootlegging from Waxey Gordon. There is also the possibility that his death could have been organized by Shultz. Two small-time Under-world crooks, Salvatore Spitale and Irving Blitz, are another possibility as they had been the victims of one of Diamond's scams. They had given him $200,000 to set up an overseas drug deal, but in true form he had invested the money in himself. No one was ever charged for the murder of Jack 'Legs' Diamond.

Dutch Schultz

Dutch Schultz, the notorious 1920s and 1930s New York gangster, died in 1935 of a single gunshot wound. Dutch was supposedly responsible for up to 135 murders before his death and was considered one of the most vicious gangsters of all time.

Arthur Simon Flegenheimer was born on August 6, 1902 in the Bronx. His parents were both German Jews and his mother, Emma, tried to raise little Arthur in the orthodox faith. Growing up in the tough section of the Bronx, Flegenheimer soon joined a street gang for protection.

When Flegenheimer was fourteen, his father left home. Schultz never admitted to any of his friends that his father had abandoned the family, he preferred to tell people that his father was a fine person and died during Schultz's teenage years. Shortly after his father left, Flegenheimer quit school and worked in a variety of odd jobs. Realizing that an honest job was not going to make him happy or rich he started hanging out at a place called the Criterion Club. This was where Marcel Poffo, a local thug with a police record, befriended him. Flegenheimer began his criminal career by holding up craps games that refused to pay a percentage to Poffo in the hope that he would impress his new-found friend.

124

When Flegenheimer was seventeen, he received his first and only prison sentence. He was arrested for breaking into a Bronx apartment, and was sent to Blackwell's Island, a brutal prison located in the middle of the East River. Flegenheimer was not a model prisoner, and in fact was so unruly that he had to be transferred to a tougher prison, West-hampton Farms. He managed to escape from there for a few hours only to be returned with an additional two months added to his sentence. On his eventual return to the Bronx, his old Bergen Gang buddies nicknamed him 'Dutch Schultz', much to the annoyance of his loving mother.

In was in the mid-1920s that Schultz realized bootlegging was the way to make serious money. He got involved in the beer trade working as a muscle man for some of the bigger operators. He was known to have driven a beer truck for the legendary Arnold Rothstein, and at one time he and Charles 'Lucky' Luciano were members of the Jack 'Legs' Diamond gang.

In early 1928, Schultz worked behind the bar in a speakeasy owned by a childhood friend Joey Noe. Schultz quickly gained a reputation for brutality, which came to the fore if someone was fool enough to trigger his temper. This brutality gained him admiration from Noe who took him on as a partner. The two men were soon on their way to building a beer empire.

With the money they made from their speakeasy Schultz and Noe opened more operations. They bought their own trucks to avoid the delivery costs, and obtained their beer from Frankie Dunn, a New Jersey brewery owner. Schultz would ride shotgun to protect his trucks from being hijacked.

The two partners realized they could increase their profits if they supplied beer to their rivals. Other speakeasy owners were soon 'persuaded' to purchase beer from the Schultz/Noe enterprise or else they would not like the consequences. Joe and John Rock were brothers who wouldn't be threatened by Schultz. John weakened after several threats, but his stubborn Irish brother refused to give in. One night Joe Rock was kidnapped by members of the Schultz/Noe gang. He was beaten, hung by his thumbs on a meat hook, and allegedly had a gauze bandage covering his eyes that had been smeared with the discharge from a gonorrhoea infection. His family supposedly paid $35,000 for his release, and shortly after Joe Rock lost his sight.

Word of the brutal attack spread and instilled fear among Schultz's competitors. His ruthless reputation made it easy for the partners to muscle in on the beer trade in the Bronx.

The modest operation which began in the Bronx, was now expanding over to Manhattan's upper West Side into the neighbourhoods of Washington Heights, Yorkville and Harlem. Schultz and Noe moved their headquarters out of the Bronx and onto East 149th Street in Manhattan. This move, however, brought the gang into direct competition with Jack 'Legs' Diamond.

It wasn't long before the Diamond gang responded. On October 15, 1928, at seven o'clock in the morning, Diamond's men ambushed Joey

Noe, while Schultz was thought to be having a meeting with rumrunner William V. 'Big Bill' Dwyer. Even though Noe was wearing a bullet-proof vest, the bullets ripped through his chest and lower spine. Noe apparently fired a number of shots in return, and witnesses reported seeing a blue Cadillac bounce off a parked car, losing one of its doors before speeding away. When police found the car an hour later, they discovered the body of Diamond gunman Louis Weinberg dead in the back seat.

Noe was rushed to Roosevelt Hospital but died three weeks later due to the severity of his wounds.

Following his partner's death, Schultz was bent on revenge. On November 4, 1928, the financier of the New York underworld, Arnold Rothstein, was shot in the Park Central Hotel and died two days later. It was rumoured that Schultz may have been involved in the shooting because of Rothstein's friendship with Diamond.

It now meant that Schultz was working on his own, and in fact never took another partner. He moved freely in the New York underworld as an independent operator, and by the late 1920s his influence became so great that he was invited to meetings called by Lucky Luciano and his associates as they began to build a national organized crime structure.

In May 1929, Schultz took part in the Atlantic City Conference. The meeting was attended by dozens of mobsters of various ethnic and religious backgrounds from all around the country. The main topic of the conference was co-operation between the gangs and the cities they represented, and to discuss plans for the day Prohibition was repealed.

Due to his working relationship with Luciano, when the Castellammarese War began in February 1930, Schultz joined forces with Giuseppe 'Joe the Boss' Masseria. Salvatore Maranzano was opposed to the Masseria set-up, and the war raged between them for fourteen months. It came to an end when Luciano set Masseria up to be murdered in a Coney Island restaurant. Still not satisfied, Maranzano put together a hit list of people he wanted out of the way. On the list were Luciano, Adonis, Frank Costello, Vito Genovese and Schultz himself. Maranzano hired Vincent 'the Mad Mick' Coll to carry out these murders. Coll at that time was in the middle of a gang war with Schultz. When Luciano was informed of the hit list from traitors inside the Maranzano organization, an assassination team was put together to murder the treacherous newly-crowned 'boss of bosses'. The hit squad dressed as police officers, murdered Maranzano in his Park Avenue office on September 10, 1931. It is thought that one of the members of the hit squad was Schultz's man Bo Weinberg.

THE WAR WITH COLL

1931 was not a good year for Schultz. On January 24 at Club Abbey, Schultz got involved in a fight with Charles 'Chink' Sherman, an associate of rival bootlegger, Waxey Gordon. Sherman was beaten with a chair and stabbed seven times with the shards from a broken peanut bowl. Schultz did not walk away from the fray unscathed, as he had taken a bullet in the shoulder, but quickly recovered. It was later revealed that the fight broke out over a joke about a girl one of them was seeing.

Shortly after, Schultz's gunman Vincent Coll decided he wanted a more important role in the gang and told Schultz he wanted to be taken on as a full partner. Schultz rejected him and Coll split from the gang and branched out on his own.

Before the split, Schultz had provided $10,000 to bail Coll out of prison, where he was being held for carrying a concealed weapon. When the trial date arrived in the spring of 1931, Coll did not appear forcing Schultz to part with the money. Schultz responded by having Coll's older brother Peter murdered. Coll was so incensed by the killing of his sibling, that he went on a rampage of hijacking Dutch's beer trucks and declaring war on Schultz gang members. Within weeks, four of Schultz's associates were killed at the hands of Coll and his men.

Coll had a flagrant disregard for the gangland hierarchy. Not very politically-minded, Coll conformed to the Irish bootlegging stereotype, thinking only in the short term and resorting to violent solutions. His reckless, gun-wielding approach led to gang warfare, which made the public angry and forced the authorities to intervene. This upset the equilibrium of gangland, for by and large, bootleggers operated with the support of the man in the street.

On the night of February 8, 1932, Vincent Coll was shot dead in a telephone booth on the West side of New York City. The authorities and the underworld alike greeted the news with relief, for Coll was the most vicious and unpredictable of all the gangsters in the Prohibition era, cutting a swathe of terror through New York society and its bootlegging underworld.

The war had been a costly one for Schultz. He lost gunmen, had numerous beer shipments hijacked, and several of his speakeasies had been shot up. His greatest loss being Danny Iamascia, a close friend and his bodyguard. With the Schultz–Coll War over, Dutch had more pressing matters to attend to in Harlem.

HARLEM POLICY RACKETS

The end of Prohibition didn't slow Dutch down at all. He was still extorting thousands of dollars from local businesses and it was then that he took over most of Harlem's policy rackets, or 'numbers' as it was often called. The policy was a kind of lottery, reducing the policy's top men to little more than salaried servants. The law wasn't any trouble either, at least as far as policy was concerned, as Dutch managed to get Jimmy Hines on the payroll. Hines was the Democratic boss of the 11th Assembly District, effective ruler not just of Harlem, but of the entire Upper West Side and a powerful force in the corrupt Tammany Hall. Once Hines was in his pocket, raids on policy games quickly became a thing of the past. Policy in

1920s Harlem was seen as a harmless vice, and many reputable citizens both played policy and operated numbers banks.

The profits from Schultz's policy operation were tremendous. The odds of winning were 999 to 1, but the house only paid off at 600 to 1. It was estimated that the average daily take was $35,000 of which only 25 percent was being disbursed to the winners. Of course out of this balance came the payoff to the police and politicians for protection, but that still left Schultz with an impressive profit margin.

While Schultz was making a fortune in the policy rackets, he devised another moneymaking venture involving union racketeering in the restaurant industry.

In 1932, a Schultz lieutenant, Julius Modgilewsky, called 'Modgilewsky the Commissar', but better known as Jules Martin, opened a small 'greasy spoon' diner. This diner acted as a front for gaining access to Local 16 of the Hotel & Restaurant Employees International Alliance. Local 16 handled the waiters in Manhattan north of Fourteenth Street. With the backing of Schultz, Martin's employees ran for union offices, fixing the ballot boxes in order to obtain the positions of president and secretary-treasurer. Their efforts were so effective that they received 38 more votes than the entire membership of the union.

The next move was to take over Local 302. This time instead of supplying his own candidates, Martin and another Schultz associate, Sam Krantz, simply advised the union's leadership to join them, or else. The final step was to establish the Metropolitan Restaurant & Cafeteria Owners Association to sign restaurant and cafeteria owners and muscle them into signing certificates of membership stating that they were doing so of their own free will.

No one realized that it was Schultz who was behind the scenes. Restaurant owners were told that the waiters' union was demanding a doubling of the wages, but this could be avoided if they joined and paid tribute to the association. One owner who refused to pay tribute to the association was Hyman Gross. Having already invested $100,000 in his new restaurant, Gross refused to give in to the Schultz mobsters. One night a stink bomb was dropped down the restaurant's chimney and Gross was forced out of business losing his entire investment.

The restaurant racket was so successful that it continued to thrive until an investigation by Special Prosecutor Thomas E. Dewey resulted in the indictments of ten men. The trial, which began on January 18, 1937, lasted two and a half months with forty prosecution witnesses and sixty defence witnesses taking the stand. The jury took just six hours to return a verdict of all guilty on all counts.

TAX EVASION

In 1933, the State of New York caught up with Dutch and a tax evasion suit was filed against him. Dutch was indicted on January 25, 1933 and for the next twenty-two months was a fugitive from the law. During his months in hiding, in broad daylight Schultz visited his wife Frances, had dinner and attended nightclubs with Jimmy Hines and Dixie Davis, and was a frequent guest at Polly Adler's midtown house of sin. All of 1933 passed without law enforcement finding Schultz who was still operating freely right under their noses.

On November 1, 1934, LaGuardia received a telephone call from Henry Morgenthau, Jr., Roosevelt's Secretary of the Treasury. Through this conversation Morgenthau teamed LaGuardia with FBI Director J. Edgar Hoover to put pressure on finding Schultz. Hoover made Dutch his 'undercover' Public Enemy No. 1. Schultz's first reaction was to send his legal team to Washington to negotiate a settlement but Morgenthau's reply was, 'We don't do business with criminals'. With that, twenty-two months as a fugitive came to an end as Schultz gave himself up.

The trial of Dutch Schultz started on April 16, 1935. His lawyers felt it would be better if the trial were held away from New York city where he stood less chance of being known as an infamous gangster. It was held in Syracuse and his laywers made no secret of Schultz's illegal activities. But the lynch pin of the case was not his criminal activities, but the fact that he had made his money illegally and goods obtained by this manner cannot be taxed. The jury was unable to reach a verdict, so a retrial was scheduled for July in the small town of Malone.

Dutch decided to stay in Malone one month before the trial and started to boost his own reputation. He bought everyone drinks night after night in the local bar and befriended the Mayor and the local Sheriff. When the day of the trial arrived, the jury found him not guilty. The judge was completely flabbergasted.

However, Dutch's legal troubles weren't over yet. Outstanding warrants barred him from immediately returning to New York, and the government filed another suit against him – eleven counts of failing to file his tax returns. Dutch took up residence in New Jersey until his new troubles could be cleared up.

New York District Attorney Dewey began to be a serious problem and Dutch wanted him killed. He went to the Syndicate, Lucky Luciano's powerful Mafia organization, about his problem. The Syndicate wouldn't allow it, wisely fearing the attention it would draw to them. Dutch wouldn't let up though and threatened to kill Dewey without the consent of the Syndicate. Rather than let this happen, the Syndicate decided to put an end to Dutch Schultz.

OUT OF THE WAY

On October 23, 1935, Murder Inc. hitmen came in through the back entrance of the Newark Palace Chop House Restaurant and Tavern, a known hangout of Dutch Schultz. Dutch and some of his men were indeed there, discussing some plans. The hitmen shot the three men at the dinner table but Dutch Schultz was not one of them. Charles 'the Bug' Workman, one of the assassins, put two and two together and headed to the men's toilet. He found Dutch there, shot him once, in the back, and fled. Dutch staggered back into the restaurant and asked for an ambulance. One of his companions, Lulu Rosencratz, despite having been shot seven times, went to the bar and got change for a quarter to make the call on a public pay-phone.

Dutch was taken to Newark City Hospital where he survived for two days in a guarded hospital room. He babbled and raved like a lunatic until he eventually died of internal bleeding.

At the cemetery there were only three mourners, Schultz's mother, Mrs. Emma Flegenheimer, his sister, Mrs. Helen Ursprung, and wife, Mrs. Frances Flegenheimer. Two state troopers and Father McInerney who had baptized Schultz just before his death accompanied them. At his mother's request, the traditional Jewish *talis*, or praying shawl, was draped over his shoulders. Schultz was buried in consecrated ground due to his deathbed conversion to the Catholic faith.

Frank Costello

*Frank Costello was one of the most famous Mafia bosses.
Costello was part of Lucky Luciano's crew as a youngster
and rose alongside his friend to become one of the most
powerful Mafia bosses the United States had ever seen.
Unlike most Mafia bosses Costello used his brains more
than his muscle, and he made contacts with judges,
police officials and politicians. It was through these
contacts that he received the nickname
'The Prime Minister'.*

Costello was born on January 20, 1891, in
Calabria province, Italy. He was born Francesco Castiglia and in 1895, with his sister and
mother, sailed for America. They settled in East
Harlem, New York, where he grew up in the Italian
ghetto. By the time Costello was 13 he was a
member of the notorious 104th Street Gang,
eventually working his way up to becoming head.
His first name became anglicized to Frank.

From an early age, Costello was involved in
crime, robbing his landlady at the age of fourteen.
He was arrested three times as a youth for assault
and robbery, but was released each time. At 24 he
was sentenced to eleven months in prison for
carrying a gun. It wasn't so much the gun that got
him sentenced, but rather the three other times
he'd been released. The judge saw his previous

releases for more serious crimes and decided to send him away. After that, Costello decided to make his living with his brains rather than a gun, which kept him out of jail for the next 37 years.

POLITICAL CONNECTIONS

After his release from prison, Costello began making contacts in the political rings. During the age of Prohibition, these contacts would prove vital to the operations set up between his childhood friends, Charles 'Lucky' Luciano and Meyer Lansky. The group, along with Benny Siegel would become the most powerful force of underworld crime the country had known, even though they were all still in their twenties. Costello was the eldest of them all, using his maturity to his advantage when dealing with the mayors, governors, police and judges that ran the city. The gang were involved with bootlegging, slot machines and gambling, and Costello himself generated huge amounts of money from a wide range of illegal operations. He also developed a reputation as an advisor and a bridge between the legitimate world and the mob. If a politician had to be reached or a judge fixed, Costello would get the assignment. He built up a solid reputation as a man who had the right contacts and could organize a fix. He proved to be of major impor- tance to Luciano and was very close to the core of the future power of Organized Crime in the United States.

While the others were plotting takeovers,

Costello was 'doing favours' for people. These favours allowed the group to operate freely around New York City, and, before long, the rest of the country. He gained them the protection they needed, something they could not operate without. His contacts came in handy when disposing of Abe 'Kid Twist' Reles in 1941. Reles, the top informant in the Murder, Inc. cases, and probably the most important mob informant in history, died somehow falling out a two-storey hotel window while under 24-hour police guard. There are many theories as to how this all took place: that Reles was playing a practical joke and messed up; that he was trying to escape; or that the mob had arranged to have him killed.

When Prohibition ended in 1933, Costello needed a new way to earn his money along with the rest of the Syndicate. Costello became more involved in gambling and casinos with contacts in Louisiana, namely Huey Long, Meyer Lansky in Cuba and Miami, and Benny Siegel in Las Vegas. He set up storefronts, such as grocery stores and butcher shops, to act as a cover for craps games and card tables which were placed in the back of the stores. He even resorted to setting up stools for kids so they could drop their coins into his slot machines.

KEFAUVER COMMITTEE

The Syndicate hit some rough times during the 1950s due partly to the Kefauver Committee. The Kefauver Committee was the first committee made up of senators from around the country organized to gain not only a better understanding of how to fight organized crime, but also to expose organized crime for the conglomerate empire that it was.

Headed by Estes Kefauver, Democratic Senator from Tennessee, the committee included several members of Congress: Lester C. Hunt (Wyoming), Alexander Wiley (Wisconsin), Charles W. Tobey (New Hampshire) and Herbert O'Conner (Maryland). Six hundred witnesses were brought before the committee which included the likes of governors, policemen, such as Captain Dan Gilbert, chief investigator for the state's attorney's office for Cook County in Chicago, major racketeers like Frank Castello, to Hollywood actress Virginia Hill, lady friend and reputed bag woman for the mob.

The committee travelled the country, investigating all levels of corruption. Frank Castello and Longy Zwillman appeared before the committee in New York, revealing their links to powerful political figures such as Governor Harold G. Hoffman and Elmer Wene and William O'Dwyer. Through each of these public figures, it was revealed that organized crime was receiving special accommodations from prosecuting attorneys to governors across the country.

It was during these hearings that Costello became a nationwide celebrity for his 'finger ballet'. Costello agreed to appear in front of the committee only if the camera did not focus on his face. With not much else to show, the cameras concentrated on his hands, which nervously danced around on the table. Despite his attempt to remain anonymous, Costello became famous for his raspy voice and dancing hands. As for the Syndicate, they had lost valuable members of their empire after the hearings due to either death or deportation.

After the Kefauver Committee, Costello was investigated for tax evasion and sent to prison. With Luciano having been deported and his other partners, such as Joe Adonis, either facing the same fate or worse, Costello started to make some moves to remain in power. Vito Genovese, an underboss for Luciano and Costello, started to make takeover moves for the Luciano crime family.

Normally, Costello would have been backed by Willie Moretti, a crime boss just over the border in New Jersey, who had fifty to sixty men to help him keep the balance and peace. But Moretti was suffering from syphilis and began to lose his mind. The Syndicate feared that if Moretti should be called in front of the Kefauver Committee, he may let out secrets that protected their entire organization. Genovese warned the Syndicate that if he should be called to testify that they should dispose of him. Costello needed a new ally so he turned to Albert Anastasia, 'the Mad Hatter'.

Anastasia was the chief executioner of Murder, Inc. and would be next on the witness stand during the hearings if Abe Reles continued testifying. Costello saved him once and decided to call in the favour. Costello convinced Anastasia to kill Vince Mangano and take the helm of the Mangano family, backed by Luciano and himself. With

Anastasia's backing, Costello was able to keep power for several years and fend off the greedy Genovese. But that peace was not to last.

In 1957, Genovese convinced Carlo Gambino to topple Anastasia, once again, shifting the power back to Genovese. During that same year, Genovese put out a contract on Costello, hiring Vincent 'The Chin' Gigante, to kill the 'Prime Minister'. The cocky Gigante fired but missed Costello, calling out to him before he fired, 'This one's for you Frank!' Costello, hearing his name, turned, and the bullet just grazed his head.

Costello took the hint and soon started to move out of power, paving the way for Genovese to move in. This was something which he had been trying to do ever since Luciano was put in prison back in 1936. However, Costello was not quite finished – he still had one trick left before he would officially retire.

Firstly in 1957, the New York State Police uncovered a meeting of major Syndicate figures from around the country in the small upstate New York town of Apalachin. This gathering has become known as the Apalachin Conference. Many of the attendees were arrested and this event was the catalyst that changed the way law enforcement battled with organized crime. This is also where Genovese was to proclaim his stature as 'boss of bosses'. As mobsters from all over the country showed up, policemen burst on to the scene making a mockery of Genovese's announcement. Those absent from the conference of note were Costello and Lansky, who were already plotting with

Gambino to overthrow Genovese. Gambino, realizing that the majority of the underworld was against Genovese becoming the 'boss of bosses' knew that it was time to change his allegiance and work with Costello and Lansky. The older mobsters convinced Gambino to set up a fake drug deal and then tipped off the police of his involvement, sending Genovese to prison for fifteen years, where he would eventually die. Costello, along with the other Dons had beaten Genovese at his own scheming.

In due time Costello made it clear that he wanted peace and would step down. Genovese agreed to let Costello live, but first he had to prove something to his peers. He reduced Costello to the rank of a humble soldier, stripping him of his gambling interests in Las Vegas, Florida and the Caribbean. He even made Frank give up his points in The Copocabana nightclub. And finally, he extracted a promise from Costello that he would get out and never again be involved in the rackets. Costello agreed, then retired gracefully from the scene. Costello went on to live the rest of his life in a quiet and uneventful retirement.

After a heart attack, he was admitted to Doctors Hospital on East End Avenue, Manhattan, and there, died peacefully in his sleep at 7.30 a.m. on February 18, 1973. He had lived to the ripe old age of 82.

George 'Bugs' Moran

A virtual legend in his own time, Chicagoans read his name in the newspapers almost weekly during the 1920s, when gangsters made the headlines with their bootleg wars.

George Moran was born in 1893 to Irish and Polish immigrant parents. He grew up on the North Side of Chicago where he soon became streetwise and ran with several gangs. Before he was twenty-one years old he had committed more than twenty known burglaries and had been imprisoned three times. He earned the name 'Bugs' when he felt that he was being ripped off by a tailor. He left the man on the floor of his shop with two broken arms and two broken legs, and from that moment on he was known on the streets as 'Bugs' a pseudonym for 'crazy'.

As Bugs started moving up in the underworld he started to run booze rackets and hosting craps games in Chicago. At that time there were around a dozen rival bootleggers, and Moran's businesses were small-time compared with those of his rivals Johnny Torrio and his new recruit Al Capone.

To gain more power, Moran became a member of Dion O'Banion's North Side gang and Bugs

143

learned a lot from his mentor. The pair got on well together, both sharing the same sick sense of humour. The press always made light of Moran's wicked humour which portrayed him as a 'jolly' murderer who always walked with a skip in his step. It was probably this publicity which made the North Side gang so popular in the 1920s.

The bootlegging business was thriving, which the gang ran from their headquarters above Schofield's Flower Shop at 738 North Slate Street. Moran and his associates were able to keep a tight grip on the booze scene, however, there was constant pressure from the outside.

O'Banion was killed in 1924 by Torrio's men and this made Moran second-in-command of the North Side gang, behind Earl Weiss. The bootlegging operations run by the North Side gang were now a real challenge to Capone's own liquor operations, and he was starting to get really pissed off.

On January 25, 1925, Weiss and Moran tried to wipe out Johnny Torrio by firing on him as he got out of his car. Fortunately for Torrio, Moran's gun mis-fired and he survived the attack, but it had shaken him badly. Torrio decided to retire and handed over his entire operation to Capone.

Starting in 1926, the North Side gang began paving its way into legitimate business – albeit, in an illegitimate way. They knew that Prohibition would have to come to an end eventually and that they would have to find another way of earning easy money, so they took over businesses like the Dry Cleaners Union. A friend of Moran, Maxie Eisen, was their stepping stone into the unions, and he was appalled at how the relationship between Chicago gangs had deteriorated over the years. He was concerned that Moran may be the next target for assassination and told his friend in no uncertain terms to make peace with Al Capone.

Strangely enough Capone agreed to a meeting, and what resulted was not only a meeting of the North Side gang, but of all the gang bosses in Chicago. As a result of this meeting a pact was drawn up saying that there would be no more crossing of territories by rival outfits. It was decided that everyone would share the profits of Chicago's booze industry, and that members of opposing gangs were tocease fighting. For the first time in years, there was actually peace.

In fact, the next major underworld death – that of Vinnie Drucci – was not the result of gangland fighting, but an argument with a Chicago policeman. His death left Moran as the last and solo leader of the North Side Irish – with Capone still out there, larger than life. Bugs had now taken the top spot and was the leader of the North Side gang.

Despite the peace treaty, Capone was jealous of Moran's dealings with Chicago's entrepreneurs. They still didn't trust Capone and refused to buy their liquor supply from him.

Bugs Moran hated Capone with a passion and often referred to him as 'The Beast'. Having taken so much of the liquor business away from his rival, Moran now prepared his organization for a fight. With Hymie Weiss and Vinnie Drucci gone, his forces, and possibly confidence too, were depleting. He made friends with a man named Terry Druggan, a

South Side fellow Irishman who had fallen out with Capone. He also hired Ted Newberry, a sharp rum-runner who knew the business, along with a small band of new gunmen including Billie Skidmore, Jake Zuta and Barney Bertsche, with Willie Marks heading up his union campaign. Also added to his force were the Gusenberg brothers, accountant Adam Heyer, speakeasy operator Albert Weinshank, bodyguard James Clark and liquor driver John May. May also doubled up as the gang's mechanic for their fleet of vehicles.

They kept up a constant vigil and, as another precaution, in 1928 Moran moved the gang's old headquarters above Schofield's Flower Shop. The owner of the shop had been making too much fuss over the bad reputation his place was receiving in the newspapers, following the deaths of Deanie O'Banion, then Weiss. Moran relocated to an office space at 127 North Dearborn in the heart of the Loop, as he agreed that they were far too easy to find. The new offices were much less conspicuous as they were well hidden amongst residential rooming houses as well as private homes.

127 North Dearborn was more of a decoy because their main gang business was run from an old S-M-C Cartage Company garage on North Clark Street in the Kilgubbin district. Moran had left the name of the old firm on the front window, as it was an excellent cover-up for his unmarked beer trucks to deliver at all hours of the day and night.

From their respective vantage points, Moran and Capone, who was now back in Chicago, simply waited and watched each other keenly.

The violence all culminated in the St. Valentine's Day massacre. Although one of the most spectacular gangland slayings in mob history, it was actually somewhat of a failure (see page 79 for details). Moran escaped unhurt as he saw the killers walking into the North Side gang's warehouse as he drew up outside. He fled as quickly as he could.

Throughout the 1930s Moran's power started to lose its credibility, even though his nemesis Capone was in jail.

THE DECLINE

After the massacre Moran's power was broken and his luck started to run out. For the next couple of years, until the repeal of Prohibition in 1932, he and what was left of his gang made sporadic attempts to regain the North Side, but Capone had moved in and could not be moved. Moran quit Chicago in the mid-thirties and moved to Wisconsin, followed by Minnesota.

Reduced to near poverty, he resorted to robbing banks and filling stations in the Illinois area. Around 1940, he moved to Ohio to join the Virgil Summers-Albert Fouts gang. They were only petty thieves and not comparable to Moran's earlier acquaintances. The Federal Bureau of Investigation eventually caught up with him in 1946.

Moran served ten years in Leavenworth Penitentiary, and when released in 1956, was immediately re-arrested for an earlier bank holdup in Ohio, which had only netted a paltry

$4,000. He was convicted and sentenced to serve another ten years.

George 'Bugs' Moran died in prison of lung cancer on February 25, 1957, receiving the Full Last Rites of the Roman Catholic Church. Moran was given a paupers burial in a wooden casket in a potters field just outside the prison.

THE OTHER SIDE OF BUGS MORAN

Behind the mask of a gangster, George Clarence Moran was something of an enigma. There is no doubt he was a tough guy, but he also loved to laugh and had a wicked sense of humour. He was a devout Catholic and attended Mass on a regular basis. Like the rest of his North Side gang, Moran carried rosary beads in his trouser pocket and would use them to pray before they hit on a target. He had a hatred of prostitution and as Capone and his men were involved in that line of business, it only strengthened his strong dislike for the man.

To the outside world he was a follower of fashion and was always extremely smart in appearance. He liked to wear a blue or brown, serge, slightly pinstriped suit, which would be finished off with a milk-coloured or brown fedora. For an evening out at the opera or dining with friends he would wear tails. In contrast, in the comfort of his own home, he liked to wear loose clothing and pair of old floppy slippers.

He always favoured brunettes and in 1926 married a showgirl who went by the name of Alice Roberts. She was a full-blooded Sioux and Moran treasured the time he spent with her. He was very proud of his wife and would show her off at every opportunity. On one occasion he cut a dashing scene on the ice rink, taking his wife along as a celebration of their wedding anniversary. He was certainly a strange sight to behold as he raced around the rink with two guns bulging beneath his expensive jacket.

Moran and his wife lived in a very upper-crust apartment on Belden Avenue, later moving to the more secure Parkway Hotel at 2100 Lincoln. By all accounts they were a very happy couple, and unlike most of his gangster friends was totally loyal.

Behind this façade as a jovial, smart, married man was the character who was ruthless, an adept businessman and above all a gangster.

John Gotti

John Gotti was the ruthlessly brutal but stylishly dressed New York Mafia chief who revelled in the public spotlight under the pseudonym 'Dapper Don'. Looking back at Gotti's reign one can see that his only true achievement as a Mafia chieftain was to captivate the public's attention. At this, Gotti had few equals. But as a leader he lacked the ability that characterized the careers of such mob luminaries as Capone, Luciano, Lansky, Torrio, Costello and Gambino. In the end it was Gotti's ego and carelessness that led to his downfall.

John Gotti was born on October 27, 1940 in the Bronx, New York. When Gotti was around twelve he and his family moved to a rough neighbourhood in Brooklyn. It was here that he discovered life on the streets.

At any early age, young 'Johnny Boy' learned to use his fists. He had a quick temper and a burning anger as he looked on in contempt at those who had a better life. Instead of striving to better himself, his goal was to be one of the kids he saw on a daily basis hanging around the Brooklyn street corners. Gotti had not even reached his thirteenth birthday before he was caught up in the street activities of the local mobsters. Together with his brothers Peter and Richard, Gotti became part of a gang that ran errands for the gang leaders. In school he was considered a classroom bully and a disruptive influence. Consequently his teachers showed little concern over his absence, and he preferred to obtain his education on the street rather than in the classroom.

In 1954, Gotti was injured while taking part in a robbery for some local hoods. He and some other kids were in the process of stealing a portable cement mixer from a construction site when the mixer tipped over and crushed Gotti's toes. After spending most of the summer of his fourteenth year in hospital, Gotti was back on the street with a new gait that would last him for life.

Gotti quit school for good by the time he was sixteen, becoming a member of the Fulton-Rockaway Boys, thus named from an intersection in Brooklyn. Gotti soon became leader of the gang. They differed from other teenage street gangs in that the crimes they committed were of a more serious nature – stealing cars, fencing stolen goods and rolling drunks.

Gotti, along with his brothers Peter and Richard, teamed up with two other young men who would become life-long friends. The first was Angelo Ruggiero, whose incessant talking earned him the nickname 'Quack-Quack'; second was Wilfred 'Willie Boy' Johnson, an amateur boxer of American–Indian origin. Johnson was constantly being teased about his roots, and consequently could never become a true member of the Mafia.

Between the years 1957 and 1961, while still a member of the Fulton-Rockaway Boys, Gotti was arrested five times. Each time the charges were dismissed or reduced to a probationary sentence.

When he was twenty, Gotti met and fell in love with Victoria DiGiorgio. They were married on March 6, 1962, almost a full year after the birth of their first child, Angela. The marriage proved to be a stormy one, with many fights and periods of separation. Yet despite their problems, the couple went on to have two more children in rapid succession: a second daughter, Victoria, and John A., who became known as 'Junior'.

GAMBINO FAMILY

In 1966, Gotti made the fateful move to Ozone Park in Queens. Gotti became an associate of a Mafia crew run by Carmine Fatico and his brother Daniel called the Bergin Crew. The Faticos had to answer to Gambino Family Underboss, Aniello Dellacroce. The Gambinos were a powerful crime family headed by Mafia godfather Carlo Gambino. Gotti quickly graduated from small-time heists to big-time felonies. Gotti's 'job' was hijacking trucks, and he made loads of money for the Gambinos by hijacking freight from Kennedy Airport. Gotti quickly moved up in status within the Gambino Family. While he was not known as a great hijacker, Gotti was successful enough to move his family to a nicer apartment in Brooklyn. He and Victoria soon had their fourth child, a second son, whom they named Frank.

On November 27, 1967 Gotti along with another crew member, forged the name of a for-warding company agent and then took a rented truck to JFK's United cargo area and drove off with $30,000 worth of merchandise. Four days later, on another heist at a Northwest Airlines cargo terminal, the FBI swooped in and arrested the crew, finding Gotti in the back of the truck hiding behind some boxes. During the investigation that followed, United employees identified John Gotti as the man who had signed for the stolen merchandise. He was arrested for the United hijacking in February 1968. In April, while out on bail, he was arrested a third time for hijacking. This time it was for stealing a cargo of cigarettes worth nearly $500,000 outside a restaurant on the New Jersey turnpike.

John pleaded guilty to the Northwest hijacking and was sentenced to four years at the Lewisburg Federal Penitentiary in Pennsylvania. Prosecutors dropped the charges in the cigarette hijacking and Gotti served less than three years of his sentence at Lewisburg, from May 1969 to January 1972.

When Gotti was released from prison, he decided the best course of action would be to get a legitimate job. John was put on the payroll of Victoria's stepfather's construction company. Shortly after his release Victoria was pregnant with the couple's last child, another son whom they named Peter.

At the age of 31, Gotti became the acting head of the Bergin Crew. The Bergin Crew under Gotti were young and hungry and, looking to make money, started dealing in narcotics. It was a rule in the underworld that a portion of the money from drug deals was always handed over to the bosses.

In return they chose to look the other way as long as the money rolled in and no one associated with the family ended up in jail.

By May 1972, as Gotti assumed more and more control of the Bergin Crew, several members had already or were about to become confidential informants for the FBI. This group included Willie Boy Johnson and William Battista and over the years, the government received conflicting reports from Johnson and Battista as to John Gotti's actual involvement in narcotics.

THE DEATH OF MANNY GAMBINO

Gotti, although not in total charge of the Bergin Crew, took great pride in relaying orders from Don Carlo. One such order was to ban the kidnapping of rival mobsters, a popular practice in the 70s. This change was most probably motivated by the kidnapping, and assassination of Manny Gambino, Don Carlo's own nephew. It was long believed that Gotti had avenged Don Carlo by murdering Irish mobster Jimmy McBratney, who was suspected of the kidnapping, but it was later revealed that Manny Gambino's true killer was Robert Sentner, a loan shark to whom he owed a lot of money. Nonetheless, McBratney was gunned down by Gotti and his associates Ralph Galione and Angelo Ruggiero in a Staten Island restaurant. The gunmen were later identified by eyewitnesses, and on October 17, Gotti was indicted by a grand jury for murder.

Gotti's in-laws were instrumental in putting up

the collateral for his release on a $150,000 bail. Victoria's family, which had already provided John with a visible means of support, also purchased a home for the couple in Howard Beach. Once out, Gotti went right back to the Bergin to attend to the overseeing of the crew and his new holdings, which included a restaurant and motel.

Just before the trial, Galione was murdered, and Ruggiero provided the court with a solid alibi. Gotti, however, was sentenced to four years in jail, two of which he served before being released on parole.

He was released from prison on July 28, 1977, having served less than two years for the murder of McBratney. To celebrate his return the Bergin Crew purchased a brand new Lincoln Mark IV for him. He soon found out that, while he was away, there had been a change in the leadership of the Gambino Family.

During Gotti's absence, Don Carlo Gambino passed away, leaving Paul Castellano in charge. Aniello Dellacroce was now the underboss, supervising many of the operations, including Gotti's Bergin Crew. John Gotti, now hungry for power, set his sights on climbing into Carmine Fatico's position as head of the Bergin Crew. Fatico had recently beaten two loansharking cases, but he and his brother Daniel, along with crewmembers Charles and John Carneglia, had been convicted of hijacking. The Faticos pleaded guilty in the hope that they would receive probation. One of the government informants reported that Gotti was hoping that his former mentor would be sent away, enabling him to move ahead. Carmine Fatico received five years' probation, but his reign as *capo* of the Bergin Crew was over. The terms of his probation stated that he was not to associate with any known criminals. On occasion Gotti was to seek the elder Mafioso's counsel, but they would never meet again at the Bergin.

Gotti at this time was still considered an associate and could not officially become the 'acting *capo*' of the crew until he became a made member of the Gambino Family. Some time during the first half of 1977, Angelo Ruggiero and Gene Gotti (who acted as crew boss in his brother's absence), were both made full members. In a second rite later in the year, Gotti and eight other men took the Mafia oath of 'Omerta', which is the Code of Honour of the Italian Mafia.

Now a made member of the Gambino Family, Gotti's hijacking career officially came to an end. He avoided what were considered 'riskier crimes' and settled instead on gambling and loan sharking. Since Gotti was still on probation, he ordered Bergin crewmembers to be on their guard and not to draw attention to the themselves or the club.

THE DEATH OF FRANK GOTTI

Frank Gotti was John and Victoria's fourth child. On March 18, 1980, he borrowed a friend's motorized mini-bike and took a ride around his Howard Beach neighbourhood. John Favara, a neighbour of the Gottis, was driving down 157th Avenue. A dumpster had been placed outside a house that was under renovation. Favara did not notice the boy on the mini-bike dash into the street from the other side of the dumpster, and his car struck and killed Frank Gotti.

Both John and Victoria were devastated by the death of Frank, who was only twelve years old at the time of the accident. Favara received death threats and abuse from Victoria, who was incensed every time she saw his car. He sought advice from a childhood friend, Anthony Zappi, whose father, Ettore, had been a *capo* in the Gambino Family. Zappi advice was for Favara to move out of the neighbourhood post-haste.

Favara took Zappi's advice and put his home up for sale. However, on July 28, three days before he was to complete on the sale of his house, Favara was abducted while leaving work. Several people watched as Favara was clubbed over the head and thrown into a van. He and his car were never seen again.

John and Victoria had conveniently been in Fort Lauderdale, Florida, when the abduction took place. When the couple returned from the south, detectives questioned them, but although they showed no remorse they denied any involvement in Favara's disappearance. No one was ever arrested for the abduction and possible murder and in 1983, Favara's wife had him officially declared dead.

TIME TO MAKE A MOVE

After the death of his son, John Gotti's gambling habits became more reckless. Paul Castellano, the boss of the family, voiced his own concerns to Dellacroce. Although Dellacroce passed it off as Gotti's way of dealing with grief, Castellano was still unhappy. It was during the early half of the 1980s, that the relationship between Castellano and the Dellacroce/Gotti crew started to deteriorate steadily. Unbeknown to Castellano, Gotti was already a potentially deadly rival. A lot of the tension between the two groups arose because of a dispute over Gotti's alleged involvement in heroin trafficking. Castellano didn't want to be involved in drug trade for fear there would be too much heat from the FBI against the family, which was making more than enough money controlling discreet businesses such as construction and private sanitation services.

It was time for Gotti to make a move. He decided to kill Castellano and assume leadership of the Gambino family.

On December 16, 1985, Gotti and a small band of Gambino family co-conspirators waited for Castellano outside the Sparks Steak House in Manhattan. Castellano never made it out of his car before he was pumped with bullets.

Within weeks, Gotti was appointed the new Godfather of the Gambino family. Operating out of the Ravenite Social Club in Manhattan and the Bergen club in Queens, Gotti quickly consolidated his power.

THE BEGINNING OF THE END

John Gotti emerged unscathed from three criminal cases brought against him starting in 1986. The charges ranged from assault to racketeering. In the end, it was Gotti's love for being in the limelight and public exposure that would bring about his downfall.

It wasn't long before prosecutors were ready to file a new racketeering indictment. Although Gotti had proved untouchable in past attempts to convict him, this time the government had a secret weapon – the testimony of Sammy 'the Bull' Gravano, who was second in command in the Gambino family.

Gravano, a suspected killer, cut a deal with the government, trading his testimony, which would clearly define the Gambino family crime operations, for a lighter sentence. The government also had tapes proving Gotti could be heard ordering mob hits.

On February 12, 1992 the trial of John Gotti commenced. By the time Gravano's testimony was complete the trial was over for all intents and purposes. The only witness the defence put on the stand was a tax attorney for Gotti, who was ripped apart during cross-examination. After final arguments the case went to the jury and on April 2, 1992 they returned with their verdict. Gotti was convicted on charges that included five murders, and was sentenced to life without parole.

The Gambino family now seemed to be without a leader. In the Mafia, a boss either has to resign or be killed, but, despite his prison sentence, Gotti was not about to retire.

From jail, Gotti appointed a committee that included his son, John Jr., then 28, to run the Gambino family, eventually naming him the acting boss. And in time, older, more experienced family members began to resent the younger Gotti.

On December 3, 1999, John Gotti Jr. was charged with racketeering, leaving the Gambino family in the care of the senior Gottis brother, Peter.

John Gotti died of cancer in the Springfield, Missouri Federal prison hospital, on June 10, 2002.

Sam Giancana

Murder dominates the story of Sam Giancana. He used people like rubber balls – to bounce when thrown – he would discard those people with bullet, knife and bomb when their purpose had been dissipated. The one emotion he was capable of feeling, was the joy of killing.

Sam Giancana was born on May 24, 1908 in the 'Patch', which was an Italian ghetto on Chicago's West Side. His mother, Antonia Giancana, died when he was two years old, and his father Antonio Giancana remarried a short time later to a girl named Mary Leonardi. Sam Giancana was beaten by his father almost routinely on a daily basis. It seemed he blamed Sam for any troubles or misfortune that had come his way in life.

Sam Giancana stopped attending school at the age of fourteen, and it appears he never held a legitimate job during his lifetime. He became a member of the 42 Gang, a gang who ran wild on Chicago's West Side. He made a living as a burglar and a car thief, and served his first jail sentence when he was seventeen – a thirty-day term for car theft. He was arrested on two occasions for murder and walked free on both occasions. In the 1920s Giancana had gained the reputation of being a good wheel-man having once worked for 'Machine

Gun' Jack McGurn as his chauffeur. He was in later years to become wheel-man to another up and coming young 'turk' who was a major player in the Chicago crime scene, Anthony 'Big Tuna' Accardo. Sam's criminal career came to a temporary halt in March 1929 when he was sent to Joliet prison for a term of three years on a burglary charge.

When he was released from prison on Christmas Eve in 1931 Giancana joined up with some old buddies from the 'Patch' who had been members of the 42 Gang. By this time they had elevated their status in Chicago by working for Al Capone. Prohibition was over but there was still some cash to be made from cheap untaxed alcohol. Giancana and his buddies started to produce thousands of gallons of illegal alcohol in a still out in the suburbs. They sold it to wholesalers who were only too glad to buy the cheaper product from them and sell it off at a nice profit. The operation went well for a year, but on January 17, 1939, the still was raided. Giancana was caught and charged with nine alcohol violation offences. He was found guilty and ordered to be detained for four years at Terre Haute Prison.

THE NUMBERS RACKET

It was at Terre Haute that Giancana met Edward Jones. Jones was a black guy from the South Side who had made a fortune from the nickel-per-bet policy game. Jones made the mistake of bragging to Giancana that the numbers racket was a licence to print money. The outfit had little or no interest before in these rackets and neither at first did Giancana. Jones, however, kept on about the easy money to be made, and Sam Giancana was becoming more and more interested by the minute. What Giancana had always considered to be just a nickel and dime operation, was much more it seemed once the figures were explained to him by Jones.

When Sam Giancana was released from prison in 1942 he was at a crossroads in his life. He was married to Angeline and had two daughters. He was earning cash by stealing and counterfeiting rationing stamps and selling them on.

Sam received his draft papers from Uncle Sam. But when asked by the medical examiner what he did for a living, Giancana replied, 'I steal' as if it were the most natural reply to give. The examiners rightly decided Giancana was not fit to serve with the US army and rejected him, stating that Giancana had an 'inadequate personality and strong anti-social trends'.

William Skidmore was a bail bondsman and gambler who had been around the Chicago crime syndicates for years. He had dealings with Johnny Torrio and Jake Guzik on a close business level. He had befriended Sam Giancana from his time in Terre Haute Prison, and it was Skidmore who introduced Giancana's ideas for the Policy racket at a board meeting where Tony Accardo was in attendance. Accardo was now boss of the outfit. He immediately liked Giancana and felt he was someone with good potential. He made Giancana his driver. Accardo also gave him the go-ahead to move in on the Jones brothers' lucrative rackets operation once Giancana had explained to him just how profitable it could be.

Sam Giancana soon came up with a plan to gain control of the Policy rackets. He kidnapped the main Jones brother, Eddie, the guy who explained the operation to him in Terre Haute and held him to ransom. The ransom was, of course, the policy 'Wheels' and control of the numbers rackets. Jones was held by Giancana and his associates for a week, being released when the 'ransom' was finally paid. Following his release Edward Jones took flight to Mexico, which left Giancana in command of the largest numbers operations in the City.

It wasn't all plain sailing though for Giancana, because there was another numbers operator in Chicago, a newcomer by the name of Theodore Roe. Roe had established a pretty good sized operation for himself among the poor in the black neighbourhoods. Giancana was not pleased with having to share his territory and insisted on having it all. He began using intimidating tactics on Roe in a bid to scare him off, but Roe didn't scare easily. In retaliation Roe hired two police detectives to act as his bodyguards and made sure he didn't get kidnapped like Jones, or get taken out of the picture more permanently by Sam Giancana.

As reward for his enterprise and endeavour in running the numbers rackets so profitably and successfully for the Outfit, Accardo awarded Giancana a place on the 'board'. It was reported that the rackets had earned the underworld an

164

estimated $150million. By this time Giancana was already running the day-to-day operations of the elder gangster Louis 'Little New York' Campagna. With Willie Daddano and Fifi Baccieri, two of the most feared hitmen in the Outfit, at his side, he took control of other lucrative rackets. He quickly spread the mob-controlled gambling operation even further afield, taking control of Chicago's loansharking, jukeboxes and prostitution operations along with labour racketeering.

As a sign of his increasing advancement within the mob Sam Giancana moved his wife and two daughters into a house in the suburb of Oak Park, which was more in keeping with his new status. In 1957 Louis Campagna died while in Florida, from a heart attack, paving the way for Tony Accardo to appoint Giancana boss to handle the day-to-day running of the Outfit. Accardo had long wanted to take a less active role in the daily running of the operations. Although he wanted to be seen to be in a semi-retired role, he watched from the sidelines and was never far away when there was a decision to be made.

Giancana was now seen to be the 'king' of the Chicago mob. Any small-time crook wanting to set up business on mob territory had to apply to Sam for a 'licence' to operate, and the standard fee was fifty per cent of the take. It was obvious that only those paying the mob operated their business without problems – the rules were simple – no pay no play!

Giancana liked to live well, and loved being around the celebrities. He dated night club dancers and singers and lavished them with expensive tokens of his 'love'. Although he was not considered a good looking man, Giancana was dating some of the most beautiful woman around. He had a much publicised romance with one of the McGuire Sisters who were famous and beautiful singers of the time.

In the fifties he became involved with the Outfits move into Las Vegas. The Outfit siphoned off cash from union pension funds which, at that point in time, was estimated to be over $100 million. Men were placed in the new casinos to operate the 'skim' where they would cream money from the casinos' huge profits to send back to the outfit in Chicago.

NAME DROPPING

Johnny Roselli was the mobs man on the West Coast, and Giancana made numerous trips back and forth to Las Vegas to liaise with Roselli. Sam's daughters were treated like royalty whenever they came to Vegas with him and were taken on guided tours of all the major Hollywood film studios. In the meantime Giancana had struck up a friendship with the singer Frank Sinatra. Giancana would arrange celebrity charity benefits at the bequest of his wife who at that time was very sick. Frank and the rest of his buddies would turn up every summer and pack out the Chicago stadium. Frank and Giancana were spotted together frequently in the early sixties, Sinatra having given Sam's girlfriend Phyllis McGuire a small part in the movie *Come Blow Your Horn*. Sam was on the set almost every day.

On November 14, 1957, Sam Giancana had represented Chicago at the ill-fated mob meeting in Appalachin, New York. Hoards of Mafia men were captured by the police, some managed to escape through the woods, Giancana being among them. Sixty-three members of La Cosa Nostra from all parts of the USA were eventually rounded up by the police. The FBI Director, J. Edgar Hoover, ordered a huge intelligence-gathering operation. He told his agents to focus on the top ten mobsters in each major city, and Giancana filled the feds' number one slot for Chicago.

John F. Kennedy around this time had declared his candidacy for the 1960 presidential nomination. His father, Joe, had made millions from importing whisky across the border from Canada in the days of Prohibition, and still had many mob connections from those days. Joe was a smart guy, and knew he would need to enlist the help of the Outfit to put his son in the White House. He realized that his son's friendship with Frank Sinatra was the ideal link to the mob via Sam Giancana.

It would be tough even for someone like Sinatra to swing this for Joe Kennedy. Sam Giancana hated Joe Kennedy's younger son Robert since in his position as council to the McClellan committee Robert had given Giancana a rough ride in questioning.

Giancana and Joe Kennedy met in the chambers of a Chicago judge. Sam took Old Man Kennedy's proposition to the outfit's 'board of directors'. Kennedy had promised that his men would back off their interest in the Outfit's Las Vegas casino operations. Sam also bragged to his friends that he'd have a 'hot-line' to the White House and that they might possibly get Cuba back. For this to happen they would have to raise money for John F. Kennedy's Virginia primary which was crucial, and would also provide help with the campaign in Illinois. Kennedy won the Virginia primary by a 60–40 margin. Kennedy won the election by the smallest of margins, one tenth of one per cent, and was propelled into the White House due to Giancana's control over the key Chicago wards and labour union votes.

At one time Sam Giancana shared a girlfriend with JFK. Frank Sinatra had been sleeping on and off with a dark-haired beauty named Judith Cambell. She had been introduced to Frank by Johnny Roselli. In February 1960 Frank Sinatra introduced Judy as she was known, to John Kennedy, and they hit it off straight away. Kennedy and the young divorcee started on what was to become a serious long-term affair. Cambell had also been introduced to Giancana, and for a period of about two years she slept with both Giancana and Johnny Roselli while still carrying on an affair with John F. Kennedy.

It came to light later on that Cambell had been carrying bags of cash from JFK to Giancana to be used in Kennedy's West Virginia primary.

In the meantime J. Edgar Hoover had spotted a pattern emerging that linked Sam and Johnny

Roselli to the President because of the relationship all three had with Judy Cambell. Hoover had no great love for the Kennedys, but decided to wait and see what would emerge. During the summer of 1961 Agent Bill Roemer set up a team of Federal agents with the principle duty of pressurising Giancana into making errors. His first task was to serve Giancana's famous girlfriend Phyllis McGuire with a subpoena to appear before a Federal grand jury. Roemer and his agents stopped both Giancana and Phyllis at Chicago's O'Hare airport. They tackled Giancana hitting him with a barrage of questions so as to distract him long enough for the other agents to whisk McGuire away for inter-rogation.

Giancana and Roemer were involved in a war of words at the airport which left the agent in no doubt that Giancana was now feeling the pressure. Giancana was being hounded constantly by the Feds and didn't like it. He was also losing face with the Outfit because when Kennedy was elected he did not keep his promise. In fact the President had elected his own brother as attorney general who, in turn, quickly pushed through congress a number of anti-racketeering laws.

Sam Giancana was undeterred, his pact with Old Joe Kennedy could still swing things in his favour. He enlisted the help of his old friend Sinatra. Sinatra visited the Kennedys at their home in Hyannis Port, and while alone in a room with Robert Kennedy, passed him a piece of paper with the name Giancana scribbled on it. It said. 'This is my buddy. This is what I wanted you to know Bob'. Robert Kennedy said nothing, and from that silence Sinatra knew the future did not look bright for his friend Giancana.

Sinatra stalled in giving his friend the verdict of the meeting which angered Giancana.

J. Edgar Hoover, who was not a fan of the Kennedys, sent a carefully worded note to Bobby Kennedy in February of 1962. The note gave details of what Hoover knew about The President, Judith Cambell and Sam Giancana. Hoover and the President met for lunch, and the aforementioned note was the main focus of conversation. Later the same afternoon the President phoned Judith Cambell. The Kennedys had double-crossed Sam Giancana, and Robert the Attorney General was hell bent on nailing Sam's head to the wall.

Robert Kennedy sent a team of more then fifty agents to Chicago. They targeted forty mobsters with Sam Giancana considered number one priority. Phil Alderisio of the Chicago mob was the first to fall. He was arrested, convicted and jailed. Rocco Pranno was convicted of extortion. By now the mob was starting to get a little shaky and it seemed that Sam Giancana was losing his grip. The mob felt that Sam Giancana was shirking his responsibilities and neglecting his position. Johnny Roselli was also missing when he was needed in Las Vegas. Sam Giancana and Johnny Roselli were both beginning to fall foul of Accardo and the Outfit.

By the summer of 1963 Giancana was being hounded day and night by the FBI. Giancana went to court with a harassment charge aimed at the FBI. He won his case, but in doing so he brought even more attention on the Outfit. Accardo and Paul Ricca were furious, it seemed that the claims that Giancana was falling apart and panicking, appeared to be coming true.

ASSASSINATION OF JFK

November 22, 1963 saw the assassination of John F. Kennedy. His brother Bobby resigned his position as Attorney General a year later, which at least was some good news for the Outfit.

However, the absence of the Kennedys from the picture brought no respite for Sam Giancana. Giancana claimed to have influenced Chicago's vote on Kennedy's behalf in the presidential election of 1960, but felt he had been betrayed when the Kennedy brothers subsequently tried to break up the Mafia's business interests and targeted him, amongst others, for prosecution. The Chicago branch of the FBI increased their already considerable effort to get Giancana, but this time they had a new strategy.

Giancana was summoned to a Federal grand jury in Chicago. Giancana appeared for the trial smartly dressed, smiling and unconcerned. He went before Judge William J. Cambell and was granted immunity from any prosecution that could result from his testimony. Giancana, however, would not speak to the grand jury, and the judge ordered him to be held for the duration of the sitting. He was placed in the cells at Chicago's Cook County jail.

Three weeks later Murray 'The Camel'

Humphreys, a top associate of the Chicago mob, was subpoenaed. Humphreys held a lot of sway within the mob, and was a survivor of the Capone era. Murray Humphreys' forte was Labour racketeering and political fixing, and his expertise in these fields had been invaluable to the mob for years. Humphreys assumed he would be granted immunity like Giancana, but he was wrong and in desperation took to his heels and fled. He was arrested the very next morning attempting to buy a ticket at a train station in Oklahoma. He was put in leg-irons, taken to court and questioned with no grant of immunity. Humphreys gave testimony but lied in answer to every question. On November 23, 1965 he was indicted for perjury, some six hours later he was dead from a massive heart attack.

Giancana never spoke to the jury and after spending a year in jail was freed. He fled to Mexico in June 1966, where he bought a luxurious villa in the town of Cuernavaca. From there he toured all over the world, looking after mob investments. He lived a grand lifestyle, visiting the French Riviera, Switzerland, the Bahamas and Beirut. He had his suits hand-made by Mexican tailors costing around $400 a time. Meanwhile back in Chicago Tony Accardo had reclaimed his position as head of the Chicago mob. He managed to calm things down after the bloodshed years of Giancana's leadership, keeping a lower profile, and aiming to keep the mob out of all newspaper headlines.

Giancana stayed in Mexico for ten years before being forcefully taken to the airport and put on a flight bound for the United States. His exile in

Mexico was assured by the bribes he had been paying Mexican government officials for the privilege of living in their country. Somewhere along the line, however, he had managed to upset one of these officials and now his bribes were no good.

He returned to his home in Oak Park. By this time, although Accardo was still in the shadows, Joey 'Doves' Aiuppa was the street-boss.

Giancana was ordered to attend another grand jury and like before he was granted immunity from prosecution. On this occasion he took advantage of it, but actually gave very little away on the stand. Investigators from the Senate Committee had been probing the Kennedy administration's plan to murder Fidel Castro and wanted Johnny Roselli and Giancana to testify. Roselli volunteered to give evidence, if Giancana testified also. This would make for huge headlines, something Accardo didn't want – headlines brought attention, and attention brought trouble.

THE DEMISE OF SAM GIANCANA

In May 1975 Sam Giancana was taken ill while on a trip to Houston visiting a girlfriend. He had to have an emergency operation on his gall bladder and was still a very sick man when he returned home to Oak Park. On the evening of June 18, 1975, he was given a 'welcome home' party by his two daughters. His two sons-in-law along with Butch Blasi and Chuckie English, two long time friends, also attended. The last of the guests left around 10.00 p.m. Reportedly, one of Giancana's daughters returned to the house to pick up her handbag which she had forgotten. As she left her father's house for the second time that evening, she spotted Butch Blasi heading back towards the house but thought nothing of it.

Later in the evening Giancana decided to cook himself a snack. Sausages and greens had always been a favourite of his, and he went down to his basement kitchen and began cooking. Before he had finished cooking, however, he was shot in the back of the head. As he lay on the floor, the pistol was placed in his mouth and another shot fired; then placed under his chin, and once more the killer pulled the trigger. The hitman had used seven bullets in total and then vanished into the night. Sam Giancana was found around midnight by his old friend and neighbour Joe Di Persio.

Few, if any, mob figures attended Giancana's funeral, a final show of disrespect by his mob friends. Butch Blasi was in attendance though and helped carry the coffin. The main source of enquiry at the police investigations into the death of Giancana focused on Butch Blasi, as it was he whom Francine, Giancana's daughter had seen return to the house that night. He was a close friend of Sam's and Giancana would have felt safe around him, safe enough to turn his back on him to cook a meal. The murder weapon was a gun with around forty holes drilled in its barrel, making the silencer even more effective. The gun was discovered on the driveway in a nearby suburb, on a route that Blasi would have used to get home.

Blasi was put before a grand jury, granted immunity, but refused to say anything by way of testimony. He spent eighteen months in jail, still refusing to utter a word of testimony. He was released, but never again took any part in mob activity.

Johnny Roselli, just six days after Giancana's death, gave testimony to a Senate Committee. He appeared on several more occasions giving a lot of information. He later vanished when he was holidaying in Florida with his family.

Roselli's revelations to the Senate Committee were not released for another twenty years, such was the magnitude of his testimony. The mob of course had by this time decided that Johnny had already said too much. Roselli's remains were found when a metal oil drum was washed up on the shore, he had been strangled, dismembered, stuffed in the drum and dumped at sea.

Tony 'Big Tuna' Accardo died of natural causes on May 27, 1992, aged 86.

'Baby Face' Nelson

Lester Gillis was to emerge from the rough Chicago Stockyards district as 'Baby Face' Nelson, one of the toughest, and definitely the most heartless, of the Depression-era gangsters. Cold and brutal, he enjoyed killing, even his criminal peers were wary of his path.

Lester M. Gillis was born on December, 6, 1908, in an area of Chicago known as 'the Patch'. His parents, Joseph and Mary Gillis, were both Belgium immigrants, and Lester was their seventh child. Joseph was a hard-working tanner and left his wife to the raising of his children. His father only had one strict rule and that was that his children were never to touch or play with guns, even toy ones were totally forbidden.

Despite the fact that Lester came from a secure and loving family, he started to roam the streets of Chicago at an early age. He very rarely went to school and his teachers were quite surprised if did actually turn up for his lessons. In his early teens he teamed up with a boy called Jack Perkins, and together they hung about on the streets with a gang of juvenile hoodlums. By the time he was fourteen, Lester had become an accomplished car thief and due to his youthful appearance was given the nickname 'Baby Face' by fellow members of the gang. They extended their range of criminal activities to stealing tyres, running stills, bootlegging and even armed robbery and Gillis was starting to emerge as a character that was not to be messed with.

In 1922 Gillis was arrested for car stealing and was committed to a boys' home. He was released after two years, but within five months he was back again after being caught stealing another car.

Gillis's father, partly due to the shame that his son had bought on the family, had become a heavy drinker. While Gillis was in jail his father committed suicide, something for which he always blamed himself. In an effort to try and relieve the feelings of guilt, Gillis started giving a portion of his illegal takings to his mother.

HIS LOVE FOR HELEN

In 1928 he met a petite Chicago salesgirl by the name of Helen Wawzynak. Gillis was completely obsessed with her appearance and quick wit, while she was impressed by his boyish manner and confident style. Within a year the couple were married, despite Helen's parents strong objections. They had two children, a son, Ronald, born April 4, 1930 and a daughter, Darlene, in 1932. The couple remained devoted to one other and their children for the rest of their lives, and even when Gillis was being hunted down by the law they still travelled round as an entire family unit. His wife retained the name Helen Gillis throughout their marriage.

As his criminal activities increased, Gillis started to adopt a number of aliases. When he was arrested and tried on a bank robbery charge in January 1931 he used the name George Nelson. He was sentenced to a term of one to ten years in the infamous Illinois State Penitentiary at Joliet. While serving his term, he was tried and convicted in the Du Page County Circuit Court on another bank robbery charge in Wheaton, Illinois. This time he was sentenced to a year to life. As his prison terms began to add up, so did his plans for freedom.

On February 17, 1932, Nelson managed to escape prison guards while he was being returned to Joliet Penitentiary. The train bringing him back to Joliet from Wheaton was late, and the prison car had already left. Rather than wait for another car to be sent to the station, Nelson's guard decided to take his prisoner back to the prison by cab. At the Joliet train station, they jumped into a yellow cab for the short ride to the prison. The time was a few minutes after 8 p.m. when the cab turned north on Collins Street. That was when Nelson made his move. With his hands cuffed in front of him, he pulled a revolver out of his overcoat pocket and ordered the guard to 'Unlock the cuffs, or I'll kill you'. The gun had apparently been slipped into his pocket on the crowded train. He then ordered the driver, who was preparing to turn into the prison entrance, to drive on to Chicago.

In Chicago's Resurrection Cemetery, Baby Face robbed both men of their cash and drove off alone in the cab. His daring escape was front page news in the *Joliet Evening Herald News*, which described him as 'a desperate gunman'. The little bandit was already known in newspaper headlines, which had nicknamed him 'Baby Face'.

After his prison escape in Joliet, 'Baby Face' Nelson formed a gang that robbed a series of banks in Iowa, Nebraska and Wisconsin. One of these gang members was John Paul Chase, a small-time thief and bootlegger, who would remain Nelson's close friend for the remainder of his life.

JOHN PAUL CHASE

John Paul Chase was born on December 26, 1901, and lived the majority of his life in California. He stayed at school until the fifth grade, then took a job at a ranch near San Rafael, California. Chase had another couple of minor jobs, but in 1930 became associated with an alcohol-smuggling operation, which was known to have connections with the underworld. The two men became close friends when Nelson took a job as an armed guard, alongside Chase, on one of the trucks used for illegally transporting the liquor.

Nelson liked his new life in California and he asked his wife to join him, where they remained until May 1933. Although Chase stayed in Sausalito, Nelson moved to Long Beach, Indiana, where he lived for several months. It was here that he met several criminals, including Charles Fisher, Earl Doyle, Tommy Carroll, Edward Bentz and Homer Van Meter, together with a relatively unknown bank robber, John Dillinger.

In December, 1933, Nelson contacted Chase again and they stayed together for almost a year. During this time, a man was shot and killed in Minneapolis and it is believed that Nelson and Chase were responsible for his death.

Nelson and Chase's next move was to Reno, Nevada, during which spell Nelson killed a man during an argument. It later turned out that the victim was apparently a material witness in a United States Mail Fraud case.

THE DILLINGER GANG

In April, 1934, Nelson, Helen Gillis and John Paul Chase went to Chicago, Illinois, where they joined up with the Dillinger gang. The Dillinger Gang didn't actually come into being until a man called Harry Pierpont and nine other men escaped from the Michigan City Prison in Indiana on September 22, 1933. Dillinger had organized their escape by smuggling guns into the prison.

The gang became famous for its violence and they terrorized the Midwest. They killed at least ten men, wounded several others, robbed banks and police arsenals, and were responsible for three other jail breaks.

While Chase remained in Chicago, Nelson and his wife had a holiday with the Dillinger gang at the Little Bohemia Lodge in northern Wisconsin. The FBI who were on the look out for members of the Dillinger gang, learned of their location on April 22, 1934, and Special Agents proceeded to the Lodge. The gangsters were warned of the FBI approach by barking dogs and managed to escape into the dark, leaving a few women friends, including Helen Gillis, behind.

Nelson ran to a nearby house and took the two occupants hostage. However, it wasn't long before Special Agents J. C. Newman and W. Carter Baum arrived at the house with a local police constable. When the car stopped outside the house, Nelson, who was only five feet four inches tall, rushed to the car and ordered the men to get out. However, before they could do anything, Nelson shot all three men, instantly killing Special Agent Baum with a series of shots from his automatic pistol.

A little while later Chase and Nelson met up again. One month later Helen Gillis, who by this time been released on parole, joined her husband and Chase, and for several days they stayed near Lake Geneva, Wisconsin. On June 23, 1934, Attorney General Homer S. Cummings offered a reward for Nelson's capture or information leading to his arrest.

On June 30, 1934, there was a robbery at the Merchants National Bank, South Bend, Indiana, during which a police officer was shot and killed. The raid was carried out by 'Baby Face' Nelson, John Dillinger and Homer Van Meter. After the robbery the men fled to Chicago, Illinois, and two police officers were shot on Wolf Road, outside Chicago, when Nelson opened fire as they approached the gang's meeting place.

On July 22, 1934, the notorious gangster leader John Herbert Dillinger was killed.

IN PURSUIT OF NELSON

As soon as they heard of Dillinger's death, Nelson, Helen and Chase headed once more for California, along with two associates. That summer the two chums made several trips between Chicago and California, and on one occasion were stopped for speeding and fined $5. Luckily for them their car was not searched for it contained machine guns, rifles and ammunition.

The daunting task of trying to track down 'Baby Face' Nelson had been given to Inspector Samuel P. Cowley of the FBI's Chicago Office. On November 27, 1934, Cowley was informed that Nelson had been seen driving a stolen car. Two agents came across the vehicle near Barrington, Illinois. Nelson reacted quickly and turned his car around so that it was now behind the car the agents were driving. Chase, meanwhile, fired five rounds from an automatic rifle into their car. One of the agents returned fire and managed to pierce a hole in the radiator of the car Nelson was driving.

Inspector Cowley and Special Agent Herman Edward Hollis took up the chase in another car. All of a sudden Nelson turned off Northwest Highway and stopped in front of North Side Park. Before Cowley and Hollis could get out of their car, Nelson and Chase began firing at them.

The gun battle only lasted a few minutes, but Special Agent Hollis was killed and Cowley was wounded, and died the following morning. Nelson himself was riddled with seventeen bullets and had to be lifted onto the back seat of the car by his wife and Chase. They rushed him to a priest, but all the man could do was offer him prayer, he was too badly injured.

THE END

'Baby Face' Nelson died about eight that evening. The FBI received an anonymous phone call and his body was discovered near a cemetery in Illinois.

After the death of his friend, Chase returned to Chicago. Because Chase had only been arrested once for drunken behaviour in 1931, their were no photographs or fingerprint records in circulation, which meant that he was able to take a legitimate job driving cars in Seattle, Washington.

In early December, 1934, Special Agents of the FBI's San Francisco Office contacted Chase's former employers and associates, and they were instructed to notify the FBI if Chase was spotted. On December 27, 1934, Chase tried to borrow money from employees at the Mount Shasta, California, fish hatcheries, where he had worked in 1928. The FBI and local police were immediately notified, and Chief of Police A. L. Roberts apprehended Chase.

On December 31, 1934, Chase was taken to Chicago, and tried for the murder of an FBI agent. He was found guilty of murdering Inspector Samuel P. Cowley and on March 31, 1935, he was imprisoned in the United States Penitentiary on Alcatraz Island. He was transferred to the United States Penitentiary, Leavenworth, Kansas, in September, 1954. Twenty years on Chase had still not stood trial for the murder of Special Agent Hollis, and the United States District Court, Chicago, Illinois, demanded immediate trial on this indictment or its dismissal. However the charge did not stand and he was dismissed, and Chase became eligible for parole. Chase was finally released from Leavenworth on October 31, 1966. After his release, Chase lived in California, where he was employed as a guardian for over six years. John Paul Chase died of cancer in Palo Alto, California, on October 5, 1973.

Nelson's widow was arrested on November 29, 1934. Having violated the terms of her parole, Helen Gillis was sentenced to serve one year and one day in the Women's Federal Reformatory in Mila, Michigan.

John Herbert Dillinger

John Dillinger lived up to the title 'Public Enemy No. One' bestowed on him by J. Edgar Hoover of the FBI. By the time he was thirty years old Dillinger had become a household name throughout the United States. He was the most famous criminal the United States has ever seen.

John Herbert Dillinger was born on June 22, 1903, in the middle-class residential area of Oak Hill, Indianapolis. John's father was a hard-working grocer, who bought his son up under strict disciplinary rules. John was only three when his mother died, and although his father remarried after six years, John resented his stepmother.

As an adolescent John was in and out of trouble and the flaws in his personality started to become apparent. After leaving school he got a job in a machine shop in Indianapolis. He was a good and intelligent worker, but the job bored him and he took to staying out all night. His father became concerned that there were too many temptations for a young boy in the city, and so he decided to sell his property in Indianapolis and move to a farm near Mooresville, Indiana. The move didn't quite work out as his father had planned, and it wasn't long before his teenage son started to run wild once more.

Following trouble with the police over a car theft, and a break down in his relationship with his father, John decided to enlist in the Navy. However, it wasn't long before he got into trouble again and deserted his ship when it docked in Boston.

John returned to Mooresville in 1924 and married sixteen-year-old Beryl Hovius. The bright lights and excitement of the city led the two newlyweds to Indianapolis. Dillinger was unable to find a job in the city and joined the loan shark, Ed Singleton, in his search for easy money. Their first crime together was a botched robbery attempt on a grocer's store in his hometown of Mooresville, on September 6, 1924. The robbery went terribly wrong and they were quickly apprehended. Singleton pleaded not guilty, stood trial, and was sentenced to two years. Dillinger, following his father's advice, confessed, was convicted of assault and battery with intent to rob, and conspiracy to commit a felony, and received joint sentences of two to fourteen years and ten to twenty years in the Indiana State Prison in Michigan city. Shocked by the severity of the sentence, Dillinger became a bitter man, which festered while he was in prison. It was while he was serving this sentence that he met his future partners in crime Harry Pierpont and Van Meter.

THE GREAT ESCAPE

By mid-1932, Dillinger had become part of a

group of prisoners intent on escaping. This group included Harry Pierpont as the leader, along with Charles Makley, John Hamilton, Russell Clark and later Walter Dietrich and James Jenkins. Since Dillinger's parole date was approaching he was chosen to be their connection on the outside, carrying out robberies to raise funds for their escape.

Dillinger was released on May 10, 1933, after having served eight-and-a-half years of his term. As arranged with his friends inside the prison he started a series of holdups to fund their venture. He drew attention to himself by leaping over the teller's barrier and wearing a straw hat. His spree lasted until September 22 when he was arrested for robbing a bank in Bluffton, Ohio. The police caught up with him at his boarding house where he now lived with his girlfriend Mary Longnaker. He was taken to the county jail in Lima, Ohio, where he waited for his case to come to trial.

When he arrived at the jail, the Lima police frisked John and found a piece of paper in his pocket that appeared to be a plan of a prison break. John vehemently denied any knowledge of such a plot, but four days later, using the same plans, eight of Dillinger's friends escaped from the Indiana State Prison. They used shotguns and rifles that had been smuggled into their cells, and ended up shooting two prison guards.

All the escapees managed to get away with the exception of Joseph Jenkins. Jenkins, having been thrown from the getaway car, managed to commandeer another car driven by a youth. Jenkins was later shot and killed by local posse members who had been put on alert in Beanblossom, Indiana.

On October 12, three of the escaped prisoners and a parolee from the same prison showed up at the Lima jail where Dillinger was being held. They Informed the sheriff that they had come for Dillinger, because he had violated his parole and needed to be returned to Indiana State Prison. The sheriff asked if he could see their credentials, but one of the men pulled out a gun, shot him and beat him until he was unconscious. Taking the keys to the jail, the bandits freed Dillinger, locked the sheriff's wife and a deputy into the cell, and left the sheriff, Jesse Sarber, dying on the floor.

The sheriff's office requested the assistance of the FBI in identifying and locating the criminals. The four men were identified as Pierpont, Clark, Makley and Copeland. Their fingerprint cards in the FBI Identification Division were flagged with red metal tags, indicating that they were wanted men. The gang then proceeded to Chicago to avoid the intense manhunt throughout Ohio.

Meanwhile, Dillinger and his gang pulled several bank robberies. In Auburn and Peru, Indiana, they robbed police arsenals acquiring a cache of weapons including machine guns and also bulletproof vests.

With publicity mounting on the Dillinger gang, on November 20 they carried out a daring robbery in Racine, Wisconsin. Although shots were fired, they escaped unharmed behind a shield of hostages. On December 14, John Hamilton, a Dillinger gang member, shot and killed a police detective, Sergeant

William Shanley. The sergeant had tried to capture him in a garage where he had been following a lead on a gang vehicle being repaired there.

With the heat now well and truly on and the development by the Chicago police of a special unit called 'The Dillinger Squad', it was decided by the gang that they should lay low for a while. Dillinger reportedly dyed his hair red and grew a moustache. Dillinger, with his girlfriend Billie Frechette, joined Makley, Clark, and Hamilton in Daytona Beach, Florida. On Christmas Eve, Dillinger and Billie had a violent argument which culminated with Dillinger beating her and throwing her out the following morning, providing her with $1000 and the keys to his car as a parting gesture.

Dillinger returned north two weeks later to go after Billie in her home state of Wisconsin. He and Hamilton decided to rob the First National Bank in East Chicago, Indiana, on January 15. During the getaway Patrolman William O'Malley fired shots at Dillinger only to have them bounce off the bulletproof vest the outlaw was wearing. In the exchange of fire that followed Dillinger shot and killed the officer. Hamilton was wounded by police fire and was helped by Dillinger to the getaway car.

A month later, the Dillinger gang killed a police officer during the robbery of the First National Bank of East Chicago, Indiana. Then they made their way to Florida and, subsequently, to Tucson, Arizona.

On January 23, 1934, Makley and Clark were forced out of hiding at the Hotel Congress in Tucson, Arizona, by a fire that broke out in the hotel that morning. One of the firemen, having

189

recognized them from a crime magazine photo, notified the sheriff. The same day, Dillinger and Billie Frechette arrived in town for the reunion of the gang. They did manage to meet on the 25th, but acting on a tip, the police first arrested Makley, and then Clark, at the house they had been staying in since the hotel fire. Later, following leads, the police were able to capture Pierpont. Dillinger, unaware of these events, arrived at the house where Makley and Clark had been grabbed, and was subsequently arrested by officers just as they were setting up their stakeout.

Dillinger was sequestered at the county jail in Crown Point, Indiana, to await trial for the murder of the East Chicago police officer. Authorities boasted that the jail was 'escape proof'. But they were soon proved to be wrong and on March 3, 1934, Dillinger intimidated the guards with what he claimed later was a wooden gun he had whittled. He forced them to open the door to his cell, grabbed two machine guns, then locked up the guards and several trustees, and fled.

THE MISTAKE

It was then that Dillinger made the mistake that would cost him his life. He stole the sheriff's car and drove across the Indiana-Illinois line, heading for Chicago. By doing that, he violated the National Motor Vehicle Theft Act, which made it a Federal offence to transport a stolen motor vehicle across a state line.

A Federal complaint was sworn charging

Dillinger with the theft and interstate transportation of the sheriff's car, which they managed to recover in Chicago. After the grand jury returned an indictment, the FBI became actively involved in the nationwide search for Dillinger.

In the meantime, Pierpont, Makley and Clark were returned to Ohio and were convicted of the murder of the Lima sheriff. Pierpont and Makley were sentenced to death, and Clark to life imprisonment. However, Makley was killed in an escape attempt and Pierpont was wounded. A month later, Pierpont had recovered sufficiently to be executed.

In Chicago, Dillinger once again joined his girlfriend, Billie Frechette. They proceeded to St. Paul, where Dillinger teamed up with Homer Van Meter, 'Baby Face' Nelson, Eddie Green and Tommy Carroll, among others. The gang's business prospered as they continued robbing banks of large amounts of money.

Then on March 30, 1934, an Agent talked to the manager of the Lincoln Court Apartments in St. Paul, who had reported two suspicious tenants, Mr. and Mrs. Hellman, who acted nervously and refused to admit the apartment caretaker. The FBI began a surveillance of the Hellman's apartment. The next day, an Agent and a police officer knocked on the door of the apartment. Billie Frechette opened the door, but quickly slammed it shut. The Agent called for reinforcements to surround the building.

While waiting, the Agents saw a man enter the hall near the Hellman's apartment. When questioned, the man, Homer Van Meter, drew a gun. Shots were exchanged and Van Meter fled the building and forced a truck driver at gunpoint to drive him to Green's apartment. Suddenly the door of the Hellman apartment opened and the muzzle of a machine gun began spraying the hallway with bullets. Under cover of the machine gun fire, Dillinger and Frechette fled through a back door. They, too, drove to Green's apartment, where Dillinger was treated for a bullet wound received in the escape.

Back at the Lincoln Court Apartments, the FBI found a Thompson submachine gun with the stock removed, two automatic rifles, one .38 calibre Colt automatic with twenty-shot magazine clips, and two bulletproof vests. Across town, other Agents located one of Eddie Green's hideouts where he and Bessie Skinner had been living as 'Mr. and Mrs. Stephens'. On April 3, when Green was located, he attempted to draw his gun, but was shot by the Agents. He died in a hospital eight days later.

Dillinger and Frechette fled to Mooresville, Indiana, where they stayed with his father and half-brother until his wound healed. Then Frechette went to Chicago to visit a friend and was arrested by the FBI. She was taken to St. Paul for trial on a charge of conspiracy to harbour a fugitive. She was convicted, fined $1,000, and sentenced to two years in prison. Bessie Skinner, Eddie Green's girlfriend, got fifteen months on the same charge.

Meanwhile, Dillinger and Van Meter robbed a

police station at Warsaw, Indiana, of guns and bulletproof vests. Dillinger stayed for a short time in Upper Michigan, departing just ahead of a posse of FBI Agents dispatched there by aeroplane. Then the FBI received a tip that there had been a sudden influx of rather suspicious guests at the summer resort of Little Bohemia Lodge, about fifty miles north of Rhinelander, Wisconsin. One of them sounded like John Dillinger and another like 'Baby Face' Nelson.

From Rhinelander, an FBI task force set out by car for Little Bohemia. Two of the rented cars broke down enroute, and, in the uncommonly cold April weather, some of the Agents had to make the trip standing on the running boards of the other cars. Two miles from the resort, the car lights were turned off and the posse proceeded through the darkness. When the cars reached the resort, dogs began barking. The Agents spread out to surround the lodge and as they approached, machine gun fire rattled down on them from the roof, and the Agents swiftly took cover. One of them hurried to a telephone to give directions to additional Agents who had arrived in Rhinelander to back up the operation.

While the Agent was telephoning, the operator broke in to tell him there was trouble at another cottage about two miles away. Special Agent W. Carter Baum, another FBI man, and a constable went there and found a parked car which the constable recognized as belonging to a local resident. They pulled up and identified themselves.

Inside the other car, 'Baby Face' Nelson was

holding three local residents at gunpoint. He turned, pointed a revolver at the lawmen's car, and ordered them to step out. But without waiting for them to comply, Nelson opened fire. Baum was killed, and the constable and the other Agent were severely wounded. Nelson jumped into the Ford they had been using and fled.

When the firing had subsided at the Little Bohemia Lodge, Dillinger was gone. When the Agents entered the lodge the next morning, they found only three frightened females. Dillinger and five others had fled through a back window before the Agents surrounded the house.

The entire raid came to be seen by the public as a disaster, bringing heavy criticism on the FBI and J. Edgar Hoover, the FBI Director.

Back in Washington, Hoover assigned Special Agent Samuel A. Cowley to head the FBI's investigative efforts against Dillinger. Cowley set up headquarters in Chicago, where he and Melvin Purvis, Special Agent in Charge of the Chicago office, planned their strategy. A squad of Agents under Cowley worked with East Chicago policemen in tracking down all tips and information they received on the gang.

Late in the afternoon of Saturday, July 21, 1934, the madam of a brothel in Gary, Indiana, contacted one of the police officers with information. This woman was Anna Cumpanas, better known as Anna Sage. She had entered the United States from her native Romania in 1914, but because of the nature of her profession, she was considered an undesirable alien by the

Immigration and Naturalization Service, and deportation proceedings had been started. Anna was willing to sell the FBI some information about Dillinger in return for a cash reward, and the FBI's help in blocking her deportation.

At a meeting with Anna, Cowley and Purvis were cautious. They promised her the reward if her information led to Dillinger's capture, but said all they could do about her deportation was to inform the Department of Labour about her co-operation. Satisfied, Anna told the Agents that a girlfriend of hers, Polly Hamilton, had visited her establishment with Dillinger. Anna had recognized Dillinger from a newspaper photograph.

Anna told the Agents that she, Polly Hamilton, and Dillinger would probably be going to the movies the following evening at either the Biograph or the Marbro Theatres. She said that she would notify them when the theatre was chosen, and that she would wear a red dress so that they could identify her.

On Sunday, July 22, Cowley ordered all his Agents to stand by for urgent duty. Anna Sage called that evening to confirm the plans, but she still did not know which theatre they would attend. Agents and policemen were therefore sent to both places. At 8.30 pm, Anna Sage, John Dillinger and Polly Hamilton strolled into the Biograph Theatre to see Clark Gable in *Manhattan Melodrama*. Purvis then phoned Cowley, who moved all the other agents and police to the Biograph Theatre.

Cowley also phoned Hoover for instructions.

Hoover told them to wait outside rather than risk a shooting match inside the crowded theatre. At 10.30 pm, Dillinger, with his two female companions on either side, walked out of the theatre and turned to his left. As they walked past the doorway in which Purvis was standing, Purvis lit a cigar as a signal for the other men to close in. Dillinger quickly realized what was happening and acted by instinct. He grabbed a pistol from his trouser pocket as he ran towards the alley. The FBI Agents fired five shots, three of which hit Dillinger and he fell face down on the pavement. One shot had entered his neck and exited under his right eye.

At 10.50 p.m. on July 22, 1934, John Dillinger was pronounced dead in a little room in the Alexian Brothers Hospital. From there his body was transported to the Cook County Morgue, where a huge crowd gathered and a number of photographs were taken. The FBI checked his fingerprints, and in spite of his attempts to have them obliterated, were able to make a positive identification. Newspapers the following day were filled with stories of his betrayal by a 'woman in red', soon identified by the press as Anna Sage.

Dillinger was buried in Crown Point Cemetery in Indianapolis, Indiana. Due to countless rumours that it wasn't Dillinger's body in the ground, John Dillinger Snr. made arrangements to have three foot of reinforced concrete poured into the ground above the grave, lest anyone attempt to dig up the coffin.

Of his surviving companions, Van Meter was trapped and killed a month later in St. Paul. Shortly thereafter, Makley was killed and Harry

Pierpont was wounded in a failed jailbreak, and was subsequently executed by electric chair. Russell Clark received a life sentence for his part in the Sarber killing.

The passing of John Dillinger and his gang marked the beginning of the end of an era of lawlessness in American history. His short life had ended violently, but his legend would continue to grow with the passage of time. Little would he have imagined that, in the end, he would be remembered as the most notorious outlaw of his time.

Bonnie and Clyde

Clyde Champion Barrow and his companion, Bonnie Parker, were shot to death by officers in an ambush near Sailes, Bienville Parish, Louisiana, on May 23, 1934, after one of the most colourful and spectacular manhunts the Nation had seen up to that time.

Bonnie Parker was born October 1, 1910, in Rowena, Texas. She stood 4 feet 11 inches in her stockinged feet, weighed 90 pounds, had strawberry-blonde ringlets, was freckle-faced and, according to those who knew her, was extremely pretty. When she was sixteen, Bonnie married her childhood sweetheart Roy Thornton. Though it was a troubled marriage, they did not divorce, even after Thornton was sentenced to five years in prison in 1929. Parker had a tattoo above her right knee that said 'Roy and Bonnie'.

Clyde Chestnut Barrow was born on March 24, 1909, and was the fifth child of seven. He was 5 feet 7 inches tall, weighed 130 pounds, and had slicked back thick brown hair in the style of the day, which parted on the left. His eye colour matched his hair, and women found him irresistible. Clyde committed his first crime with his brother just before Christmas of 1926 by

198

attempting to sell stolen turkeys. The thrill of this first offence never left Clyde, and soon after this 'great turkey heist', Clyde graduated to armed robbery. He held up a drug store and the Buell Lumber Company with his brother and various other associates. Soon after, however, the group was arrested and questioned, but released without being charged. Despite this, Clyde's reputation as a hood was set, and he and his brother were accused of most of the crimes committed in the area in which they lived.

HOW THEY MET

Bonnie and Clyde met in Texas in January, 1930. At the time, Bonnie was nineteen and married to an imprisoned murderer. Clyde was twenty-one and unmarried. Clyde got word that a friend of his by the name of Clarence Clay, had injured herself after slipping and falling on icy steps. Clyde paid a visit to his injured friend, but unbeknown to him, Clarence had another visitor. She was pretty and flirtatious, and answered to the name of Bonnie Parker. Clyde had never met her before, but by the end of the day, he and this mysterious girl would form a bond that would last for only four years, but would be remembered forever.

Soon after they met, Clyde was arrested for a burglary and sent to jail. He managed to escape by using a gun Bonnie had smuggled in to him, but was soon recaptured and sent back to prison.

After his parole in 1932, Clyde began seeing Bonnie on a regular basis and their love affair intensified. While dating Bonnie, Clyde formed a gang of new friends, who were thieves and former Eastham prisoners Ray Hamilton and Ralph Fults. Determined to never be parted again from her beloved, Bonnie went along with them on their first robbery. It was to be a hardware store in Kauffman, Texas. This was the beginning of a crime spree, and to Bonnie it sounded like fun, adventures, and more than anything else, romance.

Taking part in her first criminal act with Clyde had been thrilling to Bonnie. She served as lookout while Clyde, Hamilton and Fults broke into the store with weapons in their hands. That was until she heard the alarm. A night-watchman inside the store had spotted the trio at the cash register and set off the alarm. Clyde darted through the front door motioning to Bonnie to get into the car as quickly as possible. Following him, carrying sacks of money, were Fults and Hamilton who somehow resembled Keystone Kops rather than robbers. Clyde drove the getaway car at great speed and, once clear of town, ordered Bonnie to get out. He crammed a wad of stolen money into her purse and told her that he didn't want her involved. The stolen Buick disappeared into the night.

Realizing why Clyde had ejected her, and appreciating his intentions, she nevertheless felt somehow humiliated as she walked back into the village. By this time squad cars had answered the ringing alarm at the hardware store.

Clyde, Hamilton and Fults split up further out of town and laid low in separate hideouts. Clyde made his way to Hillsboro, where he planned another robbery. He needed cash as the last heist had yielded little money. When he eventually met up with Hamilton after several days, he learned that Fults had been arrested. As they could be next Clyde felt it was time to run, but not before breaking into a local grocers.

On the evening of April 30, Clyde and Hamilton woke up the grocer and his wife from bed, demanding that they open the storeroom safe. While Bucher meekly fumbled with the lock of the safe, Hamilton held his revolver against Bucher's cheek, with Clyde standing back and holding Mrs. Bucher. As Bucher pushed open the iron door of the safe, the edge of it jerked Hamilton's hand and the gun went off. The grocer grabbed his chest and fell face downwards to the floor. The robbers grabbed only a handful of money and escaped.

In a very short time both Clyde and Hamilton had escalated from being thieves to murderers, and had become wanted fugitives.

Clyde knew he had to run and at this point asked Bonnie if she wanted to join him. Although she knew their future would always be as fugitives, she responded with a smile and an embrace. She then jotted a message to her mother, packed a few minor articles in a bag, and made the promise to remain at his side till the end of the road.

Several other thefts followed and also a couple of robberies which culminated in murder. At this point Hamilton was arrested in Michigan and sent back to Dallas. He was given a sentence of 263 years.

The next person to join the gang was W. D. Jones, a petty thief.

IVAN 'BUCK' BARROW

Clyde's brother, Ivan M. 'Buck' Barrow, was released from the Texas State Prison on March 23, 1933. He too joined Clyde, bringing his wife, Blanche, so the group now numbered five people. The five set up house in a garage apartment and stayed there until April when the police, thinking they had found a gang of illegal gin brewers, closed in. In the ensuing gun battle, Clyde was shot as was Jones, and two police officers were fatally wounded.

This gang continued to embark upon a series of bold robberies which made headlines across the country and, despite various encounters with the law, they managed to escape capture. However, their activities made law enforcement efforts to apprehend them even more intense.

From here on, however, it was all downhill. Near Wellington, Texas, their stolen Ford plunged off a bridge under construction and Bonnie was pinned underneath, resulting in a badly damaged leg. The car then caught fire. They were rescued by some farmers, who saw the arsenal of weapons in the car, and one ran off to call the police. One of the women neighbours who came to help was shot by a nervous Jones, who blew her hand off. When two policemen came to investigate, the Barrow gang overpowered them. Along with Bonnie, they were loaded into the car but were later released. Bonnie's leg would never be the same again.

Their next place of residence was the Red Crown Tourist Camp in Platte City, Missouri, where they rented a double cabin with a garage in between. It was here that the police paid them another visit. In the ensuing gun battle Buck was hit in the forehead and Blanche was hit in the eyes by flying glass. The gang put a set of sunglasses on her face to cover the injuries. Once again, they escaped but were found three days later in a park in Dexter, Iowa, after a waiter tipped off the police that a man had for the past few days ordered five meals and taken them into the woods. Clyde, in his haste to escape, ran his car into a stump and the police riddled it with bullets. Buck was hit several more times, this time in the hip and shoulder.

Clyde and Jones took Bonnie and escaped through a stream and crossed a cornfield to a nearby farm. Holding the farmer and his son at bay, they stole his car. Buck was captured and died from his wounds a few days later in a Perry, Iowa hospital. Blanche, probably the most innocent of all, was sent to the Missouri State Penitentiary.

THINGS GOT WORSE

As if things weren't bad enough, the next few months were probably the worst ever for Bonnie and Clyde. W. D. Jones left the gang but was later captured in Texas. He claimed that towards the end he was kept captive by a pair of desperadoes for fear of squealing on them. He appeared to be scared to death after his capture, after all he was only seventeen years old.

Bonnie's leg became deformed because of lack of good medical attention. In November, while trying to visit their parents, sheriff Smoot got wind of it, set up an ambush and with other law officers, blasted the car. Bonnie and Clyde, both hit in the legs, once again escaped; it appeared Clyde had more lives than a cat.

On January 16, 1934, Clyde and Bonnie sprang Raymond Hamilton and a fellow prisoner, Henry Crowson, from the Eastham Prison Farm in Huntsville, Texas. Two guards were shot by the escaping prisoners with automatic pistols, which had been previously concealed in a ditch by Barrow. As the prisoners ran, Barrow covered their retreat with bursts of machine-gun fire.

Between January and March, several banks were robbed and were attributed to the Barrow gang. In March, Hamilton split from the gang, but was later captured and sent to the electric chair in 1935 for the murder of the guard at Huntsville.

In January, Clyde and Bonnie sprang Raymond Hamilton from the Eastham Prison Farm in Huntsville, Texas. Along with Hamilton was one Henry Methvin. Another police officer, Major Crowson, would not see the days end. Between January and March, several banks were robbed and were attributed to the Barrow gang. In March, Hamilton split from the gang for reasons that are uncertain. Hamilton would later be captured and sent to the electric chair in 1935 for the murder of the guard at Huntsville.

THE LAST MONTHS

On Easter Sunday, 1934, on a side road off Highway 114 in Grapevine, Texas, Clyde and

Methvin killed two police officers who had stopped to offer them help. Five days later they kill police officer Cal Campbell and kidnap Chief Percy Boyd in Commerce, Oklahoma. Percy was later released, but little did the couple know that they had less than a month to live.

The law enforcement authorities now started really putting on the pressure. They constantly harassed Clyde and Bonnie's relatives and tried to seek indictments on anyone who had tried to conceal or help the couple. Lee Simmons, who at that time was head of the Texas Prison System, was enraged at the Huntsville break. He received permission from Texas Governor Miriam Ferguson to hire a special agent. That special agent was retired Texas Ranger Frank Hamer.

Hamer immediately took to Clyde's trail on February 10. He used a Ford V8 which he knew Clyde was partial to and picked up their trail in Texarkana. But somehow he always seemed to be a day too late. While the chase was on, Clyde killed three more policemen.

Ivan Methvin, Henry's father, had in the past let Bonnie and Clyde use his place to hide, but, fearing for his son's life, he made a deal with Lee Simmons. He was offered a full pardon for his son in Texas, in exchange for information on the Barrow gang. Hamer was told about a 'post office' that was used by the Barrows. It was in fact a large board which lay on the ground near a large stump of a pine tree on a farm along Market Road, several miles from Plain Dealing, Louisiana. The 'post office' was used for communication among the Barrow gang and their friends and relatives. The scene was set.

At this time, Hamer picked up his old friend B. M. Gault. The other men who were in on the kill were Bob Alcorn, Ted Hinton, Henderson Jordan and Paul Oakley. At 1.30 a.m. they set up lookouts using tree branches approximately 25 feet from the road, so that they could look down on the road. They placed themselves approximately ten feet apart – and then they waited.

After approximately seven hours and at about 9.10 a.m. they heard a car approaching at great speed. It is unclear whether Hamer or Alcorn stepped into the road to challenge them. When the car stopped they were told to give up. They reached for their guns but never had a chance to use them because the posse opened fire first. The car leaped ahead and came to a halt in a ditch beside the road. The firing continued even after the car came to a halt.

The officers, even after pumping 167 rounds of ammunition into the car, approached carefully. Bonnie Parker and Clyde Barrow were dead – some fifty rounds had hit their bodies. Some even went through the driver's door, through Clyde, through Bonnie and out the passenger door. She died with her head slumped between her legs, a gun across her lap. Bonnie was 23 years old, Clyde 24.

Inside the car, Hamer found the following: 1 saxophone, 3 Browning automatic rifles, 1 10 gauge Winchester lever action, sawn-off shotgun, 1 20-gauge sawn-off shotgun, 1 Colt .32 calibre automatic, 1 Colt .45 calibre revolver, 7 Colt automatic pistols, and approximately 3,000 rounds of ammunition. They also found licence plates from Illinois, Iowa, Missouri, Texas, Indiana, Kansas, Ohio and Louisiana.

The car was towed away with the bodies still in it to Arcadia, Louisiana.

Clyde was buried in a West Dallas cemetery on May 25, next to his brother Buck.

Bonnie's mother had refused to have Bonnie buried next to Clyde and so she was buried on May 27, at the West Dallas Fishtrap cemetery.

Frank Hamer received thousands of letters of congratulations and was also honoured by Congress. Hamer died in 1955.

THE AFTERMATH

Henry Methvin received his pardon from Texas as promised, but not from Oklahoma. He was arrested for murder, sentenced to death which was later reduced to life. He served twelve years, was released, and was subsequently run over by a train in 1948.

Twenty-three people were brought to trial on charges of harbouring Bonnie and Clyde. Clyde's and Bonnie's families tried to gain ownership of the guns that they were found with because they realized they would become valuable collector's items, but they never did receive them. The grey Ford V8 was shown for years after that at State Fairs for 25 cents a look.

It is said that Bonnie never killed anyone. No matter how much it is debated, the truth will probably never be known.

Gangster's Wives

All good Mafia wives 'don't need to know nothin'.'
Basically as long as her husband can bring in enough
money to support his family and maintain a respectable
lifestyle, the wife shouldn't care or indeed know where it
all comes from, and ... if she's smart she won't ask!

Mafia wives and girlfriends, or indeed most of them, live in a complete state of denial. To an outsider, these women swear that their husbands are not thieves or killers. They are respectable businessmen and independent contractors who are constantly harassed by law enforcement officers. They are unfairly tarred with the Mafia brush because they happen to be of Italian descent.

However, Mafia wives exhibit a different kind of denial when they are talking to each other. They all know what their husbands do for a living, even if they do not know any of the details, but they rarely acknowledge the obvious. They will socialize together, shop together, discuss their children and share their personal problems, but they do not discuss mob business.

Mob wives are always prepared to visit their husbands in time of incarceration. They seem to know the good prisons and the bad ones. They never talk about what their husbands had done to get sent to prison, but they would discuss how the prosecutors and the cops had lied and set them up. In their heads it appeared that people picked on their husbands. Their husbands only did something that everybody was doing, but had had the misfortune to get caught out.

In order to survive and prosper Mafia wives must obey the code of silence, just like their husbands, who must abide by the rules of 'omerta'. They are bribed daily by large houses, luxury cars, expensive clothes, sumptuous restaurant meals and copious amounts of spending money, to make sure that their lips remain sealed. It appears that, as long as the goodies keep coming, the wives are happy. What they don't know they can't possibly tell.

Over the years law enforcement officers have gleaned a lot of information on the domestic life inside a gangster's family. This information is never made public knowledge because it is only material pertinent to the charges brought against the accused that can be used in a court of law. All the other information is kept safely locked away.

ANN COPPOLA

The underlying rules of many Mafia marriages is that the wife should be seen and not heard. Ann Coppola, the second wife of New York boss Michael Coppola, suffered much more than most.

Coppola, who was known for his violent temper, ran lucrative narcotics and numbers operations in Harlem in the 1940s and 1950s. They were married in 1955 after the tragic passing of his first wife Doris. Coppola told Ann that Doris had died giving birth, but very soon Ann suspected that Doris's death was more sinister than her husband had revealed.

When Ann became pregnant, Coppola told her emphatically that he did not want any more children. Doris had given him two children, and Ann's daughter by a previous marriage was living with them as well. Coppola told Ann not to worry and that she was to leave everything to him.

One day a physician arrived at the house after the children had left for school. Coppola introduced him to his wife as simply 'Dr. D'. The doctor spread a sheet over the kitchen table and performed an abortion on Ann while Coppola just stood by and watched, apparently with a grin of his face. When it was all over he made sure that Anne knew how much the abortion had cost him.

Within three months Ann was pregnant again. Once again Coppola called 'Dr. D' and watched the whole procedure, apparently with great enjoyment. After two more abortions Ann started to realize that the only reason her husband had sex with her was to get her pregnant so that he could watch the abortions. Doris, whose remains were cremated at Coppola's insistence, possibly had had one abortion too many.

Ann put up with regular beatings from her husband, but he was always lavishing her with fine jewellery and clothes. She felt that by giving her fine material things it made him feel big and powerful.

Ann finally walked out on him and filed for divorce after five years of unspeakable abuse. At about the same time, Coppola was indicted on four counts of tax evasion. He pleaded guilty on orders from the mob hierarchy, who feared what Ann would reveal if there was a trial and she was called to the stand. Coppola was sentenced to serve one year and one day.

While Coppola was in prison, Ann moved to Italy. She took her own life one day in a hotel room, overdosing on Scotch-and-barbiturate cocktails. Among the many goodbye notes she left was a last request to be cremated and have her ashes dropped from an airplane over Mike Coppola's house.

THE GOOD ONES

Ann Coppola's marriage was an extreme example of the hazards of being married to the mob, but they were not all so bad. In fact many gangsters have been known to treat their wives very well. It sometimes happens that a mob wife is charged with crimes along with her husband. When this happens many mobsters will agree to a plea bargain in order to get their wives off the hook. One such person was John 'Porky' Zancocchio, who really was a nice guy when it came to his wife and family.

Zancocchio ran a major bookmaking operation in New York. In 1990 Zancocchio was taken to court on federal tax evasion charges. In order to put pressure on Porky, the feds charged his wife

Lana with fraud. They also threatened to charge Porky's mother, because she had allowed her son and his capo to buy a pizzeria in her name, which they called 'Mama Rosa's'. These tactics had the desired effect and Zancocchio pleaded guilty to failing to file an income tax return. He was sentenced to one year in prison with a fine of $100,000.

Eleven years later, in 2002, Zancocchio was again charged with tax fraud charges along with Lana. The charges stretched from the year 1995 to 2000, and because of the size of the alleged offences a plea bargain was impossible. They both pleaded guilty, although the charges against Lana were lighter. Lana could have been sentenced to 16 months, but her attorney was able to negotiate a deal where she could serve her sentence at home and continue to raise her children. Porky, on the other hand, faced up to 71 months in prison and fines of up to $300,000.

Henry Hill, the mob associate, was the inspiration for Martin Scorcese's classic Mafia film, *Goodfellas*. Hill, who was an associate in the Lucchese crime family, had an extremely loyal wife. Henry could never become a 'made' member of the Mafia because he wasn't 100 per cent Italian. However, that did not stop him from participating in some major crimes in the New York City area. This included the infamous 1978 Lufthansa heist in which more than $4 million in unmarked cash was stolen from a warehouse at Kennedy Airport.

Henry's wife Karen endured many hardships.

All the time Henry had money, life was sweet, but when his scams didn't come to fruition, they had to scrounge like paupers.

When Henry went away to prison, Karen was left alone to fend for herself and raise the kids. Worst of all though was Henry's cocaine dealing which led to addition and eventually sucked Karen in. In 1989, Henry and Karen Hill separated after twenty-five years of marriage.

THE MISTRESS

The inevitable bane of every mob wife is her husband's mistress or 'goomatta'. This is the Americanized corruption of the Italian word *comare*.

How a mob wife reacts when she learns of her husband's goomatta is usually determined by the wife's age. The younger wives tend to lash out and demand their husband's fidelity, but they soon come to learn that the goomatta is a fact of mob life. To keep all the good things like the house, the cars, the furs, the jewellery, etc, the mob wife has to put up with the mistress. The glamorous mistress is as much a status symbol as, say, a Rolex watch. Having a woman on the side is a symbol of the man's success and power. In the ideal world this is how the man would like it to be, however, in reality it is sometimes quite different.

Mistresses do not always play by the rules. It often seems that the higher in rank the mobster is, the more trouble his mistress becomes.

Ralph Natale, former boss of Philadelphia's Bruno-Scarfo Family, was a little too public with his girlfriend, and as a result lost the respect of many of his subordinates. Natale came to power following the prosecution of his predecessor, Sicilian-born boss John Stanfa. Natale's induction ceremony took place in a hotel room near Philadelphia's Veteran Stadium after he was paroled in 1994. With the old boss Stanfa in prison and out of the picture, Natale was free to realize his mob dreams.

Natale's daughter Vanessa had a good friend who spent a lot of time at the Natale's New Jersey home. Her name was Ruthann Seccio, a slender blonde who had seen some tough times on the streets of South Philadelphia. A former drug addict and gang member, Ruthann had turned her life around and was now supporting herself as a waitress. Natale found the outspoken young woman irresistible despite the fact that she was 34 years younger and three inches taller than him.

Natale romanced Seccio shamelessly and set her up in an apartment in Voorhees, New Jersey, only ten miles from the home he shared with his wife Lucy. After a while Ruthann started asking why Natale wouldn't leave his wife. Natale told her that Lucy was very ill with both Parkinson and Alzheimer diseases, that her hearing was terrible, that she had to wear a heart monitor all the time and, after 42 years of marriage, there was no way he could just dump his wife. Ruthann was later to find out that Lucy Natale in fact suffered from none of these afflictions.

Despite his decision to stay married, love blossomed with Ruthann. He gave her extravagant

214

gifts, which included a Cadillac and a long-haired Himalayan cat named Dusty, and took her to the best restaurants. Ruthann was so infatuated with Natale she had a red rose tattooed on her left hip with the word 'Ralph's' engraved in blue underneath. But their romance was soon to be cut short. In 1998, Natale's parole officer caught him meeting with other mobsters at restaurants where he claimed to be selling fish, which supposedly was his legitimate job. Natale was sent back to prison for violating his parole. He called Ruthann every day, and often several times a day. He asked his associate Joey Merlino to take care of Ruthann as well as his wife Lucy while he was away.

But what should have been a short stretch in prison turned far more serious when federal agents threatened to charge Natale with financing a drug ring. If Natale was convicted on another drug charge, he would spend the rest of his life behind bars. The feds made the boss an offer – testify against Merlino and the rest of the Philly mob and they would put him in the Witness Protection Program. This way at least he'd have his freedom. Natale, having only served five years in his position of honour, decided to take their offer and rat on the mob. The government was delighted. Natale, they crowed, was the first sitting boss to turn state's witness.

Ruthann, who in her heart would always be a street tough, was stunned when she read the headline in the newspapers on August 20, 2000. Her boyfriend was being called 'King Rat'.

Unlike Ralph's wife who suffered in silence,

Ruthann agreed to do interviews with several local reporters. Even though she had never been popular in Philly mob circles, she took the mob's side against her old lover once it was revealed that he would be testifying against Merlino and four of his mob cohorts. Another reason Natale decided to turn state's witness was because Merlino had reneged on a promise. It appeared Merlino had discontinued the agreed-upon monthly payments of $3,500 to Lucy and $1,000 to Ruthann.

In April 2001, Natale took the stand for two straight weeks. Merlino and his co-defendants were ultimately convicted but not on the most serious charges brought against them.

Ruthann was offered a place in the Witness Protection Program, but she adamantly refused. Her decision was not greeted by applause by the mobsters she had so staunchly defended. To them she was still Natale's mistress, and since Natale was King Rat, she was no more than the rat's girlfriend.

THE COLOMBIAN MAID

From 1976 to 1985, Paul Castellano was the *capo di tutti capi* of New York's Gambino crime family. Castellano lived in a mansion nicknamed the White House in the exclusive Todt Hill section of Staten Island. Castellano's choice for his mistress, his Colombian maid, Gloria Olarte, was not a popular choice with his supporters.

Olarte was a most unlikely candidate for a boss's mistress. She wasn't the normal kind of flashy beauty that most mobsters wanted to show off. She was small and dark with coarse black hair, and hardly spoke a word of English. She was a shy immigrant who had been hired by Castellano's wife Nina to work as a domestic. But for reasons that only Castellano could have known, at the age of seventy, he became hopelessly infatuated with the maid.

The affair was quite open and even took place in Castellano's own home in the presence of his wife. When it comes to the women in their lives, the Mafia hold a double standard. While a real man must have a mistress, the mother of his children remains sacred. Affairs should always be conducted outside of the house, and wives should be spared the embarrassment of their husbands' whims as much as possible. By the Mafia rules of etiquette, Nina Castellano deserved the respect of her husband. His inappropriate, lovesick behaviour with Olarte was proof to his enemies that he was not sticking to the rules and needed to be replaced.

Gloria Olarte started working at the Castellanos' mansion in September 1979, and it wasn't long before Castellano started flirting with her. Nina had bought a handheld electronic English-Spanish translator so that she could communicate with the maid and tell her what chores she wanted done. It was quite a different matter though when Castellano got hold of the device, he used it to send little messages to Olarte in Spanish, paying her numerous compliments.

Castellano's infatuation with the maid soon

217

turned into a full-fledged love affair. They both acted like teenagers, completely unconcerned as to whom may be watching. Gloria became quite outspoken around her lover's associates, which made her very unpopular. Castellano took her on holidays and even bought her a hot sports car, even though she was unable to drive. While all this was going on Nina Castellano stood her ground. The White House was her home, and she wasn't going to be pushed out by anyone, let alone her own maid.

Castellano's feelings for Gloria were so strong, however, it even surprised the FBI. On St. Patrick's Day 1983, after two years of planning, FBI agents managed to bypass Castellano's security system and successfully planted a listening device in a lamp on the boss's kitchen table. They had been watching him for a long time and knew that Castellano often conducted business from his home. In the three months that the bug operated, agents listened in on conferences between Castellano and his mob associates. The agents, quite by accident, also heard personal conversations between Castellano and Gloria, and what they overheard one day left them completely speechless.

Castellano had gone to Tampa, Florida for elective surgery, but on further investigation the true nature of this surgery was revealed. Paul Castellano had received a penile implant, a device that when unfolded would give him a mechanical erection. This bit of information raised more than a few eyebrows within law enforcement. Castellano, who had never been known as a ladies' man, was presumably getting himself fixed to satisfy his new love. This information made the FBI more intent on listening to the exchanges between Castellano and the maid.

Eventually Nina Castellano was forced to move out of the White House. Gloria, whose English was improving, was triumphant. In her mind, she was now the lady of the house, but her victory was to be short-lived. Within one year Castellano's body was found sprawled on a Manhattan sidewalk.

LINDA MOLITO

Louie Milito grew up as a member of the Junior Rampers, a tough-minded gang from his Brooklyn neighbourhood. From his teenage gang he moved up to a more prominent rank, a 'made' member of the Gambino family, at which time he became responsible for some of the infamous family's most bloody work. Louie was also a trusted friend and colleague to family underboss Sammy 'the Bull' Gravano.

Lynda was born in 1947 and raised in Brooklyn, New York. She had a bad start in life and was neglected almost to the point of abuse by her mother. She was desperate to find love and the only way to find it seemed to be marriage. She met Louie at the age of sixteen, just after she had dropped out of school. He charmed her with his powerful character and the intoxicating feeling of danger that seemed to surround him. Linda and Louie were married for twenty-two years and they had a son, Louis, and a daughter, Deena. However, even though the marriage lasted for all those years it was still fraught with danger and deception. She was constantly turning a blind-eye to his illegal activities, his gangster buddies, and his bursts of violence. Lynda suffered from life-threatening bouts of mental illness which caused strained relationships with her children. But she knew the Mafia had strict rules about honour and loyalty to your husband, regardless of the wife's own health and safety. For a while she managed to live on the edge of the exciting, risky, exhilarating adventures but she soon learned that it was all about money, and dirty money at that.

Their home life was constantly interrupted by phone calls at all hours of the day and night and peculiar coded messages. For a while Lynda did not understand about his strange disappearances, but then she found out he had taken the strange blood oath of the Omerta and joined the notorious New York Gambino family. She knew she had to remain silent and loyal, but in doing so she nearly lost her mind.

In 1988, Louie Milito disappeared and his body has never been found. Lynda was suspicious and did a bit of her own investigating, soon discovering that Louie was killed by the very people who were supposed to protect him.

PART TWO

UNITED
KINGDOM

Introduction

500 years ago, the East End was no more than green fields through which an old Roman road from Colchester to the City of London passed. But by the beginning of the 1600s the unpleasant, smelly and dirty trades were being established – slaughter houses, fish farms, breweries and factories. This happened on the east side of London because the dominant west winds kept the smells away from what was to become the rich, fashionable and aristocratic West End.

London has always had criminals. The biggest city in Britain, it acted as a magnet, drawing into its fold those anxious to make money without the respectable inconvenience of working for it. In the early part of the twentieth century, the Odessian and Bessarabian gangs preyed on Russian immigrants in the Whitechapel quarter of the East End. The Blind Beggar Gang, a team of skilled pickpockets, operated out of a public house that would become famous in later years as the site of a gangland shooting. Street thugs formed into groups and called themselves 'The Titanics' or 'The Hoxton Mob' or 'The Vendetta Mob'. Early drug rings were formed in the early 1920s by the Jamaican, Eddie Mannings and a Japanese called Sess Miyakawa.

The Siege of Sidney Street on January 3, 1911,

was one of the most famous incidents in East End history. The robbery of Harris's Jewellery Shop in Houndsditch by a Russian Anarchist group intending to raise funds went seriously wrong. The gang dispersed to lodgings in the surrounding streets, one of which was 100 Sidney Street. Two of the gang members, Fritz Svaars and 'Josef' died in the house when it burned down in the much publicised shoot out with the police. A third member Peter Piatkov, nicknamed 'Peter the Painter' miraculously escaped.

The first of the British gangs that had any real international connections were the Sabinis, led by Charles 'Darby' Sabini. They operated around the racecourses of South England and also ran protection rackets with clubs as well as operating highly organized teams of robbers. The Sabinis flourished for almost twenty years, often import-ing Sicilian criminals to help them in their clashes with other groups such as the Elephant and Castle Mob.

Probably the closest to the Syndicate in the United States of America would be the Kray Twins in the East End of London. They maintained a fairly rigid system and hierarchy in and around Bethnal Green from the mid 1950s until their career ended in 1969.

There is another, less well known set of brothers in England, the Richardsons, who also built a gang network to work the protection/extortion racket. The Richardsons were even more depraved than their more famous counterparts, the Krays.

MAFIA CAVIAR RACKET

Caviar, at more than £2,000 a kilogram, is becoming a real money-earner for members of the underworld. A recent investigation by the British authorities into caviar smuggling into the United Kingdom, covered an illicit multi-million pound trade linked to the Russian Mafia.

The investigation was code-named 'Operation Ribbon' and a swoop made on three exclusive London shops, produced a quantity of illegal caviar. Officers believed that the haul was just the tip of the iceberg of a trade linked to murder, extortion and corruption carried out by criminal gangs in three continents.

Nearly all the world's caviar – the eggs of the female sturgeon – comes from the Caspian Sea. A female Beluga, which is the mostly highly-prized variety of sturgeon, can take anything from fifteen to twenty-five years to mature and produce eggs, and these eggs can be worth around £60,000. It is greed, and the demand for their roe, that has brought the species to the brink of extinction.

Although the species are protected under international treaty, since the break-up of the Soviet Union, the trade has now spiralled out of control. The Russian Mafia has realized that there are vast fortunes to be made out of the supply of this exotic delicacy, and they are making their move.

Authorities in the United Kingdom have been suspicious about the growth of the illegal trade for years, but there has been little evidence. However, with the threat of extinction, the National Wildlife

Crime Intelligence Unit was created, and they uncovered its links with organized crime. When they raided the London shops they seized around two hundred tins of caviar, labelled Iranian Sevruga, Osietra and Beluga, but when it was analyzed it revealed that it was illegally smuggled from Russia.

Over the last five years customs have made sixty-seven seizures of illegal caviar which totals around £3 million. Experts have estimated that around 30 million pounds worth of caviar has been smuggled into the United Kingdom since 1998. Just another case that highlights where there is money to be made it can usually be linked in some way to organized crime or the Mafia.

The Grizzard Gang

At the turn of the century and for the first decade of the 1900s, Joseph 'Cammi' Grizzard was renowned as being the receiver of stolen goods and the organizer of burglaries throughout London.

Joseph Grizzard was born in 1867. He was described as being of medium height and somewhat portly build, supported a blond moustache and wore diamond rings on his fingers.

Grizzard's first conviction was at Thames Police Court on May 1, 1880, where he received fourteen days for larceny. He managed to stay out of the courts for the next twenty years. The next time he did appear, however, he was charged with grand larceny which included 78 gold watches, 24 gold chains and 70 diamond, pearl and sapphire rings from a jeweller's shop in Richmond, Surrey. Also involved in this heist was a cutter named David Jacobs, or 'Sticks'. Despite the evidence of an eyewitness who claimed to have seen him outside the shop on the night of November 19, 1902, Grizzard was acquitted. Over the next few years Grizzard was to become known as one of the highest quality receivers in London.

His greatest achievement came six years later

when he masterminded a jewel robbery at the Café Monico in Regent Street. This was the first time that John Higgins and Harry Grimshaw came into the picture.

On June 20, 1909, a French dealer by the name of Frederick Goldschmidt, arrived in London bringing jewellery with him. He was staying at De Keyser's hotel, and although it is not clear how Grizzard came about the information, he started to have him watched.

Through thorough observation it became clear that Goldschmidt never let go of his case except when he washed his hands. On July 9, he was followed to the Café Monico. When he went to the men's room he put his bag down beside him. As he reached for the soap he was pushed off balance and Grimshaw managed to snatch it. Goldschmidt gave chase but his path was blocked by Higgins. The jewels, which were worth some £60,000, were never recovered. The police knew that this had all the markings of a Grizzard heist, and within a matter of hours had obtained a warrant to search his home. When they arrived they found him at dinner with three guests – three potential buyers. Grizzard and his guests remained seated while the house was searched, but nothing was found. After the police left, Grizzard drank his now cold pea soup and at the bottom of the bowl was a diamond necklace.

Higgins received 15 months imprisonment and Grimshaw three years' penal service to be followed by five years' detention.

But Grizzard's luck was starting to run out. The

following year he was back in the dock having been arrested and charged with receiving stolen jewellery from a burglary in Brighton, and for harbouring Samuel Barnett who had failed to appear at court some fourteen months previously. This time the police managed to find a criminal who was prepared to give evidence against him. Arthur Denville Sassoon Collinson claimed to have worked as a burglar for both Grizzard and Barnett.

Grizzard was given five months on 8 March, 1910, for feloniously harbouring Barnett.

Grizzard was also known to be behind the theft of jewellery from Vaughan Morgan. He was the son of Sir Walter Vaughan Morgan who was the City Alderman. Morgan's butler from 1904 until 1911 was a man called Frank Ellis, until he left to set up as a bookmaker. Before he resigned he was asked to find another footman to replace him, which he managed to do through an agency. His name was Robinson, and in the three weeks before they were to change over Robinson began betting with him. Ellis also knew one of Grizzard's gang who was a known jewel thief, William Bangham. By November, 1911, Ellis's business was not going well and he was raided and heavily fined as an illegal bookmaker. He then persuaded Robinson to let him into his former employer's house. They did a trial run where nothing was taken, but on the second raid they were successful. The police were convinced it was an inside job rather than a break-in and Robinson was arrested and discharged after naming Ellis. Ellis was arrested but remained silent, and no amount of persuasion would make

Ellis point the finger at Grizzard. He received 21 months' penal servitude.

The loyalty from Ellis was most probably because Grizzard was renowned for helping friends and their families if they were caught by the police. He also had an unswerving loyalty to those with whom he worked. Many times his associates tried to talk him into retiring, but although a comparatively wealthy man, he still enjoyed the thrill of the chase.

Grizzard's men included the burglar James Lockett who was known as 'Lockett the lion-hearted – the man who never knew fear'. He had convictions both in Italy and America and on February 14, 1906, received five years at Liverpool Assizes for the attempted robbery of a travelling jewellery salesman. His partner in this crime was 'Long Almond', or Arthur Norton, who was regarded as one of the finest safe-crackers of the period. During the winter of 1911 to 1912, Lockett was known to be involved in a series of substantial jewellery shop burglaries in the West End.

Grizzard's greatest blunder came in 1913. This was the theft of a string of sixty-one pearls with a insurance value of £130,000.

The international jewel dealer, Max Mayer, had offices in Hatton Garden and on June 20, 1913, sent the string of pearls to his agent in Paris, Henri Salomon. On July 15, the necklace together with two drop pearls and a round pearl in a leather case, were returned by registered post. This was not unusual, for it was regarded as far safer than having a messenger carry it around. Mayer received a letter to say that the pearls were on their way and, in fact, the box arrived in the same post.

However, when the parcel was opened instead of the pearls there was only the considerably less valuable package of eight lumps of sugar on a bed of cotton wool. This culminated in two problems. First, for Salomon to explain just what he had done to eliminate himself from the enquiries, and second for the thieves to dispose of such identifiable pearls.

Salomon immediately left for England producing a receipt for the package. After much investigation it seemed there was no possibility that the box had been tampered with whilst in the hands of the postal services. The police were also willing to rule out Salomon, a reward of £10,000 was posted and an extensive description of the pearls circulated.

At the beginning of August, two jewel dealers in Paris, Mayer Cohen Quadratstein and Samuel Brandstatter, who were in fact cousins, heard that Leiser Gutwirth in Antwerp might have knowledge of the whereabouts of the pearls. Brandstatter visited Gutwirth and was told the pearls were indeed available, but not for £20,000 which he was offered, he wanted double. Brandstatter said he would have to consult with his partner who was now in London. He was immediately summoned from Paris, but the price had now gone up to £50,000.

The cousins, who were only interested in the reward, met with Gutwirth, Grizzard and one of his colleagues, Simon Silverman, in a Lyons teashop in Holborn. Grizzard took out a cigarette and asked an apparent stranger for a match, at which point a box was thrown to him. When opened there were three separate pearls. For amateur detectives the cousins acted with great skill. They managed to keep the negotiations going for the next ten days whilst they contacted the assessors. The police, who were unwilling to arrest the men without the pearls, bided their time.

On August 25, another meeting took place in Holborn. The cousins, now joined by Spanier, a French jewel expert employed by the assessors, met Silverman and Grizzard. The necklace was produced and the three stray pearls were purchased for 1,000,000FF. Over the next few days the police watched Grizzard and his team like hawks.

In the meantime Grizzard was taking some precautions himself. He was beginning to sense that the whole set-up was a trap. On September 3, Grizzard, Silverman and Lockett were followed to an underground station. The trap was sprung and after a fight the three were arrested. The prisoners were taken to Bow Street, but when searched there was no sign of the necklace. Their houses were searched, they were charged with stealing and receiving the necklace, but by the evening there was still no sign of the pearls.

In fact nothing was found until about a fortnight later when a matchbox containing pearls was found in the gutter in St Paul's Road, Islington. The man who discovered them, a piano maker, thought they were imitation, but nevertheless took them to the local police station. They were sent to the Lost Property Office at Scotland Yard where an officer who had been on the case recognized them as genuine. Apparently, when Lockett's wife had heard of her husband's arrest, she had simply thrown the pearls away. And so it was that Mayer received most of his jewels back.

Lockett and Grizzard received seven years and Silverman five when the case came to trial in November, 1913.

HIS TIME IN JAIL

Grizzard found life in prison difficult. Like so many thieves, he had received a long prison sentence late in life. His health was deteriorating and he spent much of his time in prison hospital. He wanted out and to make life easier for himself he became an informer. So he reneged on the principles which had kept so many men loyal to him. But his disloyalty got him nowhere and he was told that the information he supplied was of no use to the police, and that he would have to remain where he was until he had completed his sentence.

Despite his dwindling health and his distaste for prison Grizzard just somehow could not stop doing what he knew best. In 1922, he was charged with receiving the proceeds of an ingenious fraud on a firm of London jewel dealers. Grizzard had arranged for Major Harrison to purchase jewellery on approval from Bedford & Co. He advanced Harrison £3,000 to establish a line of credit. The jewellery was to be shown to a Colonel who would shortly be returning to India. It was a simple, and well-established confidence trick. The initial purchases were paid for and more jewellery was bought and then £10,000 of jewellery was handed over for approval. However the scam backfired and Grizzard and another member of the conspiracy, American-born Michael Spellman, received only £900 for it in Antwerp. Foolishly he returned to England where he was found to have another collection of stolen jewellery in his possession. Even more gems were traced back to Grizzard.

In August, 1922, Grizzard and Spellman were arrested and both received twelve months. The major fled to Canada where shortly afterwards he received two years for a similar fraud. While Grizzard was awaiting trial his health deteriorated, and he was found to be suffering from both tuberculosis and diabetes in advanced form. He was taken home where he died on September 15, 1923.

He left a note for his partner in crime, Spellman, leaving him 'all the spoils you have done me out of and my place in the underworld as Prince'.

The Sabinis

The Sabinis were a force to be reckoned with. They'd started in about 1910 and based themselves in the Yorkshire Grey, Clerkenwell. There wasn't an English man amongst them so they became known as the Italian Mob and their business was conducted at the racetracks.

There were six Sabini brothers beginning with Frederick who was born in 1881. According to police files he traded as Bob Wilson at the Harringay Greyhound Stadium and took no part in his brothers' 'affairs'.

Next in line was Charles who was two years younger. He was a list supplier working for the bookmaker Joe Levy in what was considered to be a protection racket. He owned shares in West Ham Stadium and was considered, by some, to be mentally deranged. He had certainly spent some time in mental institutions.

Then came Joseph who, on paper, was the villain of the family. He had served in the Royal Welsh Fusiliers during the First World War, followed by the Cheshire Regiment. He was wounded whilst in France and consequently invalided out of the forces, receiving a 12 shillings a week pension. On October 12, 1922, he was given a three years' penal servitude for his part in the shooting of Fred

Gilbert in Mornington Crescent. After he split from his brothers there is no evidence that he was operating any rackets. He was known to have traded as Harry Lake at Harringay.

George Sabini was the youngest of the brothers. He had no convictions and worked at both Harringay and White City. He was never regarded as part of the gang, but just having the name Sabini meant that he would always be provided with protection.

Of all the brothers it was principally Darby and Harry who provided 'protection' or, in reality, demanded money with menaces from the bookmakers. Ullano, better known as Darby Sabini, was born in 1889 in Saffron Hill, Little Italy. His father, who was Italian, died when he was only two which meant he and the rest of the family were raised by their Irish mother. Leaving school at the age of 13, Darby joined a small-time boxing promoter and bookmaker named Dan Sullivan. Later he was employed as a strong-arm man by George Harris, who was a leading bookmaker at the time.

Harry, known as 'Harryboy', went to work for an optician after leaving school. During the First World War he worked in a munitions factory. Then he became a bookmaker's clerk, working first for Gus Hall and later Walter Beresford. When Beresford died he became a commission agent and by 1940 had become a wealthy man.

When the war was over attendance numbers at the racecourses rocketed. Before the war the Birmingham gangs had established a hold on racecourse protection, and they now sought to enlarge their empire. Under the leadership of Billy Kimber and Andrew Townie they transformed themselves into the Brummagen Boys, despite the fact that most of the members came from the Elephant and Castle area of London. Their organized racecourse protection began around 1910 and for a time Kimber's mob took control of Newbury, Epsom, Earls Park and Kempton. They had a fearsome reputation and the southern bookmakers seemed to accept their imposition without too much opposition.

The racecourse protection worked in a variety of ways. The Sabinis and their rivals would simply bully the unfortunate bookmakers away from their sites and then either sold or let them to their associates. One way of preventing a bookmaker from attracting any business was to surround his stand with thugs so that the punters could not get near to it to place their bets. Then there was something called the bucket drop. If a bookmaker wished to be left alone he simply dropped 2/6d into a bucket containing water and a sponge which was carried up and down between the races. The same sponge could also be used to wipe out the odds on the bookmakers' boards. If they did not pay up then the odds would simply be wiped off at the most inconvenient of times. There were other under-hand manoeuvres used on the tracks and, although the amounts involved might seem trivial, they all mounted up to quite a lot of money. The racecourse business was certainly a profitable one.

The Sabini brothers, otherwise known as 'The

Italian Mob' started to put their organization together. They were even said to have imported gangsters from Sicily. With the arrival of the Sabinis and their more skilful handling of the police, Billy Kimber and his gang retreated to the Midlands.

The next five years saw an on-going battle over who was going to control the bookmakers. On the one side the Sabinis and on the other the Kimbers. Kimber's boys did not give in easily and the fighting continued throughout the year.

One bookmaker, who was under the protection of the Sabinis, was threatened at Sandown Park and beaten up when he refused to pay a £25 pitch fee. Darby Sabini immediately retaliated and sent some of his men to Hoxton. He was almost caught himself at the Greenford trotting track on March 23, 1921, but managed to escape a beating by shooting his way out of trouble. This was one of the few occasions that Sabini was arrested. He was charged with unlawfully and maliciously endangering life, but was acquitted after claiming it was self-defence.

On March 27, Billy Kimber was found shot on the pavement outside Sabini's house in Kings Cross. He had apparently gone to Collier Street to settle an argument with Alfie Solomon and had pulled out a gun. Solomon grabbed the gun from Kimber and shot him with his own weapon. Solomon was acquitted of attempted murder when the jury accepted his claim that it was an accident.

The fight between Sabini and the 'outsiders' continued throughout the summer and culminated on Derby Day. It was the result of a complaint from the publisher (and later convicted swindler) Horatio Bottomley. He said that it was wrong that Italians such as the Sabinis should deprive the Brummagen Boys out of a living, particularly after their valour in the First World War. The outcome was the Brummagen Boys were out for revenge.

After the Derby was over the Boys left the course, blocked the road and lay in wait for Sabini and his friends. Unbeknown to them the Sabinis had already left the track, and when the Brummagen Boys attacked the first cab in sight, it turned out to be their allies from Leeds.

A VINTAGE YEAR

The year 1922 turned out to be a vintage year in the battle for supremacy. On 23 February two Brummagen Boys, Michael Sullivan and Archie Douglas, were slashed in Coventry Street by a Sabini team of thugs.

On Good Friday Fred Gilbert was slashed about the legs in a club in Jermyn Street by the Sabinis, but he declined to press charges. Two months later, however, the Sabinis were back in court charged with firing shots at Fred Gilbert in a fight in Mornington Crescent.

Trouble did not stop and the Jockey Club gave consideration to shutting down the courses on which there was trouble. The Sabinis and their rivals fought for leadership on street corners, on trains, on the roads, at the racecourses, nowhere seemingly out of bounds.

Meanwhile most of the Sabini gang involved in the Gilbert shooting had been acquitted. Joseph Sabini was not quite so lucky, he received three years which he served in Maidstone.

The next trouble that occurred at the Doncaster St Leger meeting where the Brummagen gang sent word that no bookmakers or their employees would be allowed to attend. As a result of this, in open defiance, Sabini and his men offered Walter Beresford protection and promptly put him on a train to Doncaster. He was met there by Kimber's men who then allowed only him and his staff to go to the racecourse.

The racecourse wars eventually died down when the Sabinis and Kimber agreed to divide the race-courses between them. Now, with the Sabinis con-trolling the south and Kimber and his friends the rest, the bookmakers were truly in their hands.

But just as things died down trouble broke out within the Sabini gang. Some of his men decided that they would like a higher percentage of the takings. The four Cortesi brothers (Augustus, George, Paul and Enrico) acted as shop stewards and put their case forward. At the same time the Jewish element in the gang, who became known as the Yiddishers, also formed a breakaway group. The Sabinis were prepared to negotiate and offered the Cortesi's a greater percentage, and the Yiddishers were given permission to lean on one of the bookmakers under their protection.

Peace did not last for long, however. The Cortesis and the Yiddishers joined forces, and the Sabini positioned was considerably weakened. By the autumn of 1922 the new team had effectively commandeered the Sabini protection money from the bookmakers at Kempton Park. Payback was swift, and as a result Harry Sabini was convicted of an assault on George Cortesi. One of the other leaders of the breakaway group was also attacked which resulted in the imprisonment of five of the Sabini gang for attempted murder.

On November 19, 1922, Darby and Harry Sabini were trapped in the Fratellanza Club in Great Bath Street. Darby was punched and hit with bottles whilst Harry was shot in the stomach. The Cortesi brothers, who lived very close to the Fratellanza Club, were arrested the same night and each received a three year jail sentence.

Without their leaders the Cortesi band started to fold. Gang fighting in London was rife in the year 1925, but died away just as suddenly as it had started. Darby Sabini moved to Brighton where, in October 1929, he was fined for assaulting a bookmaker, David Isaacs.

By the 1930s the Sabinis had expanded their territory into greyhouse racing, and it was then that they came under threat from a rival team. This threat came from their former ally Alf White whose gang had been getting stronger and stronger over the years, and who were now ready to challenge their previous allies. The Sabinis had been branching out. Their interests now included West End drinking and gambling clubs and the installing and running of slot machines. They were also extending their protection to criminals. If a burglary took place the Sabinis would send round for their share. Burglars and thieves didn't stand a chance. If they happened to go into the West End, they needed to go mob-handed. They also had to be prepared to pay out if they were met by any of the Sabinis.

THE BULLION ROBBERY

The Sabini family were also undoubtedly behind one of the finest bullion robberies of the 1930s. This was a very carefully planned snatch which took place at Croydon Airport. On March 6, 1936, three boxes of gold bars, sovereigns and dollars, which were being shipped from the airport to Brussels and Paris, disappeared. The boxes had been put in a safe room and amazingly only one man, Francis Johnson, stayed at the airport overnight. He had to leave the building at 4.15 the next morning in order to receive a German plane that was landing. An impression had been made of the keys to the safe room and, while Johnson was dealing with the plane, the gold was stolen.

The boxes were loaded into a cab which was hired from King's Cross and brought back to Harringay. Cecil Swanland, John O'Brien and Silvio Mazzardo along with a Sabini man, were arrested. The police discovered wrappers and seals from the gold in Swanland's room but there was no trace of the gold itself. None of the gold was recovered.

THE EMPIRE CRUMBLES

By 1937 there were five major London gang

districts: Hackney, Hoxton, North East London, North London, and the West End. Apart from these gangs there were a few offshoot teams such as the squad of pickpockets who worked the nearby City.

With regard to the racecourses, the last major fight took place at Lewes racecourse on June 8, 1936. The Bethnal Green Gang in alliance with the Hoxton Mob ran riot. In retaliation for an incident at Liverpool Street when a member of the whites had his throat cut, thirty members of that firm went to the races with the sole intention of injuring two of the Sabinis. They did not find them and set upon the bookmaker, Arthur Solomons, and his clerk instead. After a running battle sixteen men were arrested.

It was after this confrontation that an agreement was reached whereby the Sabinis would have the West End, while the Whites would cover the King's Cross area. They became known as the King's Cross Gang.

The Sabini empire effectively crumbled by their internment at the outbreak of the Second World War. Their business interest were now up for grabs and for a while were shared between the Whites, Jack Spot, and the Elephant Gang, with the Whites becoming the dominant force.

Jack Spot

*There have been some legendary figures at the head of
East End gangland over the decades. From the mid-
thirties to the mid-fifties the main man was Jack Spot,
though like many others, much of his legend
was self-proclaimed.*

Jacob Colmore, John Colmore, Jacob Comacho,
Jack Comer – he was known by a multitude of
names, but is best remembered as Jack Spot. He
claimed it was because he was always on the spot
when trouble needed sorting. More realistically,
however, it was probably a childhood alias given
for the mole on his cheek.

Born on April 12, 1912, in Whitechapel's Myrdle
Street, Spot was the son of Polish immigrants. His
brother was a tailor and his sister a dressmaker.

At the age of fifteen he became a bookie's
runner, and the next year joined forces with a
leading figure running protection rackets on the
Sunday morning stalls in Petticoat Lane. Strictly
small-time, together they protected the Sunday-
morning stallholders in Petticoat Lane. Times
were tight, and the stallholders' main concern was
to prevent new traders moving in and diluting
their takings.

Spot soon showed an aptitude for gangland
activities. However, it was not long before he fell

out with his senior partner, fought him, and took the protection business for himself, emerging as the self-styled 'King of Aldgate'.

Following a short spell as a partner with Dutch Barney, an East End bookmaker, he then took a more direct route – acting as a lookout and minder to a successful housebreaker. This ended up with him being arrested and admitting to more than forty offences. Amazingly, though, he was bound over. Not being able to believe his luck, Spot then returned to bookmaking and the racecourses.

For a while he ran a typical fairground con called 'Take a Pick', where punters paid sixpence (2.5p) to pull a straw with a winning number from a cup. The lucky winners (and there were very few) won a cheap prize, whilst Spot pocketed around £40 a day. Surprisingly, he continued to operate successfully at the racetracks for some time, relying on the never-ending supply of mug punters, backed up by the unspoken threat of violence. He also took his 'Pick' game back to Petticoat Lane where, on a good day, he could earn as much as £50.

THE BLACKSHIRTS

Jack Spot will probably be best remembered for his protection of Jewish shopkeepers against the Blackshirts on their marches down Brick Lane. They were obliged to pay up to £10 to ensure their premises were not damaged during the demonstrations. His protection certainly worked and stall-holders would be queueing up to donate money to

Spot's 'Market Traders Association', which was in fact just another protection racket.

In 1937 he was sentenced to six months' imprisonment for causing grievous bodily harm to a Blackshirt during one of their marches. It was to be the only prison sentence he received during his career. On his release he became an enforcer, collecting subscriptions for an East End Stall Traders Fund run by Larry Sooper. This was a private association formed by stall owners who kept the Depression at bay by refusing to let any other new trader break in and set up a stall.

During the Second World War Spot served for a short time in the Royal Artillery stationed in Cornwall, but was given a medical discharge in 1943. After his discharge he returned to the East End and then the west, to where the real money was to be made.

It was during this period Spot became involved in a fight in a club in Edgware Road. The man involved, Edgware Sam, ran out of the club, some said to get a gun. Spot, fearing a prison sentence, flex north to a land where the black market and organized crime were rife. He worked as a minder around Leeds and Newcastle, helping up-and-coming gangsters beat or intimidate the old guard out of their nightclubs, gambling dens, or racecourse pitches.

Spot helped a club owner, Milky, of the Regal Gaming Club in Chapeltown, Leeds, clear out a Polish protection racketeer from his club, then became the owner's bodyguard. As a reward he was given a pitch at the local greyhound track. He returned to London after he heard that the man with whom he had fought, Edgware Sam, had been jailed for fraud.

Now in great demand, Spot was regularly called back to the North to help club owners in the major cities. Shortly after the end of the Second World War Spot ran the Botolph Club in Aldgate, reputedly pocketing up to £3,000 a week from illegal gambling.

Jack Spot now saw himself as 'the Robin Hood of the East End', travelling to Leeds, Manchester or Glasgow to beat up villains who threatened Jewish businesses. He even claimed that rabbis would advise their frightened people to call for his services. He was still making a good living from the races, meeting anyone who crossed him with instant and brutal retribution.

The White family who had had control of the major southern race courses at Ascot, Epsom and Brighton, were constantly harassed, attacked with knives, bottles, machetes and finally routed in a fight at Harringay Arena.

HIS NEW PARTNER

The date was now 1947 and Spot teamed up with gangster Billy Hill. He was younger, smarter and even more ruthless, and all serious opposition had to be crushed. The two gangleaders settled down as businessmen, living well on the proceeds of protection in West London.

Spot's attempts to portray himself as a legitimate businessmen and a sophisticated elder statesman of crime were doomed to failure. His teaming up with Billy Hill was to be the catalyst for the decline of the self-style 'king of the underworld'. This decline was to be as dramatic and humiliating as it was sudden.

His downfall started when a robbery went disastrously wrong. The job on July 29, 1949, which was to have been the first major post-war robbery, took place at Heathrow Airport. Some members of Spot's gang targeted a bonded warehouse at what was then called London Airport. The warehouse contained nearly £250,000 worth of goods including diamonds, and was due to receive £1 million in gold the next day. The job had been meticulously planned with inside help, and the gang kept a constant vigil over a two-month period.

The plan had been to drug the guards at the warehouse and at first the raid seemed to go according to plan. But the Flying Squad had been tipped off by the chief security officer who reported that he had been offered £500 to dope the coffee of the warehouse staff. At the last minute the guards had been switched and replaced by members of the Flying Squad. The gang were arrested and the heart was torn out of Spot's team.

Although the police could never prove that Spot was the organizer, his interests were disrupted and under pressure his gambling club in St Botolph's Row was closed. Billy Hill, was already serving two years in prison, and on his release in 1949, the balance of power was already starting to shift. Spot had been Hill's protector when he was on the run in the mid-forties – now it was Hill who was on the up-and-up. One by one Spot's men moved over to Hill's side.

Hill cemented his reputation with the Eastcastle Street Great Mailbag Robbery which took place on May 21, 1952. £287,000 in hard cash was stolen from a Post Office mail van by Hill's men. In contrast to the botched heist at Heathrow, the robbery was carried out with immaculate precision. The mail van had been followed every night for months as it left on its journey to Oxford Street. Cars had been stolen specifically for use in the raid. In the early hours of Wednesday morning one of the team had disconnected the alarm system on the mail van whilst the staff were taking their tea break.

As the van turned into Eastcastle Street two cars blocked the driver's path. Six men attacked the Post Office workers and then drove off in the van leaving them on the pavement. The van was driven to the City where the cash was transferred into boxes on a fruit lorry. Surprisingly enough only thirteen out of a total of thirty-one bags had been taken, and the reason, according to Hill, was because there wasn't any more room in the lorry.

Hill was seriously suspected of organizing the robbery, but despite intense police activity they were never successful in obtaining any convictions.

Spot was now in serious decline and, to make matters worse, his big source of income, on-course betting, was being hit as the big bookmakers prepared for the legalization of off-course betting. The on-course bookies, resentful of being milked by Spot, were now refusing to pay. The fact that the ageing gangster was being deserted by his troops, allowed the bookies to defy him. Spot was losing his reputation, but worse still, he was now despised by other criminals for his reputation as a police informer.

There is no doubt that by the summer of 1955, Spot's career as a gang leader was just about in ruins. The effective end of Spot's reign came on August 11, 1955 when hardman Albert Dimes sent word that he wanted Spot to come and see him. This must have been the crowing insult. A fuming Spot, humiliated by the summons, ended up in a brutal knife fight with Dimes in Soho's Frith Street. Both men were badly injured. Spot had been stabbed over the left eye and in the left cheek as well as the neck and ear. He had four stab wounds in the left arm and two in the chest, one of which penetrated his lung. Dimes had his forehead cut to the bone requiring twenty stitches, a wound in the thigh and one in the stomach.

Dimes got away in a taxi, while Spot picked himself up off the pavement and staggered into a nearby barber's shop. Both the men went to hospital and were arrested as they left their respective beds. Eleven days later their wounds had healed sufficiently for them to appear before Marlborough Street Magistrates' Court, charged with wounding with intent to commit grievous bodily harm and affray. Neither man ended up in jail.

THE DECLINE

From then on Spot went very swiftly downhill. His

assault on the *Sunday People* journalist Duncan Webb cost him £732 in damages, a new nightclub was burned out and by the late fifties he was working as a meatpacker. Estranged from his wife, Rita, the final humiliation came when he was fined for stealing from his employer. The days when he had modelled himself on the Chicago gangsters of the thirties, right down to the handmade clothes, seemed long gone.

Towards the end, Spot was humbled about his past. Billy Hill was now in control, but a generational shift was soon to occur. In the sixties knives would give way to guns and a new set of gangsters prepared to use even more brutal methods. The day of the Krays and the Richardsons was about to dawn.

The Kray Twins

London in the 1960s was dominated by two main gangs – the Krays and the Richardsons. It is said by some that they terrorized the communities in which they lived. It is said by others that they controlled these areas better than the authorities and that petty crime was kept to a minimum due to their influence.

The Twins, known universally as Ronnie and Reggie, were born in Bethnal Green in the East End of London, in the year 1933. Reggie was the younger by forty-five minutes.

The family was part Irish, Jewish, gipsy and Austrian. Their father was a secondhand clothes dealer and their mother Violet made them the centre of her world and they worshipped her in return. The Kray family became very much a part of a vanishing Dickensian world. The older family members were well-known and distinctive local characters. 'Mad' Jimmy Kray, the paternal grandfather, was a stallholder in Petticoat Lane, renowned for both his drinking prowess and his ability as a bar-fighter.

On the other side of the family, the maternal grandfather, Jimmy Lee the 'Southpaw Cannonball', had in his youth, been a bare-knuckle boxer, and then a music hall entertainer. He was a rarity in the family in that he was a non-drinker.

GROWING UP

Growing up, the twins were identical, dark-eyed like their father, and tough little nuts. The twins caught diphtheria and measles, after which Ronnie seemed slower and more socially awkward than Reggie. Reggie seemed to find it much easier to get on with people than his brother did.

Charlie taught the twins to box and they proved so good at this that they got through to the finals of the London Schools Boxing Championship three times. In December 1951, all three brothers appeared on the same billing at a middle-weight boxing championship held at the Royal Albert Hall.

The twins were always inseparable. They would often fight each other, but would never allow a third party to come between them. Somehow they seemed different to the other tough little kids in the neighbourhood.

The twins were basically reared by a household of women during the period of World War II. Their father was on the run from the law, having refused to join up for military service. So Ronnie and Reggie's formative years were strongly influenced by their mother Violet, her two sisters, and their grandmother.

By the age of twelve they were both attending Daniel Street School, where Reggie excelled in English and Ronnie's forte was general knowledge. Three times a week, their father would take them to the Robert Browning Youth Club for boxing lessons.

When they reached fifteen and left school, they

worked in the Billingsgate Fish Market for six months. This turned out to be the longest legitimate employment they ever had. Reggie trained as a salesman, and Ronnie worked as an 'empty boy', which entailed scouring the market each day, and collecting empty fish boxes for his employer. They also worked at the weekends, helping out their Granddad Kray on his stall in Petticoat Lane.

By the time they were seventeen, the Twins had become professional boxers. Both were dishonourably discharged from National Service in 1954 after spending much of their time in military prisons.

LIFE OF CRIME

A year after they were discharged from the Army, the twins went into their first business venture. With a loan from their elder brother Charlie, they bought a seedy fourteen-table billiard hall, which had been converted from an old movie theatre called The Regal in Eric Street, off the Mile End Road in Bethnal Green. It was the type of club that always had trouble, fights all the time, getting smashed up on a regular basis, and no self-respecting person would ever set foot inside it. They called it the Regal and in no time at all the club was turned around, the fighting had stopped and the clientele had improved.

It was at the Regal that a Maltese mob tried to collect protection money from the Twins. One of the gang had a bayonet thrust through his hand.

The others were lucky to escape with their lives.

The Twins started using a club called The Vienna Rooms, off Edgware Road. The club was frequented by two of the Twin's heroes, Jack Spot and Billy Hill, who between them ran the whole of London. Ron and Reg would sit for hours with them listening and learning everything they could.

They worked for Jack Spot for a while at the racecourses providing protection for the Bookmakers. Jack Spot would provide boys to wash the chalk off the boards and the minders would make sure that the Bookmakers didn't get any trouble from irate punters or rival gangs.

They had learnt well from their brief time with Jack Spot and Billy Hill but it was time to move on. By now the Twins reputation went before them, they were into every scam you could think of. They hi-jacked lorries carrying anything from furniture to cigarettes. They dealt in National Service exemption certificates and Dockers Tickets. These tickets allowed men to work on the docks for short hours and massive amounts of pay.

By 1956, their twenty-second year, the twins were a formidable pair. They had established the biggest criminal racket in London's East End, with the homosexual Ronnie as the violent, dominant force and Reggie providing the business brains.

The twins generated cash by 'poncing' off local villains. Basically this meant that they demanded a share of illegal profits resulting from thieving and robbery committed on their patch.

Illegal bookmaking and gambling dens also

became a major potential source of corruption. Thieves, anxious to off-load their spoils, would make the twins their first contact point. They became experts at working scams which involved manipulating paste rings and jewellery and screwing victims out of their money before they discovered their mistakes. But the twins were after much more than the small time stuff – they wanted to be the barons of crime, rather than the serfs.

Despite their violent associations, however, they were also popular with the rich and famous and associated with the likes of Judy Garland, Diana Dors, George Raft and Lord Boothby.

SERVING TIME

In 1957 Ron was sent to prison for three years for grievous bodily harm on a man called Terry Martin, outside a pub in Stepney. He was also charged with possessing a fire arm. Reg was also charged with GBH but was found not guilty.

While Ron was away, Reg opened up another club in Bow and called it The Double R. Charlie. Charlie, who was usually kept in the background away from any wheeling and dealing, put some money up for the club, for which he was given a percentage of the takings. The club flourished. Reg gradually acquired many clubs that had previously been mysteriously firebombed, and so the Kray empire was slowly being built.

The business seemed to operate a lot more smoothly without Ronnie's interference. The problem with the Kray 'Firm' as it came to be known was that there wasn't just one Boss. Ron and Reg argued constantly about what they were doing and how they handled the proceeds. Ronnie, being the dominant twin usually won the arguments, sometimes at a cost to the business.

THE FIRM

The Kray 'Firm' consisted of the Colonel Ronnie Kray, his twin brother Reg Kray, Ronnie Hart their cousin, Albert Donoghue, Ian Barrie, Pat Connolly, Big Tommy Brown, known as 'the Bear', Billy Donovan, Connie Whitehead, Sammy Lederman, Dave Simmonds, Nobby Clark, Scotch Jack Dickson, John Barry, Tony and Chris Lambrianou and Ronnie Bender.

Charlie Kray didn't play a very large part in the Firm and was often left out of many of the Twins enterprises.

Leslie Payne and Tommy Cowley were the brains of the outfit, giving respectability to many of their seedy deals.

Other gang members were recruited after acts of violence had been inflicted upon them by the Twins. For example Albert Donoghue had been shot in the leg by Reg for uttering a threat against them. Weeks later, however, he was welcomed into the Firm and put on a pension, and was to become one of their most trusted members.

The Firm worked on an information basis. The Twins would always help small time crooks who had just been released from prison or when they were down on their luck in return for favours. They acted as the eyes and ears of the Kray Firm, and in fact nothing happened in London without the Twins knowing or without them getting their piece of the action.

The Firm also worked on a sort of franchise system where certain members of the gang, such as Tony and Chris Lambrianou, used the Kray name and reputation to conduct their business activities. The Lambrianou brothers operated all over the country happy in the knowledge that they had the backing and the muscle of the Firm. The Twins weren't interested in what they were doing just so long as they received their percentage.

The Twins eventual downfall came about with the help of many of the 'loyal and trusted' members of their the Firm.

SCHIZOPHRENIA

Although Ronnie could be vicious and unforgiving, there was another side to his nature. He would always help people down on their luck. He was regarded as a soft touch for those in real need, especially those people who were just coming out of prison. He would quite willingly open up the tills and hand over some cash to a deserving cause. Although very commendable, it was not good for business and it was to be the cause of constant rows between the brothers. Once Ronnie had made his mind up to do something, he would go ahead and do it regardless of the consequences. It was probably this part of his personality, coupled with

257

his oncoming schizophrenic tendencies that made the Krays as feared as they were.

So, inevitably, when Ronnie was imprisoned it reflected favourably in their business dealings.

Ron first went to Wandsworth prison, then he was transferred to Camp Hill prison. While he was inside his favourite aunt Rose died, which seemed to tip him over the edge. He was sent to the psychiatric wing of Winchester prison where he was declared insane.

He was diagnosed as a paranoid schizophrenic and his health slowly deteriorated. Reggie put this down to the different drugs they were giving Ron and decided to get him out of prison. Luck was on his side, they moved Ron to Long Grove mental hospital which gave him a better chance of being freed. The idea was to get Ron out and keep him out long enough for an independent psychiatrist to assess his state of mind. If the doctor found him to be sane then the authorities would have to re-assess him when he was captured or returned to the hospital.

Reggie visited Ron and simply changed places with him. Ron walked out of the hospital, while Reg sat reading a paper. The hospital orderlies assumed that the man sitting in the chair was Ron. When they realised what had happened it was too late – Ron had long gone and they had to release Reg as well.

Ron remained on the run for five months, but it wasn't too long before they realised what a dreadful mistake they had made. Ronnie really was ill. There were times when he didn't recognise

Reg or his parents, believing them to be imposters.

For his own sake it was essential that he was taken back to the hospital. One night when he secretly returned to Vallance Road, the police raided the house and he was arrested. His condition was re-assessed and he remained in prison until his release in May 1959.

When he came out in 1959 he had terrible mood swings and it was clear that he was still ill. He was uncontrollable, he would rant and rave, pace up and down, and thought that everyone was plotting against him. The family took him to hospital to get him the help he so desperately needed. Part of this help meant that he would have to take drugs and injections for the rest of his life.

He not only had a mental Illness but the treatment that was to keep him calm and subdued affected him physically. He put on weight, his speech was slow and he walked laboriously. He was not the man he used to be.

Unfortunately for Ron, Reggie was arrested in 1959 for demanding money with menaces. He was sentenced to 18 months in prison even though the victim retracted the allegation under oath. He was sent to Wandsworth where he first met Jack the Hat McVitie and The Mad Axeman Frank Mitchell, two men who were to play a major part in their eventual downfall.

TOGETHER AGAIN

At the start of the sixties all the brothers were together again. Ron appeared to be getting back to his old self. By now the Firm had truly established itself, business was good, and they were making inroads into the West End gambling and club scene.

They made their first inroad into this area with an upmarket gaming club called Esmeraldas. It was fronted by Lord Effingham, the sixth Earl of Effingham, who was paid by the Krays to welcome the customers as they entered the club.

They also invested a lot of their own money in a seaside development in a place called Enugu in Nigeria, but unfortunately the project collapsed and the money disappeared.

Ronnie Kray met Lord Boothby through one of the many gay parties that they both attended. He realised he was gay at a very early age when he fell in love with a boy across the road from where he lived. He didn't try to hide his sexuality but it wasn't until the sexual freedom of the sixties that it became widely known.

The Krays were now mixing with some very influential people and it was thought, by some, that they were getting too powerful. They were being watched constantly by the Authorities.

One of the reasons for their eventual downfall was their love of publicity. Ronnie in particular loved being photographed with celebrities and sports stars – displaying himself as the stereotypical American Gangster. The difference, however, between the Krays and their real life, American counterparts, the Mafia, is that they kept a low profile and let others do their dirty work.

In 1965 the Twins were arrested for demanding

money with menaces from a man called Hew McGowan, who owned a club called the Hideaway. They were remanded in custody to Brixton prison.

Their influence was so far-reaching that questions were asked in the House of Lords as to how long they were going to keep the Twins locked up. These questions, asked by Lord Boothby, caused a sensation and when they went to court the Twins were cleared of all charges.

In less than a month they owned the Hideaway club and changed the name to El Morocco.

On April, 1965, Reggie married the love of his life, 20-year-old Frances Shea. She was the sister of his good friend Frank, but it was a marriage which would end in disaster.

Ronnie and Reggie went to America for a week, to forge links with the Mafia. Although they made some very useful connections on their trip, they didn't do as much business as they had hoped. They provided protection, on behalf of the Mafia, for many American celebrities visiting or performing in England, and protected their gambling interests in the West End as well as entertaining them when they came to London.

THE RICHARDSON GANG

The Krays shared control of London with the Richardson gang who came from South London. The main body of the Richardson gang consisted of, brothers Charlie and Eddie, 'Mad' Frankie Fraser and George Cornell. They were already entrenched in the West End, supplying most of the clubs with one armed bandits, and the Krays wanted parted of their action.

In March 1966 a gun battle took place in a club called Mr Smiths in Rushey Green. It has been said that the Richardson gang went there with the intentions of wiping out the Krays, but there was only one member of the Kray gang present. He was shot dead. Frankie Fraser was shot in the hip and Eddie was shot in the backside. They were taken to hospital and on their release they were charged with affray and sentenced to five years in prison. Frankie Fraser was originally charged with the murder of Dickie Hart but was found not guilty.

On the 9th of April 1966, Ronnie Kray walked into the Blind Beggar public house and shot George Cornell in the head. It has been said that Ronnie felt Cornell was responsible for the death of Dickie Hart. Some time after the killing of Cornell, the Twins were arrested and put on an identification parade. The witnesses failed to pick them out and they were duly released.

At the end of 1966, the Twins hatched a plot to free Frank Mitchell, the Mad Axeman. They had both met him on previous occasions in Wandsworth prison. Whilst serving a short term in prison he escaped and broke into an old couple's house and held them hostage with an axe. He was recaptured and sentenced to life without any release date.

It was decided that they would break him out of prison and keep him out long enough for the newspapers to run the story with the promise of his case being investigated. He would then give himself up and return to prison.

He was sprung from Dartmoor by Albert Donoghue and Billy Williams, two of the Kray Firm. But it didn't go exactly to plan as there was no investigation and the hunt for Mitchell continued. Frank Mitchell was subsequently killed in December 1966, and the Twins were later charged with his murder.

At the beginning of 1967 things were looking up for the Krays and Reggie in particular. By June of that year, it looked as if he was getting back together with his wife Frances. However he didn't know that Frances was very ill. She had been mentally unstable before they married but the break-up, masterminded by her parents, caused her to have a mental breakdown. When she came out of hospital Reggie arranged for the two of them to go on holiday. The strain of the constant battles between her parents and Reg, who they disliked intensely, took it's toll. On the day they were to leave for Ibiza she took an overdose of pills and died.

Reggie was heartbroken and went into a deep depression for months. He was drinking all the time and it was through this very traumatic period in his life that he killed Jack 'The Hat' McVitie.

Jack 'The Hat' McVitie, so called because he would never take the hat off that was covering his bald patch, worked for the Twins doing minor tasks. He was an extremely dangerous man who wasn't afraid of the Twins in any way and was often heard running them down in public. He was a drunkard, took drugs and beat up women. He had been warned by Reg on numerous occasions about his attitude but to no avail.

Jack was lured to a party in Evering Road, Stoke Newington, where he was stabbed to death by Reg Kray. This last action proved to be the end of the Krays and the Firm. While the authorities let them get on with it in the past they had now gone 'beyond the accepted parameters' and had to be stopped at all costs.

THE END OF AN ERA

On the May 8, 1968, the Kray Twins were arrested. The raid on Brathwaite House in Old Street was headed by Inspector 'Nipper' Read. Two of the many charges they had to answer to were the murders of George Cornell and Jack McVitie. Their arrest and continued confinement before their trial, loosened the grip of fear they had on the community. It wasn't too long before the East End code of silence had been broken. Within the next few months, with the help of some of the most respected members of the Firm, the police had made more arrests. All of those arrested pleaded not guilty with the exception of Albert Donoghue, a leading gang member. He was tried separately and was imprisoned for two years.

The trial started in January 1969 and lasted about six weeks.

The ten men who stood in the Dock were all convicted of various charges except for Tony Barry. He was acquitted of being an accessory to

the murder of McVitie. The remaining nine men
were charged as follows:

Ronnie Kray, aged 35
- for the murder of George Cornell – guilty
- for the murder of Jack McVitie – guilty
- sentenced to Life imprisonment with a recommendation to serve at least 30 years
- for the murder of Frank Mitchell – not guilty

Reggie Kray, aged 35
- for the murder of Jack McVitie – guilty
- for being an accessory to the murder of George
  Cornell – guilty
- sentenced to Life imprisonment with a recommendation to serve at least 30 years
- Reg Kray, received 5 years for freeing Frank
  Mitchell from Dartmoor and another 9 months
  for harbouring him, to run concurrently with
  his other sentences.

Charlie Kray, aged 41
- for being an accessory to the murder of Jack
  McVitie – guilty
- Sentenced to 10 years in prison
- the charge of murder was later dropped

John 'Ian' Barrie, aged 31
- for the murder of George Cornell – guilty
- sentenced to Life imprisonment with a recommendation to serve at least 20 years

Tony Lambrianou, aged 26

- for the murder of Jack McVitie – guilty
- sentenced to Life imprisonment with a recommendation to serve at least 15 years

Christopher Lambrianou, aged 29
- for the murder of Jack McVitie – guilty
- sentenced to Life imprisonment with a recommendation to serve at least 15 years

Ronnie Bender, aged 30
- for the murder of Jack McVitie – guilty
- sentenced to Life imprisonment with a recommendation to serve at least 20 years

Freddie Foreman, aged 36
- for being an accessory to the murder of Jack McVitie – guilty
- sentenced to 10 years in prison
- for the murder of Frank Mitchell – not guilty

Cornelious 'Connie' Whitehead, aged 30
- Carrying a gun – guilty
- Complicity in the murder of McVitie – guilty
- Sentenced to 2 years for the gun and 7 years for the Complicity charge

On March 17, 1995, Ronnie Kray died at the age of 61 of a massive heart attack in Wexham Park Hospital in Slough, Berkshire.

On July 14, 1997, Reggie married a 38-year-old called Roberta Jones. She was a bright, intelligent, successful businesswoman, who was involved in marketing and media fields. She first met Reggie to discuss details about a proposed video on his late brother. Less than a year later they were tying the knot behind the prison walls at Wayland. She was not, however, the first one to fall under his spell. In 1993 Sandra Wrightson divorced her husband citing Reggie as the other man in her life. While in 1995 it was the turn of schoolgirl Sophie Williams. He was also the godfather to singer and actress Patsy Kensit.

Even in his sixties and from behind prison bars, Reggie Kray exerted a transcendent influence on people, particularly women. Roberta devoted her time and energy in fighting for the release of Reggie.

At the age of 67 Reggie Kray was released from prison in August 2000 on compassionate grounds, after being imprisoned for 31 years. Reggie Kray died on Sunday, October 1, 2000, from terminal cancer.

Charlie Kray, the eldest brother, died after complications due to heart trouble at about 9 p.m. on the evening of April 4, 2000.

The Richardsons

Most people, when they think of English strong-arm rackets, think of the Kray twins, Reggie and Ronnie, who dominated the British underworld for much of the 1950s and 1960s.

The boxing Krays ruled London's East End. From the docks they started out as a couple of youth gang leaders and after deserting from the British army, fought their way to the top of organized crime through standard mob activities.

There is, however, another, less-known set of brothers in England who also built a gang to work the protection/extortion racket – and they were called the Richardsons. These brothers were even more depraved than their more famous counterparts.

Compared to the Krays, Charles and Eddie Richardson were almost amateur in their criminal endeavours, but in cruelty and violence they were every bit equal to the Krays. Their big scam was buying foreign items like nylon stockings on credit and skipping out on the bill.

Charles was the older of the two and the so-called 'brains' of the outfit, whilst Eddie was the most violent. They operated on London's South

Side in a nightclub they dubbed 'Club Astor'. In addition to the credit ruse, the Richardsons liked to threaten their way into partnerships with legitimate businessmen who would be intimidated into co-operation by threats of terrible violence. Wars were going on all over the West End between rival gangs, because everybody wanted a slice of the action.

TORTURE CHAMBER

In the basement of the Club Astor, the Richardsons had a torture chamber that rivalled the Inquisition. One of their favourite tools of torture was an electric shock machine which they used on several occasions.

One story goes that as the brothers sat down to dinner, the rest of their gang was working over a businessman who unwittingly came to the club to collect money that Charlie owed him.

During Charlie's trial in 1967 Derek Harris was reported to have said, 'On Richardson's order they removed my shoes and my toes were wired to a generator. Roy Hall turned the handle and the shock caused me to jump out of my chair and I fell to the floor. . .'

Harris further testified that the shock was repeated on other parts of his body and that as he was recovering Charlie pinned his foot to the floor with a knife. In court, Harris removed his shoe to show the scars on his foot. Harris told the court that his torture lasted six hours, after which Charlie apologized and paid him £150.

Where the Krays were willing to murder to maintain order, the Richardsons seemed to like torture and were never convicted of murder. Some of their victims did disappear, however, but police were unable to locate them, so consequently no charges were ever brought.

One member of the Richardson gang, petty criminal Jack Duval, told an Old Bailey courtroom about how the Richardsons maintained control of their minions. He reported that Edward Richardson had punched him in the face, then when he fell down he was beaten with golf clubs. When Jack asked what he had done to deserve such treatment, he was told in no uncertain terms 'You just do as Charlie tells you.' Duval's offence, as it turned out, was that he had failed to complete work on a nylon-importing scam with the skill Charlie Richardson expected.

THE CONVICTIONS

It took a task force of 100 Scotland Yard detectives to finally bring the Richardson brothers to justice. The leader of the squad apparently said the hardest part was finding witnesses who were willing to talk. In the end the prosecutors were able to put together a case and the brothers were charged with various racketeering and assault counts.

However, the brothers were not going to give up without a fight, and in the middle of their trial, every juror was contacted by someone and threatened with bodily harm if the gang was convicted. Scotland Yard set up a special telephone number just for the jurors if they were threatened again and rather than declare a mistrial, the judge told the jurors it was probably just a crank who made the calls since all of the Richardson gang had been locked up for months. In their defence, the Richardsons merely claimed they were victims of a conspiracy.

After a lengthy trial filled with gruesome details of torture and assault, the case was given to the jury who, despite the threats they had received, convicted the brothers.

Charlie received a twenty-five-year sentence and Edward received ten years. They dropped out of sight soon after entering Her Majesty's prison system.

The Great Train Robbery

On August 8, 1963, Ronald Biggs and 29 other members of a gang smoothly pulled off a daring holdup of the Glasgow to London postal train and in the process became nearly $3 million richer.

A well-drilled gang of about thirty masked bandits ambushed a mail train on Thursday, August 8, 1963, at Sears Crossing in Buckinghamshire. The gang escaped with loot estimated at millions of dollars in perhaps the biggest robbery of all time.

THE GANG

The holdup actually took place at 3.15 am, forty miles north of London. It was done with such precision and teamwork that the police suspected an underworld mastermind to be the brains behind the heist. It was in fact the ingenious plan of a man called Bruce Reynolds, known as the 'Prince of Thieves'. The gang was actually made up of two different London gangs and the main characters were Buster Edwards, Bruce Reynolds, Gordon Goody, Charlie Wilson, Jimmy Hussey, John Wheater, Brian Field and Ronnie Biggs.

The gang fitted the stereotype of a Hollywood

crime movie, with each member providing a particular skill. Firstly, there was Buster Edwards, the small-time thief, fraudster and ex-boxer – a man definitely known for his 'brawn'. Bruce Reynolds was the next member – the 'brains' behind the operation – an antique dealer who liked to live well beyond his means, and drove an expensive Aston Martin car.

The remainder of the gang were a mixture of skills and muscle needed to carry out Reynolds' meticulous plan. More muscle came courtesy of Gordon Goody, a man whose huge figure and tattooed arms, gave him a fearsome reputation amongst his fellow thieves. Then Charlie Wilson, a well known 'face' in the London underworld, and local bookie who was known for being straight and uncomplicated. He proved to be the connection with Jimmy Hussey, a big man who had a long list of convictions.

The safe house was provided by the respectable face of the gang, John Wheater, a public school educated solicitor who used his proper appearance to lease Leatherslade Farm in Oxfordshire. This was where the gang went to hide out after the robbery. The connection between John Wheater, his accomplice Brian Field, and the rest of the gang is not known.

Finally there was Ronnie Biggs. He was the youngest member of the gang at the time of the heist, and as a friend of Bruce Reynolds, he was in the gang largely because of his connections to a retired train driver. As the most inexperienced criminal, Biggs' friendship with Reynolds was the only thing that eased the doubts that the rest of the gang might have had about him.

FORWARD PLANNING

With all elements in the gang brought together, they set about planning the perfect crime, and waited for the right moment to strike. Using information regarding the movements of cash and valuables on postal trains out of London, Reynolds put together a perfect plan for robbing the night train.

First, the location had to be found. Reynolds was ideally looking for somewhere close enough to London so that the police would not be alerted to changes in the routines of the gang members, both before and after the robbery. They also needed a secluded spot near to main routes in and out of London that was regularly used to carry heavy goods, so that their own vehicles didn't arouse the suspicion of the locals.

They finally settled on a site near Bridego Bridge, between the villages of Cheddington and Linslade in Buckinghamshire. A position close enough to the RAF base at Haughton to allow for residents that were used to unfamiliar heavy goods vehicles driving to and fro.

The robbery was originally planned for June, but to take advantage of the extra money that a bank holiday would have brought in, they postponed the date to August.

The preparations for the raid, in actual fact, had started months before, beginning with the blue railway-maintenance overalls that were bought to provide a visual alibi for the presence of the gang on the railway line. Roy James, the gang's get-away driver, even managed to research the workings of the mail train's engines by posing as a schoolteacher planning a lesson.

By August 8, 1963, they gang were ready.

THE ROBBERY

Reynolds' plan hinged around a set of rigged signals that would stop the train at a point on the track, just near to where the members of the gang would be waiting. A glove was used to cover the real green 'go' signal at Sears Crossing and the train driver would instead follow the instructions of a pack of lights powered by six volt batteries.

The simplicity of the props used by the gang suggests an over-confidence in their plan, and in the likely risk they were taking. The gang presumed that if they were caught, the sentences given for recent robberies of this kind were only as little as four years, so they probably weren't too worried about it.

The heist began at 3.03 am. In the grey light of morning, the train pulled to a stop at the false signals, and a group of 'railway workers' appeared on the tracks wearing uniform blue overalls. David Whitby was a fireman on the mail train that day, and he got out of the cabin to enquire what was going on. The first of the railway workers he came to was Buster Edwards, who by all accounts frog-marched Whitby down the embankment at the side of the track. Whitby quickly grasped what was happening and offered no further resistance, allegedly commenting: 'It's all right mate, I'm on your side'.

Jack Mills wasn't so lucky. When the unlucky train driver ventured into the darkness after his fireman, other members of the gang were there to meet him, and after a brief struggle he was hit violently over the head. The injured train driver collapsed bleeding from his head wounds, and never returned to work. He died in 1970 from leukaemia, the lone victim of the Great Train Robbery.

After this dramatic incident, things went from bad to worse for the train robbers. The midsummer's night slid into an increasingly bright morning, which meant that more and more light was shining on the gang's attempt to complete the robbery.

In order to get the mailbags full of money off the train, they needed to move it further down the track, but Ronnie Biggs' connection to a retired train guard failed to deliver. The old man wasn't used to mail trains, so they couldn't get it to move, and when they needed him most, their back-up man was no use at all.

Mills, who was still bleeding at this point, was forced to take over the controls, and move the train in front of four gang members. They quickly broke into the Post Office Sorting Coach, and faced little resistance from the staff inside. Then the money was quickly unloaded by human chain down from the coach and away from the track, with over 120 sacks taken in total. Some money was allegedly offered to Mills, who refused it, and the gang left approximately half a dozen sacks behind, and fled to Leatherslade Farm.

The barn at Leatherslade in Oxfordshire was reached by Land Rover. After laying low for a while and passing the time with tea and Monopoly, the gang became aware that the police were closing in on them, and they scattered. The gang's quick exit proved crucial to the police investigation. Forensic experts found fingerprints on cups, in the bathroom, on a cat's bowl, and of course on the Monopoly set. And to make matters worse, Jim Hussey had left a handprint on the train itself. So after a relatively successful robbery, the gang's luck was running out, and it was clear that they wouldn't evade the police for long.

ESCAPE TO THE SUN

To avoid the impending prison sentence, the gang members fled to all corners of the globe. One of the first to leave the country was Ronald 'Buster' Edwards. He immediately went on the run after the heist and lived in Mexico for over three years before he gave himself up to the authorities. Other gang members tried to evade the authorities in similar style, but the initial thirteen Great Train Robbers were eventually caught and brought to justice.

When they finally appeared in court, only one of the gang ever pleaded guilty. It was Roger Cordrey who admitted his crimes, returned his £80,000 share of the money, but was still given a twenty year prison sentence.

The judge who presided over the case, Mr Justice Edmund Davies, focused on the violence against Jack Mills when delivering his judgement. He stated ' . . . this is nothing less than a sordid crime of violence inspired by vast greed . . . anybody who has seen the nerve-shattered engine driver can have no doubt of the terrifying effect on the law-abiding citizen, of a concerted assault by masked and armed robbers in lonely darkness.'

The trial was held in the offices of Aylesbury Rural Council, and the case attracted a huge amount of public attention, with the public gallery of the chamber always being full. The gang members received between twenty and thirty years each, totalling 307 years. A far longer sentence than even murderers or spies got at the time.

PLANS TO ESCAPE

As thirty years was basically a life sentence, most of the gang looked at ways to escape. Charlie Wilson was first out of the door on August 12 1964, and he was followed over the wall by Ronald Biggs on July 8, 1965. Biggs had succeeded in escaping from the maximum security wing of London's Wandsworth prison.

The escape would not have been possible without the help of one particular man, Paul Seabourne. When Biggs first met Seabourne, he was at the end of a four-year sentence in

Wandsworth. A similar sense of humour and outlook on life, meant they quickly became good friends. It was to be Seabourne who would convince Biggs that he had to try and escape and together they masterminded the break. The actual escape took place on Thursday, July 8, one year and eleven months to the day since the robbery, and it went perfectly to plan. Sadly, Seabourne was picked up and ended up serving four-and-a-half years for getting Ron out of prison.

Following the escape, Biggs used plastic surgery to change his appearance and moved first to Spain, then Australia, before settling in Brazil. Biggs stayed in Brazil making money from his fame as the one member of the Great Train Robbers who actually escaped. Biggs remained on the run for thirty-five years.

This was until May 2001, when he returned to England, only to be arrested on arrival, and forced to serve the remaining twenty-five years of his original sentence in Belmarsh Prison.

Buster Edwards gave himself up in September 1966, then Charlie Wilson was re-arrested in Canada in January 1968 and Bruce Reynolds was finally captured eleven months later in England after five years on the run.

The evidence found on the Monopoly set at Leatherslade farm remains one of forensic science's greatest breaks in cracking what could have been the most successful heist ever.

The Yardies

They drive top of the range BMWs, flaunt designer jewellery and carry automatic guns. They are called 'The Yardies' and have a reputation for ruthless violence that could one day rival that of the Mafia or Triads.

The term 'Yardie' is merely a name given by the Jamaican people themselves to a person who recently arrived in the United Kingdom from Jamaica, which is referred to as 'back yard'.

During the 1950s while England was enjoying a post-war economic boom, the British Government encouraged immigration into the country to help fill existing job vacancies. As a result of this, many Afro-Caribbeans immigrated in search of a better standard of living. Most of the employment was of an unskilled nature with very low wages, and consequently the immigrants had to find cheap housing in the rundown inner-city areas. When the country's economic situation changed, many in this new work force felt the pinch of the recession.

Crime in these inner-city areas became rife, due to the squalor and the fact that many of the inhabitants were now unemployed. Over the years police relations with these residents has become strained and, on occasion, violently confrontational. The situation became even more serious when there was a new influx of immigrants during the late 1970s. Unlike those who preceded them, these immigrants did not come to seek work or a better standard of life. Rather, they came as criminals, often fugitives, to earn a living out of crime. Gradually these 'Yardies' distinguished themselves from the local communities.

WHAT IS A YARDIE?

Yardies are usually single males between the ages of eighteen and thirty-five. They are normally un-employed, very often by choice, although some will make the claim that they are involved in the music business. When these people enter the country as tourists or 'to visit relatives', they usually assume a false identity and carry forged credentials. Many already have criminal convic-tions or are actually wanted by the police. Because they are only known by their street names to their associates, they are extremely difficult to identify. It also known that some will even travel on false or fraudulently obtained British passports.

Unfortunately, with this immigration of convicted criminals and fugitives, a criminal infrastructure arose within the community that became hostile towards the police. Clubs, bars and house parties, that tended to imitate Jamaican street life, became the venues for illicit activities.

Even though Yardies find support in these established communities, the United Kingdom is probably not their first choice of destination, preferring to go to the United States. However, as Jamaican violence and drug trafficking has grown,

US immigration authorities and other Federal agencies have become aware of the dangers posed by these gangs. Consequently, the United States has made it increasingly difficult for Jamaican criminals to gain entry into their country. This means they are forced to look elsewhere for sanctuary, and in most cases the United Kingdom has simply become the staging point to gain entry into the United States on fraudulently obtained passports.

DRUGS AND FIREARMS

Once in the United Kingdom, the Yardies who blend into the community, usually become involved in drug-related crime. Drug sales are made predominantly to other residents and the violence, which is usually drug-related, is directed towards those who live there. However, the crime spills over into other areas of the community with burglary and robbery being committed outside the defined areas.

The traditional use of marijuana has now given way to cocaine and 'crack cocaine'. Heavily armoured doors, alarmed and protected by locks and grills, define the perimeters of the drug houses. The use of pagers and mobile phones are common amongst the dealers, but the greatest concern of all is their increased use of firearms.

British police, for the most part, are unarmed, but alarmingly it seems that more and more Jamaican drug dealers settle their disputes with a firearm. The fatal shooting of 'Yardie Ron' on the streets of a busy London suburb during a drug dispute, is evidence of this fact. Eight shots were fired from three different weapons, an occurrence which is totally alien to the United Kingdom.

It is difficult to ascertain whether Yardie crime is organized and comparable to other gangs like the Costra Nostra. One key element of organized crime is evident however – providing illegal goods or services. Without question these groups are involved in the supply of drugs and to a certain extent, prostitution. They also use force and violence. In contrast though, there is no central control or brotherhood structure, so Yardies have few affiliations or loyalties. Gangs appear to be very loose knit and often fall out with one another. Members are mostly linked to drug and arms dealing as well as robbery. It is a lifestyle synonymous with violence – impulse shootings and gangland-style executions are used to sort out internal squabbles.

Since then their reputation for ruthless violence has grown with each shooting. In 1993 the Yardies were blamed for the cold-blooded murder of PC Patrick Dunne, who was on patrol in Clapham when he stumbled across a shooting incident.

The gangsters hit the headlines again in 1997 when police tactics to infiltrate the underworld were exposed in a television documentary.

THE YARDIES TODAY

A network of drug dealers, with direct links to the notorious Yardie gangs operating in the English Midlands, has moved into Fraserburgh, Scotland.

Afro-Caribbean drug barons, supplying heroin and crack cocaine, are targeting the Banff and Buchan areas to secure a lucrative base for their operations in the north-east. The market there is estimated to be worth around £10 million a week. Their infiltration of the area has prompted fears of a violent turf war breaking out between rival drug gangs, with links to underworld leaders in Glasgow and Liverpool.

Glasgow Gangs

*It has been reported that as early as the 1700s there
used to be a weekly Saturday night stonefight across the
river Clyde. There used to be a small island in the middle
of the Clyde and gangs of boys and men used to gather
at the foot of Stockwell Street, and a similar sized gang
on the Gorbals side. Stealth was used to reach the
island, and fighting at close quarters was common on its
banks. It was only when a boy was killed that the fights
began to die away.*

There had been gangs in Ireland since the early
1700s, many of them fighting gangs in the
Glasgow tradition, such as the Shanavists, the
Caravats, and the Ruskavallas. It is probable that
a lot of the rise in gang activity in Glasgow can be
traced to the 1840s and 1850s when shiploads of
Irish immigrants, fleeing the potato famine,
landed in the west of Scotland. The catholic and
protestant divide arrived in Glasgow, a feature of
Glasgow life which still persists today.

In the late 1700s, the students of the College in
the High Street used to wage stonethrowing battles
with the uneducated youth of the city. Following
the founding of Wilson's Charity School in 1778,
the pupils there used to regularly battle with the
students of the Grammar School. In those days
there was no police force to counteract these dis-
turbances.

285

The first gangs which came to the newspapers attentions were the Penny Mob gangs of the 1870s. These gangs demanded subscriptions from their members in order to pay the fines of anyone jailed by the police – a penny a head – thus the name Penny Mob gangs. In 1883, one of these gangs, called the Ribbon Men, blew up a gasometer in Tradeston.

FAMOUS GANGS

As the century drew to a close, the courts began to stop offering fines as an alternative to jail, and the penny mob gangs died away. The small gangs began to group together for protection, and so the large area gangs came into being. These gangs were huge, and commanded the whole of a district. They were made up of many smaller gangs who fought under a common leader.

The two most famous gangs in Glasgow have got to be the Tongs and the Toi. The Toi are one of the oldest surviving gangs in Glasgow, and their origins are based in the San Toy Boys, who were recorded as active in the 1890s in the Calton area of the city. Most of the old gangs dropped their 'Boys' suffix in the late 1930s. The San Toy are thought to be named after a popular brand of cheroot sweets available earlier this century.

The San Toy in Calton were revitalized with the rise of the Calton Tongs in the 1930s, and after a renaming to San Toi, and later shortened to just Toi, they went on to become one of the legends of the gang movement.

The gang was originally a protestant gang, who fought the catholic Tim Malloys on a regular basis. One famous member was Algie Airns, who used to go to Ibrox with a Celtic scarf on, and go to Parkhead with a Rangers scarf on, so great was his liking for casual violence and fighting.

They became so big that many gangs took the name Toi in tribute, and there are over a dozen Toi gangs over the city to this day. The rise in so many copycat gangs, made the original Calton gang rename themselves THE Toi, or the Calton Toi, and they are famous for their large painted warnings YOU ARE NOW ENTERING TOI LAND, which has long since faded or been demolished. Although the original San Toi are long since gone, many Toi gangs are in existence to this day.

These gangs battled regularly, as did other gangs in Glasgow, for example, the Kelly Boys from Govan, and the Haugh Boys from Partick. A police report from the 1910s recalls that these gangs were full of men of extreme violence, in their twenties and thirties.

The coming of the First World War saw the end of the Tim Malloys. The San Toys remained in existence in various forms through to The Toi in the 1960s, when they were overthrown by the emergence of the Calton Tongs. The Baltic Fleet took over the large area catholic gang, and many Fleet gangs also survive to this day.

In 1916, the press reported on the emergence of a new large area gang, the famous Redskins. At its peak it was estimated to have had two thousand members. There was an entrance fee of two shillings, and was the most feared and organized gang of its time. They were one of the first gangs to have a dress code, whereby every member had to wear a light-coloured tweed cap. They were so large that they were not restricted to a single area of the city, and their secret whistle could bring a gang of helpers anywhere in the city.

The use of lethal force was certainly recorded before the 1920s. The Gorbals gangs, The Hammer Boys, who used hammers as their primary weapons, and the Gold Dust Gang, who had been attacking complete strangers with hammers since the turn of the century.

The late 1920s saw the arrival of the razor gangs, with the rise of the infamous Billy Boys and their various rival gangs.

ABOVE: *May 4, 1932 – Chicago, USA. American prohibition-time gangster Al Capone smiles as he smokes a cigar on his way to Atlanta Federal Penitentiary after conviction for Federal Income Tax Evasion.* BELOW: *A portrait and profile picture of Al Capone taken in 1931.* (Popperfoto)

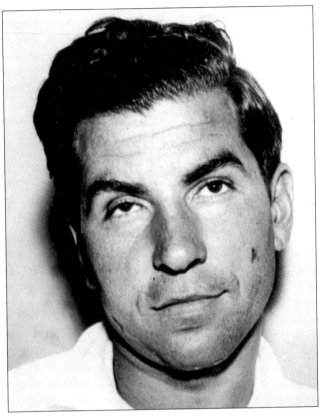

The infamous gangster, Charles Luciano was nicknamed 'Lucky' after surviving a gangland 'ride' in 1929. He had an extensive arrest record and in June, 1936, Luciano was convicted on 62 of 90 counts of compulsory prostitution and was sentenced to 30 to 50 years' imprisonment. The FBI received allegations from time to time that Luciano continued to direct criminal activities in the United States from his place of exile in his native Italy. He suffered a fatal heart attack in Italy in 1962. The above portrait of 'Lucky' was taken circa 1930s. (Popperfoto)

Circa 1932. Bonnie Parker (1910-1934) points a shotgun at boyfriend Clyde Barrow (1909-1934). Together they found infamy as 'Bonnie and Clyde' from August 1932 until they were killed at a police roadblock in May 1934. Despite their popular romantic image, they and their gang were responsible for a number of murders. (Popperfoto)

This picture of Reginald Kray was taken in January 1969, when he, his twin brother Ronald, and elder brother Charles, figured in a murder trial at The Old Bailey, London. (Popperfoto)

*Ronald Kray, aged 34. In March 1969, after an epic
trial at the Old Bailey, the twins were jailed for life
for the murders of George Cornell and Jack 'The Hat'
McVitie, both members of the London underworld.*
(Popperfoto)

Chicago, USA, February 14, 1929. The scene inside the warehouse showing dead bodies riddled with bullets after the St. Valentine's Day Massacre, a battle between rival Chicago gangsters Al Capone and Bugs Moran. (Popperfoto)

During the height of prohibition, a war between Al Capone and George 'Bugs' Moran (above) broke out in Chicago. Moran had a pathological hatred for Capone, often referring to him as 'the Beast', and this hatred culminated in the St. Valentine's Day Massacre. (Popperfoto)

WANTED

LESTER M. GILLIS,

aliases GEORGE NELSON, "BABY FACE" NELSON, ALEX GILLIS, LESTER GILES,
"BIG GEORGE" NELSON, "JIMMIE", "JIMMY" WILLIAMS .

On June 23, 1934, HOMER S. CUMMINGS, Attorney General of the United States, under the authority vested in him by an Act of Congress approved June 6, 1934, offered a reward of

$5,000.00

for the capture of Lester M. Gillis or a reward of

$2,500.00

for information leading to the arrest of Lester M. Gillis.

DESCRIPTION

Age, 25 years; Height, 5 feet 4-3/4 inches; Weight, 133 pounds; Build, medium; Eyes, yellow and grey slate; Hair, light chestnut; Complexion, light; Occupation, oiler.

All claims to any of the aforesaid rewards and all questions and disputes that may arise as among claimants to the foregoing rewards shall be passed upon by the Attorney General and his decisions shall be final and conclusive. The right is reserved to divide and allocate portions of any of said rewards as between several claimants. No part of the aforesaid rewards shall be paid to any official or employee of the Department of Justice.

If you are in possession of any information concerning the whereabouts of Lester M. Gillis, communicate immediately by telephone or telegraph collect to the nearest office of the Division of Investigation, United States Department of Justice, the local offices of which are set forth on the reverse side of this notice.

The apprehension of Lester M. Gillis is sought in connection with the murder of Special Agent W. C. Baum of the Division of Investigation near Rhinelander, Wisconsin on April 23, 1934.

JOHN EDGAR HOOVER, DIRECTOR,
DIVISION OF INVESTIGATION,
UNITED STATES DEPARTMENT OF JUSTICE,
WASHINGTON, D. C.

June 25, 1934

June 23, 1934. An American FBI wanted poster for the arrest of gangster 'Baby Face' Nelson. (Popperfoto)

A picture of Nelson (1934), a member of the Dillinger gang and regarded as the most psychotic outlaw of the 1930s, on an undertaker's slab after his assassination. (Popperfoto)

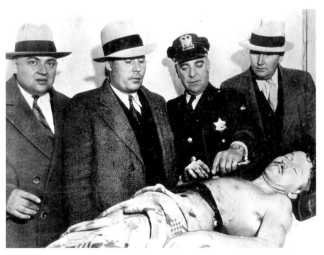

PART THREE
SICILY

The Mafia in Sicily

*For the native Sicilians, the Mafia has been accepted
as just part of life on this Mediterranean island.
It is one of the world's most enduring criminal
organizations, and one of the most serious social
problems confronting Sicily today.*

In the Middle Ages banditry and murder were
fairly commonplace in Sicily. The Mafia itself
had existed as a loose network of local criminals
only since the early nineteenth century. Its roots go
back as far as the feudal system, having humble
rustic origins not unlike those of Japan's Yakuza.
The Mafia itself developed largely as a result of
Sicilian social conditions, and there is nothing to
suggest that it existed as a hierarchical organization until the latter part of the eighteenth century.

Up until the eighteenth century many Sicilian
nobles lived on their country estates. The situation
changed, however, and by the 1700s many of the
more important titled aristocrats were now
residing in Palermo, Catania and Messina. During
their absence from their land, these nobles usually
entrusted the running of their rural estates to
managers called *gabelloti*. Before 1812, the
purchase of a feudal property made its holder the

count or baron of that fief. It was under this law that many *gabelloti* became barons themselves, by purchasing feudal lands from the men they worked for. The *gabelloti* were far worse than the aristocrats because they intimidated the poor peasants into working the estates for extremely poor wages. This often necessitated the use of local intermediaries to act as managers in such matters. These intermediaries, who today might be thought of as local Mafia bosses, rarely murdered anybody; delegating that particular job to their subordinates. Consequently the myth of the 'benevolent' mafioso was born. In fact some of the more corrupt *gabelloti* actually became important mafiosi.

When feudalism was abolished, it became even more important to control baronial interests by using force. This abolition resulted in higher rents, and by the 1850s it was clear that the mafiosi were also prepared to represent an ordinary farmer or tradesman – if they were to prepared to pay – in order to settle an argument or apparent injustice. This led to the perception of the mafiosi as being 'Robin Hoods' or even 'men of honour'. Of course, in truth, the Mafia were the complete opposite. Although the nobility may not have actually created the Mafia, it was through conflicting law enforcement that it unwittingly permitted the development of social conditions that accelerated its growth.

In Sicily the word *Mafia* tends to mean 'manhood', and is often applied to someone without necessarily meaning they were a criminal. This term has become synonymous with the Mafia's code of silence. Much of the Mafia's structure was based on those of the Catholic confraternities and even Freemasonry, coloured by Sicilian family traditions and customs. The duel, for example, gave way to the vendetta, but both were known among Sicilian feuding families in times past.

INVASIONS OF SICILY

Over the years Sicily has had to adapt to numerous invasions. In the ninth century it was the Arabs, in the eleventh the Normans, the twelfth the French, the Spanish in the fifteenth, as well as invasions by the Germans, Austrians and Greeks.

Because of these invasions secret societies were formed in the hills to resist foreign rulers. These societies were there not only to defeat the invading French but also to protect and feed the Italian families in the villages of Palermo and surrounding areas. As most of the villagers were related, each village chose a member to represent their family. These heads of families were called *capodecina* or *capos* for short. It was up to these *capodecina* to pick men from the village to take with them back to the hills. Before the men left for the hills they would have to pledge their loyalty, support and omertá.

The pledge, when translated into English, would sound like this:

'I (name) want to enter into this secret organization to protect my family and to protect my brothers "morte alla Francia Italia anelia!" with my blood. [*A knife is used to place a cut on the right index finger or hand*] and the blood of all the saints, and the souls of my children. [*The sign of the cross is made*] I swear not to divulge this secret and to obey with love and omertá. I enter alive into this organization and leave it only in death.'

Once the men were safe in the hills, all the *capos* would get together and pick someone to be in charge of all the members of this secret society. This person would be called *Capo di tutti capo* (the boss of all the families).

Conditions at this time were deplorable, food was scarce, and the French Angevins controlled everything. If the Sicilians didn't do what the French commanded, they would torture and kill the offender. Members of the society, however, would raid supplies and weapons from the French and distribute their wares throughout the villages. To protect their families from torture, it was essential that the members operated in complete secrecy. It was a totally honorable society in the fact that you had to totally believe in its cause and be willing to die to protect the members. The villagers totally honoured and respected these soldiers from the hills, because they realised it was their only chance of freedom from the French.

Joining the society was like joining a religion. It was a lifelong commitment and one that you could not possibly retire from. This society has survived through many centuries, it is secret, and only members know other members.

HOW THE SOCIETY CHANGED

Throughout the centuries the leaders and soldiers have changed the face of this society – some for the better, some for the worst. Once, the men from the hills only stole to feed and protect their families. Indeed they were so good at it that they ended up with more food and supplies than they knew what to do with. In order to get things that they could not steal they started dealing with mainland Italy and other countries. This was the start of black market trading.

By 1900, each town had its own resident *capo* or chief, and when the Fascists rose to power, Benito Mussolini's 'Iron Prefect', Cesare Mori, threw most of them into jail. In reality, the relationship between the Fascists and the Mafia was that of one group of criminals fighting against one another. It was during this time that many society members fled to America to escape Mussolini's attempt to eradicate the Mafia in Sicily.

Don Calogero Vizzini is the perfect example of an old style Mafia Don. Don Vizzini was the supreme head of the Sicilian Mafia around the same time that Lucky Luciano ran operations in America. Throughout World War II, Vizzini welcomed the help of his American Sicilian allies who had joined forces with the U.S. Navy against Mussolini. This was of great benefit to Vizzini, who was given the honorary rank of Colonel, and to many of his colleagues who were named Mayors of various small neighbouring towns. Don Calogero Vizzini was probably one of the last true

Sicilian mafiosos, soon to be replaced by a more violent, vulgar, and ill-mannered generation.

When the Allies liberated Italy in World War II, they freed anti-Mussolini prisoners, including many society members. Some were installed in positions of power and consequently began to interweave politics and organized crime in Italy. The societies moved down from the rural hills into the cities of Sicily.

In the immediate years following the war, as the Mafia set about the task of re-organizing its activities, several freelance bandits roamed the countryside. The most popular of these, Salvatore Giuliano, came closest to the image of a modern Robin Hood. Giuliano was a bandit who fought for the well-being of Sicily and its inhabitants. He was a fair, courageous, strong and intelligent leader for many Italians, and especially the Sicilian peasants. Giuliano was respected for his use of violence and seemed to fit their image of the perfect Sicilian. It appeared Giuliano was pushed into being a bandit by Sicily's unfair and harsh police force, and his mission was to make Sicily independent from Italy. Ideally he would have liked Sicily to become a state of the United States, as Sicily was already closely related to the United States due to the great number of Sicilian-Americans in America.

Men like Giuliano were not mafiosi. Indeed, the mafiosi resented and feared them. With the death of Calogero Vizzini in 1954, the Mafia slid into the realm of 'gangsterism', a more reckless American style of crime. In 1957, the Sicilian Mafia re-established ties with their brethren in the United

States and Canada. It was Lucky Luciano, of all people, who orchestrated this alliance.

Unlike Vizzini and his generation, the new Sicilian 'men of honour' were uncouth people who made no pretension whatsoever to be gentlemen. Whereas, Vizzini and people like him, maintained at least a veneer of civility in the face of the public. It was blatantly obvious that newcomers like Genco Russo, Michele Greco and Luciano Leggio were essentially vulgar by nature. 'Men of honour' and the 'code of honour' – if indeed either had ever existed – vanished in an outbreak of murders. By the 1970s, even women and children were not spared in the carnage.

During the 1960s, the Sicilian 'Cupola' and the American 'Commission' began to seriously take control of the massive drug trafficking operations, despite their expressed opinions that heroin and cocaine were somehow less 'respectable' products than extortion and murder. The Sicilian branch of the society was more ruthless than its American counterpart, often resorting to the murder of judges and other public officials whose activities they considered inconvenient or 'in the way'. Palermo's Falcone-Borsellino Airport is named after two such judges, and there is a monument in Piazza 13 Vittime (13 Victims) at the end of Palermo's Via Cavour, dedicated to the memory of people killed by the Mafia.

During the 1970s a Palermo-centred network headed by Gaetano Badalamenti had accumulated substantial profits from drug shipments into America. This provoked the wrath of a growing contingent of younger bosses from the provinces, known as the 'Corleonesi', after the rural town of Corleone which was the birthplace of their most audacious leaders. The pursuit for the control of the narcotics traffic was a vital element in the rise to power of this continent between the years 1979 and 1983. During those years they not only assassinated the leaders of Palermo's principal Mafia families, but killed some 15 police officers, magistrates and government officials who were considered to be in their way.

THE 'MAXI-TRIALS'

It was this 'Mafia war' of the early 1980s that saw a level of aggressiveness never before witnessed by the Sicilian people. This extreme violence triggered the prosecution in 1986–1987 of some 460 mafiosi in a 'maxi-trial' in Palermo.

Never before in the history of the Mafia had so many men of honour faced trial at the same time. These trials were the culmination of years of hard work by many magistrates, and most particularly judges Giovanni Falcone and Paulo Borselino. The Maxi Trial took place next to the prison in Palermo, in a bunker specially designed for the purpose. Most of the crucial evidence came from Tomasso Buscetta, who was an old school mafiosi captured in Brazil and extradited back to Italy to face trial for his own crimes. It was a tragic turn of events that made Tomasso Buscetta defect and co-operate with the Sicilian magistrates. Both of Buscettas sons had been murdered by the

Corleonesi, who continued its vendetta against Buscetta by killing several more of his relatives. So in fear for his own life and that of his remaining family, he felt the only way was to co-operate, and testify against the men to whom he once swore his loyalty.

On trial were some of the really high-ranking members of the Sicilian Cosa Nostra. Bosses like Pipo Calo, Michele Greco and many many more caporegimes, consiglieris, underbosses, soldiers and associates from all across the Island of Sicily. The magistrates had done a superb job in putting the case together and collecting all the evidence in order to deliver a crippling blow to the Mafia. For many of the Mafiosi the testimony of Tomasso Buscetta was to be the final nail in their coffin. Here for the first time was a man who had spent a lifetime inside the Mafia, and who was willing to testify against them.

The information that Buscetta gave judges Falcone and Borselino was, without doubt, priceless. He gave a new understanding to how the Mafia functioned, and how the clandestine groups of hierarchy in the Sicilian Cupola actually agreed on policy and business. For the first time the Mafia was to be prosecuted as an entity rather than a collection of individual crimes. The case took longer than first estimated, and it wasn't until November 1987 when the convictions were finally brought to bear. In total 344 defendants were found guilty and sentenced to a total of 2,665 years imprisonment. Both Michele Greco and Franchesco Madonia were sentenced to life in prison, as were Toto Riina and Bernardo Provenzano, both of whom were on the run, even though they never left Palermo.

The remaining defendants escaped judgement due to a lack of evidence, eighteen of which were murdered by the Mafia. But despite this the Maxi Trial was hailed a huge success and paved the way for further Maxi trials although none proved to be as big as this one. The Maxi Trial signified a possible turning point in the fight against the Mafia for many Sicilians and gave hope to many native Sicilians.

In 1992 judges Falcone and Borselino were brutally murdered on the orders of Toto Riina. It was this act that united the Island of Sicily against the Mafia, as thousands of native Sicilians would walk the streets, denouncing the Mafia for the first time ever.

THE MAFIOSI AND POLITICS

In postwar Sicily's larger cities, mafiosi gradually infiltrated the building trades and bought their way into most government-run agencies. Urban planning was undertaken by criminals. In fact the Mafia, directly or indirectly, built nearly half of the 'new' city of Palermo.

It is amazing that such an organization has survived into the twenty-first century. Probably high unemployment, widespread lack of confidence in the competence of law enforcement authorities, and distrust of the state, were the contributory factors. But the general secretiveness of the people

299

was one of the main reasons organized crime was still so powerful in the Italian South. The Italian ethos was based on the realities of everyday life – they presumed that their elected leaders were thieves motivated by greed; while businessmen presumed that their associates would steal at the first opportunity.

Entire economic sectors – hotels, transportation, banking, construction – were controlled by the mafiosi. Public monies were the Mafia's main target and it appeared that everything had its price. Most politicians and managers of the larger banks could be bought, while many public or semi-public jobs were sold for money or sex. Public contracts were sold in exchange for bribes and kickbacks and this was all part of 'The New Mafia'. In such a climate, the *pizzo* or protection money and narcotics trades were little more than a side line.

CLEANING UP SICILY

The mayor of Palermo, Leoluca Orlando, fought organized crime for more than sixteen years.

In 1992, the crusading judges Giovanni Falcone and Paolo Borselino were killed and police informers claimed that Orlando was to be next, but he was spared by his enemies. In some years, there were as many as 250 Mafia-related murders in Palermo. For many years, Orlando lived like a prisoner, forced to return to the safety of a police bunker after public appearances. It was not only the Sicilian gangsters who were trying to get rid of him, but many politicians wanted him out of the way as well. Apparently both the Socialist and the Christian Democratic parties were so against Orlando, they were riddled with people linked to the Mafia.

Over the years Orlando proved that in order to fight the Mafia, effective police actions were not sufficient, there was a need to build an anti-Mafia culture among the citizens.

Supporters of Benito Mussolini and his 'hard-fisted rule' claim that he showed how to crack down on the Mafia. When Mussolini was ruling Italy in the 1930s, the big Mafiosi went into exile and enjoyed the fame of political refugees, and the police arrested only low-ranking gangsters.

One strategy was to reduce the Mafia's visibility and restore an active and strong state. That's why Orlando and his team took control of the bidding for public purchases. After years when many Sicilian children were taught in rooms rented by the city from the Mafia, new schools and renovations for the old ones could now be funded by the city. The city also started to support families of imprisoned low-ranking gangsters, and these prisoners turned against the Mafia. As a member of the Italian and European parliaments, Orlando helped to enact new laws against corruption.

Palermo still has a high unemployment rate – about 28 per cent – but it is now a modern and fast-developing city. While the Mafia has loosened its grip on the city and in the region, it has not yet been totally defeated.

Bernardo Provenzano

Luciano Liggio said of Provenzano:
'He has the brains of a chicken
but shoots like an angel'.

Bernardo Provenzano was born on January 31, 1933 in Corleone. After World War II Provenzano joined the Mafia family of boss Michele Navarra and became an enforcer for Luciano Liggio within that family.

It wasn't long before Provenzano and another young man named Toto Riina, became Liggio's most trusted enforcers. Riina would later become known as one of the most vicious Mafia bosses ever. Both were soon to become greatly feared and gained a reputation for being totally ruthless. Provenzano was given the nickname 'The Tractor', because supposedly 'he mows people down'. With people like Riina and Provenzano behind him, Liggio grew more and more powerful and eventually became a threat to Navarra himself.

Navarra was aware that Liggio was a threat and decided it was time to 'remove' him so he could continue his rule uninterrupted. Navarra sent a group of his men to ambush Liggio, but they failed in the quest and only managed to wound him.

With the assistance of Riina he managed to escape.

Now it was Liggio's turn to strike, and he put together a group of hitmen including Provenzano and Riina to wipe out Navarra. This time, however, Liggio's group of hitmen succeeded where Navarra's men had failed. Liggio's group ambushed Navarra while he was driving back from a meeting. The group of young assassins riddled the car in which Navarra sat with 112 bullets, killing both Navarra and another person who just happened to be along for the ride. With Navarra out of the way Luciano Liggio became the new Godfather.

Navarra's death upset a lot of mafiosi, not only because they had lost an ally, but also because it was a breach of the Mafia code that you didn't kill your own boss. These mafiosi, along with Navarra supporters who wanted to avenge their boss, made it very dangerous for Liggio and his two enforcers Provenzano and Riina to stay in the limelight.

ON THE RUN

In the early 1960s the heat became too much for Provenzano. Sensing that he would soon be either arrested or killed he took off and disappeared in the countryside of Sicily. During his time on the run he fathered two sons, but continued to spend most his days looking over his shoulder. The Italian authorities, who had declared him a missing person, presumed he had been killed expecting any day that his body would turn up. But they couldn't have been further from the truth.

While he was on the run Provenzano had continued his criminal career, a career that came to new heights when his old pal Toto Riina became the new boss. While Riina took care of the violent aspect of mob business and stepped into the foreground, Provenzano remained in hiding taking care of the money aspect of mob business. Provenzano made sure that everybody paid and all the Mafiosi got their share.

As the drug money came flowing in, a power struggle ensued over who was to take control of it. Riina went on a rampage in a war that would leave 800 mafiosi dead. When the government decided that enough was enough and started cracking down on the Mafia, Riina hit back. Two top prosecutors were killed by bombs, and in fact anyone who opposed him was found dead. The campaign of terror that was supposed to scare off the people and government, had the opposite effect, the government went in even harder and the public was now in their favour. The people had seen the brutal image of the Mafia and were sickened by it. As the hunt for Riina became more intense, Provenzano, who was still in hiding, was presumed dead. When his wife and children returned from the countryside in 1992, talk about Provenzano's death flared up once again. However, without a body nobody could be sure.

RULE UNDER PROVENZANO

On January 15, 1993, Toto Riina was arrested by the Italian police in Palermo. The arrest of Riina placed Provenzano at the top of a criminal empire which was under fire not only from law enforcement but also from fierce competition. It was obvious that changes needed to be made.

Under Provenzano the Sicilian Mafia steered away from its terror tactics towards the government and slithered back into the underworld. Out of sight the Mafia restructured, returning to its original roots. The Sicilian Mafia, under the guidance of Provenzano, has once again become the invisible power. It has expanded its interests while managing to keep clear from law enforcement. Provenzano commands his troops via cryptic, handwritten notes carried by key members of his organization. There are occasional visits and very occasional summits with Mafia leaders, but otherwise Provenzano is a ghost – still presumed dead – but feared to be running the most powerful Sicilian Mafia in decades.

Police believe he spends most of his time in western and central Sicily going from one safe house to another. In January of 2001 police intercepted several letters by Provenzano to his family, proving that he was still very much alive. But the letters were as close as police would get to Provenzano, who seems totally unfindable even to this day. While other bosses and Mafiosi have been caught one by one, Provenzano has been on the run for almost forty years.

John Stanfa

After the Scarfo years which crippled the Philadelphia Crime Family, law enforcement and mobsters all agreed John Stanfa was going to get the Family back on its feet.

John Stanfa was born on December 7, 1940 in the tiny mountain village of Caccamo, about thirty miles southeast of Palermo. This was a region of western Sicily which had long been dominated by the Mafia. Stanfa was the youngest of four children, and he already had two older brothers and one brother-in-law who were members of the Sicilian Mafia.

John went to the United States with his wife Nicolena Congialdi and settled in Philadelphia. In 1967 their first child Sara was born, followed by Joseph four years later and finally Maria in 1976. Stanfa went by unnoticed in his early years. The FBI had seen him hanging around notorious spots but didn't even consider him a big associate of the Mafia. He was a stonemason and bricklayer by trade, and was set up in business by his friend Carlo Gambino, the New York Mafia Boss. Gambino was a friend of Philadelphia Mafia Boss Angelo Bruno, and Gambino helped Stanfa as a favour for his Sicilian friends. When Bruno was killed Stanfa was in the seat next to him. It has been said that Stanfa was in on the plot to kill

Bruno, but when questioned he didn't say anything. On May 14, 1980 he was indicted on perjury charges, but rather than face the charges Stanfa fled and went into hiding. With the help of his Gambino contacts he set himself up with a girlfriend, deserting his wife and three children. After eight months Stanfa came out of hiding and on April 21, 1981 he was sentenced to eight years in prison for lying to the grand jury.

It was during this time that Nicodemo Scarfo took over as the new boss. At the end of Scarfo's reign, around 1987, the Family was in big trouble because Scarfo had attracted a lot of attention from law enforcement officers. Eventually they built up enough evidence and Scarfo and his associates received lengthy prison sentences.

APPOINTED BOSS

In 1987 Stanfa was released from prison and for several years managed to keep a very low profile. He spent some time in Sicily and New York before returning to Philadelphia in late 1989 or early 1990. At the time Anthony Piccolo was acting boss but he made it quite clear that he wanted to step down from the position. With Piccolo's and the Gambino and Genovese families' backing, Stanfa was appointed the new boss. Piccolo became his consigliere and eventually 33-year-old Joseph Ciancaglini Jr., the son of a jailed Scarfo Capo, became Underboss.

As a boss Stanfa often talked about Scarfo's weaknesses when he was the *capo*, yet in a lot of ways he acted in the same way. Stanfa brought back street tax, whereby every criminal had to pay a tax on his activities. This generated a lot of tension and threats of violence on the streets of Philadelphia, creating an atmosphere that would not be good for business. Stanfa used a man called Felix Bocchino to collect his street tax. It appeared things were running smoothly and that street tax was an easy way to make money, but then Felix Bocchino was killed. The media went crazy and called it the first mob hit in seven years. At first both Stanfa and the FBI had no clue as to who was behind the murder but soon things became clear.

In South Philadelphia there were a group of young thugs who were relatives of Philadelphia mobsters, and who didn't feel connected to the new administration. The youngsters were led by Joseph 'Skinny Joey' Merlino, a young, flashy, good-looking thug, and the son of former Scarfo Underboss Salvatore Merlino. Other youngsters in Merlino's group were: Steven Mazzone, Marty Angelina, George Borgesi (whose father was an imprisoned Scarfo hitman), Gaetano 'Tommy Horsehead' Scafidi and Vince Iannece (whose father was a jailed Scarfo soldier). Merlino and his friends were already running things and were doing pretty well for themselves. By this time the street tax was already in place and so when Bocchino came around collecting what they felt was their money, he had to be eliminated. The Bocchino hit would be the first casualty in the war between the young mobsters and the old school Cosa Nostra gangsters.

It wasn't long before Stanfa found out about the 'young turks', as they would later be called by the media, and took appropriate action. There was an attempted hit on Merlino's second-in-command Michael Ciancaglini. Michael was 29, and the son of a jailed Scarfo *capo*. Stanfa decided that he could use some new blood and employed some Sicilian soldiers – Biagio Adornetto and Rosario Bellocchi. By autumn of 1992 Stanfa began to plot the demise of the Merlino organization. In September Stanfa held a secret ceremony in which Merlino, Michael Ciancaglini and Adornetto were inducted into the Philadelphia Family as made members. People around Stanfa warned him that these youngsters were no good and that they would bring the whole thing down, but Stanfa said he knew and would take care of it.

Meanwhile the two Sicilian mobsters that Stanfa had inducted into his Family started making advances towards his daughter Sara. Adornetto was rejected by her and this would set the stage for another attempted assassination. Adornetto started bad-mouthing the administration and Bellocchi, and consequently something had to be done, and quickly. Bellocchi went to visit his friend carrying a shotgun, but the shotgun jammed and Adornetto escaped.

Stanfa then decided it was time to get rid of the 'young turk' Merlino. Merlino had annoyed Stanfa once again, because Merlino liked to bet, but didn't like to settle his debts. Merlino, however was one step ahead of Stanfa, and on March 2, 1992, Stanfa's Underboss Joey Chang was hit in his social club. He was shot in the head, neck and chest, but somehow managed to survive his wounds. He was, however, too wounded to ever again become an active Mafia member, and at the age of 35 he retired. Stanfa was infuriated. It turned out that Merlino got advice from Joe Ciancaglini Sr. (Joey Chang's father) and his father Salvatore Merlino. Merlino had also made some contacts in prison, his cellmate being Ralph Natale, a 64-year-old Bruno Family member who was doing time for arson and drug trafficking. Natale would prove to be a serious rival to Stanfa when he was released from parole. Even more worrying was the fact that Natale had ties to New York – ties that would like to see Stanfa out of the way. Merlino, on the other hand, was backed by the Genovese Family.

Stanfa moved fast and ordered the assassination of Merlino and his two top associates. But his plan did not come to fruition because by the summer of 1993 Merlino and friends were still alive and kicking. It wasn't until August 5, 1993, in a drive-by shooting that Merlino and his second-in-command Michael Ciancaglini were shot down. Ciancaglini was dead but Merlino survived having only been hit in his backside. Even though Merlino survived Stanfa was happy because he felt he was now on top of things – but how wrong he was!

Stanfa, still high on the success of the drive-by shooting, became careless. On August 31, 1993, while he was driving to work with his son Joe and driver, went straight into an ambush. While he was stuck in traffic a van pulled up beside them, the side doors opened and bullets were pumped through Stanfa's car. Stanfa's son was hit in the face, while the driver managed to get the car away from the van and escaped with Stanfa and his wounded son. Luckily Joe survived, but for Stanfa this meant all-out war. The FBI agreed, mob hits in shady back alleys was one thing, but mob hits on a busy highway was another and so they turned up the heat on the Philadelphia mobsters. Stanfa wanted the entire Merlino faction wiped out, and for several weeks hit men from both families were on the look out for targets. Two Merlino associates were shot, which caused Merlino and his top associates to go underground. One of Merlino's men even changed sides – Tommy 'Horsehead' Scafidi, joined forces with Stanfa.

On November 15 Merlino was arrested by the FBI and charged with violating his parole, and by November 23 he was back in jail.

In the meantime, Stanfa had some other problems to deal with as he discovered he had an informer in his Family. Stanfa ordered the hit but it failed, and the man escaped with two bullets in his head. Stanfa knew that this meant big trouble for him. On March 17, 1994, Stanfa and twenty-three of his top associates were indicted on racketeering charges that included murder, murder conspiracy, extortion, arson, kidnapping and obstruction of justice. Stanfa knew he had informers but was unsure where all the information came from. It turned out that the FBI had bugged Stanfa right from the early weeks of his reign as boss. The entire war and mob business were caught on tape by the FBI. This vital evidence, along with that of the informers, would bring the entire Family down. Stanfa knew his rule as Boss was over and took it like a man. In November of 1995 John Stanfa was sentenced to five consecutive life sentences.

Tomasso Buscetta

Tomasso Buscetta knew even from an early age what he wanted from life – to be a part of the Mafiosi. But it was not long before he turned his back on the Cosa Nostra for personal reasons.

Tomasso Buscetta was highly regarded within the Mafia throughout Sicily. He was part of the Porta Nuova family, which was one of the many clans that resided in Palermo. Tomasso knew even from an early age what he wanted from life – 'I was already a Mafiosi even before I was made' he once told a Judge when being debriefed in 1984.

As a teenager he ran errands for the Mafiosi, and in his early twenties he was inducted formerly into the Mafia. Buscetta was very much an old style Mafiosi, passionately strict to his vow of omertá and living proof of what Cosa Nostra is all about. He was an incredibly vain man and kept an air of respectability with anyone he came into contact with. He impressed many throughout the world of Cosa Nostra and his reputation reached almost mythical proportions, not only in Sicily, but also across the Atlantic in America, where his name became known to many of the New York men of honour.

313

Tomasso Buscetta also attended one of the most important Mafia summits of all. In 1957 bosses from America met with the Sicilian godfathers in a hotel in Palermo. Others that attended were Lucky Luciano and Joe Bonanno who helped reshape the volatile Sicilian clans, putting in place a ruling commission that would be headed by the top bosses in Sicily. This Sicilian commission came to be known as the Cupola, and it was the Cupola that brought some unity to the extremely violent Sicilian clans.

Buscetta fled Sicily in the sixties using a false passport and spent the next ten years travelling between Canada, America and Brazil, where, according to American police, he operated a major drugs ring.

He married a beautiful Brazilian girl, but when her entire family was arrested on drugs charges Buscetta was sent back to Sicily to serve his sentence for a murder that had been hanging over his head since 1968. When he was eventually released from prison in 1980 he once again fled to his wife in Brazil, staying out of internal Mafia politics in Sicily.

TURNING HIS BACK ON THE MAFIA

In 1982 when Buscetta's two sons disappeared, the Sicilian police expected Buscetta to return to Sicily. But the next time he was actually to return, it was with a police escort. When he was arrested in Brazil, Buscetta tried to commit suicide, but when the attempt was unsuccessful he had no choice but to turn his back on his beloved Mafia.

Buscetta's defection was easy for him to make as he could now avenge the murders of his children. He was debriefed by Giovanni Falcone, and over the next few months the two men worked up quite a relationship as Falcone was the only judge Buscetta really trusted. His testimony was vital because here, for the first time, was a man that had spent a lifetime within the Mafia. In fact he was the first major Sicilian boss *pentiti* or informer who turned on his kin. His knowledge became the essential part of the Maxi Trial that took place in 1984. He gave the authorities their first real look inside the Mafia and his knowledge would also give the magistrates the chance to build future Maxi trials. As it turned out Buscetta would do much more damage to the Sicilian Mafia than he would in the trial of Badalamenti *et al*.

After the first trial Tomasso Buscetta insisted that he be moved in to the witness protection programme in the United States, as he didn't trust the Italian authorities to keep him safe.

Whilst he was in the United States he also gave evidence at the 'pizza connection' case in New York, where he testified against a huge drugs and money laundering ring. This case was brought about by Rudy Giuliani, the US Attorney in Manhattan, and once again Buscetta was the star witness.

The defence lawyers tried to make out that Buscetta was a liar, but to no avail. They had no chance, however, because his history within the Mafia was too difficult to refute.

On April 4, 2000, Buscetta died from cancer in

the United States knowing full well his debt to society had been fully repaid. It was his knowledge into the inner workings of how the Mafia worked on two continents that had been crucial in two major trials, which resulted in the convictions of major figures within the Mafia.

Salvatore 'Toto' Riina

Salvatore Riina of the Corleonesi, a peasant from
Corleone, was probably one of the most feared bosses
ever to sit on the Commission of the Sicilian
Mafia – the Cupolla.

Toto Riina was born on November 16, 1930 in
Corleone. He served his apprenticeship in the
Corleonesi under the infamous Luciano Liggio.
Toto's status within the Corleonesi soared when he
saved the life of his mentor. Liggio was ambushed
by a gang sent from a rival clan headed by Michele
Navarra. Although they both were wounded it was
Toto's instinct to protect his boss and get him to
safety that undoubtedly saved his life. Soon after
this attempt on Liggio's life the pair sought
retribution by killing the then head of the Cupolla,
Dr. Michele Navarra.

Leggio took over what Navarra left behind and
although the Cupola wasn't exactly happy with
Leggio's actions, they made no moves to punish
him. Riina began to seek power by forming a
friendship with influential men of honour belonging to respective clans, some even as far as
Napoli. His method was extremely subtle, as he
managed to fuel rifts in families in order to recruit

317

younger men of honour. This would serve Riina well when he took over the Corleonesi clan in the mid-seventies following the imprisonment of Leggio. Riina sat on the Cupola as one of three men who divided the power equally between them.

Around this time Riina was heavily involved in the distribution of heroin, and his greed sparked off a power struggle for control of the massive profits the Corleonesi were already enjoying. Toto began plotting the deaths of the men with whom he shared the power of the Cupola. First of all Salvatore Inzerello was murdered, followed shortly after by Stefano Bontade. This brought havoc to Sicily and as a result over a thousand men of honour died in a bloody war that threatened to engulf the entire Sicilian Cosa Nostra. However, after the smoke had cleared, Toto Riina became the boss of bosses in Sicily.

He was backed up by powerful bosses such as Michele Greco and Pipo Calo who became the new power on the Cupola. Riina enjoyed a couple of peaceful years but there was a dark cloud on the horizon in the shape of Tomasso Buschetta and his crucial testimony in the Maxi Trials.

Tomasso Buschetta was arrested in Brazil and returned to Italy to face his crimes. He fled to Brazil originally because he openly opposed the Corleonesi led by Riina. Buschetta, angered by the murder of his two sons, began to co-operate with the authorities as an act of vengeance on the notorious Corleonesi. Buschetta testified at the Maxi Trials in Palermo where over 400 Mafiosi were convicted. Although many of these convictions were overturned by a corrupt judge, Judge Carnevale, nicknamed the 'sentence killer'.

Riina was also convicted even though he never attended the Maxi Trials. Riina was supposedly a fugitive even though he never left Palermo. For nearly twenty years Riina avoided arrest. This was largely due to the fact that many law enforcement officers were paid off to enable Riina to walk around Sicily like a free man.

But this only lasted until 1993 when Riina was picked up in Palermo, a victim of the massive police crackdown sweeping across southern Italy. The authorities and public were outraged at the senseless murders of two anti-Mafia judges, Giovanni Falcone and Paulo Borselino. Riina became a victim of his own arrogance, thinking that he could dominate the state rather than co-exist with it.

Toto Riina is serving life behind bars and his underboss Bernardo Provenzano is now the head of the Cupola.

Luciano Leggio

Leggio is described as a violent and bloodthirsty criminal who had undeniable talents as a leader and organizer. His rise through the ranks is the story of how the Mafia transformed from good to bad.

The story of Leggio is the story of changing times in post-war Sicily. Before World War II the Mafia was under much persecution at the hands of Mussolini's fascist government who sought to abolish the Mafia. Following Mussolini's defeat, the Allied powers were anxious to find anti-fascist support in Italy, and they found it in the Mafia. As a result of the Allied invasion of Sicily in 1943 many mafioso found themselves in political positions, which helped to restore the strength of the Mafia which had been weakened by the efforts of Mussolini. Out of this newly acquired strength arose Luciano Leggio.

Whereas most up and coming *picciotto*, or lower members of the Mafia, came from wealthy mafioso, Leggio came from a peasant family which had ten children. He was born in 1925 and dropped out of school in the fourth grade. Leggio also suffered from Pott's disease, a tubercular spinal ailment, and had to wear a leg brace. At the age of 19, he was denounced for possession of illegal firearms and arrested for stealing sacks of wheat. Six months later the guard who caught Leggio was murdered, and so began the life of a fugitive, murderer, and one of the most powerful mafioso in Italian history.

HIS RISE IN THE MAFIA

After the war the Mafia was in the legitimate business of buying up land in Sicily. They would rent these estates to people and collect a percentage of the profit made from the land. Owners of these estates were known as *gabellotti* and this is how Leggio made his entrance into the business of the Mafia. At the age of 20 he became the youngest *gabellotto* in Italy. He did not go about it in the traditional sense, which would mean he would buy out the previous *gabellotto*, instead he used his own style which included killing the *gabellotto* of a large farm in Corleone and taking control of the estate. The acquisition of this estate was noticed by the mafioso in charge of Corleone, Dr. Michele Navarra. Navarra recognized the talent and determination of Leggio and appointed him his lieutenant.

After the Strasetto estate was firmly established, Leggio started up a livestock business. He organized the theft of livestock and undercover slaughtering for Navarra in Corleone. During these days as a cattle rustler Leggio was continually being investigated by a man called Placido Rizzotto, a labour agitator in Palermo. In 1948, having had enough of Rizzotto, Leggio kidnapped and murdered him. The only witness was a peasant boy who saw Leggio drop Rizzotto's body into a hole in the countryside. The boy was hysterical and went into shock upon telling his mother what he had seen. The boy was very conveniently treated by Dr. Navarra and shortly after died of toxicosis.

Working as Navarra's lieutenant did not satisfy Leggio, however. As Italy's economy recovered and expanded, so did Leggio. Over the next ten years Leggio would rise high in the esteem of many of his fellow Corleonesi members, something that wasn't to go unnoticed by Navarra. In 1958 it was decision time for Navarra and Leggio, as the two men decided Corleone was only big enough for one of them.

The first to make a move was Navarra, who sent fifteen gunmen after Leggio. However, Leggio with the help of his own lieutenant, Toto Riina, managed to escape through a tunnel designed for that very purpose, barely wounded. Over the next three months Leggio recuperated and had plenty of time to plot his revenge.

On August 2, 1958, Navarra was driving home one night from his practice with another doctor who had decided to take Navarra's offer of a lift home, when they were big by a barrage of bullets. In fact Navarra's car was hit with such force that 76 bullets ended up inside Navarra's dead carcass. Meanwhile the remainder of Navarra's followers, and indeed anyone else who had denounced the actions of Leggio, were hunted down and slaughtered as Leggio instantly made his mark on the Corleone and the rest of the Sicilian Mafia.

The Palermo Mafia now had three principle groups. The Bontate, Badalmenti, Spatola, Inzerillo, and Buscetta families were one group, Leggio and the Corleonesi were another, and the Greco family was the third. Leggio quickly formed affiliations with the Greco family, and for a while the Mafia was at peace. However, this tranquillity would only last for a short time. Leggio went on and took his place in the ranks of the Mafia's infamous, the Corleonesi clan would never be the same again and Sicily would soon see how the new regime would change the Mafia into a murderous entity that no one had seen the like of before.

MURDERS GALORE

During the next sixteen years the Corleonesi was responsible for many of the bodies that were constantly turning up in and around Corleone, Palermo, and the rest of Sicily. Leggio was now the most powerful godfather in Sicily, and even if anyone disagreed with Leggio's murderous techniques they would never dare take him on or his mighty, influential, and deadly Corleone clan. At this time the Corleone were playing a huge part in heroin refining and exportation. Having loyal underlings was always a blessing for any godfather, and Salvatore Riina and Bernardo Provenzano were just that. Leggio, Riina and Provenzano all shared the same violent and murderous tendencies. It was these three men who were the real power behind the Corleonesi's reign within the Sicilian Mafia.

In May of 1971 Mauro de Mauro, a journalist, was shot and Pietro Scaglione, attorney general of Palermo, was murdered. These two cases were surprising because this is first time that journalists and judges had been the targets. All this was carried out at the request of Leggio. These attacks, and further murders led to a divide in the Mafia. On one side was the Bontate, Badalmenti, and Inzerillo families, and the other was the Greco family and the Corleonesi. This split led to the Great Mafia war of 1981 to 1983.

In 1974 the Sicilian authorities caught up with Leggio for the murder of Placido Rizzotto. The authorities had failed in the past to successfully pin the murder on Leggio, but this time they managed to nail him down and sentenced him to a life behind bars. Leggio did not have to worry about being murdered because everyone in the prison had so much respect that they dare not touch him. Leggio's two lieutenants, Salvatore Riina and Bernardo Provenzano, known as the 'Beasts' continued to carry out Leggio's commands. Being incarcerated certainly did nothing to stop Leggio from successfully continuing his reign over the Corleonesi. His loyal underboss Toto Riina stepped up to take control of the clan with the help and direction of Leggio whilst he was serving his life sentence.

Riina went on to be even more infamous than his predecessor and mentor. He rewarded Leggio for making him godfather of the Corleonesi by winning himself and Leggio the complete control of the lucrative heroin trade that had now engulfed the entire Sicilian Mafia.

However winning the control of the heroin trade was the end result of some of the worst violence in Sicilian history. Over one thousand men of honour were slaughtered between 1979 and early 1981, a war that would change the image of the Mafia forever, as these murders would leave a deep scar in the hearts of so many native Sicilians. A scar that could be traced back to the point in time when Leggio took control of the Corleonesi.

LEGGIO TODAY

Today Leggio spends his days reading and painting landscapes of his Corleone countryside. Leggio's life is an extraordinary story of success, starting out as a poor peasant, and ending up as one of the most wealthy mafiosi in Italy. His story is one that is filled with violence, murder and ruthless acts towards humanity. Regardless of whether one thinks Leggio's behaviour is deplorable, he demands respect, if for no other reason than plain fear.

Gaetano Badalamenti

Gaetano Badalamenti was a close associate of Sicilian supergrass Tommaso Buscetta. He also became the mortal enemy of the notorious Corleonesi boss Toto 'The Beast' Riina.

Badalamenti was born in a small village called Cinisi, 15 kilometers west of Palermo, in 1923. He was the last to be born into a family of farmers and landowners, and his climb up the Cosa Nostra ladder was a spectacular one.

Before joining the Mafia, Gaetano joined the Italian Armed Forces Infantry Division. He was rumoured to have been a part of the American Invasion plan in 1942 during the collusion of Lucky Luciano and the American liberators to force back the Fascist regime of Mussolini.

After the liberation of Sicily, the Mafia went from strength to strength and so did Gaetano Badalamenti. Badalamenti proved himself as a very capable and loyal individual and his respect and stature grew in the 1950s, as he became a very cunning Mafiosi. He became involved in numerous building schemes throughout Sicily, and in 1957

326

was invited to a highly consequential meeting in Palermo. At this meeting highly respected members of the Sicilian Cosa Nostra turned out to greet their American colleagues to discuss the possibilities of joining forces to globalise the narcotics trade. From America came Joe Bonanno and his trusted aide Carmine Galante and they met up with Lucky Luciano, who had by this time had been exiled from America.

After a few days of discussion the two parties had a series of agreements, one of which was very important to the Sicilian clans. Luciano explained to Tomasso Buscetta just how he had set up the American commission and how successful it had been in helping the clans arbitrate their problems in a more orderly fashion.

Shortly after the meeting, the usually volatile Sicilian clans agreed that having some sort of governing body would be a better way of sorting out their problems. Consequently, shortly afterwards they set up their own commission which became known as the Cupola. Gaetano Badalamenti was to be its leader, for a short while anyway, before becoming the head of the Cinisi clan. His loyalty and shrewdness had paid off and he was one of the many Cupola bosses who pioneered to enter the very lucrative heroin trade that was by now completely dominated by the Sicilian Mafia. The Cupola was responsible for working out who had what territories for drug distribution, they fixed the price of drugs, and even arbitrated disputes between rival gangs. With their numerous refineries the Sicilian Cosa Nostra found them-

327

selves in a position to go on and dominate the global network of narcotics, by smuggling it to New York via Canada.

To start with everything ran smoothly and everyone was making a vast amount of money – every clan having their piece of a very big pie. But somehow instead of strengthening the Sicilian Mafia, the heroin market would be the main cause of tearing it apart.

THE CONSEQUENCES

By the mid-seventies Toto Riina began lobbying to take over the complete heroin trade in Sicily. Toto had risen to the top of the Corleonesi clan thanks to his devoted loyalty to the long time Corleonesi boss, Luciano Liggio. However, by the mid-seventies Liggio was serving a prison sentence which left Riina to run amok within the Sicilian Mafia. Riina was particularly good at manipulating members of rival clans into believing that if they were to join him they would have an even bigger share than they were receiving now. Not that they had much choice in the matter because, if they didn't go along with him, he would have them killed anyway.

Badalamenti was greatly disturbed by this turn of events. Badalamenti was well aware that Riina was gaining power, and that his actions would have an adverse effect on the Sicilian clans. By 1979, things were getting completely out of control as the Corleonesi were killing anybody that posed a physical threat to them getting their hands on the lucrative heroin market for themselves.

Badalamenti wanted Riina to explain his actions and demanded that he came to a Cupola meeting. The crafty Riina, however, having manipulated enough of the Sicilian Mafia bosses to overthrow Badalamenti, was ready to make his move. Riina ordered Badalamenti to be banished from the Sicilian Cosa Nostra forever.

Having been pushed out of Sicily, Badalamenti headed first for Spain and then onto Brazil where he met up with his old colleague Tomasso Buscetta. He asked if Buscetta would immediately return with him to Sicily and take their revenge on the Corleonesi. Buscetta, however, was reluctant to move away from his new wife in Brazil. Buscetta was well aware of the problems facing the Sicilian clans. He also knew that the Corleonesi had sanctioned over a thousand murders, many of them being Cupola bosses such as Salvatore Inzerillo, Stefano Bontate and Guiseppe Cristina. This was in fact the worst bloodshed in Sicily or anywhere else in the world of organized crime.

Like Buscetta, Gaetano set up a new home in Sao Paolo, Brazil. It wasn't long, however, before Badalamenti went back to his old habits and became involved in a new narcotics ring operating from Brazil. Badalamenti was well acquainted with the New York Mafia who operated on Knickerbocker Avenue. Most of these were immigrants from Sicily and were led by Salvatore Catalano. Catalano was heavily involved in smuggling heroin from Sicily using many Pizza parlours as cover for their drug business. But by the mid-eighties the FBI were well aware of this and were ready to bust open the massive operation. Catalano was very reluctant to do business with Badalamenti, after all, Badalamenti had been banished from Sicily and Catalano didn't want his partners in Sicily to find out that he was doing business with him.

This did not deter other immigrants on Knickerbocker Avenue from going into partnership with him though. Badalamenti had a nephew in Chicago who would do his dirty work for him in New York. But the FBI were also well aware of what Badalamenti was up to, and they knew it would only be a matter of time before they would have enough incriminating evidence to arrest him. The time came in November 1984 when he was picked up and arrested in Madrid after fleeing from Brazil.

Little did Badalamenti know that the FBI had bugged his nephew Pietro Alfano's phone and were well aware of all of his movements. Pietro had unknowingly led the FBI to Badalamenti in Madrid and the two mobsters became part of the huge Pizza Connection Case back in New York. Badalamenti was extradited back to the United States, with an agreement with the Sicilian magistrates that if they couldn't get a conviction he would be extradited back to Sicily to stand trial in the much-publicised Maxi trials in Palermo. So one way or another it wasn't looking very promising for the Sicilian don.

In March 1987 Gaetano Badalamenti was convicted of being part of the huge narcotics conspiracy along with twenty-one other defendants as part of the massive Pizza Connection Case. Badalamenti was sentenced to 45 years in prison.

Vito Cascio Ferro

Many regard Don Vito Cascio Ferro as the very first 'capi di tutti i capi' (boss of all the bosses). He is also believed to be the one man primarily responsible for establishing the communication between the Sicilian and US Mafia (or the 'Black Hand' as it was known in the early 1900s).

Born in 1862 in Palermo, Cascio Ferro grew up in traditional peasant surroundings and as a young man was hot-headed, illiterate and rebellious. In short he was a natural candidate for the life of the Cosa Nostra. By his early twenties he had been ritually enrolled into the organization as a man of honour.

Cascio Ferro was among the thousands of immigrants who got into the United States in the period before the strict quotas were introduced in the twenties. On his arrival into the United States Cascio Ferro moved in with his sister over a shop on 103rd street, New York. He had skilfully hidden his criminal record, which began in 1894 with a charge of assault and extended through 1899 when he was accused of kidnapping Baroness di Valpetrosa, fleeing to New York to escape trial.

Before arriving in New York, Don Vito was

credited with having established a sliding scale of local tax 'protection'. Within three years Don Vito had perfected his system as every business man in his area became a victim of the illustrious 'Black Hand'. Don Vito gained a reputation as a man who would act as a local arbitrator, sorting out any disputes of the many people under his protection.

THE PURSUIT

Joseph Petrosino, a New York detective, soon began to take a big interest in Don Vito. By 1904 the New York police had linked the Don to a number of crimes, including the murder of an Italian, Benedetto Madonia, whose mutilated body was found stuffed into a barrel. Madonia had apparently been trying to establish a counterfeiting ring in Don Vito's territory without permission or authority. Don Vito fled to New Orleans before the police could apprehend him, where he spent time organizing his own counterfeiting ring along with establishing a connection for heroin smuggling with Sicily.

Lieutenant Petrosino pursued Don Vito from New York down to New Orleans forcing Don Vito to return to Sicily where he quickly established himself as head of all Mafiosi. His power was derived from his strength and not by instilling fear in the local business owners and small farmers. He was known for his generosity and kindness but also for his brutality towards those he considered weak and worthless. Don Vito is attributed with being the first to introduce a system by which the

Mafia collects small amounts of payment from all businesses as a form of tribute or for protection. If the payment was not made then Don Vito would have these business owners' shops or homes destroyed and their farms burnt down.

In 1909, Lieutenant Petrosino had gone to Sicily in hopes of gathering evidence to expose the connection between the US and Sicilian mobs, and hopefully to have certain criminals extradited back to the United States, Cascio Ferro being one of them. But everything did not go as planned and, following, Joe Petrosino was shot twice as he sat on a fence, patiently waiting for two informers to show up. Don Vito was arrested on the April 3, 1909, but he had a solid alibi, a local VIP who stated that Don Vito was at his home in Palermo at the exact time of the murder.

The killing of Lieutenant Petrosino further cemented Don Vito's stature in both the Sicilian and US underworlds and also helped establish him as a well-respected legitimate businessman in Palermo. It was not uncommon to see him well received by bankers, politicians, judges and even foreign dignitaries. In the remaining years of the pre-Mussolini era he had established a major criminal network. Always keeping in touch with his associates in New York, kidnapping, extortion, murders and smuggling all headed the statistical charts in Palermo between 1921 to 1925.

THE THREAT OF MUSSOLINI

In January 1925, Mussolini took control of Italy

which was bad news for the Mafia. Mussolini would bring the first real attack on the Mafia, with the help of Cesare Mori who was appointed the police prefect. He was ordered to clean out the Mafia presence on the island of Sicily. One after another associates of the Mafia were rounded up, while Cesare Mori turned his attentions to the bigger bosses.

In 1927 Don Vito was arrested for murder, something that he got used to over the years as he was arrested on suspicion of murder 69 times. Somehow he would always be acquitted, thanks to there not being enough evidence or indeed any witnesses who were deranged enough to testify against a Mafia boss. Ironically though this time Don Vito was innocent. The evidence was contrived by Cesare Mori and his fascist dictator Mussolini who set out to get him at all costs.

So the first boss of bosses had been taken down and was sentenced to life imprisonment in Palermo. In 1945, after WWII, the Don had asked to be pardoned and released, but the pardon was refused. He continued to run his empire from his luxurious prison cell where he died peacefully in 1945.

Michele Navarra

Navarra was a ruthless, cold-blooded killer who resorted to bribery and extortion during his reign as a Mafia boss.

After the war, Dr Michele Navarra held the position of Mayor of Corleone. He was held in high regard by many of the Corleone villagers, as he was not only their mayor but their medical practitioner as well. However, this was only one side of Dr Michele Navarra, the other side was very different indeed. Not only was he a ruthless Mafia boss, he was also a cold-blooded killer, using bribery and extortion to build up his assets within the honoured society.

Whilst working at the hospital he saved many lives, but on the other side of the coin he had no qualms in ending the lives of those who opposed his positions as Mayor of Corleone and boss of his Mafia clan from his beloved town. In fact, in his first two years as mayor, there were fifty-seven murders in the town of Corleone alone, all of them connected to Mafia business in some way or another.

Without doubt the most underhanded murder in Navarra's reign was the murder of a young shepherd boy called Placido Rizzotto, who helped

335

to organize the local trade union. He had arranged to meet with Dr Navarra on the March 10, 1948 with the purpose of discussing the possibility of forming co-operatives for peasant workers, something which had already been done successfully in several other towns. Plans for the co-operatives were to boost employment by taking over vacant, uncultivated land left unwanted by many landlords. However, Dr Navarra's attitude towards the young Rizzotto was cool to say the least. Perhaps it was that Navarra was jealous because he had not thought of the idea himself. Or maybe it was because the co-operatives would have made the young Rizzotto – who still lived at home with his parents – a very popular individual. Many of the villagers were already thankful of his efforts in finding job opportunities for the local population.

Navarra did not like being upstaged by this young man with bright ideas, who in turn had lots of people backing him. So Dr Navarra began to take steps to dispose of Placido Rizzotto. He started off by harshly criticizing the youngster in public, by letting it be known that he was a Communist. Communists were very much despised in Sicily, particularly by the men of honour. On the same day that Rizzotto had the meeting with Michele Navarra, at around 7.00 pm, Rizzotto was murdered by three men, one of whom was the future head of the Corleonesi, one Luciano Liggio. (Corleonesi was the name the Corleone Mafia came to be known by.) This murder epitomizes the sort of Mafia boss Dr Michele Navarra was – someone who would kill without provocation.

AT WAR WITH LUCIANO LIGGIO

Despite his reputation, Dr Michele Navarra was soon to be on the wrong end of someone else's vendetta.

Luciano Liggio was an arrogant killer and was eventually arrested for the murder of the young Rizzotto. Liggio went through three trials, the last one being an amazing seventeen years after the event. In the meantime Liggio committed many other crimes, with murder being his particular favourite. Liggio was becoming a very respected figure in the underworld, but although he had been the hired gun of Dr Navarra, his true mentor was Frank Coppola. This got under the skin of Navarra and, with Navarra becoming more and more power hungry by the day, trouble was on the horizon for the gangs of Sicily.

It wasn't long before Navarra went to war with his former hitman Liggio. Liggio, however, who was now vying for more power himself, wasn't about to give up without a fight and so the first major Mafia battle after the war was now under way.

Between the years of 1954 and 1958 there were 153 Mafia murders around Corleone. Navarra, desperate to be rid of his arch enemy Liggio, arranged for a team of hitmen to kill him. At the time of the shooting Liggio was with his trusted bodyguard and friend, and future successor of the Corleonesi, Toto Riina. Although Liggio was shot, Toto managed to save his life by taking him to a nearby town where he was nursed back to health. So incensed by this attack, it wasn't long before he started plotting his own revenge.

Liggio was now even more hungry for power, and started to make plans to take over the entire Corleonesi. He knew that the key to his success would be the elimination of Dr Navarra. His chance finally came in 1958 when Liggio assembled fifteen men armed with machine guns. They ambushed Navarra one night when he was on his way home from his practice accompanied by another doctor who had innocently accepted a lift home. The two men were riddled with 210 bullets between them.

This was the end to Navarra's reign as boss of the Corleonesi, who had totally underestimated the influence of the ruthless Liggio. Liggio went on to cement his position by killing a further 28 close associates and supporters of Navarra, while the remainder became his loyal supporters.

Calogero 'Don Calo' Vizzini

Don Calo was one of the first Dons of the Sicilian Cosa Nostra. He was also one of the last true Sicilian Mafiosos, soon to be replaced by a more violent, vulgar, and ill-mannered generation.

D on Calo was born in the small village of Villalba in southern Sicily in 1877. The young Calo was not a good student and his digression into crime seemed inevitable.

Don Calo was only seventeen when he had his first brush with the law, being unsuccessfully charged with assault. At the age of eighteen he went into business with some local farmers, where he would charge protection for safely escorting shipments of grain across the bandit riddled countryside of Sicily. He even formed a partnership with some of the gangs of bandits and cut them in on a share of his profits, thus ensuring that they remained his allies.

Don Calo ended up spending a number of years with a certain gang because he was so impressed with the way they operated. Paolo Versalona's gang was one of the most wanted gangs in Sicily, which intrigued the rising young mobster from

Villalba. The gang was eventually caught and
detained by the police on a charge of murder, but
Don Calo was acquitted due to a lack of evidence.

MAKING AN IMPRESSION

By this time Don Calo had made quite an
impression on some of the more important Mafiosi
in Sicily. They saw that he was a very capable
young man, and it wasn't long before he was
inducted into the 'The Honoured Society'.

By the outbreak of World War I, Calogero was
given the title of 'Zu' (meaning uncle) and was
given the leadership of the province of Caltanisetta.
This was a remarkable achievement for someone
who was still only 25 years old. Throughout the
war years Calogero made a large amount of money
by selling ageing horses to the Italian army, while
charging farmers within his province guarantee
money to provide them with fit and young horses.

Shortly after the end of the war the Italian
authorities endeavoured to put Calogero on trial
after claims that he had supplied the Italian army
with stolen goods. Once again, however, Calogero
was acquitted of all charges. This acquittal earned
Calogero even more prestige as his growing
amount of influence was there for all to see.

During the late 1920s Calogero was bestowed
the title of Don, and after Don Cascio Ferro, Don
Calo was the second most important Mafia figure
in Sicily.

During the 1930s, the fascist dictator Bennito
Mussolini had sent his second-in-command,

Cesare Mori, to clean up the island of Sicily, and get rid of the Mafia's influence once and for all. Thousands of Mafia figures were sent to jail, while some managed to escape and fled to New York and Canada. Even Don Cascio Ferro fell victim to this clean-up operation.

Don Calo was sentenced to five years imprisonment, but the sly Sicilian Don had already fostered good relations with Fascists and was released a few days later. It seemed that Don Calo was a very popular man. Don Calo was always on hand to help out the people of Villalba and Caltanisetta, especially during the time when the Sicilians got very little help from the government. He looked after them very well, he gave them jobs and often acted as arbitrator in family disputes. In truth Don Calo was the last of the great Mafia Dons, in what was without a doubt a romantic period of Mafia life.

PUTTING THE MAFIA BACK ON THE MAP

By the time the Second World War came round, Don Calo found himself in a position to help out the American invasion of Sicily. Don Calo knew full well that the Americans, grateful of any help that he and his Mafiosi could provide, would put the Mafia back in power in Sicily. It was a master plan because the Mafia provided food and supplies and made the invasion a lot more comfortable than it would have otherwise been. As the fascist government of Italy was overthrown, hundreds of Mafiosi were released from prison. They were appointed mayors and police captains and given many more positions of power.

Don Calo was even made a Colonel in the American army. This was to be Don Calo's finest hour. He saved the Mafia when it was on the brink of what looked like defeat to the Fascist government and Mussolini.

A PEACEFUL END

In 1951 Don Calo died peacefully. On his way to Sicily one day Don Calo asked that the car be stopped on a bank at the side of the road. He is said to have laid down and rested his head in his hands behind his neck. Whilst in this position and totally at peace with the world Don Calo is reported to have said, 'how beautiful life is', then he passed away.

His funeral was attended by many people, almost as if a head of state had died. But Don Calo would be remembered as temperate, forbearing and tireless in his defence of the weak, and above all else, Don Calogero Vizzini will be remembered as a gentleman in every sense of the word. Don Calogero Vizzini is the perfect example of the old-style Mafia Don; bound by the Omertà, or code of silence, these men of honour usually solved their own problems in a discreet, albeit sometimes violent way.

Vincenzo Napoli

Vincenzo Napoli first came to light when the legendary New York undercover detective, Douglas Le Vien, first discovered him.

Vincenzo Napoli was born in Villabate, Sicily in 1947. In his late teens, Napoli was sworn-in as a made member of the Sicilian Mafia, due mainly to his growing ability to make money. When Napoli made money it was always on a big scale. Not much is known about Napoli's criminal career in Sicily, but it does seem that he was a very smart man as he didn't appear to have much of a criminal record.

It is not clear exactly when he arrived in New York, but one thing is certain, he was operating with the Gambino crime family in the early 1970s. It was around the time when Carlo Gambino was the boss and the Gambino crime family had a stranglehold on most of New York.

Napoli set up a hugely successful illegal gambling den in Brooklyn, where strippers were the sideshow. This venture was so successful that 'Fat Andy' Ruggiano and his people from the Gambino family tried to cut in on a piece of the action. Napoli, however, had the guts to stand up to them and told them in no uncertain terms that there was no way he was going to be run out of business. Due to the amount of native Sicilians that helped Napoli run his den, Ruggiano's people backed off and left well alone.

The size of Napoli's empire was very impressive and, according to reports, Napoli had men working for him in Munich, Paris, Amsterdam, Milan, London, Hong Kong and Bangkok. During their investigations, the FBI had even tapped into telephone calls to and from Morocco.

The sheer range of Napoli's interests was also intriguing. It appeared the truth behind Napoli's illicit amount of wealth and seemingly endless list of international contacts was partly due to his activities in the heroin trade. It was, allegedly, Napoli himself who negotiated with the five New York families in order to bring in the vast amounts of heroin that found its way to the streets of New York. However, unlike most Sicilians that trafficked heroin into the United Sates, Napoli was not just tied to his interests within the narcotics trade.

DOUGLAS LE VIEN

Detective Le Vien was an undercover New York detective who posed as a businessman from Detroit. Le Vien sold himself to Napoli as a man that could afford to throw around a lot of money. Le Vien got to know Napoli quite well, but at the outset was unaware of Napoli's role in the global heroin network. But what Le Vien did find out was that Napoli was interested in just about anything that could make him large sums of cash. Napoli asked Le Vien if he was interested in buying stolen goods, items that included violins, paintings such as Rembrandts, watches, cars and so much more. It wasn't until Napoli asked Le Vien if he was interested in buying heroin that his case was handed over to the Drug Enforcement Administration. The DEA arranged around the clock surveillance on Napoli and arrested one of his couriers in Bangkok who was attempting to bring back what would have been just a sample for Napoli. Napoli was also arrested in 1977 for his involvement and was sentenced to jail for being in possession of just one kilo of narcotics. An ironic situation considering the size of his narcotics empire.

Napoli was sentenced to eight years imprisonment, but ended up only serving four. He was released in 1981 and disappeared completely from the criminal scene.

Many believe that Napoli returned to Sicily, having already set up the heroin pipeline into America. Other people are convinced that he has changed his identity and is now living in California, no longer needing to play an active role in organized crime because of his bulging bank accounts.

Whatever and wherever he went, Napoli is listed in the FBI reports as being the first and biggest single importer of heroin into the United States and is known to be responsible for opening the heroin pipelines into the United States.

The French Connection

Michele Zaza, or the 'crazy man' as he was known to his friends, was a Camorra boss that operated from Marseille. He was involved in the narcotics trade where he had links with the cocaine cartels from Columbia.

Not much is known about Zaza's early days, but he really came to prominence when he started smuggling large amounts of cigarettes. It was through this tobacco racket that Zaza made his first black market fortune, and heightened his reputation as a high Camorra earner.

Michele Zaza (or the crazy man as he was known to his associates), was a Camorra boss that operated out of Marseille. The Camorra were renowned for tobacco smuggling, but later provided heroin to the Sicilian Mafia. Zaza made huge amounts of money from his illicit trading and laundered his ill-gotten gains by buying restaurants and casinos along the South of France.

THE NEW FAMILY

Michele Zaza formed his own clan in around 1980, which became known as the Nueva

Famiglia, or the new family. He set up his family on the French Riviera and it was from here that he controlled his operations. Zaza had his fingers in many rackets including drug trafficking, arms trafficking, gambling, prostitution and some major money laundering operations. All these rackets added to the enormous sums of money he was already making from his legitimate business ventures, such as restaurants and casinos. In truth Zaza was in control of his own little melting pot and only had to answer to one other person, his own boss, Carmine Alfieri. Alfieri was the overall boss of the entire Neapolitan Camorra, and he was more than pleased with the huge amounts of money that Zaza sent back to him every month.

SICILIAN ALLIES

Michele Zaza wanted to make sure that he had allies in Sicily, so he formed an alliance with the Fidzanti family. He felt sure that this would prevent any war from ever erupting should their two paths cross in the future. By taking this action Zaza knew that he was well covered in case there was any indiscretion between the Camorra and the Sicilian Cosa Nostra.

In the mid-1980s Zaza was arrested in Italy, but with the Mafia-controlled Christian Democrats still in power in Italy, it wasn't long before he was once again a free man. Complaining of a heart defect, Zaza was transferred to a prison hospital where he simply climbed out of bed and walked out. A month later he turned up again on the

French Riviera.

Zaza negotiated a deal with the number three man in the Cali Cartel, Franklin Jurado Rodrigues, which allowed him to handle the European smuggling routes for the Cartel. This earned Zaza and the Nueva Famiglia even more money. But in 1989 Zaza was arrested once again, this time for smuggling cigarettes. Again, Zaza had no problem in escaping whilst he was on remand.

By the early 1990s, Michele Zaza had built up a remarkable empire that stretched from the Northern Italian Ligurian coastline and onto the borders of Monaco. This stretch of coastline had numerous restaurants, properties and casinos, all of which Zaza knew would make him huge amounts of money. Michele Zaza was now at the peak of his criminal career.

OPERATION 'GREEN ICE'

It had taken many years for Zaza to reach his position in the Mafia, but his demise was a completely different story. He was arrested in May 1993 after being implicated in the operation 'Green Ice' that targeted a major international money laundering ring.

Operation Green Ice at the time was a major event in international crime fighting. For the first time a huge sting operation was carried out in unison, in various countries throughout the world, tying a number of criminal organizations together. Major money launderers were arrested as large portions of the Cali drug cartels cocaine money were seized in an operation that stretched over three continents and eight nations. This was to be one of the finest and most calculated operations of its kind in the world.

It was only a matter of time before Zaza's name would appear in the investigations. The French were already looking into his casino businesses and other international operations. Zaza was eventually picked up in his luxury villa on the outskirts of Nice. This time Michele Zaza was unable to escape as the clean-up operation swept through the French Riviera and Northern Italy. His bank accounts were investigated along with his connections with the Columbian drug cartel, all of which proved that he was a big time drugs trafficker. A total of $36 million in drug funds was seized and Michele Zaza was put away for a period of 25 years.

PART FOUR

JAPAN
&
CHINA

The Yakuza

The Yakuza is an organization that has been around for over 300 years. This group has as much honour and principle as the Mafia and is just as strong – if not stronger.

The yakuza can trace its origins as far back as early 1612, when people known then as *kabuki-mono*, 'crazy ones', started to attract the attention of local officials. They stood out from the crowd due to their peculiar clothing, haircuts and general behaviour, along with the fact that they carried longswords at their sides. It was common practice for the kabuki-mono to antagonize and terrorize anyone at their leisure, even to the point of violence for just sheer pleasure.

The kabuki-mono were in fact eccentric samurai, using outrageous names for their bands and speaking in an unusual slang tongue. One thing that could not be broken was their amazing loyalty to one another, protecting each other from any threat including those against their own families.

In reality the kabuki-mono were no more than servants of the shogun, or hatamoto-yakko, meaning literally 'servants of the shogun'. This group of people comprised of nearly 500,000 samurai who were forced into unemployment during the peaceful Tokugawa era. Without the control of a master, many turned into bandits, looting towns and villages as they wandered around freely throughout Japan.

The yakuza see the machi-yakko 'servants of the town' as their ancestors rather than the hatamoto-yakko, because it was the machi-yakko that took up arms and defended the villages and towns from the threats of the hatamoto-yakko. The machi-yakko consisted of such occupations as clerks, shopkeepers, innkeepers, labourers, homeless warriors and other ronin 'wave man' or masterless samurai. Each member also seemed to be an adept gambler and they formed a closely-knit relationship with each other and their leaders, very much like the present-day yakuza.

The machi-yakko, although untrained and weaker than the hatamoto-yakko, were praised by the townspeople for their actions against the hatamoto-yakko and soon became mythical heroes. They could perhaps have been likened to Robin Hood, many becoming famous as subjects of stories and plays.

YAKUZA ORIGINS

It wasn't really until the middle to late 1700s that the early yakuza started to come to the fore. There are three major origins of yakuza, and their operation is basically based on the origin of their family. These members included the *bakuto* (traditional gamblers) and the *tekiya* (street peddlers). These terms are still used today to describe yakuza members, but a third group *gurentai* (hoodlums) has been added after the end of World War II. All the members came from similar backgrounds – poor, landless, delinquents and misfits. The groups stuck closely in the same small areas without any problems, as the bakuto stayed mostly along the highways and towns, while the tekiya operated the markets and fairs of Japan. The yakuza started organizing their groups into families, adopting a relationship known as oyabun-kobun (father-role/child-role). The oyabun being the 'father', giving advice, protection and help, while the kobun acted as the 'child', swearing total loyalty and service whenever the oyabun demanded it.

It was about this period in time that the initiation ceremony for the yakuza developed. Unlike the bloodletting ceremony that was practiced by the Mafia and the Triads, the yakuza exchanged sake cups which symbolized their entrance into the yakuza and the oyabun-kobun relationship. The amount of sake poured into each cup would depend upon the individual's status, i.e. whether the participants were father-son, brother-brother, elder-younger, and so on. This ceremony would normally be performed in front of a Shinto altar, giving it a religious influence.

THE TEKIYA

The history of the tekiya is unclear, but the most widely accepted theory is that they came from yashi, which was an early word for a peddler. Basically the yashi were travelling merchants of medicine, very similar to the snake oil merchants of the American West, and over the years attracted a wide assortment of both merchants and peddlers.

The tekiya united with each other basically for protection, but also because of the mutual interest from the Tokugawa regime. They took control of the booths at local fairs and markets, and they soon gained a reputation for shoddy merchandise. Their salesmanship was extremely misleading, lying about both the origins and quality of their wares. They would pretend to be under the influence of drink and make a show of selling their goods cheaply, in the hope that it would appear they were not really aware of what they were doing, thus deluding their customers. They were clever salesman, offering incredible deals too good to be true. Some items were hacks, others are actually of reputable quality, but it usually takes another tekiya to tell the difference.

The tekiya followed the normal yakuza organization – oyabun, underboss, officers, enlisted and apprentices. The oyabun were in control of the kobun, the allocation of stalls, as well as the availability of the merchandise. He was also responsible for the collection of rents and protection monies, pocketing the difference between the two. Despite their somewhat underhand methods, everything the tekiya did was legal work. In the middle 1700s the feudal authorities recognized this fact and consequently increased the power of the tekiya. The oyabun were promoted to the position of supervisor, which meant they were now able to have a surname. This also earned them the right to carry two swords – similar to the samurai – in order to reduce the threat of turf wars which were spreading due to widespread fraud. Despite their move up in the hierarchy ladder the tekiya still had many criminal traits, including protection rackets, the harbouring of fugitives and known criminals and constant fighting with other tekiya and local gangs. Despite all of these traits, the tekiya held a great deal of respect within Japan. They are influential people, holding officials in their back pocket, and given rights almost equal to that of the samurai.

THE BAKUTO

The bakuto were first recognized during the Tokugawa era at a time when the government hired them to gamble with construction and irrigation workers in an effort to regain a portion of the substantial wages the workers earned.

The bakuto contributed greatly to Japan's tradition for gambling. They were also instrumental in the yakuza's traditional 'finger-cutting', and the origin of the word 'yakuza'. The word actually comes from a hand in a card game called *hanafuda* (flower cards), which is a game very similar to blackjack. Three cards are dealt to each player, and the last digit of the total counts as the number of the hand. A hand of 20, being the worst, gives the score of zero. One such losing combination 8–9–3, or ya-ku-sa, which began to be widely used, actually denoted something useless. This term was used about the bakuto as they were, basically, totally useless to society.

356

The custom of finger-cutting or *yubitsume*, was also introduced by the bakuto. If a gambler couldn't pay back a gambling debt or was required to expiate a wrongdoing, the top joint of the little finger would be ceremoniously severed. This signified a weakening of the hand, which meant that the gambler could not hold his sword as firmly. Yubitsume was generally performed as an act of apology to the oyabun. Further violations would either mean the severing of the next joint or, alternatively, the top section of the next finger. It was also used as a lasting punishment before expulsion from the yakuza.

The tradition of tattoos also came from the criminal aspect of the bakuto. Criminals were usually tattooed with a black ring around an arm for every offence that he had committed. The tattoo also was the mark of a misfit, someone who was unwilling to adapt themselves into society. However, over time this tradition became a test of endurance as a complete back tattoo could take anything up to 100 hours to complete.

THE GURENTAI

The gurentai modelled themselves on American gangsters, using threats and extortion to achieve their ends. They were the yakuza assassins, leaving chaos in their wake. They were butchers for hire, cold-blooded killers, and seemed willing to perform any job, leaving a trail of carnage as their calling card.

The gurentai could be described as the step-children of the yakuza family, given no respect, and recognized as only a gruesome reminder of the by-product of a torn land. Their savagery became a useful tool and over the years the gurentai grew, their trade becoming a valued commodity.

Despite their gruesome reputation, the gurentai were not without a sense of family. Albeit, their family consists of only fellow gurentai. It is a father-son (oyabun-kobun) and brother-brother business relationship. The oyabun, or father, is usually a warlord of a given region, being a veteran gurentai that has earned this position (usually through the killing of the prior oyabun). The oyabun only asks for a small 'donation' from the townspeople in his territory, a small price to pay for protection. The kobun, or son, is also under the oyabun, and is obliged to release a portion of his earnings out of respect.

In most cases the oyabun was truly a foster father to the kobun, taking young children off the streets and training them in the ways of killing. They progressed through the use of numerous weapons for the sole purpose of killing, as they did not believe in the concept of prisoners or hostages. It is a lifelong education, and the gurentai have long since forsaken any morals and heed no laws, as this would only divert their path. It appears that the concept of good and bad have no meaning to these men, who only understand the need for money and power, and the only way to achieve these goals is death.

Having said that, they do possess other skills. Many gurentai are fluent gamblers. Although they are not formerly trained in a specific style of martial arts, the apprentice does learn a wide variety of attack forms and techniques. A large part of a gurentai's life involves taking repeated blows to vital points of the body, to rid them of weak points. In time, they become partially devoid of feeling in some areas of their body. The training given to a gurentai is extremely rigorous and bestows with it certain gifts.

The gurentai are also able to sense when another is near death and will go into a frenzy to help the 'soul' on its way to the land of the dead.

Like the bakuto, gurentai members favour body tattoos, but theirs are elaborate body murals that often cover the entire torso, front and back, as well the arms to below the elbow and the legs to mid-calf. Naked, a fully-tattooed gurentai looks like he is wearing long underwear. The designs include dragons, flowers, mountainous landscapes, turbulent seascapes, gang insignias and abstract designs. The application of these extensive tattoos is painful and can take hundreds of hours, but the process is considered a test of a man's mettle.

THE MEIJI RESTORATION

Starting in 1867, the Meiji Restoration gave Japan a rebirth and was a contributory factor to its transformation into an industrial nation. This saw the creation of political parties and a parliament, as well as the formation of a powerful military force.

It was also around this time that the yakuza

started to modernize, to keep in pace with a rapidly changing Japan. They started to recruit construction and dock workers, and they even began to control the rickshaw business. Gambling, however, had to be kept undercover as the police were starting to crack down on the bakuto gangs operating in the city. The tekiya, on the other hand, thrived and expanded, as their activities were legal – or so they appeared on the surface.

The yakuza started to dabble in politics, taking sides with specific politicians and officials. The reason behind this co-operation with the government was purely to obtain official sanction, or at least to gain some freedom from harassment. The government did find a use for the yakuza, as an aid to ultranationalists who took a militaristic role in Japan's change over to democracy. Various secret societies were formed and trained in military combat, languages, assassination and even blackmail. The ultranationalist reign of terror lasted right into the 1930s, and included the assassination of two prime ministers, two finance ministers, and many attacks on politicians and industrialists. The yakuza provided both muscle and men to this cause and played a part in the 'land development' programmes in occupied Manchuria or China.

However, the bombing of Pearl Harbor changed all that. The government no longer needed the ultranationalists nor the yakuza. The members of these groups were given the option of working with the government, join the military forces, or alternatively go to jail.

THE AMERICAN OCCUPATION

The American occupation forces in post-war Japan saw the yakuza as a threat to their work and started investigations into their activities. They stopped their investigations in 1948 as they felt the threat was over, or at least diminished. What they didn't realise was, that food rationing introduced by the forces had encouraged black market trading which kept the gangs in wealth and power. The gangs were able to operate quite freely as the civil police were not armed, and it seemed that some occupation officials even assisted the yakuza.

It was during the occupation that the gurentai began to form. There was a power vacuum in the government because the occupation had simply swept away the top level of control in both government and business.

The gurentai could be likened to Japan's version of the Mob – its leader similar being compared to Al Capone. They mainly dealt in black marketing, but were known to resort to threats, extortion and violence in the pursuit of their activities. Their members were made up of the unemployed and repatriated.

The occupation forces began to realize that the yakuza were a well-organized society and allowed them to operate under two oyabun who were supported by unknown high-level government officials. In 1950 the forces admitted defeat, as they realized there was no way they could protect the Japanese people from the power of the yakuza.

In the post-war years the yakuza became more and more violent, not only as individuals but also operating as gangs. Swords, which were once their main weapon, had become a thing of the past, and guns were now becoming the weapon of choice. They now turned on the ordinary citizen as their targets, instead of the vendors, gamblers and specific groups they once turned on. Their appearance also changed, using the American movie gangsters as their role models. They started to wear sunglasses, dark suits and ties, and even sported crewcut hairstyles.

Between the years 1958 and 1963, the number of yakuza members rose by over 150 per cent to 184,000 members (this was even more than the total of the Japanese army). There were some 5,200 gangs operating on the streets of Japan and the yakuza gangs began to stake out their territory. What ensued was a series of bloody and violent wars.

YAMAGUCHI-GUMI

The Yamaguchi-gumi is Japan's most powerful syndicate. Their symbol is a rhombus-shaped pin worn on the lapel of their suits. By wearing this pin and displaying their tattoos, this faction could demand anything they wanted.

From the mid-1940s until his death in 1981, Kazuo Taoka was the oyabun to the Yamaguchi-gumi. He was the third oyabun of the faction.

Taoka had survived many attempts on his life, including one in 1978, when he was shot in the neck by a member of the Matsuda during a limbo dance exhibition at the Yamaguchi-gumi household. The Matsuda were a rival yakuza clan who wanted revenge for the death of their oyabun.

In the year 1980 the Yamaguchi-gumi tried to expand their territory into Hokkaido. This time the displaying of the pin did not seem to work. They were met at the Sapporo airport by 800 members of local gangs who had united in an effort to keep the Yamaguchi-gumi out of their territory. It took nearly 2,000 anti-riot police to keep the two groups apart. They were, however, successful in their quest and the Yamaguchi-gumi were prevented from opening their headquarters in Sapporo.

In July 1981, Taoka died from a heart attack, ending his 35-year rule as oyabun. The funeral was a very grand affair in the finest yakuza style. It attracted members from nearly 200 gangs, singers, actors, musicians and even the police. Following his death, police raided many Yamaguchi-gumi homes and offices across Japan, arresting more than 900 members and confiscating such contraband as firearms, swords and narcotics.

Yakamen had been Taoka's number two man, and was to be his successor. The only problem was that at the time of Taoka's death he was serving a prison sentence and was not due to be released until late 1982. During his absence, to everyone's great amazement, Taoka's widow, Fumiko, assumed temporary control. However, before Yakamen was able to take over as leader he died of cirrhosis of the liver, which left the entire structure of the Yamaguchi-gumi in complete chaos.

Under Taoka's long reign, the Yamaguchi-gumi had control of over 2,500 businesses, operated sophisticated gambling dens and loan-sharking, and invested heavily in sports and other entertainment. They operated using the same standards that had existed for the yakuza for over 300 years, and that was basically that the oyabun-kobun relationship controlled the day-to-day running of the syndicate. The syndicate was earning well over $460 million per year, and their management style was envied by such organizations as the Mafia and General Motors.

The Yamaguchi-gumi had over 500 gangs with around 103 bosses or various ranks. Each of these bosses was said to have been earning over £130,000 a year. The Yamaguchi-gumi now progressed to dealing in narcotics, primarily amphetamines. Other ventures that earned them a lot of money were moneylending, smuggling and pornography. It was commonplace for the yakuza to rig baseball games, horse races and even public property auctions. They were also known to seize real estate, entertainment halls, hospitals and even English schools.

Under Taoka's rule, the membership of the Yamaguchi-gumi rose to 13,345 members, coming from 587 different gangs. By the end of 1983 their control stretched to 36 of Japan's 47 prefectures. A council of eight high-ranking bosses took control under the guidance of Taoka. However, now it was time for the syndicate to select a new godfather. There were two candidates: Masahisa Takenaka and Hiroshi Yamamoto. Takenaka was appointed the oyabun as it seemed everyone preferred his military style over that of Yamamoto's intellectual yakuza. After losing, Yamamoto, in a fit of anger, took 13,000 men from the Yamaguchi-gumi and created the Ichiwa-kai, which was to become one of Japan's top three syndicates. In 1985, Ichiwa-kai assassins killed Takenaka, provoking another bloody gang war.

Kazuo Nakanishi was appointed the new oyabun for the Yamaguchi-gumi and immediately declared war on the Ichiwa-kai. Police intervened and arrested nearly a thousand mobsters, confiscating a great number of their weapons. So desperate were the Yamaguchi-gumi to win the battle, that they turned to the United States to fund their war. They managed to get hold of many highly illegal weapons which included rocket launchers and machine guns, in exchange for narcotics. However, before their weaponry could be put into use, the conspirators were arrested. Among those arrested were Masashi Takenaka, Masahisa's brother and Hideomi Oda, who was the syndicate's financial controller. Once again the Yamaguchi-gumi was thrown into a state of chaos.

THE YAKUZA STRUCTURE

To explain the yakuza structure in simple terms it is easiest to break it down into two types: the clan yakuza and the freelance yakuza.

Like the Mafia, the yakuza power structure is a pyramid with a patriarch on top and loyal underlings of various rank below him. The yakuza system is similar but a little more intricate. The guiding principle of the yakuza structure is the *oyabun-kobun* relationship.

The clans head chief is called *oyabun*, which means 'father'. Beneath him he has his children (*wakashu*) and brothers (*kyodai*). These are not his real children and brothers, only designations of rank and position they have within the clan. All the members in the clan obey the oyabun and in return he offers them full protection. The oyabun is considered to be almighty within the clan and his word is law. All obey him without hesitation or concern for their own life. Beneath him, the oyabun has an adviser called *saiko-komon* who has a staff of advocates, accountants, secretaries and advisers. The children's (*wakashu*) boss is called the *waka-gashira*. He is number two in the clan after oyabun, not in rank but in authority. He acts as a mediator to ensure that the oyabun's orders are being fully accomplished.

The children become leaders over their own (sub)-gangs and over time can move up in the structure. In that way the clan becomes an offshoot with several sub-families. The boss of the oyabun's 'brothers' or *kyodai*, is called *shatei-gashira*. *Shatei-gashira* is of higher rank than *waka-gashira* but does not have more authority. The 'brothers' have their own 'children' or 'younger brothers' known as the *shatei*. Shatei, has its own sub-gangs etc. etc. Everyone obeys its gangleader, but it is always the oyabun's word that counts. To help you fully understand the structure of command of a yakuza clan, the Yamaguchi-gumi

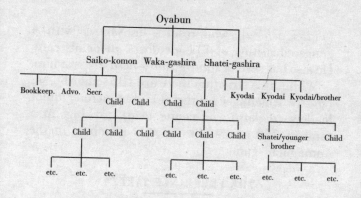

will be used, as it stood in November 1991.

The *oyabun*, Yoshinori Watanabe, is the head of the clan, residing at their headquarters in Kobe.

The *saiko-komon*, or senior adviser, is Zakuo Nakanishi. He resides at Osaka and has 15 sub-gangs under his control, giving him a total of 439 members.

Saizo Kishimoto is the *so-honbucho* (or head-quarters chief) resides at Kobe with 6 gangs, comprising of 108 members, under his control.

Masaru Takumi is the *waka-gashira*, or number-two man. He controls 941 members in 41 gangs in Osaka.

Tetsuo Nogami is the *fuki-honbucho*, or assistant, with 8 gangs comprising of 164 members in Osaka.

Under the *kumicho* (supreme boss) are various *komon* (advisers), *shingiin* (counsellors), *kumicho-hisho* (secretaries), *kaikei* (accountants) and *wakagashira-hosa* (underlings of the second-in-command).

Keisuke Masuda is the number three man

(*shateigashira*), who resides in Nagoya with 4 gangs consisting of 111 members under his care. He also has several *shateigashira-hosa* to assist him.

Within this structure there are 102 senior bosses (*shatei* or younger brothers) and numerous junior leaders (*wakashu* or young men), making up a total of 750 gangs with 31,000 members in the Yamaguchi-gumi.

THE FREELANCE YAKUZA

Freelancing yakuza are generally wannabe yakuza that don't get involved in serious crimes. They are usually little more than a group of hustlers. However, they do have some difficulties surviving since the clan yakuza do not afford them any protection or assistance and generally do not permit them to operate within their territories. Clan yakuza have even been known to tip-off the police about crimes that the freelance yakuza have commited. If the freelance yakuza is found to be earning too much money, the clan yakuza will kill the freelancing yakuza or make him disappear without leaving a trace.

Having said that, the clan yakuza do have certain uses for a freelance yakuza. If the clan yakuza needs something done that they do not want the clan to be associated with, they can turn to a freelancer. Who, for appropriate remuneration, will do the job for them. A freelance yakuza can also be used as a scapegoat for crimes commited by the clan. A freelancer is truly a genius if he can manage to start up his own clan and stay alive. It is normal for a freelance yakuza to become a clan member, unless, of course, he gets killed.

The Yakuza in Modern Japan

In a society where traditions are highly valued, the yakuza, or Japan's native organized crime group, really goes against the grain.

The yakuza have been active in extortion, illegal gambling, prostitution-related activities and drug trafficking for decades. But over the years they have become involved in new forms of crime, such as financial crime involving big corporations, firearms smuggling, large scale swindles and corruption. Furthermore, new types of criminal groups have emerged in recent years. These include organized criminals from neighbouring regions as well as cult groups which carry out various illegal activities from fraud to murder.

To try and eradicate this type of organized crime on March 1, 1992, the Japanese government passed the Act for Prevention of Unlawful Activities by Boryokudan (yakuza or criminal gang) Members. This act describes the term *boryokudan* as a group with more than a certain percentage of membership as having a criminal record. This new commercial law also put much tighter controls on the *sokaiya*, a racketeer who extorts money from companies by causing trouble at stockholder's meetings. The sokaiya would harass companies, sometimes resorting to blackmail by unearthing scandals involving the management of the company. Another way they would extract money was by playing the role of protector at the stockholder's meeting to stop any tough questioning by stockholders.

This revision in the law made it a rule to arrest not only the sokaiya who received payment from their victim companies, but also the corporate management who paid them. As the sokaiya could no longer make a profit from their traditional business, they associated themselves with yakuza groups to work on projects such as publishing a magazine which specialized in exposing corporate scandals. This was just one of the way they got round the new law and were able to still receive money from companies in the name of subscription fees. Of course in such cases, the powerful support of the yakuza group helped to increase the amount of subscription fees they could extort from the companies. The smarter ones in the yakuza and sokaiya groups, managed to obtained inside information from these companies regarding the stock market, and this was an assured way of making a profit.

Despite their associations with the boryokudan, the yakuza tries to maintain a respectable reputation by using legitimate businesses as fronts. They have also published a book called *How to Evade the Law*, which was distributed amongst the members of the Yamaguchi-gumi. Around 77 gangs who are affiliated with the Yamaguchi-gumi are now registered as businesses or religious organizations.

In the spring of 1992 there was a march through the streets of Ginza by the wives and daughters of yakuza members, protesting against the new laws. In April of that year, high-ranking yakuza argued that they were not an evil organization, and in fact lived by the code of chivalry and old samurai values. They pointed out that their conduct expresses their noble values, not violence. But this statement was proved to be worthless, when members of the yakuza ambushed and stabbed filmmaker Itami Juzo over an anti-yakuzi movie entitled *Minbo no Onna*. A *boryokudan* defector who commented on the attack was later found shot in the leg.

Even people outside the yakuza organization have protested against the new laws. Over 130 lawyers, professors and Christian ministers proclaimed that the Act infringed on basic rights, such as freedom of assembly, choice of occupation and the ownership of property.

However, the yakuza, it seems, were not even wanted by the ordinary citizens of Japan. Residents in the neighbourhood of Ebitsuka, 130 miles south-west of Tokyo, certainly didn't want any yakuza activity in their district. At the time the yakuza were operating out of a green building which neighbours had nicknamed *burakku biru* or 'black building'. The local residents made video tapes of everyone that went in and out of the building, paying particular attention to those who were wearing flashy suits, dark glasses, crewcut hairstyles and hints of tattoos on their arms. The yakuza retaliated to this intrusion on their privacy by smashing the windows of the local garage, stabbing the town's lawyer in the lung, and slashing another activist in the throat.

The police arrested about half of the Ichiri Ikka gang, who were forced to abandon the *burakku biru* in an out-of-court settlement, as they did not wish to stir up further trouble for gangster in other areas.

Since the aftermath of World War II, violence among the different yakuza factions has increased and the organizations have degraded from their original stature. However, a prominent rise has been seen in the *boryokudan*, or violence gangs, and in the *bozozoku*, the biker gangs. These minor factions have introduced quite a considerable amount of discord into the traditional criminal underworld system. Older members of the yakuza are disturbed by the decline of moral values and the increasing use of guns among the up and coming generation of their numbers, a problem which Japan has never really had to face up to in the past. Recent crackdowns by law and enforcement agencies has worked hard to alleviate this situation, but as many of the criminals are released without prosecution, it appears, in fact, that they have had very little impact on the problem.

FINANCIAL TIES

The yakuza have always maintained a very close relationship with Japanese political and corporate entities in their growth through the years. The group has always been hungry for more power and money, when and wherever they can find it.

During Japan's booming economy in the latter half of the 1980s, the yakuza's businesses and investments were extremely profitable. It was possible for them to borrow substantial amounts to finance real estate and high-finance deals. One example of their underhand dealing was a practice called *jiageya* (or land turner). Those that were involved in the jiayega would visit small, old-style shops which were concentrated in the shadows of high-rise buildings in a downtown area. They would persuade the owners to sell their premises and, in this way, the jiageya would clean the area block by block and then sell it on to major real estate companies or developers at a premium price for the erection of commercial buildings.

Another way the jiageya came in useful was when a farmer or landowner was unwilling to part with his land that was situated in the middle of a proposed development, the developer would call on the services of the jiageya. They would 'persuade' the landowner by any means they felt necessary – blackmail, threats, demolition, or even arson. If they succeed in getting the landowner to sell, they are considered skilled jiageya. Many of these jiageya, but not all, are related to the yakuza.

Once firm connections were built with financial institutions, the yakuza was no longer content with just jiageya business, and they started to run real estate businesses, develop buildings and golf courses of their own. The financial institutions seemed to have no qualms and just kept lending them money. In that way a base was established for direct and indirect transactions between the yakuza and security firms and banks.

Today Japanese gangsters still have a hand in the stock market, real estate and even national politics. Their structure resembles that of a multinational corporation. It seems the days are gone when the yakuza's activities were confined to gambling dens, construction sites and control over their local neighbourhoods.

WHERE DOES THE FUTURE LEAD?

The future of the yakuza remains uncertain, but it is highly unlikely that this organization – who can trace its roots back over 300 years – will disappear overnight. Perhaps the gangs will still survive in Japan, moving back into the underground where they hid during the occupation. Or perhaps they will just move their operations elsewhere – only time will tell.

Yoshio Kodama

*In his prime, Yoshio Kodama was considered the
most powerful post-war yakuza godfather.*

Yoshio Kodama was the man who brought peace
to the warring factions and unified the yakuza
in the 20th century.

Kodama came from a poor background and
spent most of his unhappy childhood living with
relatives in Korea. At the age of 21 he formed an
extreme right-wing, ultranationalist group called
Dokuritsu Seinen Sha (Independence Youth
Society), with the main objective of assassinating
the Prime Minister and top cabinet ministers.
However the authorities found out about his plan
and he was arrested and imprisoned for three and
a half years.

Kodama has a gift for balancing his affiliations
between both right wing political groups and
criminal gangs, and he put this skill to use over the
years. He was a political fixer who served his
government through corruption, espionage and
other dirty dealings.

Recognizing Kodama's skills and contacts, the
Foreign Ministry made use of his underworld
connections sending him to North China on a fact-
finding mission. There he cleverly established a
network of spies and informants, feeding

information back to the Japanese government.

In 1942 the Naval Air Force commissioned him to collect raw materials for the Japanese war effort. He procured large shipments of materials, such as nickel, cobalt, copper and radium, sometimes bartering for these supplies with heroin. The Japanese government were so grateful that he was awarded the title of rear admiral. By the time the war was over in 1945, Kodama was worth an estimated $175 million, making his the second wealthiest man in Japan.

The occupation forces, however, were not so impressed, and after the Japanese surrender Kodama was arrested and imprisoned as a high-risk Class A war criminal. He was unexpectedly released in December 1948 as part of a strategic move by the occupation forces to try and eliminate the yakuza. The yakuza had gone underground and were thriving on the proceeds of their rationing and blackmarket activities. There were more than 5,000 rival gangs fighting each other for supremacy in the absence of a clear leader. Clearly the yakuza were out of control. This is where Kodama came into the picture with his contacts, money and leadership potential. Personally Kodama hated warfare and loathed street hoods, even though they were such an important part of his power base. Ironically, it was his dream to secure peace in Japan.

Ultimately, this was the pinnacle of his career. He succeeded in realizing a truce between the warring factions, uniting them under the collective title yakuza. He was given the title 'The Kingmaker' and emerged as Japan's most powerful underworld figure. His wealth and powerful connections earned him respect from all quarters.

In 1949 the CIA paid Kodama $150,000 to use his underworld connections to smuggle a shipload of tungsten out of China. The load never arrived, and Kodama claimed it sank while carrying its cargo, but he kept the fee anyway. In the same year Kodama ordered the Meiraki-gumi gang to disrupt a labour movement at the Hokutan Coal Mine.

Kodama was also involved in the notorious Lockheed scandal which started in 1976. The Lockheed Corporation wanted to break into the Japanese market with their military and civilian aircraft, which included the new TriStar. The Corporation paid the godfather more than $2 million to influence the Japanese market away from McDonnell-Douglas and Boeing and towards Lockheed.

To do this, Kodama sent a gang of sokaiya to disrupt a meeting of Nippon Airways stockholders. The sokaiya spread rumours of an illegal million-dollar loan made to the president of the company, Tetsuo Oba, who had rejected Lockheed's bid for a new fleet of passenger aircraft. The pressure mounted and Oba was forced to resign making way for someone who was more receptive to Kodama's and Lockheed's interests. His replacement was hand-picked by Kodama, and the new president was surprisingly in favour of purchasing Lockheed's wide-bodied jets. Boeing and McDonnell-Douglas were not impressed.

When the scandal actually broke in 1976, tax officials started to dig a bit deeper and found an additional $6 million in evaded taxes. Carl Kotchian, Lockheed's president, was called to testify before a United States Senate committee who were investigating the scandal. The shock-waves from his shocking testimony reached as far as Japan, spurring the national police to investigate Kodama's participation in the scandal.

Although the police were unable to find enough evidence to prosecute Kodama for the Lockheed incident, they did uncover the fact that he had evaded paying taxes to the value of $6 million. The general public were outraged by the enormity of his tax-fraud scheme. So much so that a young actor, Mitsuyasu Maeno, who had been a staunch supporter of Kodama, flew a small plane into Kodama's Setagaya home in a semi-successful kamikaze mission – only the pilot died.

Although Kodama had survived the kamikaze mission, by now his empire was crumbling. He was indicted for perjury, bribery and violation of the exchanged laws, but Kodama was too sick to stand trial. Kodama suffered a stroke on January 17, 1984 and died peacefully while awaiting trial. Fittingly, the title of his memoirs that he wrote in prison – *'I was defeated'*.

Kazuo 'The Bear' Taoka

Kazuo Taoka was boss of the most powerful yakuza family in Japan – the Yamaguchi-gumi. He was the toughest and most feared yakuza boss Japan had ever known. Under his reign the Yamaguchi-gumi grew more powerful than ever before.

Taoka was born on March 28, 1912, in Sanshomura, Japan. His parents were unable to take care of him and so at an early age he became an orphan. Taoka was forced to work on the Kobe docks where he soon turned to a life of crime in order to survive. He joined a gang under the leadership of Noburu Yamagu, and soon proved to a fierce street fighter. One of his special moves was to claw his opponents eyes with his fingers and this signature move earned him the nickname *Kuma* (the Bear). In 1936, at the age of 23, Taoka was sentenced to eight years in prison for killing a rival yakuza member. He was released in 1943 and his friends in the Yamaguchi-gumi clan welcomed him back with open arms.

In 1946 the boss of the Yamaguchi-gumi, Noburu Yamaguchi, died and, at the age of 33, Taoka took over as the new oyabun. At the time when he took control the gang had been reduced to just 25 loyal kobun, due to police arrests and the military draft. But under Taoka the gangs ranks soon started to swell. Taoka turned out to be an amazing oyabun, and his organizational genius and natural aggressiveness helped to make the Yamaguchi-gumi Japan's premier yakuza clan. Soon they were strong enough to challenge other groups in the area. First to succumb to the Yamaguchi-gumi's powers were the Honda-kai group. They were a major gambling group in Kobe. The traditional gamblers were no match for Taoka's soldiers, and soon the Honda-kai was swallowed up by the Yamaguchi-gumi.

The next targets were the Korean gang, the Meiyu-kai. The defeat of this gang gave the Yamaguchi-gumi a controlling share of the Osaka rackets. Still Taoka wasn't satisfied with his empire and so he ordered his soldiers to take on the Miyamoto-gumi. Operating like a war-time commanding general, Taoka moved in on the Miyamoto-gumi and they too were engulfed into the ranks of his clan. His clan were growing ever more powerful and finally he felt they were strong enough to tackle the great Kodama. However, his attempts were foiled following talks with Kodama. Kodama was one of the most respected yakuza oyabuns in Japan and he brokered a historic pact between the Yamaguchi-gumi and Tokyo's powerful Inagawa-kai. The deal was sealed at Taoka's home in a traditional *sakazuki* ceremony in which blood brotherhood was sworn over elaborately poured cups of sake. When the sake had been consumed, the ceremonial cups were wrapped in paper and put away inside the representative's kimonos. Then the men clasped one another's hands and a mediator declared the ceremony complete. This alliance created a yakuza monopoly with only four of Japan's prefectures free of their control.

By 1978 Taoka was living the good life. He had the power and the money and now he could just sit back and enjoy it. But the good times were to be soured. In July of that year, Taoka was relaxing in a Kyoto nightclub enjoying a limbo performance. He was, as always, surrounded by his bodyguards, but that did not stop a young man named Kiyoshi Narumi from walking up to the godfather's table. He pulled out a .38-calibre pistol and started shooting. Despite the quick reactions of his bodyguards, Taoka was hit in the neck, and the assassin managed to escape. Taoka was rushed to the hospital in his bulletproof black Cadillac. Taoka survived the attack and discovered that Narumi was a member of the Matsuda syndicate, whose boss had previously been killed in a skirmish with the Yamaguchi-gumi. Several members of the Matsuda gang, including Narumi, had eaten their oyabun's ashes, vowing to avenge his murder. This young man tried, failed, and was found dead several weeks later in the woods near Kobe.

These were the glory days for the yakuza, and under the control of Taoka the Yamaguchi-gumi went from strength to strength.

In 1981 Kazuo Taoka died from a heart attack. His funeral was a grand affair attended by high-ranking Yamaguchi-gumi members from all over the country, as well as a number of well-known celebrity entertainers. Following his death the clan had problems getting back to normal. The National Police Agency took advantage of the customary three-month mourning period and arrested 900 Yamaguchi-gumi members in the hope of weakening the gang following their godfather's demise. Although Taoka had chosen a successor before he died, a man named Yakamen, he was in prison at the time of his death. In the chaos that was created by the lack of a leader, Taoka's widow, Fumiko, took control of the reigns and prevented a power struggle within the gang. She was mainly a figurehead in a male-dominated society and, although she didn't make any major decisions, she maintained order until a permanent new oyabun could be appointed.

Hisayuki Machii

*The man who paved the way for Koreans in
Japanese organized crime was the Korean yakuza
godfather Hisayuki Machii. The Korean yakuza are
a powerful presence in Japan, despite the fact that
Koreans suffer discrimination in Japanese society.*

Born Chong Gwon Yong in 1923 in Japanese-occupied Korea, Machii was an ambitious street
hoodlum who saw an opening in Japan and seized
it with both hands. Although Japanese-born people
of Korean ancestry are a significant segment of the
Japanese population, they are still considered
resident aliens. However, Koreans who are often
shunned in legitimate trades, are welcomed into
the Japanese yakuza precisely because they fit into
the gang's 'outsider' image.

Following the Japanese surrender, Machii
worked with the United States Counter Intelligence Corps, who valued his staunch anti-communist beliefs. While many of the leaders of
the Japanese yakuza were either under close
scrutiny or serving a prison sentence, the Korean
yakuza were left alone to take over the lucrative
black markets. Machii, rather than trying to rival
the Japanese godfathers, made alliances with

them. Throughout his career, he had both Kodama and Taoka as his close allies.

In 1948 Machii established the Tosei-kai, or 'Voice of the East' gang, taking over Tokyo's Ginza district. They became so powerful in Tokyo that they became known to the police as the 'Ginza police'. Even Yamaguchi-gumi's powerful oyabun, Taoka, had to make a deal with Machii to allow his group to operate in Tokyo. Machii's enormous empire included tourism, entertainment, bars and restaurants, prostitution and oil importing. Like Kodama, he made a lot of money just on his real estate investments. But more importantly, he negotiated deals between the Korean government and the yakuza which allowed Japanese criminals to set up rackets in Korea, a country that had been victimized by the Japanese for many years. Thanks to Machii, Korea became the yakuza's second home. Machii also acquired the largest ferry service between Shimanoseki, Japan, and Pusan, South Korea, which was the shortest route between the two countries. It was a fitting tribute to his work in forming an alliance between the underworlds of the two countries.

Machii was forced to disband the Tosei-kai in the mid-1960s due to police pressure. He decided to form two outwardly legitimate businesses to act as fronts for his criminal activities – the Towa Sogo Kigyo (East Asia Enterprises Company) and the Towa Yuai Jigyo Kumiai (East Asia Friendship Enterprises Association).

It is also rumoured that he helped the Korean Central Intelligence Agency kidnap the then-leading Korean opposition leader, Kim Dae Jung, from a Tokyo hotel. Kim was taken out to sea where he was bound, gagged, blindfolded and fitted with weights so that his body would not float up to the surface. The execution, however, was abruptly halted when aircraft flew over the ship, and Kim was mysteriously delivered to his neighbourhood in Seoul. It is believed that it was the intervention of the Americans that saved his life. Following a police investigation it was discovered that Machii's people had in fact rented every other room on the floor of the hotel where Kim had been staying. Machii, however, was never charged with any crime in connection with the kidnapping. Machii 'retired' from the yakuza when he was in his 80s and was frequently seen on holiday in Hawaii.

The Biker Gangs of Japan

Japan's teenage biker gangs are young, fast and deadly and were once seen as little more than rebels. But with violent crime soaring rapidly, Japanese society is coming to regard them now with real alarm.

Teenage biker gangs in Japan are known as *bosozoku* and it is thought that these young thugs could be linked in some way to the yakuza. Not surprisingly, killings by unstable teenagers get a lot of public attention, and yet police statistics show that the clear majority of these crimes – murder, manslaughter, assault, extortion and robbery – is in fact committed by bosozoku gangs.

Information supplied by a 'retired' leader of one of the Tokyo-based teen gangs, shows that possibly as many as 80 per cent of bosozoku gangs pay yakuza mobsters cash tributes amounting to several hundred thousand yen a month.

Serious bosozoku crime has risen dramatically in recent years, in fact more than doubling since 1996. The gangs are increasingly resorting to violence using bats, steel pipes and knives as weapons, whereas only ten years ago they just used their fists. On average each gang has around 25

387

members. The ties between these gangs and the yakuza were not always close.

Apparently when the bosozoku first took to the streets in the mid sixties, they were dominated not by knife-wielding thugs but by rebellious teenage car and bike enthusiasts. Dedicated to flouting authority and driving their machines as fast as possible, they gathered at night to play hide-and-seek with the police along Japan's roads.

At the time, the yakuza gave the bosozoku a wide berth. In fact if the yakuza thought of the bosozoku at all, it would be as annoying teenagers, ill-suited to organized crime. They had no need for them in the 1960s and 1970s because Japanese law and widespread prejudice barred Japan's burakumin underclass from taking good jobs. Consequently this left a number of embittered potential yakuza recruits. Since the yakuza worked quite openly alongside the police and the ruling Liberal Democratic Party to crush left-wing dissent, they faced virtually no opposition from the officials.

However, in the 1960s and 1970s things changed quite dramatically, and the yakuza bosses were very keen to enlist bosozoku members into their clan. This was mainly because of a series of legal changes which opened up new professions to the burakumin, consequently decimating the yakuza's traditional post-war recruiting pool.

Initially the bosozoku were quite flattered that the yakuza would want to recruit them into their organization. But, over time, virtually all came to regret their ties to the big boys of Japanese crime.

It appeared that the yakuza, who now were considerably short of cash, often squeezed money from the bosozoku under the threat of violence, charging them a form of 'road tax' for riding their bikes, and also forcing them to buy amphetamines. The only way for the bosozoku to meet these financial demands was to turn to crime – typically theft, extortion and assault. In one case that came to the fore, police arrested 19 teenagers for nearly 100 muggings, assaults and thefts around Nagoya, and during their investigations discovered that a significant chunk of their ill-gotten gains had been paid to local mobsters.

Due to their associations with the yakuza, fierce battles have broken out between rival bosozoku gangs. This was due to the fact that the bosozoku needed more and more turf to meet the hefty 'protection' payments enforced by the yakuza. As bosozoku interaction with Japan's mobsters has grown, so have their crimes and also their acts of public defiance. They started to make their mark in society by driving around in late-night motorbike convoys, with their crudely-modified bikes emitting a deafening squeal. In the biggest incident so far, in downtown Hiroshima in November 1999, over 1,000 bosozoku members threw rocks and Molotov cocktails at the police, and this conflict lasted for three days and nights in a row.

Concerned that such street brawls may represent the future of Japanese youth crime, politicians, police and civic groups are working hard together to stop the bosozoku in their tracks. Last year the Japanese parliament revised the nation's juvenile law, lowering the age at which teenagers could be prosecuted from 16 to 14. The police have put more officers on the streets and are closely monitoring the bosozoku movements by helicopter. Police in Fukuoka, in southern Japan, are making use of a device made from tape, glue and rope that is laid in the road to stop the bosozoku bikes by wrapping itself around the rear tyre. Civic groups are taking their own stand by putting pressure on petrol stations and motorbike accessory dealers to turn away any customers who belong to bosozoku gangs.

Hopefully all these measures will help to put a stop to the constant problem of the Japanese biker gangs.

The Triads

*The Triads are undoubtedly the oldest criminal
society in the world, with a history over three
hundred years long and roots in traditions that go
back even further. Chinese secret societies go back
to the time of Christ and include such colourful
groups as the Red-Eyebrows Society, the Copper
Horses, the Iron Shins, The Yellow Turbans and the
White Lotus Society.*

Triads can be traced back to 1674, when secret
societies were formed to overthrow the Chinese
Manchurians and to restore the Ming Dynasty to
power. The Manchu were from a country north of
China (Manchuria) and were seen as foreign rulers.
They took over China's northern capital (Peking)
by force and established their own dynasty in 1674.

According to legend there was a group of 128
Buddhist monks who lived at a monastery near
Foochow in the Fukien province. In his thirteenth
year of rule the second Manchu emperor, Kiang
Hsi, decided to enlist the help of these fighting
monks, or Siu Lam, to defeat a rebellion in Fukien.
In return for their services the monastery received
some sort of imperial power, but these Fukien
Buddhist monks were then seen as a threat.

In the year 1736, the Manchus decided to rid
themselves of the Sonshan Shaolin Temple to

thwart the plans of Taiwanese rebel commander
Cheng-Cheng Gong. Gong had sent troops to the
temple to seek refuge with Abbott Chi Tong and his
128 warrior monks. Fearing this alliance, which
could spell the end of the Manchu rule, two Manchu
officials bribed Ma Linger, who was ranked seventh
among the warrior monks, to spy for them and help
destroy the Shaolin Temple. On a dark, moonless
night, Ma Linger opened a secret passageway to the
two Manchu officials, who set fires in key locations.
The fire spread through the temple with amazing
speed. Realizing that the 128 monks were no match
for the 10,000 Manchu troops, Ma Linger placed
sleeping draughts in the monks' food supplies.
Drugged and helpless, the monks died in their beds
from the effects of the fire.

Only five monks managed to escape that night
and between them they formed the Hung Family
League, which also became known as the Triads.
The word 'triad' in English means 'a group of
three' and denotes the sacred symbol of these secret
societies. This symbol was a triangle enclosing a
modification of the Chinese character known as
'Hung'. Hung by itself had no meaning, but its
enclosure within the three-sided geometric figure
symbolized the union of Heaven, Earth and Man.
When the monks set up their secret society they
devised the triangle-protected Hung as a holy
symbol of their purpose, which was to drive out the
conqueror and again achieve for China that perfect
union of Heaven, Earth and Man.

The remaining five monks set up a new
monastery in the village of Chuan Chow in Fukien

province to keep the Shaolin traditions alive and to form a resistance movement against the Manchus. It was here in Fukien that the five Shaolin ancestors Wu Mei, Chi Shan, Bok Mei, Feng Daode and Miao Chian gained prominence as masters of the martial arts. Shaolin Martial Arts became known as Sil Lum in Cantonese and Shorinji in Japan. The moves were based on those of five certain animals – Tiger, Dragon, Snake, Leopard and Crane. Each animal each represented the natural instincts or 'Five Essences' that the Shaolin monks felt all people possessed. The Dragon fuels the spirit; the Tiger trains bones to resist heavy blows; the Leopard develops strength and footwork; the Crane loosens sinews and ligaments; while the Snake builds Chi or internal strength.

Alongside the martial arts training, the monks developed secret codes to frustrate the emperor's spies. However, this secrecy and the martial arts training eventually led to the associations being used for criminal purposes. During this period many Hung families were seen as protectors of the people against a repressive and sometimes vicious regime of the emperor.

These secret societies played roles in several rebellions against the Manchus, notably the White Lotus Society rebellion in Szechuan, Hupeh and Shansi in the mid-1790s; the 'Cudgels' uprising in Kwangsi province from 1847 to 1850; and Hung Hsiu Chuan's Kwangsi-based rebellion from 1851 to 1865. The Boxer Rebellion in Peking in 1896 to 1900, again involved the White Lotus Society, as well as other triad groups called the 'Big Swords' and the 'Red Fists'. The founder of Republican China, Sun Yat Sen, was allied with the Hsing Chung triad society in his 1906 rebellion. Meanwhile, the Western powers and Japan virtually seduced China, by stealing gold and heritage antiques, influencing drug sales, and demanding huge rewards for their provocation.

The Manchus were finally overthrown in 1911, but there were no Mings left to restore.

Sun Yat Sen's successor was warlord Yuan Shik Kai, who worked with the triads in corruption. In 1927 the Nationalist government was set up in Nanking, and it was headed by a known killer and criminal member of the Shang Hai Green Gang, Chiang Kai Shek. The triads took over the government of southern China, and fought the Communists (later under Mao Tse Tung) for total control. Western powers used this 'Green Tang' organized crime group of suppress any labour unrests and to kill off Communists.

When the Japanese invaded most major Chinese cities in World War II, the triads offered to work for them instead. In Hong Kong, the triads ran criminal enterprises for the Japanese. The Japanese united these gangs under an association called the Hing Ah Kee Kwan (Asia Flourishing Organization). The gangsters were used to help police the residents of Hong Kong and also to suppress any anti-Japanese activities. The gangs were paid through a Japanese front company called Lee Yuen Company.

At the end of World War II, the target of the West and the triads once again became the Communists. Chiang Kai Shek's nationalist government campaigned to increase triad membership and it was estimated that by 1947 there were around 300,000 triad members in Hong Kong alone.

When Mao Tse Tung's communists were victorious in 1949, these triad nationalists were forced to disperse. They went to Hong Kong, Macao, Thailand, San Francisco, Vancouver and Perth in Australia. The communists suppressed the triads on the mainland, executing and imprisoning many of their members.

In 1956 there was a major riot in Kowloon which was exploited by the triads now resident in Taiwan. Emergency Regulations were passed by the colonial government and 10,000 suspected mobsters were arrested. During this period the triads were semi-dormant. However, the cultural revolution in China was just one of several factors which caused massive emigration and social problems. This included the resurgence of triad criminal activity, most of it concentrating in Hong Kong, but also extending to several continents.

CEREMONIAL RITES AND TRADITIONS

Triads differ from traditional organized crime, due to their elaborate system of rituals and traditions. Membership into a triad society traditionally began with an apprenticeship leading to full initiation, which involved three days of ritual called Hung Mun. On the walls of the chosen place, designated a 'lodge', were hung triad insignia including representations of the mythical triad capital city, Muk Yeung. A Heung Chu, or incense master, presided over the rites. Blood was drawn from one of each recruit's fingers by the Heung Chu, tasted first by the recruit himself, then added to a communal bowl from which everyone drank to signify blood-brotherhood. The recruits also subscribed to 36 oaths, 21 codes, 10 prohibitions, 10 penalties and 10 mottos.

Today's version of these rites has been simplified, but at least one oath of allegiance continues to be sworn. Of the original 36, most telling was number 13:

'If I should change my mind and deny my membership of the Hung family, I will be killed by a myriad of swords.'

Spoken or not, that oath never lay far from being implemented if it was renounced.

Early initiation rites often took place in temples or cemeteries, locales which fostered a sense of both spiritual and eternal commitment. It was believed that the ritual entry into the sacred bond of Taoist-oriented triad confraternity signified re-birth. Recruits took part in the ceremony of Kwa Lam Tang Lung, or 'Hanging the Blue Lantern'/ In China, a blue lantern placed outside a house would be synonymous with the black wreath hung on front doors in the Western hemisphere, signifying a recent death. One had to 'die' before resurrection into life as a triad brother.

Although joining a triad society implied a willingness to commit mayhem and murder on command, initiations after 1956 more closely resembled acceptance into a service club. The Sen Wei Yen (new soldier), was proposed for membership by a Tai Lo (elder brother), meaning mentor. The recruit was obliged to pay a fee and swear allegiance before receiving instructions in secret signs of mutual recognition. This oath of loyalty became the pressure point of a recruit's future association with the society. Once having uttered it he was locked into the triad for life, as there was no way out. Although a member might 'retire' from active duty, he could always be recalled at any time without explanation, to help in triad matters. This could involve either giving financial aid, or more sinister, to hide a fugitive 'brother', arranging complex and expensive escapes from Hong Kong, or even setting up the transfer of drugs to Europe and North America.

The Taoist numerical principles of good and bad luck were operative factors in all triad societies. Nine embodied connotations of luck, as did three and six. Four was unlucky. If the number four was used, a lucky number had to follow to offset the bad luck. The principles were even extended to initiation fees in the triads themselves. Although a new member could actually pay as much as a $1,000 for the privilege of joining, the figure recorded might only be $36.60 for luck.

For this very reason the sums demanded even now in Hong Kong extortion cases – such as HK$6600.39 (very lucky because it includes six, three and nine), HK$449.46 (unlucky four offset by lucky nine and six) or HK$9999.99 (for maximum luck) – still seem a little bizarre to the

Western mind.

The command echelon of triads was structured numerically, not just for luck, but also to facilitate mutual recognition and to avoid detection.

The chief officer (also known as First Route Marshal or Shan Chu 'Mountain Owner') was designated Four-Eight-Nine (489). Four, eight and nine add up to 21. The character Hung inside the symbolic triangle of the triads consists of three parts: an upper right, a left, and a lower right. In old Chinese script, the writing of 21 forms the upper right of Hung.

The Second Route Marshal or Fu Shan Chu 'Second Mountain Owner', became Four-Three-Eight (438). The same number could be assigned to the Heung Chu, the 'Incense Master' in the initiation ceremony, or to persons honoured with 'Double Flower', a title denoting high command. Four was ignored in the four, three and eight combination because the calligraphic symbols for three and eight comprise the left and the lower right parts of hung. Thus, the numerical designations for the two highest-ranked officials of the triad society rendered complete the central character within the holy triangle.

The counsellor, or chief of staff, was assigned the numbers Four-One-Five (415). He was also known as Pak Chi Sin or 'White Paper Fan'. His duty was to advise on organization, administration and finance. The use of four, one and five symbolized four times 15, plus four – or 64, a multiple agreeing with eight times eight, representing eight groups of eight diagrams each, which memorialized a series of military tactics used successfully by an ancient general.

Four-Two-Six (426) took charge of the fighting section of the triad. This was the Hung Kwan, the 'Red Pole', who played the leading role in battles against rival societies. The numbers four, two and six represented four times 26, plus four, equal to 108 legendary heroes who fought in a band against government oppression during the Sung Dynasty.

Number Four-Three-Two (432) was the liaison officer or Cho Hai 'Straw Scandal'. He served as chief messenger in matters such as rallying manpower to fight. He also delivered demand notes for protection or extortion fees. Four, three and two stood for four times 32, or 128, the number of monks who practiced martial arts in the Siu Lam Monastery in the 1600s.

The lowest of triad ranks was Four-Nine (49), denoting a sort of foot soldier. This combination signified four times nine, or 36 – the traditional number of oaths made by a recruit upon initiation.

The Triads Today

Triad conflicts have been part of Macau history for centuries, though the 1990s has been particularly turbulent.

There are around 50 triad groups, many of them minor localized gangs of young thugs, active in modern Hong Kong. There are several larger groups, including the Sun Yee On, Wo Shing Wo and 14K, which are syndicates of sophisticated criminals. The secretive nature of triad societies makes it virtually impossible for police to penetrate the inner sanctums of these organizations.

Probably the most feared triad group, the 14K, has more than 10,000 members locally and more than 20 factions globally involved with trafficking everything from arms to illegal immigrants. It is thought to have got its name from the Nationalist army lieutenant general, Kot Siu Wong, who originally had his headquarters at number 14, Po Wah Road, Canton.

Romanticized legends of the past are far removed from the present-day realities. Triads are menacing, cowardly thugs who prey on the weak, the innocent and the foolish. Their activities are funded by enormous profits from gambling, prostitution, pornography, narcotics, loan sharking, extortion, terror and violence. In fact no criminal act is too despicable if there is money to be made out of it.

Combatting this social cancer is one of the greatest challenges facing the police in Hong Kong. It is mainly the job of the detectives in the Organized Crime and Triad Bureau, which has significant street-level backup from every district. Triads are an extreme threat both to law and order, and also to social stability. The way they prey on small businesses extorting millions of dollars, is passed on to the public. All Hong Kong is held victim by the thugs of organized crime and local street gangs.

Although most of the gangs and organized syndicates operate independently, many triads attempt to spread the myth of one invincible, invisible and all-powerful organization. This fearsome reputation is intended to frighten their victims into silence. Day by day detectives come up against a wall of silence.

Several crime agencies – Organized Crime and Triad Bureau, Criminal Intelligence Bureau at Police Headquarters, Narcotics and Commercial Crime Business, Customs, Immigration and ICAC – are all working relentlessly in an endeavour to clip the spreading wings of triads and other organized syndicates.

THE 'GOLDEN TRIANGLE'

Chinese criminal groups are heavily involved in

the drug-trafficking trade, particularly that of opiates. The opium poppy grows extremely well in a strip of land known as 'The Opium Crescent' which is situated between Asia and the Middle East. A portion of the Yunnan region is in the so-called 'Golden Triangle' and certain parts of China's borders coincide with half of the Opium Golden Crescent's northern borders. However, despite this geographical connection, there are precise historic reasons why the triad's influence on the trafficking of drugs comes from the Golden Triangle.

The Golden Triangle is an area which includes territories under the sovereignty of many nations. In the west Burma (which is now called Myanmar), in the north some zones of the Chinese province of Yunnan, in the east Laos and Thailand, while in the south still Thailand and Burma. The whole area covers more than 240,000 hectares where the opium poppy is traditionally intensely cultivated. That part of Burma, in particular, is controlled by the Shan ethnic group, a separatist group who's main activity is the cultivation of opium. The leaders of these forces are tied at all levels to secret Chinese societies. Furthermore, Thailand has a very large Chinese community and therefore is one of the places where most drug intermediations take place.

A large community of Chinese immigrants lives in Bangkok and it represents a recruitment 'supply' for criminal organizations. In fact, Bangkok is one of the most significant intersections for heroin runners heading towards the European and Western markets.

To confirm the central role that the triads play in this drug trafficking, it should be pointed out that large drug consignments coming from the Golden Triangle usually follow land routes passing through China. Crossing the Chinese provinces of Yunnam and Guangxi, the consignments arrive in the Guangdong area, and in particular the city of Canton (or Guangzhou). From here the drugs are sent sent to Hong Kong.

It is also important to point out that many of these routes start in cities like Shanghai or Fuzhou, which are located in the south-eastern provinces. The vast majority of Chinese immigrants who form the Italian community, also come from this same area. Many of the journeys include stopovers in European cities like Frankfurt, London, Paris, Amsterdam, Copenhagen, Zurich, Moscow and Istanbul. Investigations by national and European police forces have uncovered other routes followed by the traffickers – Austria, Bulgaria, Hungary and other eastern European countries – all interested in Chinese immigration.

Before the war, opium was legally smoked in private. But a change in the law left opium addicts in the hands of the triads, who also controlled prostitution and coolie labour. The coolies paid back between 50 and 75 per cent of their wages, and in turn they pilfered the cargos. Hawkers paid protection money to be allowed to sell on the streets.

Up until 1948 addicts were still able to buy their opium at government dispensaries. But over the years patterns have changed and the highly refined 'China white' heroin is now the choice of most addicts. Far more potent than opium, heroin and a shocking assortment of other lethal concoctions fuel an enormously lucrative trade. Despite considerable efforts by police in Hong Kong, allied with international law enforcement bodies, the traffic of narcotics remains a constant threat to society. Although penalties for drug trafficking are severe, including capital punishment, it has done little to staunch the flow as the profits are so vast.

THE TRIAD'S INFLUENCE ABROAD

Chinese organized crime has been present in Europe for a long time, using many important cities as stopovers or even as final destinations for large consignments of drugs and also for undercover immigration. It is known that the triads earn vast amounts of money taking advantage of the desperation and the desire for achievement of the Chinese who hope to find their fortunes abroad. Because of this, the triads can rely on a continuous supply of criminal and cheap labour.

It is not clear when triad members started to infiltrate Great Britain. Triads have been called a 'criminal cancer' in the UK and are looked upon as a major criminal threat. The Organized Crime Unit of Britain's National Criminal Intelligence Service has carried out an extensive assessment of the level of Chinese organized crime activity on the British Isles and this assessment has been code-named Project Chopstick. The NCIS discovered that there four fully operational triad societies operating in the UK in 1990:

Sui Fong also known as Wo On Lok. Most of their members are successful businessmen, who possibly employ Vietnamese or other gangs at lower levels. Sui Fong came from Kowloon, and were founded in 1930s. They have bases in Southampton, London and Nottingham.

The *14K* are a Hong Kong-based gang and arrived in the UK around 1975 from Netherlands.

Sun Yee On whose speciality is Chinese entertainers. Only a few members have been traced in the UK.

Finally the *Wo Sing Wo.* Thought to be largest gang to be operating in the UK. They are extremely violent and are involved in gambling, kidnapping, protection rackets, video piracy and robbery. They are strongest in Manchester, and are a dominant gang in London.

A study of court cases in various parts of Britain, including Hampshire, South Hampton and Edinburgh, Scotland, show that almost all of the crimes involved only the Chinese community and Chinese people. However, the largest Chinese community in Britain is Manchester, which is one of only four cities outside of Asia with a Chinese community strong enough to have its own ceremonial dragon (the other cities are Perth, Western Australia; Vancouver, Canada; and San Francisco, USA).

The Wo Sing Wo are the strongest triad group in Manchester and London, owing to their allegiance to Yau Lap Yuen (in 1990) of Hong Kong. Yau Lap Yuen also operated in Britain as Georgie Pi (aka 'George the Duck'). The Manchester gang was believed to have 30 core associates, and possibly 200 fighters. Their leader, Georgie Pi, was a Red Pole who was forced to leave Britain, but may still possibly be in charge. It seems as though they they are not controlled from Hong Kong and they are not part of some large international criminal organization.

The main criminal activity of the triads is extortion, loan sharking, credit card fraud and video piracy. There is also some evidence of a little involvement in prostitution. Intelligence from the British NCIS indicates that the vast majority of the extortion takes place in the Chinese community. The main victims are traditionally restaurants and other small businesses. The number of reported cases is small, but again, traditionally, the Chinese have a tendency not to report crime to the authorities. Low reported figures does not mean that no crime is happening. But it is very clear and certain that the triads are involved in extortion, using the name, 'Triad', as a means of intimidating their victims.

In the United States, drive-by shootings are commonplace among rival street gangs. Among the Chinese, there are violent assaults but they take on a different form between rival triad groups. An assault called 'choppings' is done with a large knife. Most of the assaults seem to be over a 'loss of face', which is extremely important in Chinese culture.

Britain's NCIS says that Chinese organized crime activity is a cause of concern. The extortion schemes that are operated by the triads creates a climate of fear within the Chinese community. However, in essence, the Chinese triads do not pose any greater threat than other crime groups in Great Britain. The NCIS says that their intelligence does not indicate that the Chinese triads in Britain are involved in drug smuggling, which is contrary to Chinese organized crime groups in North America and Australia, which are heavily involved in drug trafficking. Triad activity appears to be increasing and bears additional scrutiny by law enforcement officials.

There is a record of Chinese presence in the Netherlands from shortly after World War I, when the British started using low-paid Hong Kong sailors to serve on merchant ships. The Dutch retaliated, using a family named Poon as their recruiters. Another major Chinese faction in Amsterdam at the time was the Sam Tin, who were supplying Sun Yat Sen with arms. This resulted in a battle on one of Amsterdam's bridges in the Chinatown area. The authorities, who were unsympathetic with the Republican quarrel, expelled the Sam Tin and allowed the Poon family to stay. Eventually they formed a rich and successful family business.

It was not until the year 1979 that anything that resembled a modern triad influence could be uncovered. It was in that year that 14K's Chung Man or Moon arrived in Amsterdam. He was present of an international club of Chinese businessmen with connections in Taiwan, Amsterdam, San Francisco and Canada. He set up a casino and then branched into the seemingly respectable business of travel agencies. On the more sinister side, though, he became involved in running brothels, extortion rackets and drug dealing.

Another group, this time a syndicate originally based in Singapore, was also operating in Europe. The leaders of the Ah Kong, Golden K and Ah Men, who were wanted in connection with Singapore gangland killings, moved into Holland and started running drugs from the Golden Triangle.

There are now signs that a group called the Tai Heun Chai, 'Big Circle triads', are moving into Britain and Holland. It is believed that they have taken control of the Dutch heroin market, ousting the 14K. In May 1995, two Big Circle gang members were found shot dead in a house in Plaistow, London. They had both been stabbed, but their deaths had gone unnoticed until neighbours complained about the smell. They were believed to be involved in smuggling illegal immigrants into the country in August when they claimed political asylum.

In Nuremberg in November 1993, an operation called 'Rising Sun' was launched in the belief that the 14K and Wo Shin Wo were behind the Chinese restaurants in the area. The authorities rounded up almost the entire Chinese community and had them fingerprinted. The police announced that they had broken a ring using restaurants as a cover for smuggling illegal immigrants. It was claimed that the route for the immigrants came from China via Moscow and Prague, and that they then walked over the forest-lined border into Germany. The police claimed that the 33,000 legal

Chinese residents were matched by a similar number of illegal ones. Guns and heroin were brought from the Burmese Golden Triangle and the funds laundered through restaurants. It was feared that it may be as many as 90 percent of Chinese-own businesses were the subjects of blackmail.

It is feared that the triad problem will get worse following the reversion of Hong Kong to China. The Chinese Intelligence Unit who are based in London's West End, are sure that triads resident in Great Britain are arranging for other gang members to join them here.

THE TONG WARS

With the first wave of Chinese immigrants in the 1800s, many Chinatowns sprung up throughout the west and east coasts of America and in various mining towns throughout the west. These Chinatowns acted as Chinese communities, with everything from shops to restaurants. Eventually, these chinatowns developed various Merchant Associations, which acted as local 'political parties' for the community, hosting various cultural/social town events for the community. However, with the introduction of the Chinese Exclusion Act, many of these 'benevolent' merchant associations soon began to focus their attention on providing vices to the Chinese population, including gambling, prostitution and opium. With the issuance of the Chinese Exclusion Act, the Chinese miners were prohibited from bringing over their wives, which effectively created a 'bachelor' society within the Chinese American community. This caused many Chinese to turn to vices which the Merchant Associations, or Tongs, provided.

It wasn't long before the Merchant Associations began to rival each other for control of the vices. The two most powerful merchant associations were the Hip Sing Tong and the On Leong Tong. As expected, this ultimately led to the Merchant Associations, or Tongs, going to all-out war with each other, culminating in what has become effectively known in history as the 'Tong Wars'.

Fights broke out in almost every major Chinatown across the United States from the mid-1800s and even right up to the 1970s. In fact, it is from these Tong Wars that various Chinatowns obtained their reputation as being neighbourhoods full of violence, opium, and just general hedonism. The foot soldiers were called *boohowdoy*, which is Cantonese for hatchet-boy, because they would always use a hatchet or cleaver as their weapon of choice.

Eventually, the competition between the Tongs began to dissipate and the all-out-wars ceased. Many of the Tongs, however, retained their criminal ways, and even today continue to engage in extortion, murder, gambling, prostitution, smuggling illegal Chinese immigrants into the US, and of course, supplying heroin, also known as China White, from the Golden Triangle.

PART FIVE
RUSSIA

The Mafiya

Although often dubbed the 'Russian Mafia', organized crime in Russia does not fit the usual picture of underworld mobsters. It is far bigger and more complicated: a three-way alliance of officials, businessmen and gangsters reaching into every level of society and the economy.

The rise of the so-called Russian mafiya can be traced back to 1956 when the *vory v zakonye* (thieves-in-law) held a conference in Krasnodar designed to divide up the country into regions which could be controlled by them. During this period, groups of organized criminals made the best out of an economy that was dominated through the rule of communism and the communist dictators that ruled over the old Soviet people with an iron fist.

Going back to the dark days of Soviet communism, syndicated crime was already around, although not perhaps as comprehensive as it is today. After the fall of communism and the wave of freedom that swept across the eastern European States, the Russian gangs of criminals found themselves in an unbelievable position, the position of having more power than the state itself. With the new state just starting to find its feet after the many years of Communism, the true

412

realization would be that the Russian mafiya were now indeed more organized and had more knowledge of how to survive the transition. This was due to the many years they had abused the law even when communism was at its height, and this is why the Russian mafiya is so powerful today.

It is also important to take into account that the Russian mafiya is not restricted like it once was under the old regime. They are now able to cross countries without any restrictions, a far cry from the dull days of communism, when the Masters of the fatherland decreed that they would not do business with foreign countries. The old attitude was that they would manufacture everything they needed, that they would stand alone, without need of any outside assistance, which left the modern Russia with terrible financial problems.

The years of communism have certainly taken their toll on the Russian people, and with the harsh Russian winters it is both understandable and excusable that the Russian people may have a negative outlook on life. After the fall of Communism and the hope of a new regime the native Russians this time had real hope and belief. But realistically, the job of having to turn a government round from the many years of Communism was going to be tough. This was when the mafiya found itself with a perfect opportunity to progress, and were able to offer the people some hope of prosperity, which was long overdue. In fact it is from this point that the Russian mafiya began to grow and prosper. For the first time the people felt that there was some sort of organizational structure within their country, a structure that was at last free of dictatorship. Like any criminal, the Russian mafiya do whatever it takes to cover up the trail of bribery, murder and any other underhand activity, which is vital to an organization of their kind to survive.

But the real question is whether the Russian mafiya is a problem or not. It is thanks to them that the Russian economy has started to pick up. They have also managed to put in place politicians that will do as they are told. They own banks and monopolize large industries, offering many of the Russian people jobs along the way. In more ways than one the Russian mafiya own Russia and some of the old Soviet states like the Ukraine, Moldova and Armenia. The Russian mafiya are probably the most cultivated criminal syndicate in the world, in the sense of governorship within their own country.

Russia is now riddled with criminal organizations and, for many young Russians, succeeding in crime has become far more glamorous than studying hard at a University. Moscow alone is thought to have up to nine different gangs, and St Petersburg, Vladivostok and Kiev are all places of major Mafia activity.

The Russian mafiya has become one of the largest networks of organized crime in the world. It feeds off the political and economical transitions taking place in Russia, undermining objectives of national reform policies. A grey area between criminal and legal business activity has allowed mafiya groups to penetrate most areas of the Russian economy, and has provided them with a disproportionate amount of influence. Between 5,000 and 6,000 gangs operate within the boundaries of Russia, including several hundred organizations whose activities span the territory of the Commonwealth of Independent States, Central and Western Europe and the United States. These transnational groups are regarded as very sophisticated and are believed to be operating in approximately 29 countries.

What really makes the Russian mafiya unique is its infiltration of key sections of the government bureaucracy. It appears that more than half of the country's criminal groups have ties to the government, and a number of mafiya organizations are fronts for the former Soviet party elites who have engaged in illegal activities – including bank fraud – to become wealthy monopoly owners. Added to this, in 1993 successive corruption scandals paralysed the Yeltsin government; senior commanders of the Red Army were caught in smuggling rings, while cabinet ministers and police officials were discovered working for shady commercial firms.

Between the years 1992 and 1994 the Russian mafiya targeted the commercial centres of power, seizing control of the nation's fragile banking system. At first the criminal gangs were content to just invest their large cash holdings in legitimate institutions, but soon they realized that the next step was the easiest of all – direct ownership of the bank itself. Banking executives, reform-minded business leaders, even investigative journalists, were systematically assassinated or kidnapped. In

1993 alone, members of the eight main criminal gangs that control the Moscow underworld murdered ten local bankers. In fact using the old name *vory y zakone*, Russian gangsters have murdered ninety-five bankers in the last five years.

The underpaid and demoralized city police are ill-equipped to curb the rising tide of violence or halt the nightly shootings. Police records show that in 1993 there were more than 5,000 murders and 20,000 incidents of violent crime. Since then conditions have got even worse and it is estimated that around 10,000 people die each year from gun violence – 600 of which are probably contract killings.

MAFIYA GROUPS

The size of the Russian mafiya is estimated at around 100,000 members who pay allegiance to 8,000 stratified crime groups. These groups control 70 to 80 per cent of all private business and 40 per cent of the nation's wealth.

The largest of these groups are the Dolgopruadnanskaya and the drug-running Solntsevskaya, with 5,000 members concentrated in the Moscow suburb of Solntsevo. This group was formed in 1980 by one of Russia's deadliest and most feared criminals, Vyatcheslav 'Little Japanese' Ivankov. The current leader of this cartel is Sergei Mikhailov. It has been alleged that the Solntsevskaya took over the Russian Exchange Bank in September 1992, supposedly replacing the accountants and financial managers with mafia employees hired to oversee money laundering, embezzlement and other illegal operations.

The Georgian mafiya, a major group based in Russia, controlled much of the black market under the Communist system and has now extended its range of activities. Two other organizations with ethnic backgrounds – the Chechens and the Azerbaijani groups – have contributed to a major upsurge in the illegal trafficking of drugs, metals, weapons, nuclear materials and even body organs.

Among the most influential mafiya groups in the United States are the Odessa mafiya, based in Brighton Beach, New Jersey, the Chechens, who tend to concentrate on contract killings and extortion, and the Malina Organizatsia, a multi-ethnic group also based in Brighton Beach, that maintains extensive international connections and is active in a variety of areas including drug trafficking, credit card and tax fraud and extortion.

For a long time now, the Russian mafiya have been branching out into Europe, making ties with Italian mafia groups. The threat of the Russian mafiya is of great concern to the United States as they have already proved that they can easily gain access to nuclear materials – materials that are sold onto terrorist organizations time and time again. Finally, because the Russians don't rely on a hierarchical structure, their efforts are pumped into sheer money-making and large operations that are turning the Russian mafiya into an organization unlike the rest. They go from strength to strength as they continue to integrate themselves into many European countries by buying into their banks giving them the financial grounding that will ensure a healthy future. Foreign companies are estimated to pay up to 20 per cent of their profits to the mafiya as the on-going price of doing business in Russia.

THE EXTENT OF CRIMINAL OPERATIONS IN RUSSIA

Narcotics, prostitution, racketeering, product diversion and counterfeiting of popular Western goods like Levi jeans, video casettes and software applications are the nucleus of businesses for mafiya gangs in the Russian republics. Other groups found a lucrative niche smuggling weapons and plundered art treasures to Europe and the Third World. The Microsoft Corporation have estimated that as much as 98 per cent of all its products in Russia are merely cheap imitations.

St. Petersburg and Moscow form the hub of the flourishing drug trade. In 1992 over 70 laboratories producing cheap, synthetic narcotics were uncovered.

Prostitution was strictly clamped down on until the dawning of Perestroika, and was viewed as a 'Western vice'. Nowadays, however, it is a buyer's market in post-communist Russia and many women choose to sell themselves while others are literally forced into the trade. The girls who work the streets only keep about 20 per cent of their earnings. Corrupt police officials and the mafiya evenly divides the other 80 per cent. It is only the fortunate few who work as highly-paid call girls, that manage to make a reasonable living. The mafiya stepped up the pressure when a move to legalize prostitution was suggested, as they did not want to see this lucrative new venture taken over by government regulators.

The local mafia also control airport taxi companies, forcing the drivers to charge customers double the going rate in order to pay the gangsters their 'service charge'. They are also known to collect between 10 and 20 percent of the takings from private shops, restaurants and kiosks.

Every day large quantities of copper, nickel, zinc, cobalt, weapons and other 'vital materials' are shipped in unmarked trucks or military aircraft, from Central Russia to various Baltic ports. The nation's natural resources are being purchased at subsidized domestic prices and being smuggled abroad for large profits. Western democrats had to stand by helplessly as the mafiya tightened its grip over the distribution of profitable export commodities like aluminium and oil from Siberia. In 1995, the mafiya murdered four executives in order to take control of the aluminium industry.

The theft of cars for the purposes of resale in Russia, Poland and other areas of Eastern Europe, is commonplace. Top-of-the-line luxury cars can now be seen on the streets of Moscow and are frequently the targets of armed hijackers.

Of course the truly frightening aspect to all this is that nothing seems to faze these gangsters despite all the public outrage or governmental crackdowns. During the Brezhnev era, the KGB managed to keep a tight lid on the mafiya.

Between the years 1983 and 1987, Moscow agents arrested and tried hundreds of high-ranking criminals in an attempt to shake up organized crime. Many of these leaders were convicted, shot or committed suicide. In June 1994 President Yeltsin initiated 'Operation Hurricane', which resulted in a 48-hour roundup of 2,200 known or suspected mafiosi and put them in jail. It was a symbolic gesture designed to impress his Western allies, but long-term efforts to stem the crime wave have not been very encouraging.

Semion Mogilevich

*Semion Mogilevich is possibly the most powerful mobster
in the world. He is the greatest evidence yet that the
Russian mafiya is becoming a major threat that the
world must stand up and take note of.*

Semion Mogilevich was born on June 30, 1946,
in Kiev, Ukraine and is said to be proud of the
fact that he is a Russian Jew. Little is known of his
early years and his first criminal credentials came
to the surface in the early 1970s. At this time he
was part of the Luibertskaya criminal organization,
that operated from a Moscow suburb. Mogilevich
was only a small-time crook, trying to stay ahead
of the Communist government, and made ends
meet by participating in petty thefts and counterfeiting. During this period of his 'career' he served
three years in prison for selling currencies on the
black market and another term of four years for
currency dealing offences.

This, however, was all petty crime and hardly
made Mogilevich a rich man. His first experience
of the big time came in the 1980s when scores of
Russian jews emigrated to Israel and the United
States. He made deals with them that he would
buy their possessions, sell them on the markets,

and then send the Jews hard cash to enable them to start a new life in the US. In reality, though, he didn't send them anything and made a lot of money out of the Jews who were so keen to leave.

From here Mogilevich set up a petroleum export company with another major Russian mobster Vacheslav Ivankov, and registered it in the tax haven of Alderney, in the Channel Islands. Mogilevich was an incredibly astute and brainy individual, who held at economics degree from the University of Lvov, earning himself the nickname 'Brainy Don'.

By the 1990s Mogilevich had made several millions. He had invested the money he had extracted from the Jews and made money through weapons smuggling, prostitution, gambling, drugs and black market items. By the start of the 90s Mogilevich found himself in a very good position to further his already massive amount of assets. The Soviet Union was collapsing and the organized crime groups were getting more powerful than ever before. Wars erupted over the Soviet treasure and Mogilevich, along with his top employees, decided to leave Moscow for Israel.

In Israel Mogilevich became an Israeli citizen and kept himself out of the limelight. He made contacts with other Russian and Israel Organized Crime groups, kept running his foreign businesses and expanded his criminal empire. He invested all of his illicit gains in companies. He bought nightclubs, precious stone factories, art galleries, liquor factories and that was just to name a few. He used some of these companies as fronts and to further his already expanding illegal empire. He settled well in Israel and set up groups in Prague and Budapest, also having important contacts in New York and California. However, it would be Budapest where Mogilevich would finally set up his base.

In 1991 he married his Hungarian girlfriend Katalin Papp, which allowed him to move to Hungary and live there on a permanent basis. Soon after settling in Budapest he started setting up his criminal organization. He bought night-clubs and restaurants and, according to the FBI, built up an organization in Budapest of 250 members following the style of the Cosa Nostra family. Mogilevich now found himself in the envi-able position to be able to control certain rackets which was not possible before the breakdown of the old USSR. Also, since he had become a citizen of Israel, he felt sure the Budapest authorities wouldn't know so much about him or what he was setting up in their capital.

Stolen art was always a favourite with Mogile-vich, and he set up a network of thieves that targeted art collectors and museums in Moscow and St. Petersburg. He also set up groups of talented thieves that did the same in East Germany and throughout Eastern Europe. Churches and synagogues were also targeted for their riches. All the plundered goods were sent back to Budapest where Mogilevich had conve-niently bought a jewellery restoration factory. It was from here that Mogilevich chose which art and jewellery he wanted to keep, while the remainder were sold on to other museums in different countries and others on the black market.

Possibly the most remarkable feat that Mogilevich achieved was to corner the entire Hungarian armaments trade, but this time legally. From his acute position in Budapest and due to his many contacts in Russia, Mogilevich was able to buy a weapons factory which was known to sell anti-aircraft guns, missiles and mortars. Nuclear arms and materials allowed Mogilevich to strengthen his reputation and control even further by selling his wares to the Hungarian army itself. This was another business that Mogilevich cornered and absolutely plundered, giving rise to much concern among the authorities. They realized that it posed as a real threat to Eastern European security. This move not only attracted the concern of NATO but the FBI also obtained permission from the Hungarian government to set up their first field office outside of the US.

By the early 1990s Mogilevich, although already a multi-millionaire, decided to look into getting into the narcotics trade. Like everything else he did this was on a large scale, and he looked into buying large amounts of heroin from some of the most powerful narcotics producers in the world today. The Golden Crescent, deep in the Burmese jungle, was the place where most of the world's heroin supply was produced, and it would be here where Mogilevich was to further his already enormous criminal empire. His main problem was, having bought the vast amounts of heroin, how to get it out of the jungle and onto the black market.

But with his astute business brain, Mogilevich soon worked out the perfect plan to pull it off. Even before buying his first shipment of heroin Mogilevich had bought an airline that was in the process of going bankrupt. He used this airline as a means of transporting high-grade heroin from the Golden Crescent suppliers and onto the black markets of Europe. Mogilevich now had groups working for him stretching even as far as New Zealand.

Like all master criminals Mogilevich had a number of loyal lieutenants. One that was well known to the FBI was a man called Monya Elson. After spending some time with Mogilevich in Israel, Elson went to New York in the early 1990s where he targeted a number of Russian immigrants for extortion. Elson was without doubt another major Russian mafiya member who had numerous contacts in Europe. He was arrested in New York for three murders and countless numbers of extortions and is currently serving time in the United States for these crimes.

Mogilevich had most of the politicians and police in his pocket, or so scared that they didn't want to do anything to upset him. He was believed to have wined and dined many Israeli officials and police that kept Mogilevich well informed of any investigations against him. This information gave him more than enough time to adjust his business interests when needed. Despite the fact that he had the authorities eating out of his hand, the Hungarian government still wanted to show Mogilevich and his criminal friends that they were not welcome. On May 31, 1995, a restaurant called 'U Holubu', that was owned by one of Mogilevich's companies, was raided by the police. Apparently two major Russian-speaking criminal organizations were meeting at this restaurant, one from Moscow and the other from the Ukraine. All the men present were arrested and later released. Mogilevich himself didn't attend the meeting and when asked about it said, "Yes, on May 31, 1995, my comrade Victor Averin had his 38th birthday". This raid was only a small hitch for Mogilevich and his organization, it was just a desperate attempt by the government and police to try and maintain some kind of authority and power over criminals that appear to have so much more power and authority than them.

MOGILEVICH'S EMPIRE TODAY

The criminal empire of Semion Mogilevich currently operates in Europe (including Italy, Czech Republic, Switzerland and Russia), the United States, the Ukraine, Israel and the United Kingdom. He also has dealings/contacts with organizations in South America, Pakistan and Japan. It is also strongly rumoured that Mogilevich has offered Interpol and Europol incriminating evidence on many of the Russian groups operating in Moscow and St. Petersburg in an effort to keep himself out of their investigations. Mogilevich is considered to be one of the smartest and most powerful gangsters in the world and so far no one has been able to put a stop to his activities.

Vyacheslav Ivankov

Vyacheslav Ivankov, nicknamed Yaponchik 'Little Japanese', was a mysterious and somewhat mythical figure. He was considered to be the most powerful Russian mobster in the United States.

Ivankov was believed to have been born in the Soviet Republic of Georgia and grew up in Moscow. He very quickly learned the harsh realities of growing up in a Communist world and, although a proud Russian, hated the Communist regime. As a youth Ivankov became a champion amateur wrestler, a toughness that would stay with him throughout his criminal career. It was for fighting that Ivankov received his first jail sentence. He was involved in a bar room brawl in which, according to his lawyer, he was defending the honour of a woman.

Following his release, Ivankov gathered some local hoods together, and quickly climbed the Soviet underworld ladder. Like so many before him he started his criminal career by dealing stolen goods on the black market.

By 1980, according to Russian law enforcement reports, Ivankov had formed a powerful Moscow gang known as the Solntsevkaya syndicate.

Among its many activities, this group used false police documents to search the homes of wealthy individuals and then steal money and other valuables. They were also involved in extortion rackets, fraud, firearms and drugs. The Solntsev-kaya syndicate went on to become the most power-ful Moscow clan in the whole of the old USSR.

In 1982 Ivankov had the taste of his second prison term. He was convicted for robbery, posses-sion of firearms, forgery and drug trafficking and sentenced to fourteen years imprisonment. He was sent to a prison in Siberia to do some real hard time. However, although he only served ten out of the fourteen years, it was in prison that he was initiated as a *vor v zakone*. This is the highest rank in the Russian mafiya. His prison activities during this period antagonized the Russian Ministry of Internal Affairs, which subsequently conspired with the FBI against him. Thanks, however, to a powerful politician and a hefty bribe for a corrupt Russian judge, Ivankov received an early release in 1991.

Ivankov arrived in the United States in March 1992 with a regular business visa indicating that he would be working within the movie industry. It seems amazing that a man with a felony convic-tion, ten years in prison, and a reputation as one of the most powerful criminals in Russia, was able to receive a visa to get into the United States. On his arrival in America he settled in the Brighton Beach section of Brooklyn, New York. It was from here that he put in place some structure of Russian organized crime. The many Russian immigrants, who had heard of him back in the old country, looked upon him as a legendary figure.

In time Ivankov became the Russian godfather in America, in fact the most powerful Russian criminal in the United States. He started out by extorting his fellow Russian comrades and from there moved into a number of different rackets including arms smuggling, narcotics and contract murder. However, it wasn't long before the FBI were onto Ivankov's activities. He had links to another huge Russian crime boss Semion Mogilevich who lived in Israel. Mogilevich had clans all over the world and a number of companies in the United States for the purpose of money laundering. He was already well known to the FBI, and it is believed that Ivankov was looking after his business interests in the United States, although there is no proof of this.

Ivankov was finally arrested in 1995 and charged with supervising the extortion of several million dollars from an investment advisory firm run by two Russian businessmen. He and three co-defendants were convicted of this extortion in July 1996 and is currently serving a nine year and seven month sentence in a US federal prison for both murder and extortion.

There is no doubt that it is thanks to Ivankov that the Russian mafiya managed to get such a strong foothold in the United States. His Brooklyn crew had over a 100 members and is still thought to be the most powerful Russian clan in the US today. Ivankov has an eight-pointed star tattooed on his chest to signify that he is of the highest rank in the Russian mafiya.

Sergei 'Mikhas' Mikhailov

*Sergei Mikhailov's power reaches from Moscow to Miami
to Geneva and the Middle East. He is the boss of the
Moscow-based Solsnetskaya organization, which is the
biggest and most powerful Russian mafiya group in
Russia and probably the world.*

Born on February 7, 1958, in Moscow, Sergei
Anatoliavic Mikhailov grew up in an atmosphere where committing a crime wasn't really a
crime. The real criminals of the day were the police
and politicians who would murder and torture
anyone who opposed the Communist regime.

He started his working life as a waiter in several
different Moscow restaurants. Realizing that there
must be a way to earn more money, he turned to a
life of crime. In 1984 at the age of 26, Mikhailov
was charged with theft and fraud and sentenced to
six months in prison. Inside the prison he came into
contact with gangsters, including members of the
vor v zakonye, the Russian mafiya. These contacts
would serve him well in the future.

By the time he was released Mikhailov was a
hardened criminal with many contacts and a
feared reputation. He was now ready to rise to
power and put together his own organization. He

named it after a neighbourhood in Moscow and it became known as the Solsnetskaya Organization. In the beginning their main activities were extortion, counterfeiting, drug trafficking and blackmail. Sometimes they crossed over into the territory of rival organizations and pretty soon gang warfare broke out. Mikhailov and his Solsnetskaya Organization were always victorious. With the rival gangs out of the way Mikhailov seized total control and soon was involved in more serious activities – arms dealing, infiltration of legitimate businesses and money laundering. It didn't take long before the Solsnetskaya were the biggest, most organized, most powerful and feared criminal organization in Moscow and indeed Russia. Mikhailov's power was enormous and the money coming in was unlimited.

Mikhailov was arrested in 1989 on extortion charges and served eighteen months in a Russian detention centre while waiting for his trial. However, when he went to trial the main witness refused to give evidence, and the case was abandoned. Mikhailov walked free and continued to expand his criminal empire. And expand it did. The Soviet Union was about to fall and the Russian mafiya were to get a whole new playing field.

When the Soviet Union fell there was total chaos, and this is where Mikhailov and the other Russian mafiya bosses took advantage of the confusion. Between them they gained control of the politicians and government resources. Without the strict control of the Communist regime, there was nothing to stop the Russian mafiya totally taking over what the government had left behind. It wasn't long before Mikhailov's organization owned banks, casinos, car dealerships and even the local Vnoekovo Airport. Operating from their new headquarters – a stylish building along the Leninsky Prospekt – the Solsnetskaya controlled prostitution, gambling and weapons dealing. Having now got a stronghold in Russia, Mikhailov felt it was time to expand and he prepared his organization for international expansion.

In 1994, while Mikhailov sent his men all over the world to set up bases, he himself decided to go to Israel. Israel was a popular place to live for Russian mobsters because, due to a certain law, Jews from all over the world may return to Israel and cannot be refused even if they are on the run from the law. Because of this law many non-Jewish Russians obtained fake passports to enable them to live in Israel – Sergei Mikhailov being one of them. From Israel he saw his empire expand, and it was now active all over the world.

He had business dealing with other criminal organizations including the Colombian Cartels and the Italian and Sicilian mafia. His power was enormous and he even had a team of hitmen based in Miami. Whenever someone needed wiping out he simply flew his professional 'combat brigade' to the required destination, the team took care of the hit and then flew back to Miami to wait a new assignment.

In 1995 Mikhailov decided to move to Switzerland where he started to build up a web of bank accounts and companies with respectable directors. According to Swiss court documents Russian mobsters had laundered around $60 billion dollars through Swiss banks. Mikhailov was enjoying the good life. He had put his children in a good private school, bought a castle near Geneva, drove a Rolls Royce, and spent more than $15,000 dollars a month on clothing. That was until the Swiss authorities decided to put some pressure on the Russian mobsters who were moving to Switzerland.

In October 1996 Mikhailov was arrested and charged with being boss of a criminal organization using false documents and breaking a Swiss law which restricted foreigners from buying property. In his castle police found Israeli military bugging equipment on which Mikhailov was able to listen in on secret Swiss police radio transmissions. The police also found many documents with names of bogus companies which had been used to launder money from drugs and weapon sales. Detectives also discovered that Mikhailov had invested millions of his white money in the United States, by purchasing nightclubs in New York and Los Angeles. In addition to this he had also bought a car dealership in Houston. Despite his denial of any criminal activities, the Swiss authorities sent him to prison to await his trial. During this period of internment a lot of things happened all over the world.

Mikhailov was considered to be a major threat to society and so he was denied bail while he waited for his trial. But, while the Swiss prosecutors were gathering evidence against him, Mikhailov was making sure that there wasn't any evidence left. Several people who were known to have done business with him, were found dead. In Holland a father and son were murdered, the father being stabbed in his eye which resulted in him bleeding to death. Meanwhile another man in Amsterdam was found shot dead. Soon after these discoveries the head of the Moscow police department fled to Switzerland, claiming that he was being threatened by some of Mikhailov's men. Even the media received threats. A Belgian journalist, who wrote several columns about Mikhailov, was warned by the local police that there was a contract out on his life. Luckily the police managed to thwart the plot when they arrested a corrupt Belgian policeman who had been hired as the hitman. Finally on November 30, 1998, after a wait of two years, the trial was set. There were eighty witnesses, wearing bulletproof vests, who were prepared to testify. If Mikhailov was convicted he could be facing up to seven years in jail.

The trial turned out to be a huge success for Mikhailov and a major blow to the Swiss authorities. Despite all the evidence found at Mikhailov's home and the large number of witnesses, the Swiss prosecutors could not convict him. The main obstacle that had been in their way was the Russian government. The Russians were asked to give certain documents that would show that Mikhailov was the head of a criminal empire, but they refused. As a result Mikhailov was found not guilty on the most serious charges and found guilty on a minor charge for which he wasn't sentenced as he has already served two years awaiting the trial.

After being freed in December 1998, Mikhailov returned to Russia and sued the cantonal authorities in Geneva for his lost income in the two years he spent in prison – he won his case. In July 1999, a Geneva court awarded Mikhailov the full amount he had claimed, although the authorities appealed against this decision.

Living in freedom Mikhailov leads his criminal empire which now stretches from Asia to Canada back to Moscow and Western Europe. There is no place in the world which is safe from the tentacles of his organization.

Aleksandr Solonik

Aleksandr Solonik was a Russian professional killer who was dubbed 'Sasha of Macedonia' because of his ability to shoot with both hands at the same time.

Aleksandr Solonik was born in 1960 in the Russian city of Koergan. As a child he always showed a great interest in martial arts and guns. When he finished his schooling he decided to join the Russian military. After serving his time in the army he signed up for the militia, which was a security unit used for special commando missions. He learned his militia skills at the Gorkovskaja Institute, but was expelled after only six months for no clear reason.

Back home Solonik gets employment as a grave-digger at the Kurgan cemetery. Solonik was married twice and had a daughter with his first wife and a son with his second. But Solonik is restless and in 1987 he is charged with rape and convicted to eight years in the Gulag (the place the Russians call 'hell'). On the day he was due to leave for the Gulag he was granted permission to say goodbye to his wife. Solonik, however, had other ideas and during this meeting he escaped. He managed to jump from the second floor and fled. After several months Solonik was rearrested 120 miles north of Kurgan. This time the authorities were a lot more attentive and he was heavily guarded on his way to the Gulag.

Because Solonik had worked for the army and had training with the militia, he was entitled to separate lockup away from the rest of the prison inmates. However, for some reason – probably due to his time on the run – Solonik was placed among the normal prison population. When they found out that he had been a soldier and had done work for the militia he was earmarked for death. Since there are no real rules in the Gulag it meant that Solonik had to take care of himself – and he survived. Even after fights where he had to take on sometimes as many as twelve hardened inmates, Solonik still came out on top. After this the other inmates left him alone, he had earned their respect. Solonik was a loner while serving his sentence, and after two years he managed to escape again.

Once again Solonik returned to Kurgan and joined the local notorious criminal organization where he was employed as a hitman. His first target was the leader of a rival gang, and he was killed in 1990 in the city Tjumen. After this hit Solonik and some fellow mobsters from the Kurgan organization decided to go to Moscow. There were plenty of jobs there for a qualified killer such as Solonik and in 1992 he is hired to kill Russian Vor Viktor Nikiforov. Six months later another important Russian moss boss, Valeri Dlugatsj, was shot down in a crowded disco despite the fact that he was surrounded by his bodyguards. Solonik was also employed to kill Dlugatsj's successor, Vladislav Vinner. These were all big-time hits, but his biggest one was still to come. In 1994 Solonik tried to extort a Russian mobster and was told in no uncertain terms that he wasn't prepared to pay anything. The mobster made a phone call and put the speaker on to Solonik. He knew that the speaker was Otari Kvantrishvili who was one of the most powerful Russian gangsters in Russian history. Solonik left without taking any money, but several weeks later Kvantrishvili is killed. Solonik had got his revenge and apparently with powerful backing from Chechnian groups.

By this time Solonik was well known among the Underworld and law enforcement figures alike. Law enforcement had a special interest especially as Solonik was supposed to be in prison. Solonik was sitting with some fellow criminals having a drink in a Moscow marketplace when they were apprehended by the Moscow militia. The militia made a big mistake and didn't bother to check Solonik for weapons, because under his jacket he was carrying an automatic weapon. He opened fire and hit six members of the militia. Solonik is hit as he tries to escape and eventually the militia managed to overpower him. Solonik was back in prison but this time in Moscow, where he was operated on to have the bullet removed. Whilst in prison he studied foreign languages and in 1995 he escaped again.

As he was so well known and had few hiding

places left in Russia, Solonik headed for Greece using a forged passport and faked identity which he obtained from the Greek consulate in Moscow. In Greece Solonik set up his own organization of around fifty men who dealt in narcotics and of course his speciality – contract killings. His new organization bought several villas but everything was done in complete secrecy. The Russian government and law enforcement agencies had no clue what had happened to Solonik and his legend as 'superkiller' grew in the public eye.

In February 1997 the legend was over. Greek newspapers published articles that said a Russian mob boss had been found fifteen miles from Athens. The man had been strangled and, although he had no identification papers on him, was later identified as Aleksandr Solonik from his fingerprints.

In the weeks after his death the Greek authorities raided the villas belonging to Solonik's organization and found an arsenal of weapons. Andrei Pylev, who was involved with a Moscow Organized Crime group was later detained in the Spanish city of Marbella and charged with the crime of killing Aleksandr Solonik. Solonik remains to this day a legend for the Russian public and is still known as a 'superkiller', which is the name for the best contract killers in Russia.

Evsei Agron

Evsei 'The Little Don' Agron was an important figure in the Russian mob, but he simply had made too many people angry in his lifetime.

Evsei Agron arrived in the United States on October 8, 1975. He was just one of the 5,200 Soviet Jews who fled Russia that year. Many of these Jewish immigrants were tough Russian gangsters who were deported by the KGB. By the time he arrived in America he had already served seven years in a Russian workcamp for murder. By the time he left the workcamp he was already a fully-fledged member of the VOR brotherhood (*vor* standing for thief, lord of crime).

When Agron first left Russia he already had some experience of the free western world, because in 1971 he ran a huge prostitution and gambling operation in Hamburg, Germany. When he arrived in Brighton Beach, New York, the people already knew who he was. His reputation and membership of the VOR brotherhood made Agron the most feared man in Brighton Beach. At first he didn't attract too much attention himself. He had an office inside the El Caribe Country Club, and it was from there that he ran a ruthless organization extorting the Russian community, from doctors to lawyers and store owners. Everyone paid up, they knew what would happen if they didn't. The other men in Agron's group were as ruthless as him, but the Russians still hated Agron the most. He was known to carry an electric stick, which was used to control cows, around with him, and he used this stick to torture his victims. It appeared that, in contrast with most Russian VORs, Agron found being feared more important than being respected, and that would turn out to be his downfall.

One night in 1980 while Agron was walking through Coney Island, he was shot in the stomach. He was taken to Coney Island hospital where he was guarded by a hired ex-policeman who belonged to the Genovese family, with whom Agron was known to have connections. When he was asked by the police if he knew who had shot him, he replied that he did but that he would take care of the matter himself. There were a lot of people who would like to see Agron dead, but whoever it was that was behind the attempt on his life, Agron resumed his life as if nothing had ever happened. His men went back on the streets and truck hijacking became their favourite occupation. Agron even bought a Russian newspaper company that provided the Brighton Beach Russians with the daily news.

Agron was now at the top of his game, his position among his group of ruthless Russian mobsters was unquestioned and his operations had even expanded to six other major US cities. Agron was also supported by two very powerful allies – the Genovese family and Ronald Greenwald, a Jewish rabbi who was active in politics. In return for their friendship the Italians were able to obtain Russian manpower and also to expand their operations to the Russian neighbourhoods. The friendship was also very important to Agron, for the Italians had an enormous army of soldiers and very beneficial political connections. Although the Italians and Russians made a lot of money by working together, there was still some friction between the two groups. Most of the Italians lived modest lives without trying to attract attention to themselves, while on the other hand, the Russians loved the attention and loved to boast about their wealth. The Russians did not live by the same code of standards as the Italians.

By the mid 1980s Agron was feared by many people and his power had seriously grown. He was doing bigger heists and making even more money than ever before. But even though he was a sort of godfather figure, working with professional crime groups, the Russian groups in his neighbourhood were still running rampant and out of control. There seemed to be no structure or control and it was quite apparent that another attempt on his life could be made at any time. In January 1984 Agron was indeed shot again. He was hit twice, once in the face and once in the neck, both from a very close range. Again Agron was taken to the Coney Island hospital and again he survived. His face, however, was severely disfigured and left him with a weird grin.

The prime suspect in this shooting was a man called Boris Goldberg, an Israeli ex-army officer from Russia. Goldberg ran a group of criminals together with David 'Napoleon' Shuster, who was a known criminal mastermind. The Goldberg group had amassed an enormous arsenal including guns with silencers, boxes of grenades and plastic explosives with detonators.

Because of their kindred spirit it was inevitable that both Agron and Goldberg would meet at some time. One of the areas that had caused friction between them had been the extortion areas. They had had several meetings to discuss who would have which territory, but every time things got out of hand. After the second attempt on his life, Agron called a meeting with Goldberg at Agron's Country Club. When Goldberg arrived with his trusted soldier, they were welcomed by fifty silent, heavily-armed Russians who sat at a round table. After a heated discussion in which Agron asked Goldberg if he was behind the hit, things started to go very wrong. Agron didn't believe that Goldberg wasn't involved and wanted to kill him, while Goldberg said that it he wanted trouble he was ready. Agron instructed one of his men to go outside and see if he was bluffing – he wasn't. The parking lot in front of the Country Club was filled with armed men. Agron decided that things were best left alone and the meeting ended without any bloodshed.

However, someone definitely wanted Agron dead, for on May 4, 1985, he was shot in the head twice from a very close range, as he was leaving his apartment to relax in a Turkish bath in Manhattan. This time, however, he did not survive.

Ludwig Fainberg

Ludwig 'Tarzan' Fainberg was the Russian Mafia leader of South Florida. He started out like every other Russian gangster with extortion and fraud, but made it to the big time when he began shipping cocaine for the Colombian Drug Cartels.

Ludwig Fainberg was born in 1958 in Odessa, a Black Sea port in the Soviet Union. His parents marriage ended in divorce when he was very young, and his mother married a man named Czernowitz. They moved to a small city in Ukraine where Ludwig sang for a national boys' choir. He trained as a boxer for the Russian army, but what really influenced the young Ludwig was his stepfather. Czernowitz worked for a factory that produced rugs and fur hats, but he was also a prosperous dealer on the flourishing black market. He provided his family with a comfortable living by trading merchandise for meat, theatre tickets and fresh vegetables.

When Ludwig was 13 the family moved again, this time to their homeland Israel. It was in Israel that he got his nickname 'Tarzan' when he jumped out of a building purely to get attention. Eventually he joined the Israeli Marines and tried to become a Navy Seal, but he didn't get through his basic training. He then tried to become an army officer, but this time failed the exam.

In 1980 Ludwig moved to East Berlin, where he joined up with a Russian crew who were involved in credit card fraud and extortion. This crew was headed by the notorious Efim Laskin, who was a man renowned for selling weapons to the Red Brigade, and it was from him that Ludwig got the assignment to shake down a certain banker. Ludwig and two other men went to the bank and pushed the banker into the trunk of their car, threatening him with death if he wouldn't pay up. The banker told him that he wasn't able to get the money straight away, but would have it by the time the bank closed. The three men waited in the car. After a while, Ludwig stepped out of the car to have a cigarette when all of a sudden four cars pulled up beside the car containing his two associates. The two men received a severe beating and, fearing for his life, Ludwig fled to America.

Ludwig settled in Brighton Beach. It was not quite the paradise that he had been expecting and he made sure that he carried a gun with him at all times. Ludwig's big break came when he married a Russian Mafia princess whose grandfather, ex-husband and brother-in-law were all Russian gangsters. Although her family were all involved in criminal activities, she wouldn't allow him to get involved, and they lived off the money her ex-husband had made through extortion, and for which he was currently serving time in a German prison. She lavished Ludwig with expensive suits and generally treated him to an extravagant lifestyle. Although Ludwig enjoyed the luxuries provided by his wife, he didn't like the feeling of being a kept man. He decided, that if he wasn't allowed to join his wife's family in their criminal activites, then he would make his own arrangements. Ludwig joined forces with another gangster named Grecia Roizes. Roizes had already served a three-year prison sentence in a Siberian prison, and was now the head of the most feared crew in Brighton Beach. Roizes had furniture stores in New York, Italy and Russia that were fronts for a heroin ring used by the Russian Mafia, namely the Gambino Crime Family and the Genovese Crime Family.

One day while Ludwig was working in one of the stores, an elderly lady came in and was treated rudely by one of the young thugs that worked for Roizes. Ludwig, disgusted by their behaviour, stepped in and offered the old woman some free furniture. The following day a muscular Italian man walked into the store and introduced himself as Frankie, the old lady's son. He told Ludwig that he owed him a favour for helping his mother and that if he needed anything at all he should call him – Frankie would take care of it. Ludwig did exactly that and arranged with Frankie to kill Frank Santora, who was a made member of the Colombo Crime Family.

In the year 1990 Ludwig moved to Florida. Florida attracted many Russians who either had money to spend or money to make. Ex-KGB agents and other government officials settled and bought entire buildings with the money they had taken when the Soviet Union collapsed. In South Florida Ludwig opened his club 'Porky's'. The pink neon club was on the fringe of Miami International Airport and was a magnet for Russian hoods who had visions of untapped criminal proceeds.

Ludwig was now heavily involved in the drug business, and owned cannabis fields in the everglades which included a landing strip for aeroplanes. But Ludwig wanted bigger and better things and he moved into the cocaine business setting up links with Colombian drug cartels. Business started to boom and now he was starting to make real money.

Ludwig had an evil side to him though, and that was that he loved to humiliate women. He would beat them, sexually assault them and on one occasion he chased a stripper down the street, beat her up and forced her to eat stones. However, it appeared that his money gave him power and influence and it seemed he could get away with anything. His Russian connections were also serving him well, and in 1993 Ludwig and his Colombian friends bought six M18 Russian helicopters for $1 million each. The planes would have their innards removed to make room for the large shipments of drugs. Not satisfied with this they negotiated to buy a Russian army submarine, including the crew, for $5.5 million. However, before the deal could be finalized Ludwig was arrested.

Suspicious of his activities, the FBI had been

keeping track of Ludwig's movements, checking into his past and his friends. They got their first break when Ludwig's friend Grecia Roizes gave evidence to the FBI so that he could get some time out of prison. Ludwig had trusted his friend and had told him a lot about his business activities. On October 17, 1999, Ludwig was convicted on RICO (The Racketeer Influenced and Corrupt Organization Act) charges. He was labelled a threat to national security and public safety, and was deported back to Israel with fifteen hundred dollars in his pocket. Ludwig said of the land he was leaving, 'I love this country! It's so easy to steal here!'

Alimzhan Tokhtakhounov

In February 2002, the Salt Lake City Winter Olympic Games were rocked by allegations that the French pairs skaters had been robbed of their rightful gold medal. Tokhtakhounov was allegedly right at the heart of the scheme to award figure skating gold to the Russian pair, rather than the French – while his mafia connections just added an extra twist.

Alimzhan Tokhtakhounov was born in 1949 in Tashkent, Uzbekistan. His first setback came when his father died, followed not long after by his mother, leaving him at the age of thirteen to take care of his younger brother. Tokhtakhounov's one love was football and he played it with a passion, eventually making the first team of the Uzbek team Pakhtakor. It was as a football player that he earned the nickname 'Taiwanchik', which means little Taiwanese. But as much as he loved playing football, it didn't pay the bills and Tokhtakhounov needed money to take care of his brother. Desperate for some cash he started playing the cards for money and to his surprise he started winning. His football career ended suddenly as the result of an injury, so he decided to try his luck at other operations in the big city of Moscow.

449

In Moscow Tokhtakhounov started to manage a football team during the day and played cards during the night. He also joined the Izmaylovo Organized Crime group. Things went well for Tokhtakhounov and he was starting to earn a good living from his criminal activities. During a holiday in the town of Sochi he even resorted to scamming tourists out of their credit card money. By now he had given up his job as a football manager and had turned into a full-time criminal. However, in 1972, this proved to be a big mistake because he was arrested for nothing more serious than being without a job. In communist Russia arrests of that nature were commonplace, and in 1980 he was arrested again on similar charges. During his years with the Izmaylovo Organization Tokhtakhounov rubbed shoulders with Russian celebrities and athletes. He met these people while he was working for the Association XXI Century company, a concern which was owned by the powerful mobster Otari Kvantrishvily. He was given the job to take care of any debtors who refused to settle their accounts.

In 1989 Tokhtakhounov decided to leave Russia and planned on setting up a business in East Germany. However, after having spent only three years in East Germany Tokhtakhounov found the attention of the German authorities too great. He noticed that people around him were being killed and the police started to question him to see if he knew the reason. Tokhtakhounov didn't know, but fearing for his own life he fled Germany in 1993. This time Tokhtakhounov headed for France and continued his criminal ways. In 1994, according to French authorities, he was involved in a money-laundering case involving $70 million. French police also questioned him in connection with the murder of a Russian man because they believed he had connections with the man behind the murder. When all the questioning was over, Tokhtakhounov had had enough and decided it was time to return to Israel. However, unable to settle he again returned to France. Tokhtakhounov once again mingled with celebrities and athletes and members of the higher class society, and it paid off. In 1999 Tokhtakhounov was made a knight in the Order of St. Constantine, a ceremony which was attended by several reputed Russian organized crime figures.

In the year 2000, Tokhtakhounov moved again, this time to Italy. Here he bought houses in Forte dei Marmi, Rome and Milan and this time the move seemed more permanent. In Italy Tokhtak-hounov kept a low profile – or so it seemed. On July 31, 2002 it became clear exactly what Tokhtakhounov was doing in Italy – he had fixed the Olympic Ice Skating games.

He was arrested on June 31, 2002, and charged with fixing the pairs and ice dancing figure skating competitions at the Salt Lake City Olympics. According to the FBI Tokhtakhounov fixed the competition for the French couple Marina Anissina and Gwendal Peizerat, and made them win by pressurizing a Russian judge to vote for them. He also put pressure on a French judge to vote for the Russian pair Elena Berezhnaya and Anton Sikharulidze. A day after the pairs medals were awarded, the French judge admitted to buckling under pressure to vote for the Russian pair. Although the judge later rescinded her statement she been suspended from judging. The FBI believe Tokhtakhounov may have arranged the fix in favour of the French ice dancing pair in exchange for a visa to return to France.

True or not Tokhtakhounov was arrested in Italy and kept at Venice's Santa Maria Maggiore prison. The US authorities have requested that the Italians hand him over but so far it seems Tokhtakhounov will stay put in an Italian prison. If the Ice Skating fix turns out to be true it is yet another example of how far the power of the Russian Mafia reaches.

Victor Bout

By the time the world took notice of Victor Bout he was safe in his home in Sharjah in the United Arab Emirates, having made enough political connections and money to make him almost untouchable.

Victor Anatoliyevich Bout was born on January 13, 1967 in Dushanbe, Tajikistan. There is very little known about his early life, but at one point he joined the military forces. After his initial training he began working at a Russian military base in Vitebsk as a navigator. After several years he increased his duties and starting training commando troops for the Russian airforce. In 1991 Bout graduated from Moscow's Military Institute for foreign languages and could now speak six languages fluently. He expanded his military duties even further and became a translator for the Russian army in Angola, Africa.

This was not to last for long, however, because in that same year, 1991, the military base where Bout was working was disbanded as a result of the collapse of the Soviet Union. This meant that Bout and his colleagues were now out of a job. However, Bout and his fellow officers were all well trained, and by now had access to all the equipment they needed, so they started up in their own business. With the help of his international contacts, Bout started the Transavia Export Cargo company which, in 1993, helped supply the Belgian peace-keeping forces in Somalia. But this wasn't the only work that Bout's company was involved with – far more sinister dealings were to be uncovered.

Bout had already made contact with an Afghani group called the Northern Alliance and was selling them vast amounts of weapons. From the years 1992 to 1995 Bout supplied several Afghani groups with tons of ammunition and weapons. Using the money he made from these deals, allegedly $50 million, Bout expanded his empire.

In March of 1995 Victor Bout started a company in the Belgian city of Ostend. This company was named the Trans Aviation Network Group. It got off to a bad start though, because their main customer – the Afghani Northern Alliance – was pushed out of power by the Taliban. In May of that year a plane carrying weapons and ammunition destined for the Northern Alliance was intercepted by the Taliban in Afghanistan. The crew of this plane were held captive until August 16, 1996, when they managed to break free. Not long after this incident, Bout secured himself a new customer – the Taliban. Actually this was not the first time that Bout had supplied the Taliban with weapons, but this time it was on a much larger scale.

Business was booming and Bout was living the good life in Ostend, where he purchased a mansion and several expensive cars. He also bought an apartment in one of the more exclusive areas of Moscow. But in 1997 thing started to turn a little sour for Bout. The Belgian newspapers published reports about Bout's shady operations and when the Belgian authorities started looking into his business activities, he moved to the United Arab Emirates.

Bout reformed his company in 1995 in the United Arab Emirates, based first of all in Sharjah, but later in 2001 in Ajman, which would be the base for all his operations. The United Arab Emirates was a perfect place for a man like Victor Bout. Firstly, it was a major financial centre and also a crossroads for East and West trade, and secondly, with its bank secrecy laws and free trading zones it was the perfect location for any arms dealer. Bout ran his empire from his base in Sharjah, and in 1995 founded Air Cess in Liberia which was the start of Bout's grip on supplying weapons to Africa. Bout was ruthless, he really didn't care who he supplied weapons to or for what cause just so long as he received payment.

United Nations officials believe that Bout may have airlifted thousands upon thousands of assault rifles, grenade and missile launchers, and millions of rounds of ammunition into Africa. Clients of his companies include – Angola, Cameroon, Central African Republic, Democratic Republic of Congo, Equatorial Guinea, Kenya, Liberia, Libya, Congo-Brazzaville, Rwanda, Sierra Leone, South Africa, Sudan, Swaziland and Uganda. Most of the weapons that arrived in Africa came from Bulgaria where Bout had made frequent trips between 1995 and 2000, and was known to have visited at least six factories there. Between July 1997 and September 1998 Bout organized 38 flights with weapons as cargo, which were estimated to be worth $14 million to African nations. In the summer of 2000, four of Bout's planes landed in Liberia with weapons on board and they were also known to be carrying helicopters, armoured vehicles, anti-aircraft guns and automatic rifles.

By this time the law enforcement agencies were beginning to understand what a major role Bout was playing in the world of arms dealing and they knew they had to deal with the matter, but that was something that proved to be far more difficult than they had first imagined. In fact, by the time the world took notice of Bout and his activities, he was tucked up safely in his home in Sharjah in the United Arab Emirates. His strong political connections and vast accumulation of money had made him almost untouchable and, on top of that, the law enforcement agencies didn't actually have any solid evidence.

While they were investigating Bout's empire they discovered that it was a maze of people, companies, planes and routes and it seemed to be impossible to check where and when Bout's planes flew and which planes actually belonged to him. When they did finally have enough evidence to bring charges against him, the law enforcement agencies discovered that Bout had the protection of UAE royalty and officials such as Sultan Hamad Said Nassir al Suwaidi. He was the adviser to the ruler of Sharjah, who apparently also co-owns one of Bout's companies. Although they desperately wanted to catch him out it seemed he was too far out of their reach and the interest and intensity of the investigation died down. That was until September 11, 2001, which suddenly changed the whole situation.

On September 11, 2001, Al Qaeda terrorists attacked New York. Al Qaeda had close attachments with the extreme Muslims of the Afghani Taliban, a group that had been supplied weapons by Victor Bout. Consequently after the terrorist attacks of September 11, Bout once again became a priority target. All the old evidence was pulled out of the archives and new evidence was collected and it looked as though this time they would be able to nail him down. His name appeared everywhere, in newspapers and on the television, until everyone knew about his arms dealing empire. Unfortunately no-one really knew where Bout was or exactly how to catch him.

By now the United States and Interpol were involved with hunting him down. He was tracked back to his homeland, Russia, where he was being successfully hidden by corrupt officials. Russia was asked to hand Bout over but Moscow decided to give a press conference in which they stated that he was no longer in Russia. This turned out to be a big mistake because, at exactly the same time as the Moscow press conference, Bout was giving his own conference on a Moscow radio station, Ekho Moskvy. In a live interview there he claimed his innocence and told the people that he was just an ordinary businessman.

Victor Bout is still free and the status of his arms dealing empire is not known at this moment in time.

The Story of Paul Tatum

The first time the Western world became familiar or in touch with the crime entangled Russian business scene was when American businessman Paul Tatum was murdered by unknown assassins reputedly over a business dispute.

Paul Tatum was born in 1955 in Edmond, Oklahoma. He graduated from Edmond Memorial High School, showing an enormous drive to succeed in whatever he attempted to do. After dropping out of college, Tatum started to hop from one job to another, and eventually ended up doing fundraisers for the Republican Party.

Tatum's first visit to Russia came in 1985 when he was 29 and with an American trade delegation. Immediately he saw the potential in the Russian market and in 1987, after two years of planning and preparation Tatum was ready to conquer Russian business. He set up a business centre for foreign firms in Moscow, which was a first for the Communist city. Soon after, he and several other American businessmen founded the Americom International Corporation. Two very important business associates in Americom were H. R. 'Bob' Haldeman and Bernie Rome, both of whom were former members of President Nixon's staff. Tatum first came into contact with these two men when he was doing his fundraising for the Republican Party. It was these two that assisted Tatum in getting 'in' with all the important people in Russia, which enabled him to set up and expand his business ventures without too much interference.

Tatum's first big break came in 1990 when his Company RedAmer Partnership joined forces with the Radisson Hotel Corporation. They signed a contract with Goskom Intourist and later the Moscow City Government that made an agreement to build an American hotel/business centre that would go by the name of Intourist RedAmer Hotel and Business Centre. The hotel opened its doors for business one year later in June 1991. It was at the many parties held at the hotel that Tatum rubbed shoulders with powerful figures from Russian business, politics and inevitably, the Russian underworld.

The Moscow underworld is a complicated mesh of different organized crime groups or gangs. In the mid-1900s the Russian Interior Ministry did some research on the amount of gangs in Moscow and came up with the amazing figure of around 200 organizations, 20 of which had branched out to other parts of the world. The Moscow underworld is known to be made up of groups from several different ethnic backgrounds – the main ones being Slavic (Russian), Georgian, Armenian and Chechen. With so many groups in Moscow, business inevitably became tangled up with organized crime and vice versa. Organized crime is said to control around 75 per cent of all private businesses in Russia.

Tatum's hotel was doing very well and business seemed to be on the up and up. The only slight inconvenience to Tatum was the August 1991 Coup but after it died down, he emerged even more powerful than before. In 1992 Goskom Intourist was liquidated and the Moscow City Government became a new partner in the deal. This was not a problem to Tatum at first because his company still owned a large percentage of the property. But with the Moscow City Government came a partner that held a lot of power. They had connections throughout the Russian government and it soon became obvious that they could put pressure on anyone to make them give in to their demands – and their demands would soon become very clear!

Paul Tatum and the Moscow City Government had a peaceful working relationship for a couple of years and then the problems started. In January 1995 the General Director of the American Partnership hadn't received his Russian visa and it didn't look like he was going to get one either. The loss of his General Director was a big blow for Tatum because it meant that the position would now be filled by someone from the Russian partnership. Umar Dzhabrailov was the new General Director. Dzhabrailov was a Chechen who had strong connections within the Moscow City Government and he used those connections to get the position of General Director. But those were not the only connections he had, as he was also a member of Chechen organized crime. A report in the Russian press even reported him as 'a known contract killer and one of a handful of Chechen Mafia bosses now operating in Moscow'. So with Dzhabrailov as General Director things went from bad to worse for Tatum.

Paul Tatum was totally unaware at this stage that the Russian partnership had made it their priority to oust him from the business by whatever means possible. While Tatum went about his normal business the Russian side started to make their mark. On St Valentine's Day in 1995 one of Tatum's bodyguards was found beaten and stabbed in the chest with a penknife. The bodyguard also had a message from his attackers: 'Tell Paul it is time he left for home'. Most men would have got the message and left town immediately, but not Paul Tatum. He was enjoying the good life in Moscow and he wasn't about to give it up without a fight.

Meanwhile the cold war for control of the Hotel and Business Centre continued. Tatum employed more bodyguards and after the attack he took extra security measures. He made sure that his bodyguards stood watch in any empty rooms so that no one could plant a bomb. He also decided to fight Dzhabrailov in the media calling him a 'genuine mafioso' who 'has threatened he can kill me at any time'. The fight turned ugly not just in the boardrooms but also on the public scene.

After many months of warfare between Tatum and Dzhabrailov, in February 1996 it looked like there might be a solution to Tatum's problems. It appeared the answer was to bribe Dzhabrailov and the Moscow City Government. If Tatum would pay the sum of $1 million to a certain person then all his troubles would be over. $500,000 would go to the Moscow City Government and the remaining $500,000 would go to Dzhabrailov so that he would resign or step down as General Director. However, instead of paying the bribe, Tatum decided to take the matter to court. He sued the Russian partners for $35 million and payment of damages. Tatum was defiant as ever in his statements to the press and things started to heat up. Tatum braced himself for the hit that he knew would come. Preferring to stay in his hotel suites, Tatum was told repeatedly by US Embassy officials to leave Russia but he said he would prefer to stay and fight it out. He went one step further on September 30, 1996, when he published a full page advertisement in a Moscow paper directed at Moscow Mayor Yuri Luzhkov:

'Yuri M. Luzhkov: I must tell you that not one person here in Russia or abroad is fooled. All know of the dangerous activities. I implore you to show the world your resolve and commitment to become the catalyst to solve these grave problems – peacefully, efficiently, with fairness and justice for the investor and for the legal agreements under which their original activities were created. The world now awaits this signal. This is your choice and your crossroads. Where do you stand, Yuri M. Luzhkov? In the shadows or the bright sunlight?'

This would be Tatum's last defiant gesture.

THE END

On November 3, 1996, at around 5.00 pm, Paul Tatum left his hotel and headed towards the Mievskaya metro station, where he had arranged to meet someone. When he arrived, accompanied by his bodyguards, the person he was supposed to meet wasn't there. In his place was a man who walked up to Tatum and shot him eleven times from about a 5-metre distance. Tatum's bodyguards did nothing to protect their boss, the killer simply dropped his weapon and fled the scene unharmed. His bodyguards rushed their wounded boss to the hospital, but it was too late and he died shortly after arrival. Following the news of Tatum's death Dzhabrailov and the Moscow City Government took undisputed control of the Radisson Slavyanskaya Hotel and Business Centre. He denied any role in the murder but did say: 'What goes around, comes around'.

Tatum's murder shows just how corrupt Russian business had become. Russian business is controlled by Organized Crime groups and powerful businessmen who use their strong-arm tactics and criminal ways to get deals done.

PART SIX

AUSTRALIA

The N'Drangheta

Organized crime is a frightening fact of life in Australia. The petty back-street racketeering of Australia's cities has become a sophisticated business of enormous proportions.

The Australian based group of Mafia-style Italian criminals is known as the Honoured Society. It would appear that the majority of these organized criminals derive from perennially impoverished Calabria, in the toe of Italy. Calabrian organized criminals are referred to variously as N'Drangheta (a Greek word meaning heroism and virtue, spelled at least three ways in English, and pronounced with a grunt), L'Onorata Societa (The Honoured Society), La Famiglia (The Family), and others. They are also known as the Calabrian Mafia, to distinguish them from their compatriots across the Straits of Messina, the Sicilian Mafia. It was the N'Drangheta that would put the early foundations to what was to follow in the years to come.

Instead of the pyramid structure of bosses used by other Mafia, N'Drangheta uses families based on blood relationships, inter-marriages, or being a Godfather. Each group is named after their village, or their family leader. The Siderno group is a leading Calabrian family, in both Italy and North America. The leader is Comiso 'The Quail' Commisso, with many other Commisso family members deeply involved – some of them in Canada, the United States, Germany and Australia. All members go through an N'Drangheta ceremony which involves a series of rather obscure questions and answers spoken rapidly in the Calabrian dialect. This ceremony is a promise of loyalty to the organization regardless of what the person is asked to do.

There appeared to be five established rules within the Society:

1. Aid was to be extended to a member no matter what the circumstances.
2. There was to be absolute obedience to the officers of the society.
3. An offence against an individual member was an attack on the Society and must be avenged.
4. No member will turn to a government agency for justice.
5. Omerta, the code of silence, must always be obeyed. No member was to reveal any of the organization's secrets.

Mob-related extortion in Queensland's cane fields in the 1930s, is generally seen as the birth of Mafia-style corruption in Australia. The N'Drangheta became infamous for taxing and extorting local farmers. Vincenzo Dagastino, who was an early Mafia boss in Australia, became notorious for this extortion and it continued with many more using this path to riches. The farmers themselves were completely helpless, as some of the farms were so remote and far away from any government authority. The N'Drangheta used this method right up until the end of the Second World War.

After the war the Mafia benefitted from the building of major cities in Australia where they could expand their businesses in areas such as labour racketeering and political corruption. They quickly turned their interest to the very rapidly growing drug trade, and in particular cannabis. This has become a huge money earner for the Society, and its role in the primary production is very strong. Members have been able to use their agricultural skills to grow crops as well as using their place in the agricultural market to transport and distribute the drug. All throughout Southern Australia the Mafia installed many cannabis plantations. This provided the Mafia with a major racket that meant they were no longer completely self-dependent. Finding the narcotics industry so lucrative, the Society made ties with Triad clans in the nineties and began to import heroin in exchange for cannabis. These ruthless gangsters have become major players in Melbourne's heroin trade and rule over fellow countrymen with an iron fist. It is thought that they have links to the Russian Mafia in New York in addition to their home country.

Time Line of Crime

The influence of Italian families and syndicates affiliated with organized crime is said to have been entrenched in the underworld of Australia's East coast since the 1930s. This section contains a brief outline of some events that occurred at the height of a struggle for control of Melbourne's Mafia.

Domenico Italiano
(Godfather, died December 1962)
Domenico was known as 'Il Papa', or 'the Pope' and was the Godfather of the Honoured Society. His trusted lieutenant was Vincenzo Muratore and Antonio Barbara, his right-hand man. Domenico was the father-in-law of notorious hit-man, Michele Scriva. Domenico Italiano died peacefully of old age in his west Melbourne home in December 1962. His funeral was held at St. Mary's Star, of the Sea.

Antonio Barbara
(Died 1963)
Antonio Barbara, or 'The Toad' as he was known, was a senior member of the Society. He was Italiano's right-hand man and was well known for his violence. His death, so soon after Italiano's, left

a huge hole in the upper echelons of the Honoured Society. He served five years in jail for killing a woman in 1936.

Vincenzo Angiletta
(Shot dead April 1963)

Vincenzo Angiletta was a gunman who migrated to Australia in 1951. He became a producer of fruit and vegetables for the Society. He wanted the Society to be like the Sicilian Mafia in the United States and called for extortion rackets to include non-Italians. This scheme was rejected by Domenico Demarte and other Society elders, and Angiletta reacted to this snub by refusing to sell his produce to designated wholesalers and going direct to the public. Although Angiletta was warned by the Society to comply with their orders, he still refused to return to the fold.

The Society reacted by having him stabbed. When this didn't work he was kidnapped and covered in excrement at Woodend. Vowing revenge he formed his own group called La Bastarda 'the Bastard Society' and recruited three hundred members. Angiletta sold his market garden in Kew to a Greek family rather than a designated Calabrian Family, and it is believed from then on that Angiletta became a marked man and started carrying a pistol for protection.

In the early hours of April 4, 1963, Angiletta, by then employed as a cleaner, was hit twice in the head by shotgun fire as he parked his car in the garage of his Stafford Street, Northcote home at 2.30 a.m.

Friends of Angiletta blamed Domenico Demarte and Vincenzo Muratore.

Domenico Demarte
(Shot November 1963)
In 1963 Demarte became head of the Society after Domenico Italiano died. Demarte, a market commission agent, experienced problems when a rival faction emerged within the Society, led by Vincenzo Angiletta.

Demarte was wounded by a shotgun blast while leaving his Chapman Street, north Melbourne home to go to market at 3.30 a.m. on November 26, 1963. This was seen as revenge for the shooting of rebel member Vincenzo Angiletta, leader of La Bastarda. The shooters were believed to have been two relatives of Angiletta. Demarte survived but decided to resign from the Honoured Society.

Vincenzo Muratore
(Shot dead January 1964)
Vincenzo was a trusted lieutenant of the 'Godfather' Domenico Italiano. He was Domenico Demarte's financial adviser when Demarte took over as Melbourne's 'Godfather' after the deaths of Italiano and Barbara in 1962 and 1963. Vincenzo was a prominent market merchant and commission agent and the father of Alfonso Muratore.

Vincenzo was killed with a shotgun outside his Avondale Street, Hampton home on the way to a supermarket at 2.30 a.m. on January 16, 1964. This was allegedly a payback for the Vincenzo Angiletta murder in April 1963. He was said to have been killed by two male relatives of Angiletta, one who managed to escape to Italy following the killing.

Antonio Monaco
(Shot dead January 1964)

Antonio Monaco was a market seller. He was shot dead on January 18, 1964 two days after Vincenzo Muratore's murder. Monaco was leaving his Dandenong Road, Braeside home at about 2.30 a.m. The attack allegedly involved three men as a payback over a domestic dispute.

Domenico Cirillo
(Shot February 1964)

Domenico Cirillo was a fruit and vegetable retailer. He was wounded by a shotgun blast when leaving his home at Ardmillan Road, Moonee Ponds, to go to market at 4.30 a.m. on February 6, 1964. Two people were supposed to have been involved in the attack, which came about as the result of a domestic and financial dispute.

Rocco Medici and Giuseppe Furina
(Found dead May 1984)

Medici was a close associate of Liborio Benvenuto. He was found tortured near the Murrumbidgee River with brother-in-law Giuseppe Furina, on May 6, 1984. Medici and Furina were both from the Melbourne suburb of East Keilor and were known associates of Laurence Sumner, one of Victoria's most notorious criminals. Sumner was alleged to have supplied the bomb which took out

Liborio Benvenuto's land cruiser and it has been said that Medici and Furina were killed as a payback for the explosion.

Sumner was an associate of several Italian crime figures and a close friend of 'The Friendly Godfather' Giuseppe 'Joe' Arena.

Giuseppe Sofra
(Shot June 1985)

Sofra was a greengrocer who was shot three times in the back of the legs at his Springvale Road fruit shop on June 19, 1985. The shop was owned by a man named Antonio Madafferi. The shootings were said to have been related to a price-cutting war in the area and was meant to be a warning to the two men.

Liborio Benvenuto
(Godfather, died May 1988)

Liborio was born in Calabria on December 15, 1927. He was involved in the fruit and vegetable industry, and the son of a man reputed to be 'in charge' of several Calabrian villages. Benvenuto was described as a small and dapper fellow, and a close associate of Joe Arena.

Liborio was the father of Frank Benvenuto, and rose to fame following the 1963–64 market murders of Muratore and Angiletta. This made him the undisputed Godfather of Melbourne. His right-hand man was Michele Scriva. Liborio was married to Domenico Italiano's daughter, while Scriva's son, Tom, married one of Benvenuto's daughters.

On May 10, 1983, Benvenuto's four wheel drive was blown up at the market. No one was hurt, but a shotgun was found in the car. Benvenuto said at the time: 'I have no enemies, only friends at the market. I don't know why anyone would do this at all. I have never done anyone any harm.'

In 1984, the bodies of close-associates Rocco Medici and Giuseppe Furina were found in the Murrumbidgee River, believed by some to be a payback for the bomb. An astute and experienced criminal, Laurence Joseph Sumner, is rumoured to have helped plant the bomb, and also allegedly supplied the gun which was used to kill Joe Arena, even though the couple were close friends at the time.

Sumner was caught in 1991 in a laboratory at his own home, where they discovered a large quantity of amphetamines. He went on to become an informant in one of Melbourne's biggest drug cartels.

Liborio Benvenuto died of natural causes in May 1988. He had not considered his son, Frank, to be a worthy successor and so close associate, Giuseppe 'Joe' Arena, was summoned to Benvenuto's Beaumaris home. Discussions were held about him becoming head of the organization, but on his deathbed Liborio Benvenuto appointed son-in-law, Alfonso Muratore, as Godfather. However, Muratore declined the offer and the next year left his wife, Liborio's daughter, Angela, for mistress Karen Mansfield. Muratore was shot dead outside his Hampton home in 1992. An inquest heard allegations that Frank Benvenuto took out a contract on Muratore's life for snubbing the Honoured Society and his family but was never charged. Frank Benvenuto was shot dead in May 2000.

Michele Scriva

Michele was born in Reggio, Calabria on June 19, 1919 and migrated to Australia in 1936. Scriva, a notorious hitman, was the right-hand man for Liborio Benvenuto. The pair were related through marriage. Michele was married to a daughter of Domenico Italiano and his son Tom married one of Benvenuto's daughters.

Scriva was a stallholder at Melbourne's fruit and vegetable markets and in 1945 was acquitted of murdering Giuseppe 'Fat Joe' Versace in what was probably Victoria's first Mafia hit. Versace had been stabbed ninety-one times. Scriva was later sentenced to hang for stabbing Frederick Duffy to death in North Melbourne, but the sentence was later commuted and he only served ten years.

Giuseppe 'Joe' Arena
(Shot dead August 1988)
Joe was known as the 'friendly Godfather' and was a close associate of Liborio Benvenuto. It had been suggested by Liborio that Arena would take over after his impending death, but this never took place.

Arena apparently retired from the insurance business he had been involved in all his life within weeks of Benvenuto's death. At the age of fifty he gave up work even though he clearly did not have enough money. Arena sold his small insurance broking business for $60,000, but his assets were not those of a man who could retire in middle age. He had a small share portfolio, a few life insurance policies, four motor cars valued at $20,500 and jewellery worth $20,000. His estate was later valued at $216,768.57, but this was simply not enough of a nest egg to retire.

About two weeks later Arena's behaviour changed and he became nervous, agitated and withdrawn. It was at this time that someone started a disinformation campaign against him. It was falsely alleged he was having an affair with the wife of a powerful Italian identity. Arena had become terrified that he was marked for death and approached his friend, Laurence Sumner, in late July who provided him with a pistol for protection.

It remains a mystery as to why Arena feared for his life and why he must have thought the threat was over, days before his murder. He was killed in the backyard of his Bayswater home on August 1, 1988, just a few months after Liborio's demise.

A man walking past Arena's home a couple of hours before the shooting reported that he felt as though he were being watched. He said he could feel eyes being focused on him from bushes in Arena's garden. The man naturally upped his pace and returned home as fast as he could. He then retired to bed only to be awoken a short time later by the sound of gun-fire. It appears the killers may have been laying in wait for some time.

Joe Arena was shot from behind with a shotgun, the traditional Honoured Society method of death with dishonour. The killing happened shortly after he and his wife came home from a wedding in Footscray. Police were told that Benvenuto picking Arena as his replacement as Melbourne Godfather had angered several of the high-ranking officers in the secret criminal organisation. Police suspected Arena may have been killed by those who wanted a slice of Benvenuto's empire. Former boxer, Dominic 'Mick' Gatto, was considered a prime suspect but he denied the allegations.

The reason Arena was known as 'The friendly Godfather' was because he was a likeable man, well known, gregarious and friendly. He was also a moderately successful insurance broker. However, police investigations have shown that Arena was anything but the straightforward insurance broker he appeared to be. Inquiries by the homicide squad and the National Crime Authority uncovered allegations of money laundering and strange financial activities.

Arena was married to Maria and was the father of two boys and one girl. He was known to have laundered around $350,000 for Italian criminals using phoney land deals organized in a Melbourne solicitor's office. On December 17, 1990, Federal police charged a Mildura man over the alleged $350,000 fraud and linked him with Arena.

The arrest of Antonia Cufari, 54, of Irymple, followed more than a year of investigations by the National Crime Authority. Cufari appeared in Mildura Magistrates' Court charged with conspiring with Giuseppe Arena and others to defraud the Federal Government. Cufari had opened twenty bank accounts in Adelaide between 1983 and 1986 in his own name and those of his children. Cufari was known to have deposited more than $350,000 in those accounts to conceal alleged illegal transactions. Cufari was remanded on bail to appear in Melbourne Magistrates' Court on March 21, 1991.

Arena was a man with many social contacts. He regularly dealt with a group of police, and once helped the son of a prominent legal figure find employment. He was convicted of manslaughter after he killed his wife's lover in 1976 and served two years. It was while he was in jail that he met Laurence Joseph Sumner.

In 1982 Arena used his family home as surety to get bail for Sumner who had been charged over a $2 million heroin deal. Sumner was later acquitted and was seen drinking with members of the jury in a hotel near the court the very same night. Sumner became an associate of several Italian crime figures and a close friend of Arena.

Laurence Sumner is rumoured to have supplied the gun that killed Arena. Unfortunately for investigating police, those interviewed stuck strictly to the unwritten law of 'Omerta' or silence, so they failed to make any charges. Arena's closest friends simply refused to acknowledge any friendship when questioned by the police.

One thing the police did discover though, is that in 1988, Arena fell out with a wealthy Italian gangster who had just bought a $1.2 million business in Melbourne.

In September 1998, Dominic 'Mick' Gatto publicly denied murdering Arena. Gatto said he was shocked at a news report he claims pointed the finger at him over the 1988 killing. The burly Mr Gatto, a friend of slain crime boss Alphonse Gangitano, said he contacted the Arena family after a newspaper report indicated he was prime suspect in the 1988 gangland slaying. He said that both he and his father were good friends of Mr. Arena and that he would have no reason to take his life.

On May 8, 1992, police announced a $100,000 reward for any information over the murder of Arena. The reward was made up of $50,000 from the State Government and another $50,000 from an anonymous donor.

John Vasilopolous
(Shot December 1990)

In 1989 a senior executive with retailer Coles-Myer called for an investigation into the Mafia-style kickbacks which seemed to becoming more prevalent at the fruit and vegetable market. He employed a man called John Vasilopolous to head an internal investigation.

Vasilopolous severely rocked the system that the Honoured Society had in place. He refused to pay bribes and also deemed some of the fruit to be of an unacceptable quality. While this was happening, Coles manager Robert Desfosses was seriously assaulted by two men in the car park of the Sunshine Fruit and Vegetable Distribution Centre on June 18, 1990.

In the same month the wife of Coles fruit and vegetable buyer, Terry Hoskin, received a call at her home claiming she would be going to her husband's funeral within a week.

Then in August 1990 Coles buyer, Paul Rizza, received a telephone call at his home warning him to watch his back. The motive for these threats was said to have been a direct attack on the efforts of Coles-Myer to clean up 'corrupt market practices'. In November 1990, Vasilopolous received a number of threatening phone calls. More of these calls were made to other investigators and members of Coles management in early December.

John Vasilopolous was blasted by a shotgun as he answered a knock at the door of his Ivanhoe home on December 19, 1990. A man with an Australian accent who claimed to be 'Tony' shot him in the stomach. Vasilopolous survived but subsequently resigned from his position.

Trouble continues for fruiterers *(1991)*
On March 26, 1991, Cheltenham fruiterer, Armedeo Di Gregorio was ambushed and robbed of $4000.

On May 16, 1991, another Cheltenham fruiterer, Jack Degillio, was ambushed and robbed of $1000 outside his home.

On June 8, 1991, arson caused $100,000 damage to Central Fruit Market in Bentleigh. The premises were doused with petrol and set alight.

Antonio Peluso
(Shot dead June 1991)
Antonio Peluso was a Glen Waverly fruiterer. He was ambushed and shot several times as he left his home on his way to the market. He died on the

veranda of his home. Peluso was robbed of $4000 although he was said to be carrying at least $7000.

More trouble for fruiterers *(1991)*
On June 27, 1991, East Doncaster fruiterer, Tabaret Louey was ambushed by two men and robbed of $2000 on the way to the market.

On July 3, 1991, Wantirna South fruiterer, Phillip Strati, was hit and robbed of $5000 outside his home.

On August 5, 1991, there was an attempt to blow up the Central Fruit Market after explosives were planted on the roof. Petrol was added but it failed to ignite.

On November 20, 1991, a similar attempt was made on the Central Market but this also failed.

On February 29, 1992, a Melbourne market fruiterer and his wife were shot and robbed of $5000 at their Wandin home by two masked men.

Santo Ippolito
(Beaten to death December 1991)
Ippolito was a retired fruiterer. He was battered to death by a man who smashed his way into the victim's Springvale home on Christmas Eve in 1991. Ippolito and his wife were in bed after a family barbecue. There were no demands and nothing was stolen. A man had broken down Ippolito's front door, entered the bedroom and began beating him with an iron bar. Ippolito's wife turned the light on but did not recognise the killer. She was also brutally attacked. Ippolito died in hospital the next day.

The seventy-one-year-old Ippolito was president of an RSL club and it was said that a dispute there led to a hitman being paid to kill him.

Robert Nancarrow
(Beaten to death March 1992)
Robert Nancarrow was the founder of the Nancarrow supermarket chain. He was beaten to death in his Northcote shop and drowned in his own blood on March 2, 1992. The motive was assumed to be robbery.

Costa's Pty Ltd
It was at this time that the big-time Geelong fruiterer Costa's Pty Ltd was called in by Coles-Myer. They were seen as very trustworthy and reputable. This was successful to a degree with company head and now Geelong Football Club President, Frank Costa, appearing on ABC-TV's *Four Corners* programme. He spoke out against the corruption and spoke of the fear many fruiterers had for their lives.

In 1992 Alfonso Muratore and Orlando Luciano met with Coles-Myer executives in an attempt to smooth things over and to advise them of some of the questionable schemes that had operated at the market. The meeting was highly secret and the city venue was checked extensively for bugs. The two were believed to be making a solid sales pitch to the executives, ensuring them that they could do a better and 'cleaner job'. However, their attempts seemed to have failed as Muratore was soon found dead.

Alfonso Muratore
(Shot dead August 1992)

The son of Vincenzo Muratore, Alfonso was married to Angela Benvenuto, the daughter of Melbourne 'Godfather', Liborio Benvenuto. When he was approached by the dying Benvenuto to take over the position of Godfather, he declined, and this was to later cost him his life.

Alfonso had carried a .22 pistol since mid-1991 after being told that a contract had been taken on on his life. In July 1992, fellow-fruiterer and associate, Orlando Luciano, met with Coles-Myer executives to discuss corruption problems at the fruit and vegetable markets and to make a sales pitch on their own behalf. On August 4, 1992, Alfonso, then thirty-nine, was shot dead in Hampton as his father Vincenzo had been twenty-eight years before.

He had left his Storey Avenue house with friend and workmate Ron Lever. Lever was shot in the legs to immobilise him but Muratore was shot four times and died instantly.

A 1995 inquest heard allegations that Frank Benvenuto took out a contract on Muratore's life for snubbing the Honoured Society and his family but was never charged. Benvenuto took over Muratore's fruit stall at the market after Alfonso was shot dead. Frank Benvenuto told the inquest he had no idea who had murdered Muratore.

Another man police saw as a suspect in Muratore's death was truck-driving fruiterer, Guiseppe 'Joe' Quadara. Represented by jailed criminal lawyer, Andrew Fraser, it was speculated that Quadara eluded a payback hit when a man of the same name was shot dead in Toorak on Friday May 28, 1999.

Joe Quadara
(Shot dead May 1999)

Joe Quadara had worked for thirty years in the fruit and vegetable industry and was known as a perfectionist. He was considered to be a good fighter when he was younger, and had gone from being a millionaire to bankrupt.

Once a generous patron of Collingwood Football Club, Quadara, aged fifty-seven, was ambushed at 3 a.m. on Friday, May 28, 1999, when he arrived for work outside a Malvern Road supermarket. Two men armed with handguns shot him repeatedly – he was the third greengrocer killed since 1992.

Quadara's funeral was attended by notable criminals including Graham Kinniburgh, the main witness in the Alphonse Gangitano shooting, as well as a man described as being Gangitano's right hand man.

The second Joe Quadara

Giuseppe 'Joe' Quadara, was a truck-driving father of three and also directly involved in the fruit and vegetable industry. Mr. Quadara was angered following accounts of his murder at the hands of an assassin in Toorak. The shooting the press referred to was that of 'Joe Quadara', a distant relative with the same name.

Giuseppe 'Joe' arrived in Melbourne in 1956

from Lipari, Italy. On October 4, 1992, he was a named suspect in the murder of vegetable whole-saler, Mr. Alfonso Muratore. Giuseppe strongly denied that he had prior knowledge of the killing.

Mr. Quadara, told the inquest that he was pressured to work at the market and left after Mr. Muratore's murder. He said he worked from one in the morning seven days a week and that he was an honest man just trying to earn a living. He further stated, 'Mafia people don't work'. It really did seem that he was just an innocent man who happened to have the same name as the murdered man.

The other Quadara's murder sparked one hundred phone calls to his home. One was from a reporter who told his wife, Giuseppina, that he'd been shot dead. Giuseppe 'Joe' was represented by Mr Andrew Fraser, the high profile lawyer, who was later jailed for cocaine trafficking.

Frank Benvenuto
(Shot dead May 2000)
Frank was the son of former Melbourne Godfather, Liborio, who became Honoured Society crime boss after winning the bloody market wars of the 1960s. Frank was related to Michele and Tom Scriva through marriage (*see* page 466). Frank was also a known associate of the notorious Moran family.

At the time Liborio Benvenuto senior was critically ill, but considered his son-in-law, Alfonso Muratore was not ready to take over the running of his empire. On his death bed, Liborio appointed his son-in-law, Alfonso Muratore, who subsequently declined the offer.

An inquest heard allegations that Benvenuto took out a contract on Muratore's life for snubbing the Honoured Society and his family but was never charged. Benvenuto had no criminal record and detectives could not link him to Muratore's murder. Benvenuto took over Muratore's fruit stall at the market after the killing.

Frank Benvenuto was shot in the chest at the wheel of his Holden Statesman outside his Beaumaris home at about 3 p.m. on May 8, 2000. His falling out with Alfonso Muratore was one avenue homicide detectives followed in trying to identify a motive for the murder. Karen Mansfield, Muratore's mistress, said at his inquest in 1995, that Frank Benvenuto had tried to hire someone to kill him.

Victor Peirce, one of the men acquitted of the 1988 Walsh Street police shootings, and a member of the Pettingill crime family, was also believed to be linked with Benvenuto's murder. Police said Peirce worked as 'hired muscle' for Benvenuto both before and after a six-year jail sentence for drug trafficking between 1992–98. Detectives said the circumstances suggested Mr Benvenuto knew his killer, who shot him in the chest through the car window. Peirce was interviewed over the killing, but said he was working on the docks at the time and is believed to have had an unshakeable alibi. Before his conviction for drug trafficking, he was reported to have fired a machine gun inside the wholesale fruit and vegetable market at Footscray early one morning.

He was working for Mr. Benvenuto then, during a period when price fixing, extortion, standover tactics and drug trafficking were reported to be rife at the market. Some detectives believed the circumstances of his murder – shot in daylight as he sat in his car – may be seen as a public warning to his supporters and family. The police expected there would be revenge killings as a result.

Richard Mlandenich
(Shot dead May 2000)

The next murder was a drug dealer and standover man Richard Mlandenich, who was shot dead at a St. Kilda flat on May 16. He had only been released from jail a month before and had shared a cell with a man called 'Chopper' Read while he was inside.

'Chopper' became the star of the Melbourne underworld after a movie about his life was released in 2000. His criminal history, which spans twenty-seven years, includes trying to kidnap a judge at gunpoint, stabbing a man with scissors, impersonating a police officer and shooting a drug dealer. Read spent twenty-three years in prison, was stabbed, had his ears cut off and had a prison baton broken over his head.

Mlandenich was said to be a giant of a man as well as being extremely violent. He had a criminal record of more than nine pages with most charges relating to street violence. He also had twenty-four aliases including John Mancini and Richard Mantello.

The Moran Brothers

The Moran name has been well known through three generations of criminals. The two half-brothers Mark Anthony Moran (formerly known as Mark Anthony John Cole) and Jason Matthew Patrick Moran had a history of criminal activities including drugs, guns and armed robbery.

Mark Moran was a former professional chef, very fit and a champion footballer for West Kensington. Jason Moran worked on the docks and was known to be a hothead. Similar to Italian crime gangs, the 'dockies' followed an unwritten set of rules which included assistance to members, rejection of conventional justice and, of course, silence. Both Mark and Jason Moran were well known in the world of organized crime. They were part of the Ascot Vale crew and they committed some of the best known crimes in Australian history. Jason was Alphonse Gangitano's right-hand man for a while, that is until the two men had a major falling out.

Jason Matthew Moran was sentenced to a period of twenty months in jail for his role in a fight that left thirteen people injured. The brawl occured at the Sports Bar, King Street, on 19 December, 1995.

Mark Moran was murdered outside his luxury home in Combermere Street, Aberfeldie, near Essendon, on June 15, 2000. Mark Moran was shot twice in the chest. An ambulance was called immediately but Moran was dead by the time it arrived. Amphetamines and cocaine were found on his body, which was surprising seeing as a series of raids had been carried out on a network of amphetamine factories in the area.

Mark left two children, Tayla and Josh.

Jason Moran was paroled in September 2001 and left Australia amid fears for his life.

The shooting of Victor George Peirce
(Shot dead May 2002)

One of the men acquitted of the Walsh Street police shootings (*see* page 492) and a member of the feared Pettingill crime family (*see* page 503), Victor George Peirce was shot dead in Bay Street, Port Melbourne in an execution style drive-by shooting on May 1, 2002.

Peirce was rumoured to have been heavily involved with the drug trade and to have started trafficking illegal guns in Brunswick. He was also known to have made several enemies over drug deals. Police believed that Peirce had moved into the pill and powder market – amphetamines, cocaine and ecstasy. The drug squad had seized a pill press used to make amphetamine-based fake ecstasy and were informed that it had been owned by Peirce.

Family members said Peirce had been afraid someone was trying to kill him. The only jobs he was known to have had before and after a long spell in jail during the 1990s were at the Footscray fruit and vegetable market and on the docks. Peirce, who had moved to Port Melbourne about six months before his death, had recently been employed as a waterfront labourer. He had been linked to thefts on the docks, but had not been charged with any offence.

In recent years he had been questioned about the murder of Frank Benvenuto, had been spotted 'casing' banks, and was linked to people involved in large-scale fraud.

On May 3, a newspaper reported that Peirce was involved in a long-running feud with another Melbourne crime family, the Morans, and was suspected of being involved in the murder of Mark Moran in June 2000. His killing may have been an act of revenge by supporters of the Morans.

Peirce had allegedly been hired by a drug baron named Tony Mokbel to murder a man that was informing against his gang. Peirce set fire to the man's car at the Port Melbourne Docks but the man escaped injury. It is believed Peirce pocketed a sizeable deposit from the group although his attempt at killing the man was unsuccessful.

Victor and his wife, Wendy, were sitting in their dark red sedan opposite the Coles supermarket, near the intersection with Liardet Street, when a car pulled up beside them at about 9.20 p.m. Peirce is said to have stepped out of the car, exchanged words with people in the second car and was then shot at point-blank range several times in the chest. Peirce was frisked and then put back into his car, then the killers sped off towards Beaconsfield Parade. Peirce died a short time later at the Alfred Hospital.

The car, a mid-eighties Commodore, was very similar to the one used to lure police to Walsh Street. It contained two men, a driver and a shooter. Police believed the 1988 Walsh Street shootings of constables Tynan and Eyre were revenge for the killing of Peirce's best friend, armed robber, Graeme Jensen, during an attempted arrest in Narre Warren the previous day. Jensen and Peirce were wanted over a string of armed robberies including one in July 1988 which resulted in the death of a security guard. Peirce and three associates were acquitted of these murders. Peirce claimed after his acquittal that he was afraid of police retribution.

The police were convinced the murder was planned and executed by an experienced shooting team of two hitmen. It had all the markings of professionals because, although the murder was carried out in a busy street, the pair did it quickly without drawing attention to themselves and the gunman appeared confident and calm. Police say the car was probably stolen and almost certainly picked because it had no distinguishing features – nothing a witness could easily remember.

Police believed that sixty numbers stored on the mobile phone of Peirce could hold vital clues to the execution-style slaying. The phone, together with an expensive watch and valuable diamond ring, were still on Peirce when he was pronounced dead on arrival at the Alfred Hospital. The mobile phone's memory bank recorded numbers of the last sixty calls made to and by Peirce. Police said they were hoping one or more of the calls could contain evidence that would lead them to the killers. Police also viewed footage from security cameras at a Port Melbourne shop in the hope of finding those responsible for the murder.

The considered opinion was that Peirce was just

a cold, hard criminal for whom violent death was an occupational hazard. Peirce lived – and died – on his reputation as a tough, violent standover man. He intimidated a lot of people, and plenty were scared of him. Victor knew how to handle himself and usually carried an automatic handgun.

A burnt-out stolen car, believed to have been used in the shooting was discovered shortly after the shooting and was tested for clues.

Kath Pettingill, Peirce's mother, spoke of retribution on talk-back radio the morning after the shooting saying that the killers 'could run but they can't hide . . . from me'. Victor was the third of Kath's eight sons to die, but probably the closest to her, and the most loved of all. She even intimated that she would shoot two people, one a 'big-mouth' the host, Neil Mitchell, believed to be a celebrity gangster, the other Mark 'Chopper' Read. She vehemently denied her son was the killer of constables Tynan and Eyre, saying he had been acquitted by a jury of the crime.

Peirce was also believed to have been linked to the murder of reputed Mafia Godfather Frank Benvenuto, who employed him as a bodyguard. Victor Peirce also engaged the legal services of Frank Benvenuto's brother-in-law and Mafia-connected solicitor, Tom Scriva during the eighties and nineties. The solicitor (who died in 1990 of natural causes) had his practising certificate cancelled in 1999 and was under investigation at the time of his death over bogus loan schemes thought to have raised up to $6 million. Peirce's solicitor a decade ago, when he was acquitted of the

Walsh Street police murders, was another disgraced lawyer – convicted drug dealer Andrew Fraser.

On May 9, 2002, a large gathering said goodbye to Victor Peirce at St Peter and Paul's church in Dorcas Street, South Melbourne. A notable appearance was made by Jason Moran, a man whose family the press have suggested could have been associated with Peirce's death. Several homicide squad detectives who were still on the hunt for Peirce's killers, were among the congregation. Mourners mingled with plainclothes police, reporters and members of the criminal world. It wasn't, however, a huge funeral by underworld standards. Possibly the killer himself was in the crowd on that day. Victor Peirce was finally laid to rest at the Altona cemetery.

When police finally returned her murdered husband's 1993 Commodore after forensic checks, Wendy Peirce slid her fingers under the front ashtray with practised ease. She immediately found what she was looking for – nearly $400 in cash – apparently it was her husband's favourite spot to hide money. Once police had finished with the maroon sedan, Wendy had it repaired, including patching a bullet hole, replacing the driver's-side window, shattered by the shots, and fitting new seat covers. It looked as good as new and her seventeen-year-old daughter learned to drive in it.

SO WHO KILLED HIM?

One theory, and there are several, is that an old

friend – a man who once shared the criminal dock with him during a trial – was the one who set him up. As the story goes, the old friend works for a South Yarra drug dealer whose supply of ecstasy was ripped off by Victor. The associate was given three choices: kill Victor, get the drugs back, or die. He took the first option.

Detectives discovered that Victor was unarmed at the time of his death – a sure sign he believed he was meeting a friend and did not anticipate trouble. They also found he had two mobile phones in the car – one was for personal use and the other purely for his 'business' dealings.

In August, following the shooting, police conducted raids and interviewed five men who were known associates of Victor. Wendy believes the killers were hired by an associate of her late husband – but as yet the killers have not been apprehended.

Gantanol 'Tom' Scriva
(1945-2000)

Born in 1945, Tom was the son of notorious hitman Michele Scriva. He was a stallholder at Melbourne's fruit and vegetable markets after migrating to Australia as a seventeen-year-old in 1936. In 1945 Michele was acquitted of murdering Giuseppe 'Fat Joe' Versace.

He was later sentenced to hang for stabbing Frederick Duffy to death in North Melbourne, but the sentence was later commuted and he only served ten years.

Michele Scriva was also a pall bearer at the

funerals of Melbourne's first Godfather, Domenico Italiano in 1962, and Vincenzo Muratore in 1964. Both of these men were shot and killed in an internal Mafia power struggle for control of Melbourne's markets.

Tom married a daughter of Melbourne Godfather Liborio Benvenuto. Affiliations between the Scriva and Benvenuto families were cemented decades ago with the two families linked through marriage. Scriva was a firm friend of the feared Benvenuto clan.

Scriva later became known as the disgraced lawyer for suspected Melbourne Mafia figures. He represented Walsh Street suspect Victor Peirce and his wife Wendy. In 1986 Scriva represented Claudio David Crupi, when he was charged with shooting with intent to murder policeman Gerard Michael Wilson at Greensborough in February of that year.

Scriva also represented a husband and wife, John William Palmer and Darlene Joy Palmer, of West Heidelberg, who, on December 6, 1986, held three people at knifepoint intent on revenge for the drug-related death of a friend. The court heard that the couple burst into a house on Moonee Ponds which was owned by a man charged with the murder of Julie Ann Dunne. A policeman told the court he went to the house and found John Palmer with a pistol and Darlene Palmer with a knife.

On June 24, 1992, police raided the offices of Constantine Vincent Kay and Co. in Bridge Road, Richmond, looking for information linked to Victor George Peirce. On November 28, 1995, eight of the police officers involved in the raid were ordered to pay $10,000 damages over their conduct which a judge said amounted to false imprisonment of staff. County Court Judge, Leslie Ross, said police had gone too far in their search, and that restrictions on the movement of staff, the control exercised over them and other security measures taken by police during the two-hour raid were not justified. He said experienced police from the fraud and tactical investigation squad searched the office looking for material relevant to the prosecution of Peirce for drug trafficking. The search was in fact part of a larger task force investigating the activities of Peirce. Judge Ross said the task force was told of two people at the firm believed to be involved in money laundering for Peirce – but no charges were laid as a result of the raid.

The head of the firm, Mr Constantine Vincent Kay, solicitor Thomas Scriva, and legal secretaries Elisabeth Mantzos and Carol Havelos, brought the civil action against the police, claiming they had suffered anxiety, loss and damage. Judge Ross awarded Mr. Kay $5000 damages, Mr. Scriva $2500 and Ms. Havelos and Ms. Mantzos $1250 each. He stated that during the raid Mr Scriva was physically detained for about fifteen minutes. Mr. Kay said he had no freedom to move around his office and was restricted in his access to phones and the facsimile machine, and one secretary said she felt intimated by such a large police presence. Staff claimed they were wrongfully locked in the premises.

In 1999 Scriva acted as a loan shark in apparent breach of a Legal Profession Tribunal decision in cancelling his licence to practise. He was under investigation by the Law Institute for trust fund irregularities. Scriva borrowed money from mostly legitimate investors with the promise of high returns and then lent the money to others. Some used the money to pay off gambling debts or for other dubious activities. An underworld source said one borrower had taken a $600,000 loan through Scriva, but had lost the money gambling and had no way to repay the debt.

It is believed that Scriva raised up to $6 million in his final months alive from both underworld and everyday investors for finance schemes. Much of the money is now believed missing. Also in 1999, Scriva was banned from practising on his own after the Legal Profession Tribunal found him guilty of misconduct. Scriva was reprimanded and had his lawyer's certificate cancelled until 2009. Scriva then worked at a Melbourne legal firm, but it is unclear what his role at the firm was.

Tom Scriva died on July 13, 2000 of natural causes at the Alfred Hospital, and millions of dollars were feared lost after his death.

He is buried less than a metre above Melbourne's most recent murdered Mafia Godfather, Frank Benvenuto.

The Walsh Street Police Shootings

At the height of the investigations, hundreds of police were working for a task force called the Ty-Eyre. The Victorian Police Bureau of Criminal Intelligence even dropped a long-term investigation into cocaine importing to assist. By November 1988, at least a dozen people were involved in 24-hour surveillance of suspects.

On October 12, 1988, Steven Tynan and another young policeman, Damian Eyre, were murdered in the early hours of the morning after answering a call to investigate a car abandoned in the middle of Walsh Street, South Yarra. The police investigation that followed Walsh Street was the biggest ever conducted by the Victorian police force. It lasted for 895 days and turned out to be one of the most extraordinary cases in Australian criminal history.

The execution-style killings of the young officers were thought to have been a payback instigated by prominent members of the Melbourne Underworld. Police believe members of a well-known group of armed robbers and drug dealers had organised the murders after two of their own were shot by police.

Perhaps to understand the Walsh Street killings you need to appreciate what it was like in the late 1980s, when bank robberies were rampant and police earned a reputation of shooting criminals dead. One gang famous for robbery was dubbed the Flemington crew. Its members – according to Wendy Peirce (wife of Victor Peirce) – were her husband, Graeme Jensen, Jedd Houghton and Peter McEvoy.

Amid the rumour, myth and claims that surround the murder of the policemen is one certainty – the killers used the same pump-action shotgun fired in a bank robbery seven months earlier. The shotgun blast that cut down Steven Tynan and maimed Damian Eyre, came from the same weapon used in an attempt to blast open a door at the State Bank in Oak Park in early 1988. The gang robbed at least four banks. At Oak Park, the robbery went wrong from the start when security screens were activated, separating the robbers from the money. Several shotgun blasts failed to open a security door and the robbers fled, leaving three empty cartridges behind them.

Armed robbery squad detectives failed to get any leads. They filed details of the robberies in a box marked 'The Flemington crew', as raids by other gangs drew their attention.

In June 1987, career criminal Frank Valastro, a known associate of the Flemington crew, was shot dead by detectives. Valastro's death allegedly started a pact among criminals to kill two policemen for every criminal gunned down. It is believed by many that this threat was carried out at Walsh Street just over one year later. Many also suggested that the Walsh Street murders were a 'payback' by the Melbourne underworld for the killing of Graeme Jensen thirteen hours before the constables were shot.

In July 1988, four months after the Oak Park incident, a security guard at a Coles supermarket in Brunswick was killed in an exchange of fire. The wounded bandit escaped with $33,000.

Graeme Jensen was kept under surveillance by police after the Brunswick robbery and shooting. Fellow gang member Santo Mercuri was later convicted of the robbery which was also said to have involved the Moran crime family and Victor Peirce. Jensen was a good friend of Peirce, a member of the feared Pettingill clan.

Acting on a tip-off, detectives discovered that another armed robbery squad crew was investigating Peirce, Jensen and Houghton. According to an informant, they were planning a big robbery. When the informant said the job had been called off, detectives decided to arrest Peirce and Jensen, mainly to ask Peirce about the Coles job and other raids, but also to determine if Jensen might have been the wounded bandit. The first arrest, by any assessment, went badly wrong. Detectives tried to grab Jensen at a Narre Warren hardware store but by the time they moved in he was already in his car and he was shot dead as he drove away. Police said Jensen had a gun, which turned out to be a non-functioning sawn-off rifle, an odd weapon for an experienced criminal.

On October 1, 1988, Hai Foong Yap was shot by police officer Steven Tynan in a hold-up in Myrtle Street, South Yarra. Yap ended up a paraplegic and according to some reports, committed suicide whilst in jail. Only a few days after the shooting, Steve Tynan was back on the beat.

Thirteen hours after Graeme Jensen's death, a police divisional van from Prahran was called to its ninth job of the evening, a car abandoned with a broken window and its lights on in Walsh Street, South Yarra. As the constables, aged twenty and twenty-two, inspected the car, they were ambushed and killed by the Flemington crew's alleged shotgun.

In the weeks that followed, police conducted numerous and sometimes brutal raids on hundreds of houses across Melbourne. The Richmond home of Victor and Wendy Peirce was raided the afternoon following the shootings. Peirce's house was demolished and the backyard dug up in a fruitless search for evidence. It was said that the demolition job on the house during subsequent raids was so thorough that all that remained of their home was rubble. Tempers were, understandably, running hot and a shot was fired by policemen in the initial raid caused the death of two pet budgerigars, who died of fright. Wendy, her nephew, and a friend of his named Anthony Farrell, were taken in for questioning.

Apparently Victor had made his escape over a back fence. Peter McEvoy, a tenant in the flat, was arrested but not charged until a later date when he was put on trial. McEvoy himself was no stranger to the police. He was facing armed robbery charges at the time of the Walsh Street shootings. The charges involved a hold-up at the National Bank in East Bentleigh in August 1988, just two months before Walsh Street. He was sentenced to seven years jail with a minimum of five years, when his case finally came to court in 1992.

Inspector John Noonan who led the task-force said McEvoy was a coward. He was represented in court by the flamboyant Victorian criminal barrister, Robert Roy Vernon, who was also Chuck Bennett's main legal representative. Vernon had an aversion to paying tax. So much so that he went bankrupt to avoid his tax debts . . . not once, but four times.

Later that afternoon police raided the Brunswick flat of Vicki Brooks (Kathy Pettingill's daughter).Victor Peirce gave himself up to police the following day and was charged with the July 11 Brunswick armed hold-up which left a guard dead. The robbery was said to have involved Jason Moran, Santo Mercuri and Russel 'Mad Dog' Cox. These charges were ultimately dropped, but Victor was charged with the Tynan/Eyre murders and spent the next thirty months in custody.

At the height of the investigations into the killings, hundreds of police were working for the Ty-Eyre task force. On many police station notice boards was a cartoon which showed a policeman face down being kicked by a group of so-called enemies, including the government, media and judges. One of the figures was labelled 'Victor Peirce'. The Victorian Police Bureau of Criminal

501

Intelligence even dropped a long-term investigation into cocaine importing to assist. The Drug Squad and the National Crime Authority in Victoria were also called in to give a hand. Within two weeks of the killings, the Victorian government passed legislation allowing phone-tapping by State police. Before this they had had to work with the Federal police, who had this power, if they wanted to use their recordings as evidence in court. Five months passed before the legislation was made public.

All of the murder suspects had long histories of criminal activity and by November 1988, at least a dozen people were involved in 24-hour surveillance of suspects.

On November 17, 1988, another gang member, Jedd Houghton, then twenty-three, was shot dead by two members of the Special Operations Group at a Bendigo caravan park. Police wanted to arrest him for questioning over Walsh Street and knowing they were searching for him, Houghton had been hiding out in a cabin with his girlfriend. Another member of the gang and close friend of Houghton, Gary Abdallah, became a Walsh Street suspect on the evidence of the prosecution's key witness, who had claimed that Abdallah's part in the killings was to provide and drive the getaway car. On October 31, 1988, Ryan gave a statement implicating friend Anthony Farrell and another friend, Emmanuel Alexandris, in the killings. Farrell was charged with murder the following day.

On November 16, Ryan listed the party of

killers as being Jedd Houghton, McKevoy, Farrell and his uncles Victor Peirce and Trevor Pettingill.

For two months Gary Abdallah eluded the police. Raids were made on all known associates including his girlfriend's family and the family of the now deceased Jedd Houghton. News filtered back that police intended to kill him if they got to him first. Abdallah kept away from police until visiting Detective John Noonan at St Kilda Road Police Headquarters on February 22, 1989.

Abdallah had arranged a meeting with the task force head and his lawyer. Noonan told him that he was not wanted for the shooting, and Abdallah said that he hadn't come in earlier because he had heard there were threats against his life. Noonan assured Abdallah that he was not wanted in any relation to the case. Abdallah's car, suspected of being used in the getaway, had been sold before the murders and, although it was later obtained by police, their tests proved nothing. Abdallah was immediately put under close surveillance for about six weeks. The police planted a listening device in Abdallah's flat in Drummond Street, and set up a permanent surveillance position in the building opposite.

One Sunday afternoon, police noticed Abdallah leaving his flat. He was followed by detectives Lockwood and Avon, who pulled him over and searched him, and then drove him back to his flat. Once there police claim that Abdallah produced an imitation pistol and pointed it at the detectives. Detective Lockwood then fired seven shots at Abdallah, including one from his partner's gun after he had used up all the bullets in his own revolver. Abdallah was critically wounded and died after 40 days in a coma.

Abdallah's family asked the Deputy Ombudsman, Dr Barry Perry, to investigate the shooting. His 329-page report was completed shortly before Christmas 1989. It said that 'the evidence seems to provide some basis for believing that there was criminal conduct' in the police shooting of Abdallah.

During the inquest, the Abdallah family's lawyer expressed a more direct view – the pistol was a plant and Abdallah was on his knees, his hands behind his head, when he was shot like a dog on a short lead. It came to light that on several occasions police went too far in investigating the Walsh Street killings.

All the key suspects in the Walsh Street shootings – Victor Peirce, Jedd Houghton, Anthony Farrell, Peter McEvoy, Trevor Pettingill and Gary Abdallah – were warned that their lives were in danger. Hundreds of houses across Melbourne were raided by police. All the suspects had long histories of criminal activity, but by the time of the trial in March 1991, the prosecution's case was too weak to obtain a conviction. It has been suggested that the Walsh Street murders were a 'payback' by the Melbourne underworld for the killing of Graeme Jensen only thirteen hours before the constables were killed.

Anthony Leigh Farrell, 21, Victor George Peirce, 31, Peter David McEvoy, 34, and Trevor Pettingill were all arrested. Each faced two counts of murder.

In earlier evidence police alleged the killing of suspected armed robber Graeme Jensen at Narre Warren the day before, may have sparked off the murders. It is alleged that Peirce and McEvoy were deeply distressed when they heard of Jensen's death and vowed that 'two police will die tonight'. Peirce's solicitor was a disgraced lawyer and convicted drug dealer, Andrew Fraser, who also represented Farrell. Ironically, the barrister who represented Peirce in that trial was Geoff Flatman, QC, later the Director of Public Prosecutions and now a Supreme Court Judge.

One of the key witnesses against the Walsh Street four was Peirce's wife Wendy, who was to give key evidence against her husband. However, after entering the witness protection scheme at a cost of $2 million, she changed sides and refused to implicate Peirce. She was later jailed for perjury.

The Peirces were reunited after Victor was acquitted. The youngest of their four children, Vinnie, was named after the Walsh Street trial judge, Justice Frank Vincent. He was born in prison while his mother was still serving time.

In a series of video interviews in 1989 that detailed a decade of crime, including several murders by her brother-in-law Dennis Allen, Wendy Peirce examined bank security pictures and identified those in them, saying she recognised her husband, Jensen, Houghton and McEvoy by their clothes, shoes, features (they wore balaclavas or stocking masks) and stance.

Victor Peirce's sister, Vicki Brooks, turned

against him and joined the witness protection programme. So did her son Jason Ryan, whose various stories about the police killings sapped the credibility of his evidence. By the time of the Walsh Street trial in March 1991, the prosecution's case was too weak to obtain a conviction.

The prosecution believed six people were involved in the ambush (including Jason Ryan and Jedd Houghton), but only two were needed to complete the killings and only two people were seen. Perhaps there were only two people present at the time of the killings. While the shotgun's link to the Flemington crew remains the only certainty in the case, circumstantial evidence and testimony suggest that one of the killers that night was Jedd Houghton, and most likely Victor Peirce was there, as well.

Victor Peirce claimed after his acquittal that he was afraid of police retribution. He issued a statement in which he professed his innocence and asked 'to be left alone to work and prove to the community I am not as bad as police and the press has made me out to be'. However, it was never going to be as simple as that. After his acquittal Victor received jail sentences for involvement with his brother Peter in a prison drug cartel, for petty theft and drug trafficking. While he was in prison Kathy Pettingill told Adrian Tame: 'I know nothing will stop the police. They will shoot Victor and they will shoot Trevor. They're in the only safe place they can be – in jail.'

Peter McEvoy was later sentenced to seven years for armed robbery and is believed to be living in northern Victoria. Victor Peirce was murdered in an execution-style killing in Bay Street, Port Melbourne on May 1, 2002. Trevor Pettingill faced drugs and burglary charges. Since being acquitted Anthony Farrell, a heroin addict, has maintained he tried to leave his past behind and get on with a life not involving crime. But he has been jailed twice for drug offences since the Walsh Street trial.

The Pettingill Family

If there was one crime family in Australia considered beyond infiltration by undercover police it was the Pettingills of inner-city Richmond.

The Pettingill Family consisted of: Dennis Allen, Kath Pettingill, Peter Allen, Victor Peirce, Jamie Pettingill, Lex Peirce, Trevor Pettingill and Jason Ryan.

The family's matriarch, Kath Pettingill, was known as 'Granny Evil' and had led a chequered life as a barmaid and a brothel madam. She had been around crime for thirty years and ran brothels in South Melbourne and later in Richmond. She had various drug-dealing convictions and she lost an eye when a woman shot her in the head.

Kath raised seven children and most of these were involved in serious crime at one time or another. Her son Dennis died in prison of a rare heart disease at the age of thirty-five. He was facing a murder charge at the time and had been implicated in another ten deaths. One of these was reportedly said to have been a biker who he shot and then dismembered so that he could squeeze the body into a 44-gallon drum. Another son,

508

Jamie, died from an overdose at twenty-one, but not before he assisted in an armed robbery that resulted in the death of a barman.

Victor Peirce and Trevor Pettingill were charged and later acquitted of the 1988 Walsh Street murders of constables Damian Eyre and Steven Tynan. Dennis and Peter Allen, were Melbourne's most notorious dealers in guns and drugs during the 1980s and were known to have a love of extreme violence.

Although the Pettingill family were blamed for the Walsh Street killings, police felt they would probably kill again if they received undue harassment. It is considered that the family had the protection of corrupt police, because several of their investigations were thwarted when the Pettingills received tip-offs of impending police raids.

Dennis Allen was left to run his 'patch' of inner city Richmond without any interference. Witnesses, including ex-girlfriends, told of phone calls from detectives giving him blatant tip-offs of forthcoming raids or observation operations. It appeared that the Pettingill family had the people and the means to do what ever they wanted and for a long time they got away with it.

In Kath Pettingill's biography *The Matriarch*, written by Adrian Tame, she told of the time when she split open the head of a detective with a bottle of perfume. At the time her son, Victor Peirce, had escaped from the Turana Youth Detention Centre and had decided to return home to celebrate his birthday. Later that evening Kath had gone to bed when she heard a lot of noise coming from downstairs. She ran downstairs to find two detectives holding her son with a gun to his head. Kath's immediate instinct was to protect her offspring and so she grabbed a large perfume bottle off a shelf and hit one of the detectives over the head. He fell to the ground like a stone with blood gushing from a wound in his head. Her son, Lex, knocked the other policeman to the ground, but by this time Kath's victim was back on his feet. He stamped viciously on his attacker's foot and then started pulling wildly at her clothes and shouting obscenities. He had to be restrained by the other detective who managed to pull him off. The detective in question later retired from the police force and became a prominent figure in both legal and sporting circles.

Victor Peirce, was shot dead on May 1, 2002, in Port Melbourne, and Kath went on local radio and spoke passionately about getting revenge on her son's murderers. She told the interviewer that if she owned a gun she would immediately kill those responsible.

COMMUNITY AWARD

Kath Pettingill had another side, though, and she was very active in community business. On September 1, 2002 she was nominated for a community award for volunteer work. Kath was given the International Volunteer of the Year Award by locals thankful for her enthusiastic support of the community. Ms. Pettingill helped run a bingo group whose profits financed street decorations and she was an avid supporter of the local community centre. Locals said that she was always willing to put her hand in her pocket at times of fundraising and the certificate she received was one of 700,000 given to community groups. Kath Pettingill has lived in Venus Bay for over fourteen years and when interviewed in recent years said that she had changed her ways but that she did not expect to go to heaven when she died.

Dennis Bruce Allen

Dennis grew up in a housing estate in Heidelberg. The estate was originally built as the 1956 Olympic Games Village and then became a major housing development. He served a ten-year jail sentence for a rape which took place in October 1973.

Dennis, and his brother Peter, raided a house in Sandringham. The occupants of the house were threatened and hit before Peter fired a handgun and Dennis raped one of the three women present. For this crime Dennis only served four years.

After Dennis' four-year stretch he moved into a flat in Walker Street, Northcote where he harboured one of his brothers, Jamie, then only fourteen, who had escaped from Turana Youth Detention Centre in Parkeville.

In 1979, painter and docker Victor Allard, a probable heroin dealer, was shot dead in Fitzroy while in the company of Dennis Allen, who immediately became the prime suspect. So added to his harbouring charge, were charges of gun possession and a drink driving conviction. Dennis appealed, even though he had committed the offences while he was still on parole, but the appeal failed and he was sent to Castlemaine jail. On one occasion, in October 1881, he managed to skip custody while on day release. He was subsequently found at a Richmond Hotel with a prostitute in a very drunk state.

Dennis built up a quite substantial heroin empire after his release from jail on July 2, 1982, and his temperament was such that he earned great respect from his associates.

In May 1983, police raided his home in Chestnut Street. At the time of the raid another drug user, and former armed robber, Victor Gouroff, was also in the house. The police had been following a girl named Helen Wagnegg (another drug user) hoping she would lead them to her dealer. She turned up at Allen's home, and Gouroff greeted her at the door. They didn't apprehend her until she was back home later, and Wagnegg was arrested with 1.5g of heroin in her possession. As a consequence of this arrest, Allen's house was raided and police discovered 30g of heroin, several bags of amphetamines, and a cache of guns and ammunition. They also discovered explosives that had been buried in the back yard.

Helen Wagnegg, who was also a prostitute, later died from an overdose during a visit to Allen's headquarters. It is believed that Allen poured Yarra River water into her mouth to simulate drowning before the body was dumped in the river.

Greg Pasche, Kathy's much-loved 'adopted' son

was murdered by either Dennis or Victor Gouroff. Greg's body was found in the Brisbane Ranges, just out of Geelong. Shortly after this Victor Gouroff disappeared and his body was never found. Police believe he was murdered by Dennis.

In September 1983, Dennis Allen was arrested for trafficking heroin and was taken to Russel Street Police Headquarters. He managed to obtain bail, and his lawyers posted a surety of $30,000.

Dennis was the leading distributor of heroin and amphetamines in Melbourne between 1983 and 1987. By the end of 1984 he had bought ten houses in Richmond and spent thousands more on renovations. Police have estimated that in the mid-80s, Dennis was making anything between $30,000 and $70,000 per week.

It is also alleged that Dennis murdered Hell's Angel, Anton Kenny. He had an argument with Dennis, ended up dead with his legs having been removed by chainsaw so that his body would fit into a 40-gallon drum. The drum was dumped in the Yarra and later discovered after police received a tip-off. It is possible that this tip came from Dennis himself in return for favours from the police. Children had used the drum as a diving board before the police retrieved it, not aware of its grisly contents.

In mid-1984, Dennis is said to have shot an associate, Allan Stanhope. He had visited Allen's home and following a prolonged drinking session with another couple of friends, Dennis shot Stanhope repeatedly. Dennis emptied the barrels of two shotguns into his head at close range and then slit his throat. The motive – he was supposed to have fiddled with Allen's stereo system! As Jason Ryan and two other frightened houseguests cleaned up the blood and glass, Dennis made some phone calls which resulted in his brothers Jamie and Trevor Pettingill arriving at his home. The police were aware that Stanhope's car had been at the home of Allen the night of his disappearance and they found it later burnt out in the Brisbane Ranges near Geelong. His body, however, was never recovered. This was, in fact, the only murder Allen was ever charged with.

Dennis' notoriety in 1984 came not only from his soaring drug empire but also from his reputation as a gun dealer, particularly to those with robbery on their mind. He allegedly supplied guns to a number of armed robbers including his own brother Jamie. Dennis was also becoming a favourite of police in their relentless search for 'gigs' or informers. Dennis, codenamed 'Gus', was said to have informed on many armed robbers who were jailed as a result of his information.

Also around this time, several armed robbers from the Flemington area were shot dead, some by police. Another criminal of note, Jimmy Loughnan (made famous in the *Chopper* movie and a later victim of the 1987 Jika Jika fires in Melbourne's Pentridge Jail) was arrested for an armed robbery in North Balwyn. He was very angry at being arrested and claimed that he had been the subject of a set-up. He escaped custody for a short period and police immediately issued Dennis Allen with a bullet-proof vest for his own protection.

Roy 'Red Hat' Pollitt escaped from a New South Wales jail in 1980 and headed to Melbourne. Pollitt was harboured for a number of years by Dennis Allen who had hired him to kill a drug supplier named Alan Williams. But Pollitt shot the wrong man, who turned out to be Williams' brother-in-law, Lindsay Simpson. Pollitt was jailed for life in 1990, but Dennis refused to pay him any money because he had not satisfactorily carried out his contract.

In late 1984 Dennis faced court on charges of carrying a handgun. He was sentenced to twelve months, he appealed, and was granted bail and was later acquitted.

In the *The Matriarch*, Kath Pettingill, says that Dennis was directly involved with a corrupt Sydney detective named Roger Rogerson. She went on to say that drugs were purchased from and sold to him during meetings at an airport. She said that a woman who claimed to be the girlfriend and close associate of Dennis was instrumental in bringing Roger Rogerson down. She is currently on a witness protection programme and therefore cannot be named. Miss 'X' was a useful source of information to police, providing the evidence that produced the only conviction recorded against Rogerson. The story in this case is that Dennis sent Miss X to Sydney Airport on May 14, 1985 to meet Rogerson. Allen gave her a black bag containing $100,000 and two tickets, to and from Sydney, under different names.

She arrived in Sydney at 11.30 a.m. and found Rogerson in the terminal close to the women's toilets. She approached the man and they exchanged bags. The bag Rogerson had given her contained books, clothing and plastic bags of heroin weighing about a kilo. She flew back to Melbourne, where the heroin was collected from her, and the next morning, an envelope containing $7,000 was placed in her letter box.

However, Rogerson's version of events was as follows: He received a phone call from Kath Flannery, Chris Flannery's wife, expressing concern over her fifteen-year-old son, who was depressed after his father's disappearance the previous week. Rogerson took the boy and his sister, together with his own two teenage daughters, on a boat trip on the Georges River, presumably at the same time the airport exchange is alleged to have taken place.

On May 21, 1985, Roger Rogerson opened two accounts in false names at the York Street, Sydney, branch of the National Australia Bank, and in three visits deposited $110,000 cash.

As a result of this chain of events Rogerson was initially convicted of conspiring with Dennis Allen to supply heroin between March and May 1985, but the conviction was overturned on appeal. Later Rogerson was charged with conspiring to pervert the course of justice by allegedly misleading a police inquiry into the source of the $110,000 deposited into the false accounts. Rogerson was convicted, but after serving only nine months of his eight-year sentence was released in 1990, pending appeal.

Rogerson's release did not please Miss X, who claimed that her years as a protected witness had ruined her life. She said she was scared of Rogerson who, she claimed, had mouthed death threats at her in court during his committal hearing. Luckily for her Rogerson lost his appeal and was returned to jail in 1992 with a reduced sentence. He was finally released in December 1995.

Andrew Fraser, a leading Melbourne criminal lawyer, was being jailed in 1999 after he was involved in the importation and distribution of cocaine. Before he was jailed he represented and assisted both Peter and Dennis Allen, and their associate, Walsh Street suspect Anthony Farrell. Fraser helped Dennis set up 'Mr D Investments' (Allen's nick-name was Mr D – short for death). He also set up a trust account for Peter in which he amassed hundreds of thousands of dollars made from his massive dealings in heroin. Not long after this Peter Allen was jailed.

During his life of crime, Dennis Allen also attempted to blow up a Coroner's Court investigating one of his alleged murders and attempted to shoot down a police helicopter.

Dennis died of heart failure due to his once massive amphetamine addiction. One of the last people to see him alive in hospital was former lawyer Andrew Fraser.

Peter John Allen

Born in 1953, Peter John Allen, spent over thirty years of his life in jail on drugs, rape and robbery charges. Peter grew up running with elder brother Dennis and, after being expelled from school at fourteen, quickly progressed into the world of crime. Assaults led to fights involving weapons and armed robbery and the time he spent in a youth training centre was just a taste of what was to come. The Allens' exploits ended violently in 1973, when they raped two Sandringham sisters aged twenty-two and sixteen while on a mission to kill a man for $500.

Allen, along with criminal Allan Rudd, went on a booze-induced shooting spree that ended with Rudd being shot by the police, and Peter Allen being jailed for twelve years. During this twelve-year term, Peter Allen managed to escape twice, and was on the Top Ten wanted list until he was recaptured.

In August 1985, at the age of thirty-two, he walked free from jail determined to make big money and live a lavish lifestyle. Within days, he was driving a flashy sports car and living with a new girlfriend in Brunswick, earning big bucks in high-quality heroin deals.

With a network of dealers, Allen began earning up to $40,000 a week. It seemed his grandiose plans to set himself up as a drugs' king were reaching fruition – he had the car, the trappings, and now he had the mansion in Lower Temple-stowe. However, as his wealth grew, his gambling habit increased and he started losing just as much as he won. Allen started to brag about his new stature and police started making investigations into how he was coming by his new-found fortune. He was arrested by detectives in April 1986, having only been out of jail for eight months. In December 1988, he was sentenced to thirteen years for trafficking heroin and conspiracy to commit armed robbery. Allen's newly gained possessions were confiscated as they were purely profits of his crime.

Even in prison, though, his criminally driven entrepreneurial spirit could not be broken. As mastermind of an elaborate syndicate involving female couriers, a corrupt prison officer dubbed 'The Postie', and his brother Victor Peirce, Allen sold drugs to fellow inmates. But police uncovered the syndicate and in March 1995 Allen was sentenced to a further six years for trafficking. Victor Peirce was also jailed for his part in the syndicate.

Peter was released from Loddon Prison in July 1999 after serving thirteen years. Now aged forty-six, with two children and five grandchildren, Peter had spent all but one of his adult years behind bars. He had spent about twenty-five years in prison since 1973 and in his case it would seem crime certainly hadn't paid off. After being paroled, he said that he just wanted to lead a normal life, but the temptation was obviously too great and it was less than three years before he again faced serious charges.

On January 21, 2002, Peter was in court again, this time to face nineteen charges including armed robbery and burglaries. Allen represented himself as he applied for bail at Melbourne Magistrates Court. Senior Detective Andrew Collins told the court – Allen broke into a Williamstown home and stole a mantelpiece on January 9. About a week later he returned and stole a television, rugs and the front door from the same house.

On January 16, Allen, his girlfriend Amber Barry, who was only nineteen, and several others, allegedly robbed a man at knifepoint after driving him to a street in North Caulfield. Allen appeared in court on April 2, but was released on April 30, having successfully applied for bail. The very next day his brother Victor Peirce was murdered.

On January 14, 2003, Peter Allen was once again up against the authorities, having been charged with armed robbery. Peter Allen represented himself during the filing hearing and bail application in the Melbourne Magistrates Court. Peter was charged with one count of armed robbery, one count of the theft of a motor vehicle, and a count of possession of a firearm.

This time the court was told that Allen, wearing a balaclava and armed with a sawn-off shotgun, went to the Australia Post building in Toorak Road, Hartwell, about 2 p.m. on January 8, 2003. He demanded cash from an attendant, and was followed by a witness when he left the building. The witness apparently hit Allen with a club lock and smashed the back window of the car in which Peter and another man drove off.

On July 19, 2003, Allen was denied bail after the judge noticed his 'appalling' six-page long criminal record going back to 1968.

Victor George Peirce

Born on November 11, 1958, Victor was Kathy Pettingill's sixth child. His father was Kathy's second partner, Billy Peirce, who died a horrifying death – buried alive while helping to dig a three-metre trench – when Victor was only ten years old.

Peirce was the prime suspect as a triggerman in the 1988 Walsh Street police shootings. He was a good friend of fellow armed robber Graeme Jensen, who, at the age of fifteen, became one of Australia's youngest bank robbers. Jensen was shot dead by detectives the day before the Walsh Street shootings.

Peirce had vast gangland contacts, including Mark Militano, Frank Valastro, Jedd Houghton and Gary Abdallah, all of whom were armed robbers and who were eventually killed by police.

The home of Victor and Wendy Peirce was raided the afternoon following the Walsh Street shootings. Apparently, the police search was so thorough that all that was left of the Peirce home was just a pile of rubble. Later the same afternoon police raided the Brunswick flat of Kath Pettingill's daughter, Vicki Brooks. Victor managed to escape by climbing over a back fence but gave himself up to police the following day. He was charged with the July 11 Brunswick armed hold-up which included the murder of one of the guards. The robbery was said to have involved Jason Moran, Santo Mercuri and Russel 'Mad Dog' Cox. These charges were dropped but Victor was charged with the Tynan/Eyre murders and spent the next thirty months in custody.

One of the key witnesses against the Walsh Street four was Peirce's wife Wendy, who was to give key evidence against her husband, but at the last minute she refused to implicate him and she was later jailed for perjury. The Peirces were united once again after Victor was acquitted.

Life was never going to be simple for Victor, after his acquittal he received further jail sentences for his involvement with drug trafficking.

The Peirce couple had an interesting marriage to say the least. On one occasion, Victor's brother Dennis Allen offered to shoot Wendy in the leg to assist Peirce in a bail application on compassionate grounds. But it turned out Wendy was pregnant and their little plan was foiled for fear of damaging the unborn child.

After the acquittal, Peirce lay low for a while, but his return to crime was almost a certainty. In the early 1990s he built up a heroin business and became one of Melbourne's biggest traffickers. Peirce was once again jailed when arrested for selling heroin to a police operative at Chadstone Shopping Centre. The evidence was conclusive as the transactions had been videotaped and shown in court. Peirce was convicted in April 1993 and sentenced to eight years in jail with a six-year minimum to be served.

Peirce was released on parole in June 1998. On his release, wife Wendy said she was confident he had reformed. 'He is not a monster. When he gets out we just want to be left alone . . . He is a family man with family values. He is one of the best fathers you could see. No one has anything to fear from us. He has had six years to think about it. He has a job lined up. I know that he is finished with crime. He just wants to live quietly with his family.'

Once free, according to his mother Kath Pettingill, Peirce lived the life of a loving husband and father and worked hard on the docks. She was quite adamant that he was staying away from his criminal past. It also seems apparent that although police loathed Peirce there was somehow a begrudging respect for him.

Peirce was quietly spoken and believed in opening his mouth only when he had something worthwhile to say. And for that reason he was invariably listened to by his more hot-headed underworld peers. Peirce was a vegetarian, fitness freak and, according to Kathy, unusually squeamish.

Peirce was murdered on May 1, 2002 whilst sitting in his car in Bay Street, Port Melbourne.

Lex Peirce

Lex was Kath Pettingill's seventh child and never committed criminal offences on the same scale as his siblings. He has lived peacefully in South Gippsland for years.

Jamie Pettingill

Jamie Pettingill was caught for burglary at the age of eleven, and by his early teens car theft was his passion. He continued his career as an armed robber, and was arrested for his fourth robbery – an Ascot Vale Supermarket – at sixteen.

Jamie was a friend of Flemington armed robber, Gary Abdallah, who was later shot dead by police. Jamie was used by brother Dennis Allen as a strong man in his many street dealings. Jamie always carried a gun and was with Dennis when he shot a bottle shop attendant during a robbery at the United Kingdom Hotel in Clifton Hill on March 5, 1980. Dennis managed to escape the scene, but his brother Jamie took the whole rap. The attendant later died from what was found to be a moving blood clot.

Jamie also shot a man whose associate threatened Dennis with a gun in their family home. He later became addicted to heroin while in prison.

Jamie died May 14, 1985 after a mysterious heroin overdose. Many, including some police, have suggested that maybe Dennis was responsible.

Trevor Pettingill

Born on February 16, 1965, Trevor's first experience of institutions was when he was only six years old. He was put under state supervision because he was seen to be in moral danger.

Trevor became a hardened career criminal. In September 1987, he, along with his mother Kath, pleaded guilty to heroin possession and was consequently sentenced to seven months jail.

A known drug user, Trevor had a long criminal history before he was charged with the shooting of the two policemen in Walsh Street in 1988. Trevor was kidnapped on November 29, 1988, during the Walsh Street investigations, when he was taken to a deserted road and beaten by masked men in an effort to force him to tell police the truth about the murders. He was later arrested and charged, but acquitted with his three co-accused.

Trevor moved away from Melbourne to the family hideaway at Venus Bay after the acquittal.

Later that year he appeared in Heidelberg Magistrates Court charged with aggravated burglary, theft, and carrying a weapon. He was granted bail. The following year he was arrested after a car chase through Northcote. The burglary, theft and weapons charges were adjourned along with dangerous and unlicensed driving charges to give Trevor a chance to beat his heroin addiction at Odyssey House.

In 1993, Pettingill was again in court, this time on a charge of growing marijuana. While on bail on that charge, with his mother and ten others, he faced further drug charges. Kath Pettingill was charged with drugs and firearms offences. Trevor was sentenced to a minimum forty-five months' jail when the case came to trial and the court was told of his thirty-two previous convictions.

In 2001 he was in court again this time charged with street offences after trying to help a man who had been tied up by railway inspectors. The magistrate fined Pettingill $500 and described him as a 'devotee of democratic justice'.

Jason Ryan

Jason Ryan was the son of Vicki Brooks, Victor Peirce's sister. Jason moved in with his uncle Dennis Allen during the height of his heroin empire and was apparently used as a carrier of drugs and guns.

Ryan was caught up in many 'Cyclops' raids in the mid-eighties including one where a pistol was found under his pillow. Jason became a witness for the prosecution in Walsh Street when taken out of

Melbourne for questioning by police.

Ryan, who exchanged his testimony for immunity, left for the country on October 24, 1988, after his first statement about Walsh Street three days before. Ty/Eyre Task Force head, Detective John Noonan escorted Ryan to the small town of Mansfield in North East Victoria, where he was interrogated with regards to Walsh Street. Ryan gave crucial, but ever-changing evidence in the Walsh Street trials and was subsequently put on a witness protection programme.

Ryan would have made a lot of enemies because it was due to him that Jedd Houghton, a family friend, was implicated in the shootings. Also a fellow Flemington armed robber, Gary Abdallah, became a suspect on the evidence that Jason Ryan put forward on October 27. Ryan claimed that Abdallah's part in the killings was to provide and drive the getaway car. Abdallah and Houghton were shot in police raids shortly afterwards.

On October 31, 1988 Jason gave a statement implicating friend Anthony Farrell and another friend, Emmanuel Alexandris, in the killings. Farrell was charged with murder the following day. Jason told police on November 16, listing the party of killers as being Jedd Houghton, McEvoy, Farrell and his uncles Victor Peirce and Trevor Pettingill.

Ryan's story changed so many times that he lost his credibility but Kathy Pettingill admits that she has now forgiven him.

Robert Trimbole

Men like Robert Trimbole were infamous as the alleged Kingpins of organized crime. In underworld terms, he has been referred to as the 'Godfather'. Not a boss but a boss among bosses.

Robert Trimbole was born on March 19, 1931, and is now recognized as the most prominent chief in the history of Australian organized crime. Trimbole has been accused of many things in his time ranging from organizing murders, marijuana and heroin trafficking, police and political corruption, race fixing and money laundering. Normal activities for most Mafia godfathers.

His rise to international notoriety began in Griffith, in the Riverina district of New South Wales. He started out in legitimate business ventures, but unfortunately these ended in bankruptcy in 1968. This made him look in other directions to earn a living. In the 1970s he gained huge wealth through setting up and distributing large amounts of marijuana in the Griffith region. He soon became known as the leader of the secret organized crime group known as L'Onorata Societa (The Honoured Society) or, as he originates from a band of Southern Italians from Calabria, N'Drangheta, as it is known locally.

Trimbole worked very hard to portray the image of a successful businessman, but not everyone in the Griffith district was taken in, and in the mid-1970s an up-and-coming politician by the name of Donald Mackay, tried to win over recognition by kicking up an anti-drugs campaign. In truth this was an anti-marijuana campaign which was targeted directly at Trimbole. However, Mackay soon found out that he had messed with the wrong guy.

Donald Mackay was murdered on July 15, 1977 for criticising the amount of money that was being made from the trading of marijuana around his home town of Griffith. A $25,000 reward for information was offered one week after his murder. Bloodstains and three spent cartridges were found near Mackay's car at the Griffith Hotel. It turned out that Mackay had been a secret informant for police action against illicit marijuana growing in the Riverina. In November 1975, he had received information about a multi-million dollar crop at Coleamby near Griffith, but distrustful of local police, Mackay has passed on his information to police in Sydney, who subsequently raided the plantation.

During the trial of those arrested, a notebook was produced in which Mackay was named as an informant. This meant that Mackay's name was now disclosed, and it became obvious that he was the police informant whose information led to the raid.

Robert Trimbole, who was not impressed by 'squealers', ordered the hit on Mackay. Before his death Mackay had publicly exposed the true ramifications of the Trimbole Empire, an empire that had been built up on the proceeds of his large-scale marijuana operation. This exposure did untold damage to Trimbole's operation, hence the eventual murder of Mackay. Trimbole, always the true businessman, had already begun to diversify his business interests as he was now involved in a heroin operation that soon became known as the Mr. Asia gang – an international heroin smuggling syndicate.

The activities of the Mr. Asia gang, operated a drug distribution network in Australasia between 1972 and 1979, and was the first sign of large-scale drug dealings with New Zealand.

The arrest and incarceration of the main members in England in 1979, spelt the end of the Mr Asia syndicate but it did not result in an end to organized crime. A huge drug market existed by the end of the 1970s, and it was thus inevitable that organized criminal distribution networks would grow. Today organized crime in New Zealand is manifest in two major areas: among motorcycle and street gangs, and within the Asian community.

In August 1980, Robert Trimbole was ordered to give evidence at the Melbourne inquest into the murder of two members of the Mr. Asia syndicate, Douglas and Isabel Wilson. The two members had been brought in from New Zealand and were eliminated by Trimbole because he had found out through his number of paid-off policemen, that the couple had turned into police informants and had become a threat to his organization.

More trouble was heading Trimbole's way, however, this time in the form of Gianfranco Tizzoni, who was arrested in June 1983 for his part in the murder of Donald Mackay. Tizzoni began to sing and gave the police all the evidence they needed on the Mackay hit, implicating Trimbole to the full. Trimbole was beginning to feel the heat as his Mr. Asia syndicate was being dismantled in both Australia and England but he wasn't going to hang around and await the consequences, so he fled Australia. Tizzoni also gave evidence on the Griffith Mafia and stated that Trimble was a major player, in fact the number two man within the N'Drangheta of Australia.

Trimbole was finally tracked down in Ireland in October 1984, after being suspected of hiding away in Italy, Switzerland and France. He was arrested on the outskirts of Dublin, where he had been hiding as a retired businessman. The legal moves to have Trimbole extradited back to Australia were stepped up, but Trimbole who had already been in hospital in Dublin, died of cancer before they even got the chance.

Bruno Romeo

Bruno Romeo was jailed for 10 years in 1994 over his role as the ringleader of an $8 million cannabis-growing operation on remote pastoral leases in Western Australia.

Bruno Romeo was born in 1929 in Calabria, Italy, and was thought to have left for Australia at the end of World War II. On his arrival he settled in Adelaide, where he set about becoming the major force in organized crime in Australia.

Romeo, along with his brother Dominico, set up an empire that is believed to have stretched from Adelaide to Perth. In 1965 a secret intelligence report listed Bruno Romeo as the leader of the Calabrian Mafia in South Australia. Romeo, like many Mafia men before him, ran the usual rackets such as extortion, and ringing stolen cars. However, the principal racket that Romeo was interested in was the growing and producing of marijuana. It was from this 'enterprise' that he managed to launder the profits into many different legitimate businesses giving him the image of a successful business man. This was an image that he tried very hard to maintain during his working career. Romeo also preferred to keep a low profile when going about his usual Mafia business.

In 1992 Bruno Romeo was charged for growing

and producing large crops of cannabis. Earlier that year ten of his men were also sentenced to fifteen years for growing cannabis. Romeo had now been on the run for several years and was considered one of Australia's most wanted men. He was eventually arrested on the New South Wales coast near a place called Lismore. He was in hiding in a caravan near a crop of 750 cannabis plants, some of which had grown as tall as four metres.

After taking out attempted contracts on two of the witnesses who were under a protection scheme, Bruno Romeo was sentenced to twenty-five years behind bars. As he was already sixty-four years of age at the time of his sentence, it is possible that he will spend the rest of his lift in jail.

Vincenzo Dagastino

Vincenzo Dagastino was one of the first, if not the very first, Mafia leaders in Australia.

Dagastino arrived in Brisbane sometime in the middle of the 1920s from Milan. He quickly set about bringing a different breed of violence to his new homeland. Australia already had a number of Italian immigrants, and a number of Italian communities. Dagastino started to get his gang together and operated out of Ingham. His gang consisted of a number of Calabrian thugs such as Dominico Belle, Vincenzo Soprano, Niccolo Mammone, Guiseppe Parisi, Guiseppe Buette and Francesco Femio.

Dagastino's first operation was to target a number of farmers for extortion, using the 'Black Hand' method which meant delivering a letter with the stamp of a black hand on it. If the farmers ignored the letter they would be paid a visit by the 'black-handers' and threatened. Needless to say, following the threats most of the farmers paid up. Anyone who didn't was beaten first, and then eventually murdered if they still declined to pay.

Dagastino was also known to use other methods

to make sure the farmers paid. He would tell his men to kill cattle, burn crops and even poison their water supplies. During the late 1920s and 1930s eleven people were murdered or maimed in the Queensland area.

The first to fall victim was a man named Nicky Patane. Patane did actually pay for nearly a full year but was facing bankruptcy after giving in to demands that were constantly growing. The authorities were unable to pin the murder on Dagastino as many of the Italians respected the code of silence imported from south Italy and Sicily. Dagastino was earning a good living out of his Black Hand victims, but his under-boss Dominic Belle was not happy about Dagastino keeping the majority of the extortion proceeds.

Belle decided that enough was enough and left Queensland to start up his own gang in Sydney. It didn't take long for Belle to leave his mark in Sydney, and he soon accumulated a luxurious life-style of his own. However on February 11, 1930, Belle was murdered following a heated argument with a fellow Italian at the Newtown Railway station. Belle was stabbed in the heart and was left for dead.

Back in Brisbane it was Dagastino's turn to witness some adversity. One of his Black Hand members, Guiseppe Parisi, was fished out of a creek near a farm in Queensland, his body having been seriously mutilated. The murder of Parisi looked like it was retaliation from Belle's people in Sydney, following the murder of Dominic Belle himself.

On February 11, 1934, following the orders of Dagastino, Mammone, Speranzo and Buette sliced off the ears of a man called Giovanni Iaconna, a farmer who had fallen behind on his payments. In hospital Iaconna refused to name his attackers. Instead he tracked down Mammone and pumped his body full of bullets. When Iaconna was arrested for the murder of Mammone, he named Speranzo and Buette as his attackers. While Iaconna received a life sentence, his attackers would only serve seven years.

Towards the end of 1936, feuding had once again erupted in a power struggle to seize control of the extortion racket. On December 12 Francesco Femio, who was now Dagastino's number two man, was shot in his sleep.

In a similar attack, a bomb was planted beneath the bedroom of Dagastino, and which exploded while he was sleeping. His funeral was a really low-key affair, as the real hatred and contempt for the man within the community was so much that no one, not even any of his men, turned up. In fact, the only person that did turn up at the funeral was the paid undertaker's assistant.

The Kelly Gang

*Few words are as menacing as 'gang' when used in
relation to crime. Reports of gang violence and
gangland crime strike fear into people's hearts. Of course,
gangs have long been a fact of Australian life – and
perhaps the most famous one is the Kelly Gang.*

Ned Kelly left an indelible imprint on Australia's criminal history, and although he was
definitely a common criminal, he was also revered
as the original Australian hero.

Ned was born in December, 1854, at Beveridge,
Victoria. His father, John, was an Irishman from
Tipperary who had been transported to Tasmania
in 1841 for stealing two pigs. When he had finished serving his time, in 1848, John crossed over to
Port Phillip, Victoria. Two years later he met and
married an Irish girl named Ellen Quinn, and they
went to live at Wallan Wallan, which is thirty miles
north of Melbourne. John and Ellen had eight
children – Mary, Annie, Ned, Maggie, Jim, Dan,
Kate and Grace. After Ned was born the family
moved to a small dairy farm near Avenel, which is
where Ned attended his first school.

While Ned was at primary school he did his first
heroic deed. He risked his own life to save that of
a drowning boy, Richard Shelton, who had been
swept off the banks of the Hughes Creek into the

raging waters below. Ned was rewarded by Richard's parents with a green silk sash as a sign of bravery, and this sash was to become one of his most treasured possessions.

When Ned was twelve he was forced to leave school because of the tragic death of his father. Times became hard for the family as they had now lost their breadwinner, but the resourceful Mrs. Kelly moved her family to a small hub on Eleven Mile Creek, an area which was later to become known as 'Kelly Country'.

Ned did everything he could to earn a few shillings for his family. He would put up fencing, break horses and drive cattle. It was probably this period of his life that determined Ned's future. Many of the settlers in the area were at constant war with the big landowners. The Kelly family along with other families in the area used to use horses for currency and they regarded all un-branded strays as fair game. The police did not take kindly to this, and the boys began to consider that they were their enemies. The Kelly house became a famous meeting place for local rogues and cattle-thieves and she was given a warning more than once by the local police. The authorities even at this early stage had it in for the Kelly gang.

When Ned was fourteen, he was arrested for assaulting a Chinaman. He was kept locked up in the Benalla jail for ten days, but was reluctantly released when the magistrate dismissed the charge. A year later Ned was arrested again on a more serious charge, that of being an accomplice to a famous bushranger by the name of Harry

Power. Again the case was dismissed through lack of any evidence. However, the police did not leave Ned alone and in the following year he was failed for six months for assaulting a hawker. The year 1871, saw disaster for Ned, when he was jailed for three years in Pentridge jail for receiving a stolen horse. Ned came out an embittered man in 1874.

THE KELLY GANG

The Kelly gang consisted of Ned, of course, Joe Byrne, Ned's younger brother Daniel, and Steve Hart.

Joe Byrne

Joe Byrne was born in 1857 to Irish-Catholic parents. His father, who had worked as a dairyman, died when Joe was only twelve. He had had minor scrapes with the law, but nothing more serious than stealing meat, and the illegal use of a horse.

At the age of twenty-one, Joe was Ned's best friend. He was reasonably well educated but had an addiction to opium. Like the rest of the Kelly Gang he was an excellent shot and also a fine horseman, and would practice riding down gullies just for fun. Joe was fluent in Cantonese which was very handy when the gang visited one of their numerous opium dens.

Joe Byrne first got to know Ned in 1876 and they became trusted friends. Joe was known as his lieutenant, the man who Ned would always consult if he needed advice. Ned looked upon Joe as wise, patient and very different to the other members of the gang.

Joe's real trademark were his high-heeled boots and he was seen as one of the more glamorous members of the gang. He had charisma, was handsome, but had strong opposition to police law and order. Joe was a learned scholar, who loved reading and was also a proficient writer. He allegedly had quite a number of girlfriends in the surrounding towns.

Joe ended up by murdering his one-time best friend Aaron Sherritt, whom he believed to be a police informer. There is no proof that Sherritt was supplying police with any information, but whatever he was doing he made the fatal mistake of not letting his friend in on his plans.

Joe lost his life when the gang had their final confrontation with the police at Glenrowan. His mother, who had always welcomed her son home, refused to claim his body and he was buried in the Benalla cemetery in an unmarked grave.

Daniel Kelly

Daniel was born in 1861 and was the youngest of the three Kelly boys. Although he was less formidable than other members of the gang, he was still a keen fighter and a very able horseman. It was Daniel's drunken pass at Daniel's sister Kate that precipitated the 'Fitzpatrick Incident' which culminated in the Kelly boys being hunted by the police. This is explained more fully further in this story.

Dan Kelly was considered to be the thinker of

the family but for some reason Ned tended to ignore his suggestions, which possibly could have saved the Kelly gang from ruination.

Dan accompanied Joe Byrne to Aaron Sherritt's hut on Saturday, June 26, 1880 where Joe shot Aaron to death. Dan was also a member of the 'Greta Mob' along with his best friend Steve Hart. At the age of fifteen Dan had his first court appearance, but was acquitted of the charge of stealing a saddle. However, by the age of seventeen he was branded an outlaw and by nineteen he was dead, his charred remains being pulled from the ashes of the Glenrowan Inn.

Steve Hart

Steve Hart was born in 1859 in Beechworth. Of all the gang, it is Steve Hart who is least well known. He was slim but took a lot of pride in his appearance and, like the others, was of Irish-Catholic blood.

In 1877 Steve was sentenced in Wangaratta to seven years on thirteen counts of illegally using horses. Steve was a really exceptional rider and was an occasional jockey, he even won the Beechworth Handicap. There is a rumour that when the gang was being hunted, Steve dressed as a woman and rode side saddle to avoid being detected.

Steve was a leading member of the 'Greta Mob' but, like Joe Byrne, became an outlaw purely by chance. Like the rest of the Kelly Gang Steve Hart died young. His charred remains were also dragged out from the embers of the Glenrowan Inn when he was only twenty-one.

THE GANG'S EXPLOITS

As previously mentioned, Ned Kelly came out of prison a very angry and embittered young man. On his release he returned home to find that his mother had remarried. Her new husband was a Californian man named George King. Ned worked with his stepfather for a while running stolen horses across the Murray River so that they could be sold in New South Wales.

Dan Kelly also fell foul of the law in his teenage years and was given three months for damaging property. On his release he returned home, little realizing that the police, who had been unable to trace the real horse thieves, had warrants against both Ned and Dan. The man who arrived at the house with a warrant, was a trooper named Alexander Fitzpatrick. On his way to Mrs. Kelly's place he had stopped at a tavern to give him courage for what he had to do. When he arrived he found Dan at home with his mother and his sisters, Will Skilton (who was Maggie Kelly's husband) and a neighbour by the name of Williamson. Fitzpatrick had only been inside the house for about five minutes when violence erupted, apparently the trooper had made a drunken pass at Kate Kelly. Dan immediately flew at him and knocked him down and, in the ensuing scuffle, the trooper's gun went off and he received an injury to his wrist. Mrs. Kelly, who was concerned, bandaged the man's wrist and invited him to stay for supper and asked him if he would be prepared to forget the incident. However, on his way back to the police station, Fitzpatrick had some more brandy and fabricated a story that Ned had resisted arrest and had burst into the room and shot him in the wrist. He went on to say that Ned offered to cut the bullet out with a rusty old razor blade, but Fitzpatrick declined his offer and removed it with his penknife.

A doctor who later gave evidence at the trial stated that he was doubtful that a bullet had actually caused the injury to Fitzpatrick's wrist, but he did accept that the wound could have been made by a penknife. Even the police had to admit that Fitzpatrick was indeed a 'liar'. Despite Mrs. Kelly's protests that Ned wasn't even at the house on the night in question and that nobody had even shot the trooper, arrests were still made. Judge Redmond Barry sentenced Skillion and Williamson to six years each for assisting in the attempted murder of a police officer, and even Mrs. Kelly was given three years.

Ned Kelly swore vengeance, but having been restrained from violence by his friends, wrote a letter instead to the Magistrate offering himself in exchange for his mother. Unfortunately the Magistrate was powerless to act, and by this time the police were stepping up their efforts to get Ned Kelly. Ned and Dan Kelly both left the district and the government put up a reward of £100 each for their capture. The two boys hid in the Wombat Ranges which was about twenty miles from Mansfield. They made a clearing in the rough ground and built a slab hut near the banks of a creek. They passed their time panning for gold.

While in hiding they were joined by their two friends Steve Hart and Joe Byrne. Both Steve and Joe had previous prison sentences, but the plans of the four men was not to carry out large scale crimes – they hoped to find a way to distil illicit liquor. They wanted to raise enough cash so that they could arrange for a retrial of Mrs. Kelly.

All the while the police hunt was intensifying. In late October 1878 four policemen, Kennedy, Lonigan, Scanlon and McIntyre rode out from Mansfield and on the 25th made camp at Stringybark Creek. They had no idea that they had set up camp just one mile away from Ned and his gang. Ned, out riding one of his daily reconnoitres, spotted the police camp and rushed back to warn the others. He believed, quite rightly, that he and Dan would be shot on sight.

The police had indeed come well armed, not only with guns, but also heavy leather straps with which to strap the bodies of Ned and Dan onto their spare horses. The following day two of the troopers, Lonigan and McIntyre, were relaxing by the campfire, while the other two were out searching the area. Ned, Joe, Steve and Dan emerged silently from the bush and took the troopers completely by surprise. Lonigan immediately jumped to his feet and drew his revolver but Ned was too quick for him and shot him dead. McIntyre, fearing for his own life, surrendered immediately. When Kennedy and Scanlon returned to their camp they spotted the gang and opened fire. A gunfight ensued and both Scanlon and Kennedy were shot. McIntyre, however, managed to escape on Kennedy's horse. Ned and his gang then covered the bodies of the troopers with blankets, took their weapons and rode away.

THE AMBUSH

Constable McIntyre reached Mansfield and raised the alarm. He told the story of a cowardly ambush by the Kelly Gang and the ultimate slaughter of his associates, which totally shocked the police and later the whole country. Ned Kelly, Dan Kelly, Joe Byrne and Steve Hart were immediately branded as outlaws – to be taken 'dead or alive'. Two hundred police were drafted into the area and they also enrolled the help of some skilled native troopers from Queensland. For a while the manhunt drew a blank, they could find no trace of the dreaded Kelly Gang.

Then, at last, the police got help from a friend of Joe Byrne named Aaron Sherritt. He told the police where they could find the gang, but Ned and his mob managed to escape by a matter of hours. Although they had no money they did still have many friends and they were able to keep one step ahead. Ned decided they really could do with some money and on December 10, 1878, the Kelly Gang invaded a station property at Faithfull's Creek.

The gang rounded up twenty-two people at the sheep station and locked them in a storeroom, while Kelly's horses had a well-earned rest. Ned, Dan and Steve left Joe Byrne to guard their prisoners while they drove into nearby Euroa in a stolen hawker's cart. Although Euroa only had a small population there was a National Bank on the main street and at 4.00 p.m. Ned entered the building with his gun drawn, while Dan came in from the rear. Ten minutes later they were on the street again richer by £2,260 in both notes and gold. They returned to the sheep station, picked up Joe and rode off again on fresh horses.

The Kelly Gang had managed to carry off the most perfectly planned and executed bank robbery in Australian history – with no violence and leaving no enemies behind them.

Following their bank raid the Government of Victoria increased the rewards on the heads of the Kelly Gang to £1,000 each and they posted guards on all the banks on the North-Eastern District. Two months later, having crossed the border into New South Wales, the gang struck again.

GATHERING FUNDS

Their next target was the Bank of New South Wales at Jerilderie. It was a Saturday night and the gang captured two policemen, locked them up, and stole their uniforms. The following day they rounded up sixty of the townspeople and assembled them in the dining room of the Royal Mail Hotel, which just happened to be right next door to the bank. He then read out a letter to his captive audience, a remarkable document that Ned had dictated to the educated Joe Byrne. The document, which became known as the *Jerilderie Letter*, was in fact an autobiography, a statement of fact and self-justification.

On Monday morning Ned went to the local newspaper to see if he could get his letter printed, but the editor had gone into hiding. Ned, after checking to make sure that all the telephone wires out of town had been cut, went into the bank and robbed it of £2,000. Before he left the bank Ned gave his letter to one of the tellers who swore he would give to a local MP, but instead he passed it on to the Crown Law Office in Melbourne. The statement was then carefully put away and was not produced at Kelly's trial.

Following the raid on the bank at Jerilderie although there were reports of the gang being seen as far away as Melbourne, they seemed to go into hiding and were not seen for another seventeen months. The bounty on their heads was increased to £4,000 by the Victorian government which was matched by £4,000 from New South Wales.

The police became increasingly frustrated by the support that the Kelly Gang were receiving and proceeded to lock up friends and relatives of the gang for months on end without any due reason. When this backfired, the police decided to draw up a blacklist of known Kelly associates and they were told they were not allowed to take up land in the north-east. This was a very unwise move and tipped the supporters into rebellion. Meanwhile Ned and his gang were making their own plans to get back at their police enemies. While all this was going on, one of the Kelly Gang's enemies, Aaron Sherritt, was making his own plans to destroy the Gang.

Sherritt, along with the police, set about a plot

which would incriminate Sherritt in the eyes of the Kelly Gang. They felt that if they broke cover to come and kill Sherritt the police felt they would at last get the chance to capture or even kill the outlaws. One night Aaron Sherritt opened his front door to find his old friend Joe Byrne standing there. Without a word passing between them, Joe shot Sherritt dead. There were four armed policemen in the house who had been placed there as protection for the Sherritt family. Joe Byrne along with his fellow gang member, Dan, ordered the police to come out and fight, but the troopers declined and took to hiding under Sherritt's bed. The two outlaws threatened to burn the house down, and then rode forty miles across country to meet Ned and Steve at Glenrowan.

On Saturday, June 17, 1880, the Kelly Gang captured the railway station at Glenrowan. The news of the Sherritt shooting had already reached the south, so Ned knew now that the time had come to stand up and fight.

The Gang's last stand was held at a tiny hotel in Glenrowan, which was owned by Mrs Ann Jones, a suspected police spy. They rounded up a crowd of people in the hotel, took captive the local constable, and cut the telegraph wires. Then the Kelly Gang proceeded to have a drink with the locals well into the night. Ned then decided to cut off the small town even further, and he ordered a railway fettler named Reardon to tear up a section of the railroad track.

The Kelly's tried to stay alert even though they had not slept for two nights. However, the resourceful Constable Bracken and a school teacher, Thomas Curnow, were able to outwit them and escape. A train, full of police, left Melbourne for Kelly Country and arrived in the early hours of Monday morning. They heard the whistle of the approaching train and the Kelly Gang waited to hear the derailment, but it never came. Curnow had run along the track waving a light shaded with a red cloth and had managed to stop the train before it reached the break in the rails.

As the police headed in force towards the hotel, Ned could be heard in a back room putting on his armour preparing for the fight that was about to come. His armour consisted of a cylindrical helmet, a breastplate with apron and a back plate laced with leather thongs, the whole outfit weighing around ninety pounds.

THE FINAL STAND

The moon was very bright and at around 3.00 a.m. the police, using the trees for protection, surrounded the hotel. As they took up their positions the Kelly Gang came out of the hotel and started shooting. Superintendent Hare, the commanding officer, was the first to be shot and he promptly retired to the safety of the post office. Joe Byrne was shot in the leg during an exchange of fire, then he, Dan and Steve retired back into the hotel. Ned Kelly, who had been shot in the foot, hand and arm, escaped into the trees.

Inside the hotel the women and children were screaming, but still the police kept up a constant barrage of gunfire. Dan ordered the townspeople to keep flat and not to raise their heads on any account. The firing continued as the night drew in, and Joe, tired from fighting grabbed a bottle of whisky, straightened himself up to drink from it, and then dropped dead from a bullet to his groin. The captive townspeople by this time were becoming hysterical and, braving the police fire, started to come out of the hotel.

It was sometime before dawn that Ned went back into the hotel only to find his friend Joe Byrne dead. He then headed off into the bush and collapsed from loss of blood. Still the heroic gang leader, instead of escaping, Ned returned to the hotel to rescue his brother and Steve Hart. Ned must have been a sorry sight as he came out of the mist, an apparition in his dented armour, and limping badly. Bullets rang against his armour as he slowly walked towards the police firing line. They fired at his legs and he eventually collapsed to the floor. The police surrounded the outlaw and as they removed his armour they realized that he was so badly wounded he probably wouldn't survive for very long.

By this time another train had arrived which carried Ned Kelly's sisters, Kate and Maggie, and a Roman Catholic priest. Ned's sisters begged the priest to see their brother and read him the last rites. Father Gibney agreed and finding Ned still conscious proceeded to comfort him. Then he left for the hotel. At around 3.00 p.m., believing that everyone was out of the hotel, the police set fire to the Glenrowan Inn. Someone cried out that there were still people trapped inside, and Father Gibney, with incredible courage walked into the burning building with his hands raised high. But no shots were fired, and when he fought his way into the back room he found the lifeless bodies of Dan Kelly and Steve Hart. The bodies lay side by side, heads propped up by folded blankets. Joe Byrne's body was dragged from the Inn but those of Dan Kelly and Steve Hart were charred beyond recognition. When the priest gave evidence later he said it was his opinion that Dan and Steve had both committed suicide, probably by drinking poison.

THE END OF NED KELLY

Surprisingly, Ned Kelly survived all his wounds and a hearing was held at Beechworth in August 1880. He was considered fit to stand trial for murder at Melbourne's Supreme Court on October 28 of that year. Inevitably a guilty verdict was reached and Ned's execution was scheduled for Thursday, November 11, 1880. Although a massive movement was launched to save his life, which included torch-lit marches, huge public meetings, and a petition with more than 32,000 signatures, Ned was hanged at 10.00 a.m. on November 11. A crowd of five thousand people gathered outside the Melbourne jail to watch his execution and his headless body was eventually buried in an unmarked grave on the ground of the Old Melbourne Gaol. It was later removed to Pentridge Prison's Cemetery.

Ned's mother, Mrs. Ellen Kelly, survived until 1923, eventually dying at the age of ninety-two.

PART SEVEN
SERBIA
AND
ALBANIA

Nasa Stvar

*The Serbian Mafia, or 'Nasa Stvar', is just another
branch of the worldwide problem of organized crime.*

The death of Serbian police chief, Radovan
Stojvic Badza in 1997, was the last in a series
of mysterious and spectacular execution-style
murders which have taken place in Belgrade in the
last five years. The actual 'style' of the murders is
almost identical, the victims' profile as well, but
the final similarity is that none of the murders has
ever been solved.

The mysterious showdowns started in August
1991 with the murder of Branislav Matic Beli at
the front of his house, in the the presence of his
wife and children. Beli owned a chain of used car
dealerships in Belgrade, had financed the
paramilitairy unit Sprska Garda (Serb Guard) and
also fiancially assisted the largest opposition party,
the SPO. Two men jumped out of a van and fired
27 bullets at Beli from machine guns. He was
killed where he stood, and the assassins sped away
and entered the history books of Serbian crime.
This was to be the first action carried out to what
would become a familiar recipe.

It is thought that all the murders are directly
connected to politics. According to a Belgrade
police lawyer, Vlada Kovacevic, the transformation

of the Serbian economy came in the nineties with the UN sanctions. The appearance of privately-owned companies, the takeover of large state-owned companies, and the transfer of business to private firms produced certain monopolies which became the source of huge profits. These mysterious murders all seem to be the result of business deals which involve a lot of money. Kovacevic also gave his opinion that everyone with a lot of money needs the support of criminal gangs, so that in the end classic and economic crime intertwine. Those deals that cannot be concluded with money are closed with threats, blackmail, rackets and, in extreme cases, murder.

The background of Beli's murder will probably never be made public. However, it will be remembered that at the time he financed a paramilitary unit named Srpska Garda. He was also responsible for financing the largest opposition party (SPO) and was a disappointed former follower of Slobodan Milosevic, the former Yugoslavian President.

Beli's murder, however, turned out to be only the beginning. His old friend, former Belgrade criminal and commander of Srpska Garda, Djordje Bozovic Giska, was killed on the front near Gospic, in Croatia. Although he was officially reported to have died fighting, the circumstances of his death were rather suspicious. For a start there was no autopsy, so it wasn't possible to find out where the bullet had been fired from and whether in fact it had come from an SAR rifle, which at the time was only used by the Yugoslav

Peoples Army and State Security forces. Giska's mother received an anonymous message the evening before his death stating 'they have gone to kill him'. But who and why still remains a mystery. Apparently Giska was just one of a number of people who, in the eighties, had contacts with the State Security forces and carried out their dirty work abroad. But what he, or the others in his line of business, didn't realize was that they would become disposable.

The next event which shocked the people of Serbia, was the execution of Aleksandar Knezevic Knele. He was known as Giska's 'boy' and was for a while the personal bodyguard to Vuk Draskovic, the once deputy Prime Minister. He was also one of the thugs who broke up the anti-government demonstrations in the centre of Belgrade in March 1993. Room 331 in the Hyatt Hotel still hides the secret of Knele's death. It could possibly have been the result of a Mafia war, although some people still believe that such a murder could have only been carried out by a specially trained professional.

RADOJICA NIKCEVIC

Radojica Nikcevic was assassinated on October 7, 1991 at 8.15 in the morning. He had come out of a huge company Mercedes and was walking towards the entrance of the First Belgrade Housing Cooperative Sumadija. The assassin and his assistant, both wearing workers' uniforms, walked towards Nikcevic. As soon as they passed him they fired two shots into the back of his head.

Nikcevic was a businessman with strong connections in the Serbian and Montenegrin leaderships, and his life was both mysterious and confusing. He brought the controversial Giovani Di Stefano (today Arkan's best man and advisor for foreign policy) to Serbia. Zeljko Raznatovic (better known as Arkan) was the man who organized a private army, the Serb Volunteer Guard or 'Tigers' in 1992. Nikcevic travelled with Stefano to Colombia – with unknown intentions. Nikcevic himself claimed that he was worth 50 million DM (US $25 million). He liked to flaunt his success and to this end he wore a valuable diamond ring and a Rolex watch inlaid with diamonds.

He maintained contacts within seemingly very different circles within the Serbian society. On the one hand, he had been seen in the company of almost all-important Belgrade gangsters, while on the other he had very good connections with the police and politicians. To put it in simple terms, he was a powerful Yugoslavian version of a 'godfather'. His murder still hasn't been solved.

GORAN VUKOVIC

Goran Vukovic was the leader of the Belgrade Vozdovac gang, and the first person to accuse the police of organizing 'death squads'. On many occasions he spoke about strange coincidences in the press. It turned out later on that two Federal policemen took part in one of the six assassination attempts that Vukovic managed to survive. Another valid point was that the guns used in several of these attempts were at the time only used by the police.

Vukovic was known to have sponsored the war in the Republic of Srpska, supported an opposition party and was a shady businessman with a lot of money which came from unidentified sources. He was murdered in December 1994 from a machine-gun 'heckler' in Serb Rulers streets.

Belgrade's mob bosses are adamant that the killing of Goran Vukovic was directly linked to his firm stands and refusal to negotiate a division of spheres of interest in drug dealing. But there are at least ten convincing reasons why someone would want to shoot Goran Vukovic, from the Vozdovac neighbourhood of Belgrade, and boss of the strongest and most dangerous group of criminals in Belgrade.

Unidentified assassins sprayed him with auto-matic weapons fire while he was starting up his car in central Belgrade. Dusko Malovic also died, who was in the back seat of Vukovic's BMW at the time of the shooting. The motives for the killing inside Belgrade's growing underworld remain purely hypothetical. Everything about the killing, however, points to the conclusion that this is part of a fight for territory where dealers working for Belgrade's organized crime groups are selling hard drugs such as cocaine and heroin.

Vozdovac residents say many owners of cafes, restaurants, boutiques and shops will breathe more easily after this killing, as Vukovic was one of the worst racketeers in the neighbourhood. People who worked with him say he couldn't resist the challenge and started trafficking drugs and taking over territory which was far from his native Vozdovac. Somewhere along the way he seems to have overlooked some vital details – many underworld figures have been trafficking drugs for a long time and doing their best not to allow their names to be published. These people aren't the least bit naive and some of them have even been charged with several spectacular murders having obvious police support. Some were released while others had their sentences cut short, and for years nothing was heard about them. However, suddenly some threatening new kids began to surface, headed by an experienced Goran Vukovic. They endangered their quiet lives and tried to take over their market. Without giving it a second thought they took out the leader, Vukovic, and seriously rattled the Vozdovac team.

Vukovic is also known to have been a soldier in the Bosnian Serb Republic during frequent visits to the front. He offered support to the Serbs in Bosnia when morale was low. Although nothing was official, he brought food, ammunition, and his people in to help fight for the cause. His good friend Dusko Malovic who was killed with him, was also a member of the Serb Republic police special forces. Many people compared Vukovic to Zeljko Raznjatovic Arkan, but there was never any love lost between the two. They are similar in some ways – both men's fathers were intelligence officers in the Yugoslav army, both were accused of crimes and tried to portray themselves as notorious patriots.

Some people believe that Vukovic was killed to prevent him from taking revenge for the shooting that happened on board the Lukas restaurant boat, on the morning of 27 November 1994. It was on this boat that one of Vukovic's soldiers, Bojan Banovic, was killed. Vozdovac gang member Miodrag Baskalovic was seriously wounded in the shooting. The man who fired the shots was Goran Mrdeljic, a former police officer who was himself seriously wounded. He was later allegedly transferred from a hospital in Belgrade to his grandmother's in Leskovac.

The story goes that the shooting was over a car. Mrdeljic allegedly sold his car to Banovic, claiming it had been stolen abroad, which meant that the whole deal was quite harmless. But the car had actually been stolen in Yugoslavia, which could possibly have caused complications for Banovic because the law says the buyer committed the crime of concealment and could face a prison sentence. Mrdeljic had grown rich in the period of just three years, one of his properties being the 'Boemi' cafe, which was the former National theatre club. He was also known as the most successful stolen car dealer in the whole of Belgrade.

Vukovic and his soldiers Zoran Dimitrov and Miodrag Baskalovic challenged the police openly in an interview, saying that they were fighting for democracy and not a political war with the police. It does seem very unlikely that the police quickly organized the assassination of Vukovic, especially as they knew the killing could be arranged without direct police involvement. There were many who were ready to have him eliminated, if the police turned a blind eye. It is a well-known fact that it is very difficult to stay alive today if someone has decided to kill you. You can avoid death for a while, like Vukovic did several times, but the final outcome is certain.

Murders were becoming increasingly frequent and mysterious. In February 1996 one of the best detectives in the Belgrade police department, Dragan Radisic, was murdered. The police arrested a man in connection with the killing, but it turned out that he had a firm alibi. Radisic's murder marked the beginning of much suffering for the police. The next victim was Miroslav Bizic, a former inspector, who was murdered in full daylight. Bizic was used as the main coordinator between the Secret Police and the criminals, and he was killed in front of hundreds of witnesses. The police were now feeling the full force of the Mafia's wrath.

ASSASSINATION OF GENERAL BUHA

The assassination of General Bosko Buha, the third most important man in the Serbian police force, represents the Mafia's most serious challenge to the authorities since the fall of Slobodan Milosevic. General Buha directed Serbia's main anti-riot unit when Milosevic, whose turbulent decade in power saw the emergence of powerful gangland figures with links to politicians, was still president of Yugoslavia. There were several assassinations during Milosevic's last year in power, including the shooting of the Serbian warlord Zeljko Raznatovic, known as Arkan, in a Belgrade hotel in January 2000 and Defence Minister Pavle Bulatovic in a restaurant the next month.

Buha, who was 42 at the time, was shot seven times on Monday, June 10, 2002, in the car park of Belgrade's Hotel Yugoslavia. In the past, and due to international pressure, the government had expressed a desire to combat the Mafia influence, at the same time avoiding any kind of showdown. However, the murder of Buha forced the authorities to change their attitude towards the criminals whose grip had been so powerful during the Milosevic era. The government knew they needed to take serious action or admit that the Mafia was in control of Serbia.

Buha, who had been appointed deputy head of Serbia's public security service at the end of 2001, spent the last hours of his life with friends in a floating restaurant on the Danube. Although no details have been released of his dining companions, it is a well-known fact that the Danube's riverboat restaurants have a reputation as meeting places for Belgrade's underworld. After leaving his friends in the car park, Buha was about to get into his car when he was shot. It is believed that two men were involved in the attack, but they immediately fled the scene. Even though his companions and a traffic police patrol were in the car park at the time, they fell to the ground at the sound of gunshots, and consequently did not catch sight of the assassins. There was one witness, however, a taxi driver who saw one of the attackers shoot the police chief. He described the man as being about twenty years of age, wearing a leather jacket but no face mask, and had opened fire using a Kalashnikov rifle.

In what must have been the largest Serbian police operation in several years, special squads raided flats and homes all over the capital, detaining dozens of suspected criminals. There was no stone they left unturned.

Although no motive has yet been determined for the killing of Buha, there are several theories that have been put forward. One is that it was a revenge killing by Milosevic supporters, who were angry that Buha had sided with the opposition when the former regime was toppled. Buha came to Serbia in 1991 as a refugee from Croatia, and was appointed commander of the Belgrade police brigade in 1998. He led this brigade in Kosovo from June of that year and returned to Belgrade twelve months later after sustaining light injuries.

In late September 2000, Milosevic sent Buha and his brigade to Kolubara to crack down on a miners' strike that marked a crucial step in the preparations for the protests that were to bring down the government. He blatantly disobeyed Milosevic's orders, and the unit refused to suppress the demonstrators on October 5, which was the day Milosevic was ousted.

Another theory to Buha's murder is that he was eliminated to prevent him from testifying against Milosevic at The Hague tribunal. The United Nations International War Crimes Tribunal met in

The Hague to question Serbian soldiers about war crimes and issuing arrest warrants for Bosnian Serb officers. It is believed that Buha knew that the court possessed compromising evidence against him, namely a radio recording of a communication between himself and Sreten Lukin, the public security chief who commanded the police force in Kosovo from 1998 to 1999. It is possible that circles close to Milosevic and Serbia's anti-Hague lobby murdered Buha because he knew too much and had agreed to share his knowledge with the prosecutors. However, his career was in decline long before his death.

After being appointed to the prestigious post of police chief in Belgrade immediately after Milosevic's fall, he was effectively sidelined by his appointment as deputy chief of public security. He was apparently dismissed as city police chief because of reports that he had been in contact with certain underworld groups, but these links were never proved. In December 2001 Buha issued a statement to a Belgrade newspaper in which he presented himself as a determined foe of the Mafia. He said that there were five large organized crime groups active in Belgrade and their bosses were mainly involved in illegal road building and other construction. He also added that the mafia had offered him and several other politicians 'various services, money, and even files that would help them compromise their political rivals'.

The new government marked its first months in office with an aggressive fight against crime, but the danger of tackling the menace of the underworld soon led to it softening its attitude. As a result, while Mafia bosses invested some of their unlawfully gained money in legal businesses, they also held on to some of their old enterprises. The tax authorities believe that around half of Serbia's financial transactions pass through illegal channels.

THE MAFIA FIGHTS BACK

An apparent attempt to assassinate Serbia's Prime Minister, Zoran Djindjic, is being viewed as a declaration of war by Mafia gangs angered at his efforts to break their formidable hold on power. A car taking the Prime Minister to Belgrade airport on February 21, 2003, narrowly missed a collision with an Austrian-registered freight truck that abruptly served in front of it. It was only the swift reaction of Djindjic's chauffeur that averted a head-on crash. Police arrested the driver of the truck Dejan Milenkovic, alias Bugsy, who apparently had a string of criminal records.

Djindjic played down suggestions that the collision was an underworld bid to kill him, but he warned on February 23 that even if it had been, the fight against organized crime would continue. Although it would appear that assassination was his aim, Milenkovic was charged with possessing counterfeit ID papers and for stealing a vehicle. A judge ordered that he should remain in custody, but he was released on bail late on February 24 after his lawyer argued that there was no legal justification for detaining him. His release infuriated the Serbian justice minister Vladan

Batic, who immediately called for a reform of the judiciary. Later, in a television report on the incident, it was claimed that Milenkovic had been informed by mobile phone that the Premier's convoy was approaching. Milenkovic apparently used to belong to the Surcin gang, but had recently switched sides to join rival Zemun mobsters.

A truck was also used in an apparent attempt to assassinate Vuk Draskovic in 1999. He was the leader of the Serbian Renewal Movement and, although Draskovic narrowly escaped serious injury, four of his party officials were killed. At the trial, the Serbian secret police were blamed, as it was felt they had been hand-in-glove with the Mafia for some considerable time.

Mafia gangs, which grew up under former president Slobodan Milosevic, have now grown so powerful that many people believe they actually wield more power than the government. Under international and domestic pressure, Djindjic has introduced anti-Mafia legislation, reshuffled the men at the top of the secret police, and issued public declarations that extraditions to The Hague War Crimes Tribunal would continue. In fact many of the current-day mobsters are thought to be war crimes suspects.

During 2002 the Mafia tightened its hold on the trade in drugs, arms and sex slaves. Gang warfare led to a series of violent outbursts in which several underworld leaders were killed. A spectacular explosion in early January at Zemun Polje destroyed a company which apparently belonged to the leader of the Surcin gang. The incident roused widespread public alarm. Although the authorities claimed it was a terrorist attack, observers suggested that it was more likely to be a showdown between the Surcin and Zemun gangs.

Several months ago, Djindjic brought in a law on fighting organized crime, a move regarded by many as too weak. The criminal law in Serbia was amended to widen the police powers and a witness protection programme was introduced. At this stage there is uncertainty as to how the anti-Mafia campaign will fare – but the authorities were clearly preparing for the worst.

They were right to be worried, on March 12 Zoran Djindjic was assassinated. His murder seems to have had the positive effect of propelling a campaign to root out corruption. In their hunt for the assassins, police rounded up thousands of suspected Mafia figures in the biggest crackdown yet on organized crime in the Balkans. Police have filed nearly 400 criminal charges against the underworld figures detained since Djindjic's death.

THE ZEMUN GANG

As a result of their investigations the Serb police confirmed that their sweep through the underworld has proved that a Belgrade criminal ring known as the Zemun gang was behind Djindjic's murder. The gang has ties to the security setup of the former President Slobodan Milosevic, whom Djindjic played a major role in overthrowing in October 2000. According to police and secret service intelligence of dozens of countries around the world, this gang is part of one of the largest organized criminal networks of cocaine and heroin dealers in the world. Zemun leaders have had a monopoly for supplying drugs to south-eastern Europe for some considerable time.

In less than six years they became the most powerful individuals in the country and among the richest in Europe, making millions of Deutsche marks each day by selling drugs.

Zemun gang members spend their money quite freely having extravagant trips, sports cars and houses around the world, presenting themselves as young businessmen and representatives of the world's jetset elite. The gang leaders often visit posh resorts including Paris, Monte Carlo, Athens, Singapore, Hong Kong, Colombia and the Dominican Republic, where they spend their holidays and hold business meetings. Two such members who had a particular weakness for luxury yachts, apartments and gambling, were Milorad Lukovic and Dusan Spasojevic.

French police arrested Dusan Spasojevic in May 2001 in Paris and deported him to Belgrade. According to French intelligence, Spasojevic and his associates were to known to spend as much as $50,000 a day prior to the arrest. Other gang members presented themselves in Serbia as patriots – honourable and respectable champions of Serbian national interests, and men who did a lot for their country, especially for powerful figures during the Milosevic regime.

More than 3,000 people were taken in for questioning and the police detained just over 1,000 of them. Not all the people who were detained would be prosecuted for their involvement in the attack on Djindjic, but for other criminal activities as well. Those arrested are known to be key members of the Zemun gang, but the three main ringleaders, including the alleged mastermind – a former commander of the Red Berets police special forces unit known as 'Legija' – are still at large.

The Zemun gang includes many former para-militaries who fought for the nationalist Milosevic in the Balkan wars of Croatia, Bosnia and Kosovo. When the conflicts were over Milosevic gave them a free hand in drug trafficking. Other Zemun crimes include kidnapping, murder and the smuggling of cigarettes, arms and people. The Serbian government believe that the murder of Djindjic was an effort by the criminal overlords to sew a seed of chaos in Serbia.

As a Prime Minister Djindjic had made many enemies. He had angered nationalists by arranging the arrest of Milosevic and his extradition to the UN War Crimes Tribunal at the Hague to stand trial for crimes against humanity. It is also widely suspected that Djindjic made a deal with some elements of Milosevic's security forces under which they would not block the overthrow, and he would leave them alone following the takeover of the democratic opposition. The slain Prime Minister's foes have alleged that Djindjic had further connec-tions with the paramilitaries-turned-Mafia, includ-ing regular telephone conversations with the Legija, and participation in the cigarette-smug-gling racket.

The dragnet to uncover the assassins has taken in several state security and police officials accused of corruption, including Serbia's deputy prosecutor. He was subsequently arrested for being on the Zemun gang's payroll.

CLEANING UP

In the year 2003 the Serbian police have arrested several of the organized criminal group suspected of being behind the assassination of Prime Minister Zoran Djindjic. The people behind the killing had a clear political plan to destabilize the state, instigate political conflicts, thwart the work of the government and parliament and induce new elections in a effort to return their forces to power. The Serbian government described these people as the greatest organized crime group in the region of the former Yugoslavia.

Members of the Zemun clan are not only wanted in connection with the assassination of Djindjic but also for some three hundred other crimes, including the kidnapping and murder of former Serbian President Ivan Stambolic in August 2000. Other crimes which they are suspected of committing include the attempted murder in Montenegro of Serbian Renewal Movement leader Vuk Draskovic, dozens of kidnappings over the past several years, more than fifty murders, organized trade in narcotics, the creation of a network of drug dealers both domestically and abroad, and last but by no means least, acts of terrorism.

The Albanian Mafia

*The ethnic Albanian rebels fighting in the hills of
Macedonia are the paramilitary wing of an
Albanian Mafia exporting drugs and trafficking
humans to Europe and beyond.*

In the Albanian world – Albania, Kosovo and the
Albanian-populated part of Macedonia – there
are clans and in those clans you have a mix of
young people fighting for the cause of national
liberation, young men belonging to the Mafia, and
young men driving their cousins or other girls
from the villages into prostitution. It is absolutely
impossible to distinguish between these groups.
They all obey the same clans, they all have the
same logic, the same view on the world and it
would appear that their excuse for standing up for
the rights of the ethnic Albanian minority is just
an excuse for their criminal activities.

IN THE CLAWS OF THE MAFIA

Business is so well organized in Macedonia, Bulgaria,
Montenegro, Kosovo-Metohija, and partly in
Greece, that the police are just left to play the role
of 'silent observer'. The view of the people is that

this is only possible if the state authorities are involved in Mafia 'dirty business'.

The people who are responsible for conducting this business, worth vast sums of money, include the members of the so-called Kosovo Liberation Army (or KLA) – that is their 'officers', but only those of high ranks i.e. captains etc. KLA terrorists are getting two percent of the profit gained from heroin and cocaine sales in European countries. There are many among the Albanian Mafia who, during the NATO aggression on Yugoslavia, spent some time in camps located in Albania, in the town of Korca. It was here that they were trained for terrorist actions against Kosmet and Macedonia. Many of them, after Kosovo-Metojiha was ethnically cleansed, were left without jobs and consequently joined the Albanian Mafia.

The Mafia is also known to bribe officers NATO-led peacekeeping force in Kosovo, KFOR, Kouchner's 'peacekeepers' and individuals from various humanitarian organizations, giving them eight to ten per cent net gain. Bernard Kouchner was the Special Representative of the Secretary-General and the head of the UN Interim Administration Mission in Kosovo (UNMIK) from July 15, 1999 to January 12, 2001. In return for these bribes, KFOR and UNMIK and the humanitarian's duty is not only to turn a blind eye to the ongoing events, but also to offer their vehicles for smuggling operations. It was not coincidental that Kouchner appealed for the Macedonian-Kosmet border to be revoked, because this would make it much simpler for the Albanian

Mafia to operate reducing the risks to a minimum. Reports show that there is now a special kind of trade, reaching even Chechnya, which involves large quantities of light and heavy weaponry, automatic rifles, pistols and machine guns and large quantities of ammunition and mines. Indeed, smuggling is the Albanian Mafia's core competency, and over the past decade they have steadily come to dominate smuggling to and within Europe, even overshadowing their erstwhile mentors, the Italian Mafia.

The conflict in Kosovo opened the floodgates of people seeking to leave for fear of their own safety. That in turn generated a smuggling boom so great that the Albanian clans had to turn desperate customers away. Aided by the consent of the Albanian government and a corrupt police force, the Mafia were smuggling more than 10,000 Kosovar refugees per month during the war.

DRUG TRAFFICKING

As if human cargo is not disturbing enough, it is certainly not the clan's only source of revenue. In 1997 Interpol stated that Kosovo Albanians held the largest share of the heroin market in Switzerland, Austria, Belgium, Germany, Hungary, Czech Republic, Norway and Sweden. Even the arrest of one or two major players provides only a brief respite, before another clan picks up where they left off. Albanian clans command approximately 70 per cent of Germany and Switzerland's heroin market.

Apparently the home base for these ethnic

Albanian rebels is in the hills of Macedonia, where they have formed a paramilitary wing of an Albanian Mafia. They are mainly refugees that have fled the Kosovo conflict, and their headquarters in the hills has made a safe power base for the Mafia to efficiently carry out its smuggling of narcotics.

It is very hard to actually distinguish between the rebels and militias on the one hand and the Albanian Mafia on the other. This is because, in Albania, Kosovo and in the Albanian-populated part of Macedonia, you have certain clans and within those clans you have a mixture of young men fighting for the cause of national liberation, while others belong to the Mafia. They appear to obey the same clans, they have the same logic, the same view of the world, and one day will be selling heroin and the next day fighting in the mountains for their cause.

In recent years the passage through the Balkans into Europe has grossly overshadowed previous drug channels from Southeast Asia's Golden Triangle. This principal drug-shipping channel, known as the Balkan Route, is worth an estimated $400 billion a year and handles 80 per cent of the heroin destined for sale in Europe. Opium grown in Afghanistan and Pakistan (the heart of the Golden Crescent) is processed in Turkey, then travels through the former Yugoslavia and the Czech Republic to reach other parts of Europe. The Balkan Route then links to England through the French port of Calais, where Albanian gangs have secured their position. In the Channel ports, the Albanians hire facilitators who, to confuse sniffer dogs, disguise the smell of smuggled cargo by loading their vehicles with meat, pet food and even fresh flowers. The clans profit doubly by piggybacking illicit trafficking operations – for example, shipping oil to Macedonia, dodging the Greek embargo, and using the shipment to cover the added cargo of heroin. Also people who are desperate to get into Europe make ideal drug-carrying mules for these clans.

TRAFFICKING OF CHILDREN

The Albanian Mafia gangs are actively involved in the trafficking of children to Italy, where they are exploited in clandestine operations, some of which are suspected of holding the victims in practices of sexual exploitation. Supposedly smuggled into Italy for fruit-picking, these thousands of children (usually aged between 12 and 17 years of age) pour out of Albania's poorer interior regions in search of a fortune in the European Union. But for many the dream soon turns into a nightmare. They find themselves gridlocked in Mafia-controlled criminal activities from which the only escape in many cases is death. It has been discovered that many of the Kosovar women supposedly fleeing from the Serbs, were actually running away from the UCK (the Albanian faction fighting in northern Macedonia), which were rounding up the prettier girls to ship off to Italy.

In the last four years the Italian carabinieri in Tricarico have rounded up 100 women and 70 children trafficked into Italy to work in clandestine prostitution rings.

ALL OVER THE WORLD

The clans run a multinational operation. The Albanian clans are dispersed in Kosovo and Macedonia as well as Albania itself. They have also confederated with their counterparts in Turkey and Bulgaria. The smugglers also forged alliances with their criminal counterparts in Italy, including La Cosa Nostra. It is an open secret that the Italian Mafia relocated to Vlore, a coastal town in southern Albania, after the recent Italian crackdown on organized crime.

These clans continue to survive because of political deterioration in Albania which has created such an ideal working environment for the illicit traffic. Organized crime thrives on a weak government, a lack of antidrug legislation, poorly equipped police forces, a cash-based economy, and fragile banking regulations – Albania has all of these.

Communist rule isolated Albania for 47 years, and with its record of corruption and abuse, it is still trying to shed its Communist skin. After becoming a democracy in 1991, Albania attempted to establish a market economy, but the economy collapsed in 1997 and has not yet recovered. The economic plunge led to rioting and looting and a general state of lawlessness. Corruption extends to the very top, so much so that the Albanian parliament has been dubbed the 'Kalashnikov parliament' because of its apparent indifference to organized crime and close ties to weapons dealers. Because of this weak political system they do not have the strength to fight these clans.

The Albanian Mafia continues to cause chaos on the borders with Yugoslavia. Under the administration of the United Nations Organisation, the situation in Kosovo has become steadily worse with US-armed Albanian Mafia turning the border regions of Kosovo into bandit country. It would be a tragic case if, in winning back Kosovo, the West were to lose Albania to the Mafia.